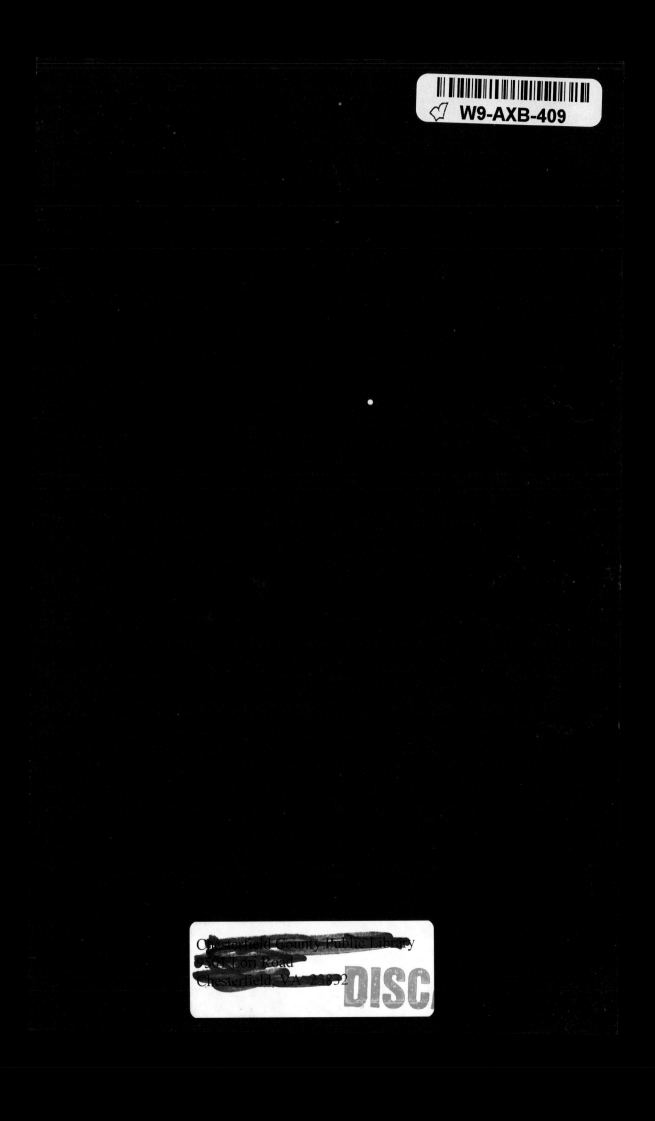

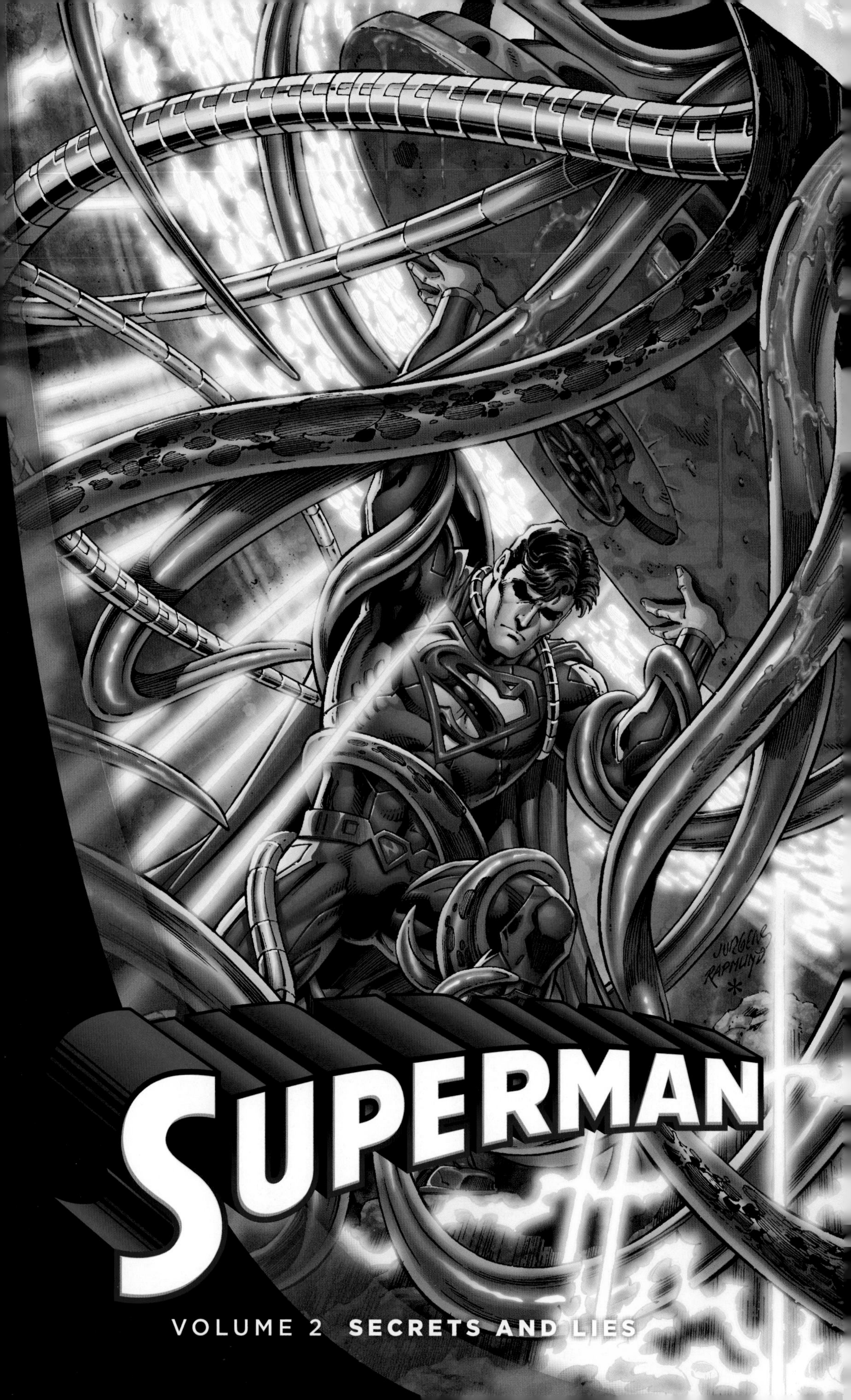
JURGENS
RAPMUND
SUPERMAN
VOLUME 2 SECRETS AND LIES

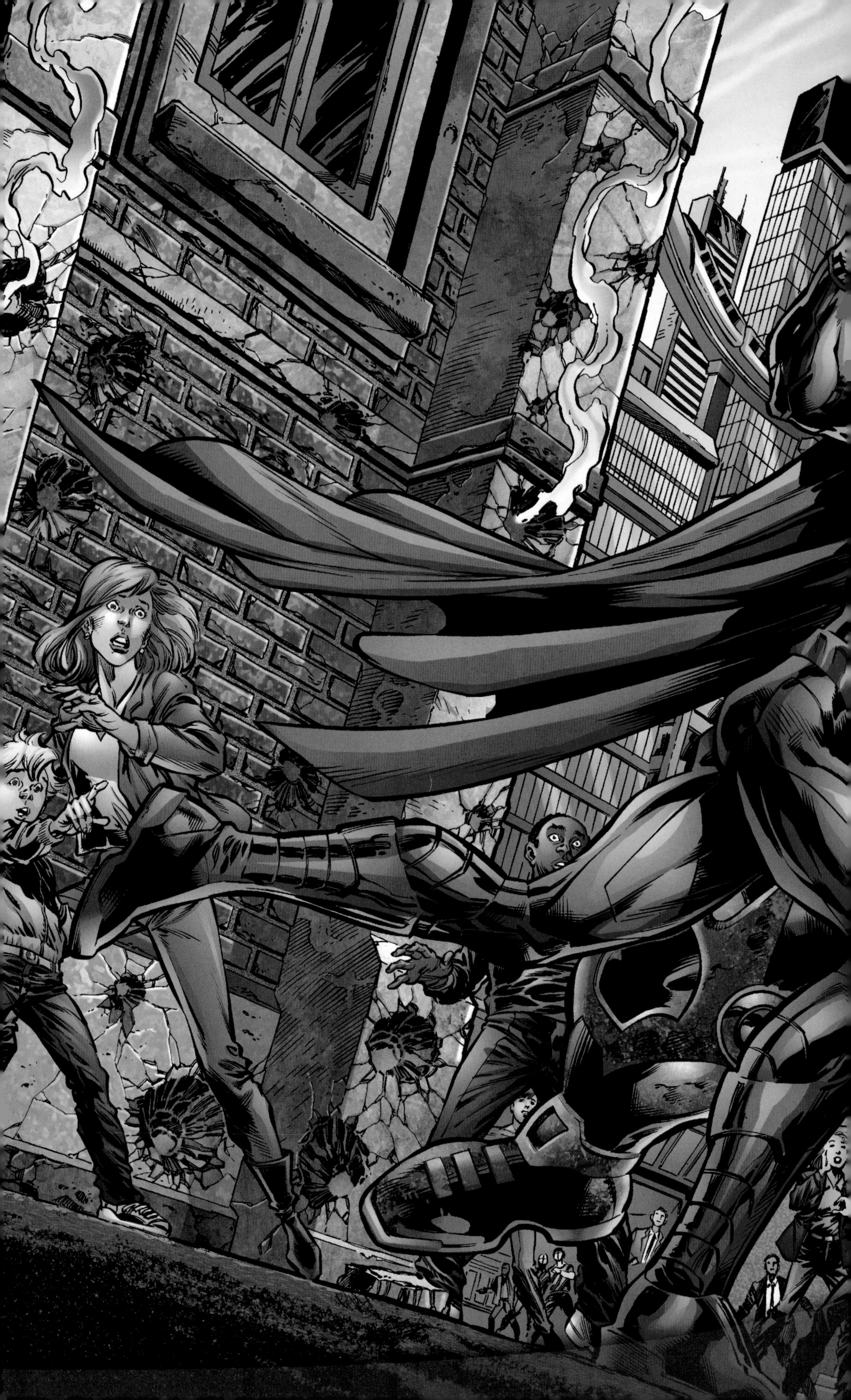

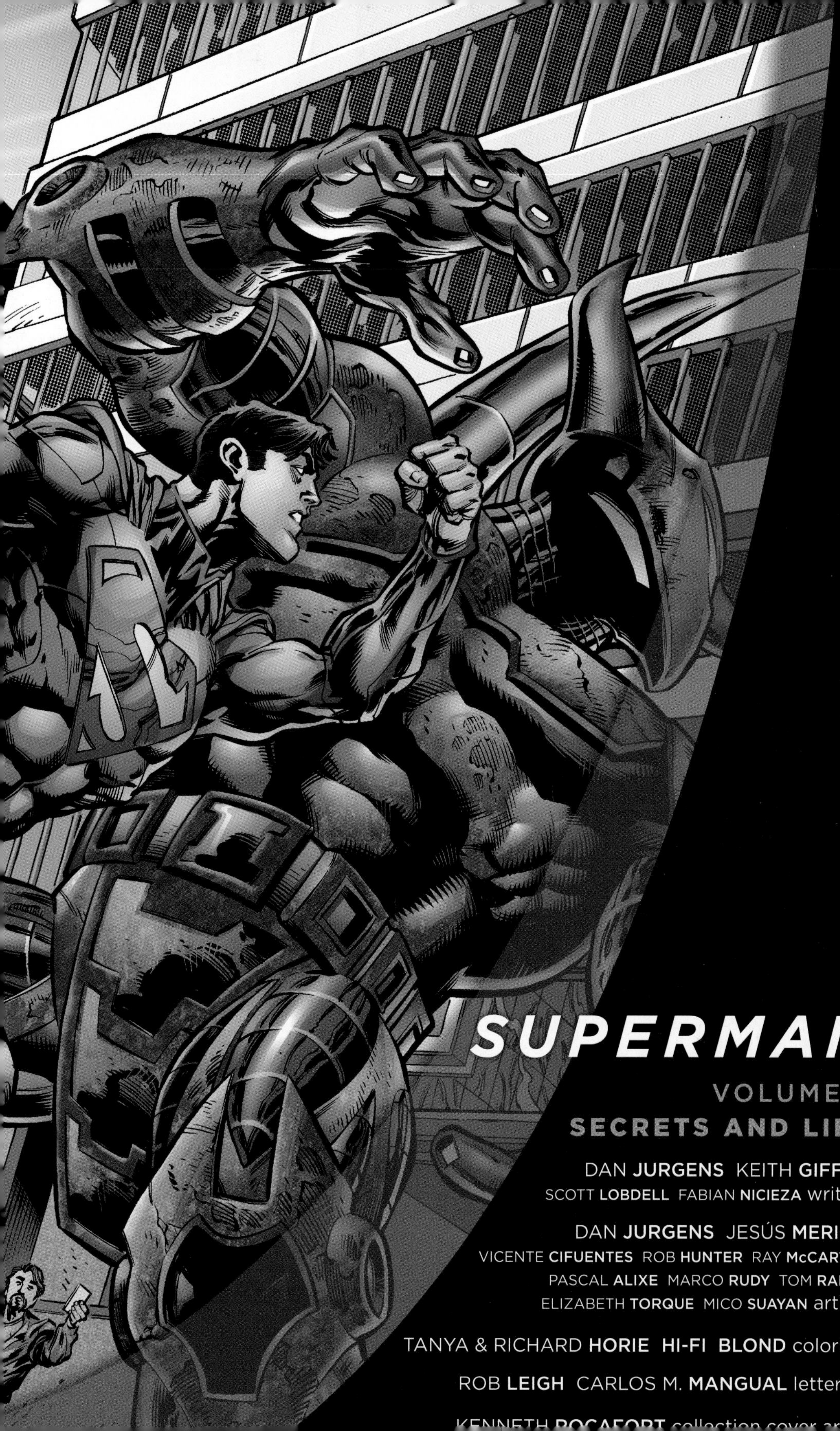

SUPERMAN

VOLUME 2
SECRETS AND LIES

DAN **JURGENS** KEITH **GIFFEN**
SCOTT **LOBDELL** FABIAN **NICIEZA** writers

DAN **JURGENS** JESÚS **MERINO**
VICENTE **CIFUENTES** ROB **HUNTER** RAY **McCARTHY**
PASCAL **ALIXE** MARCO **RUDY** TOM **RANEY**
ELIZABETH **TORQUE** MICO **SUAYAN** artists

TANYA & RICHARD **HORIE** **HI-FI** **BLOND** colorists

ROB **LEIGH** CARLOS M. **MANGUAL** letterers

KENNETH **ROCAFORT** collection cover artist

MATT IDELSON EDDIE BERGANZA Editors – Original Series WIL MOSS Associate Editor – Original Series
DARREN SHAN Assistant Editor – Original Series ROWENA YOW Editor
ROBBIN BROSTERMAN Design Director – Books ROBBIE BIEDERMAN Publication Design

BOB HARRAS Senior VP – Editor-in-Chief, DC Comics

DIANE NELSON President DAN DIDIO and JIM LEE Co-Publishers GEOFF JOHNS Chief Creative Officer
JOHN ROOD Executive VP – Sales, Marketing and Business Development AMY GENKINS Senior VP – Business and Legal Affairs
NAIRI GARDINER Senior VP – Finance JEFF BOISON VP – Publishing Planning
MARK CHIARELLO VP – Art Direction and Design JOHN CUNNINGHAM VP – Marketing
TERRI CUNNINGHAM VP – Editorial Administration ALISON GILL Senior VP – Manufacturing and Operations
HANK KANALZ Senior VP – Vertigo & Integrated Publishing JAY KOGAN VP – Business and Legal Affairs, Publishing
JACK MAHAN VP – Business Affairs, Talent NICK NAPOLITANO VP – Manufacturing Administration
SUE POHJA VP – Book Sales COURTNEY SIMMONS Senior VP – Publicity BOB WAYNE Senior VP – Sales

SUPERMAN VOLUME 2: SECRETS AND LIES

DC Comics, 1700 Broadway, New York, NY 10019
A Warner Bros. Entertainment Company.
Printed by RR Donnelley, Salem, VA, USA. 6/14/13. First Printing.

HC ISBN: 978-1-4012-4028-8
SC ISBN: 978-1-4012-4257-2

Library of Congress Cataloging-in-Publication Data

Jurgens, Dan, author.
Superman : secrets and lies / Dan Jurgens, Keith Giffen.
pages cm
"Originally published in single magazine form in Superman 7-12, Superman Annual 1."
ISBN 978-1-4012-4028-8
1. Graphic novels. I. Giffen, Keith, illustrator. II. Title. III. Title: Secrets and lies.
PN6728.S9J8786 2013
741.5'973—dc23
                    2013009122

 SUSTAINABLE Certified Chain of Custody

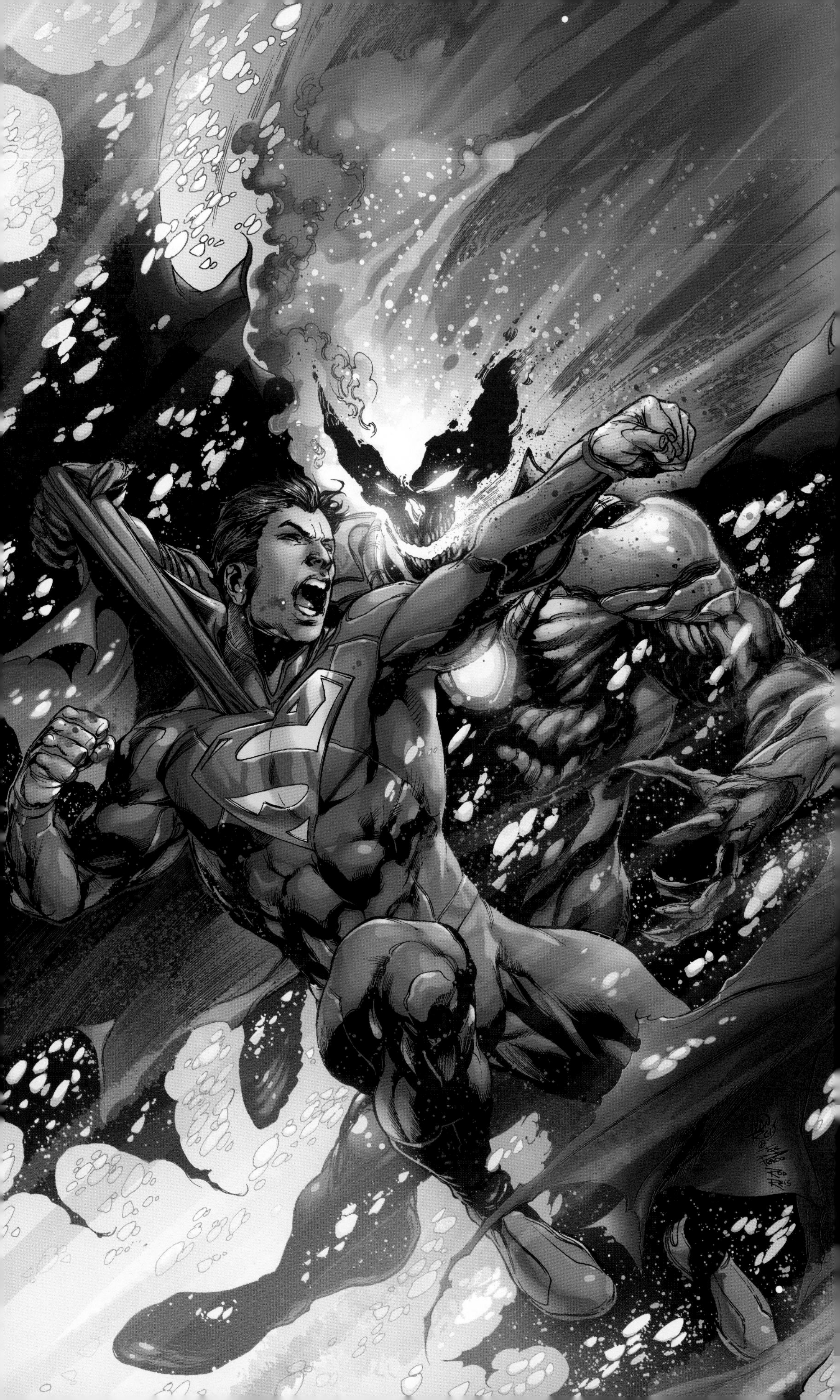

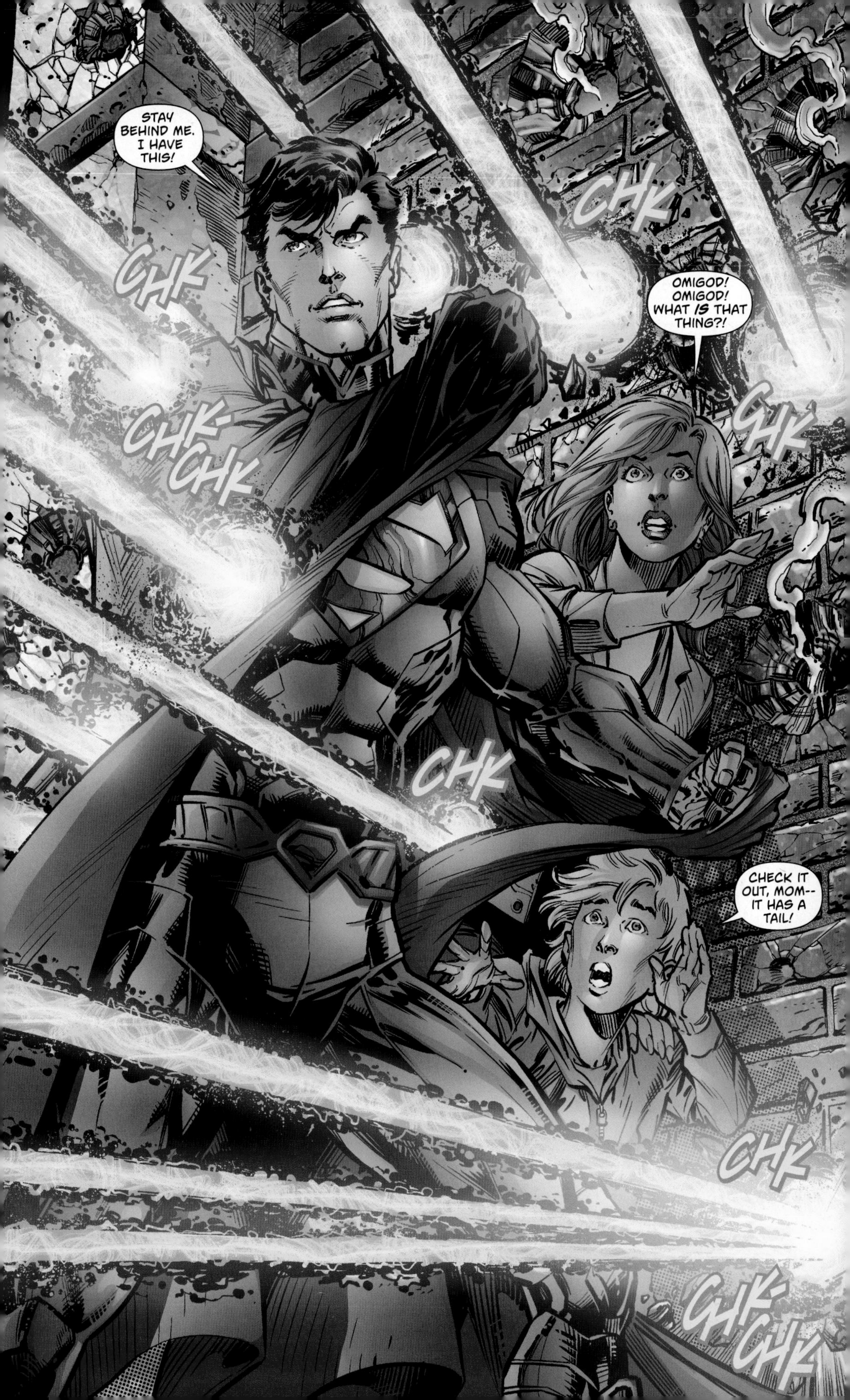
STAY BEHIND ME. I HAVE THIS!
CHK
CHK
CHK-CHK
OMIGOD! OMIGOD! WHAT IS THAT THING?!
CHK
CHK
CHECK IT OUT, MOM-- IT HAS A TAIL!
CHK
CHK-CHK

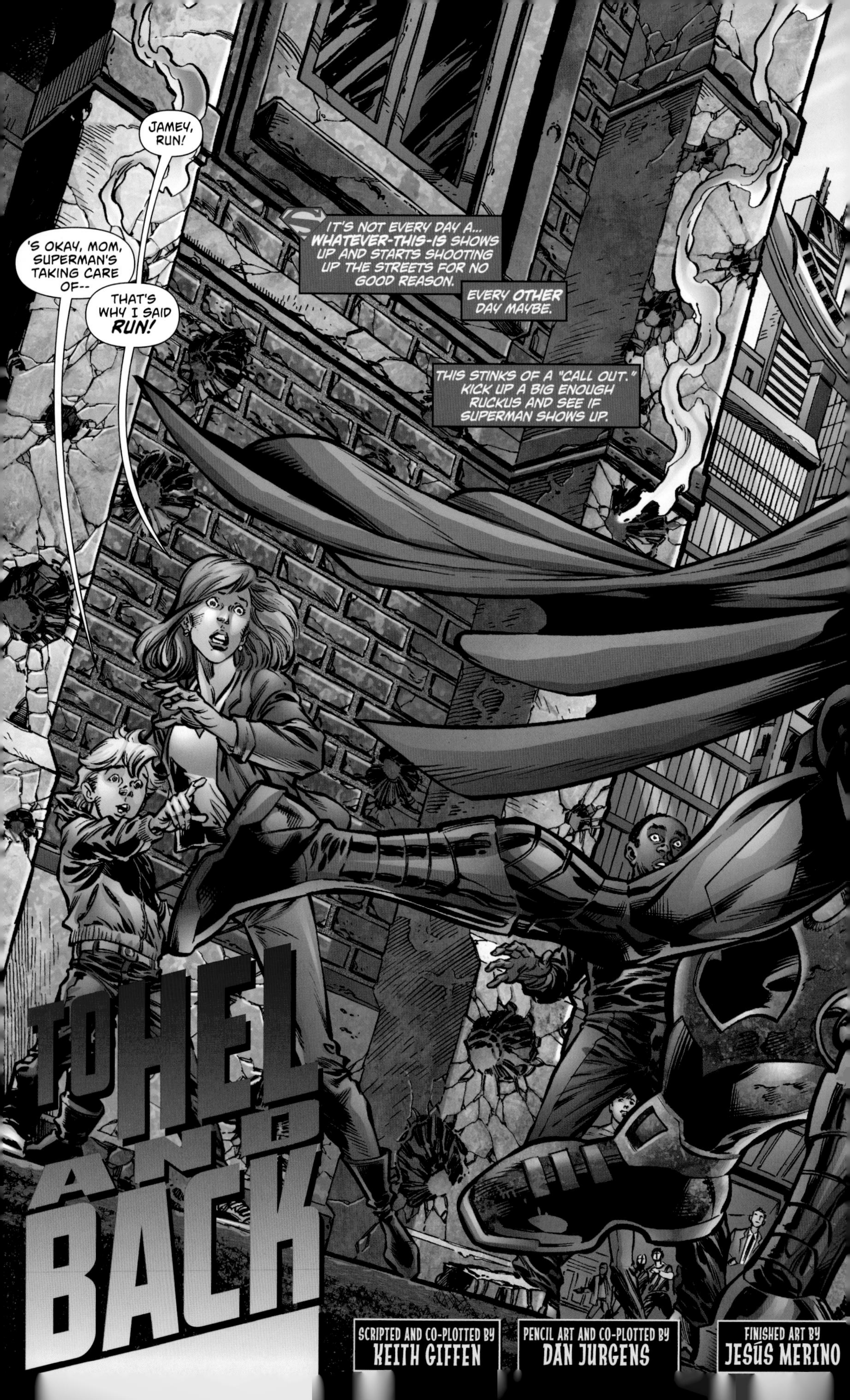

JAMEY, RUN!
'S OKAY, MOM, SUPERMAN'S TAKING CARE OF--
THAT'S WHY I SAID RUN!
IT'S NOT EVERY DAY A... WHATEVER-THIS-IS SHOWS UP AND STARTS SHOOTING UP THE STREETS FOR NO GOOD REASON.
EVERY OTHER DAY MAYBE.
THIS STINKS OF A "CALL OUT." KICK UP A BIG ENOUGH RUCKUS AND SEE IF SUPERMAN SHOWS UP.
TO HEL AND BACK
SCRIPTED AND CO-PLOTTED BY KEITH GIFFEN
PENCIL ART AND CO-PLOTTED BY DAN JURGENS
FINISHED ART BY JESÚS MERINO

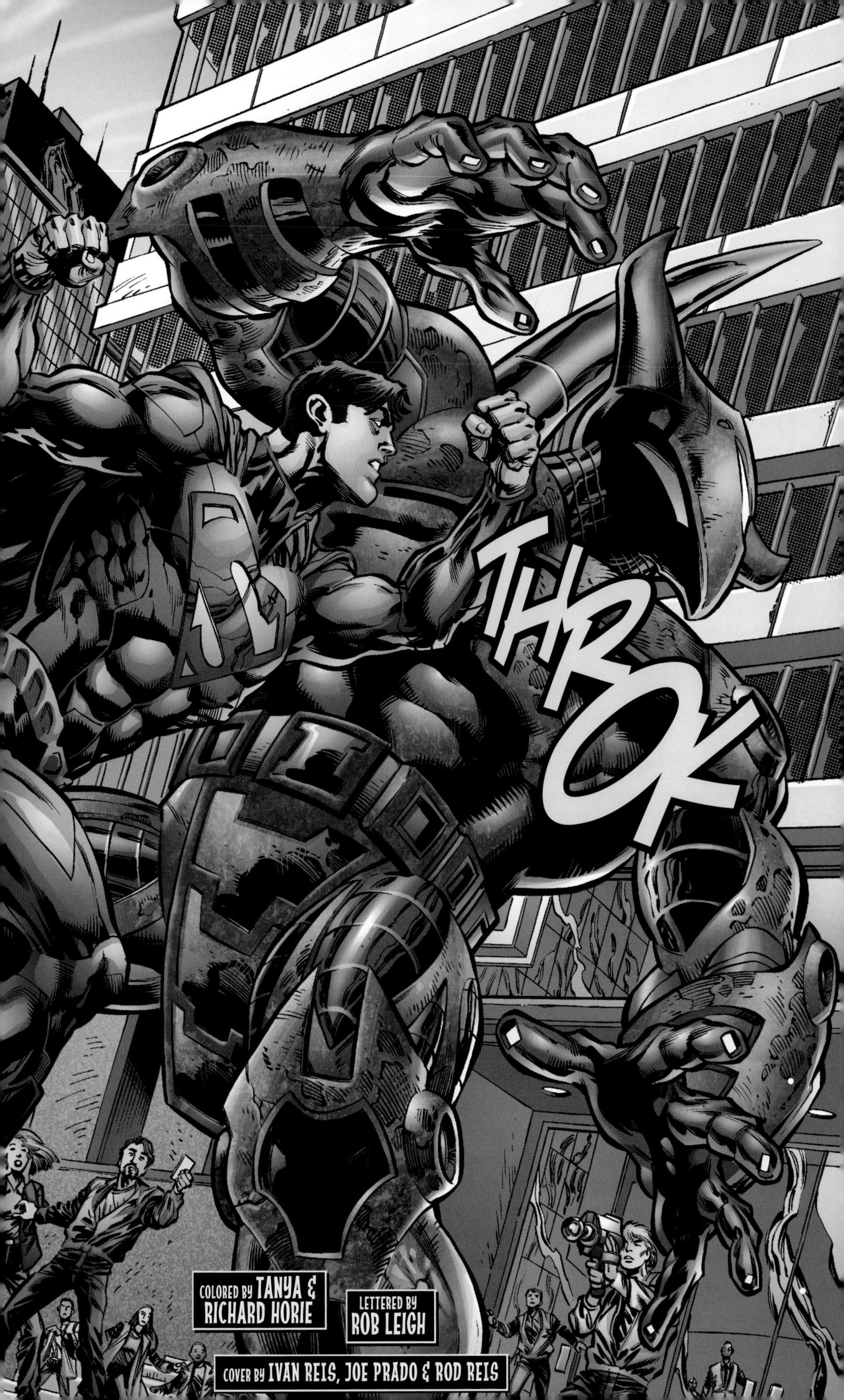
THROK
COLORED BY TANYA & RICHARD HORIE
LETTERED BY ROB LEIGH
COVER BY IVAN REIS, JOE PRADO & ROD REIS

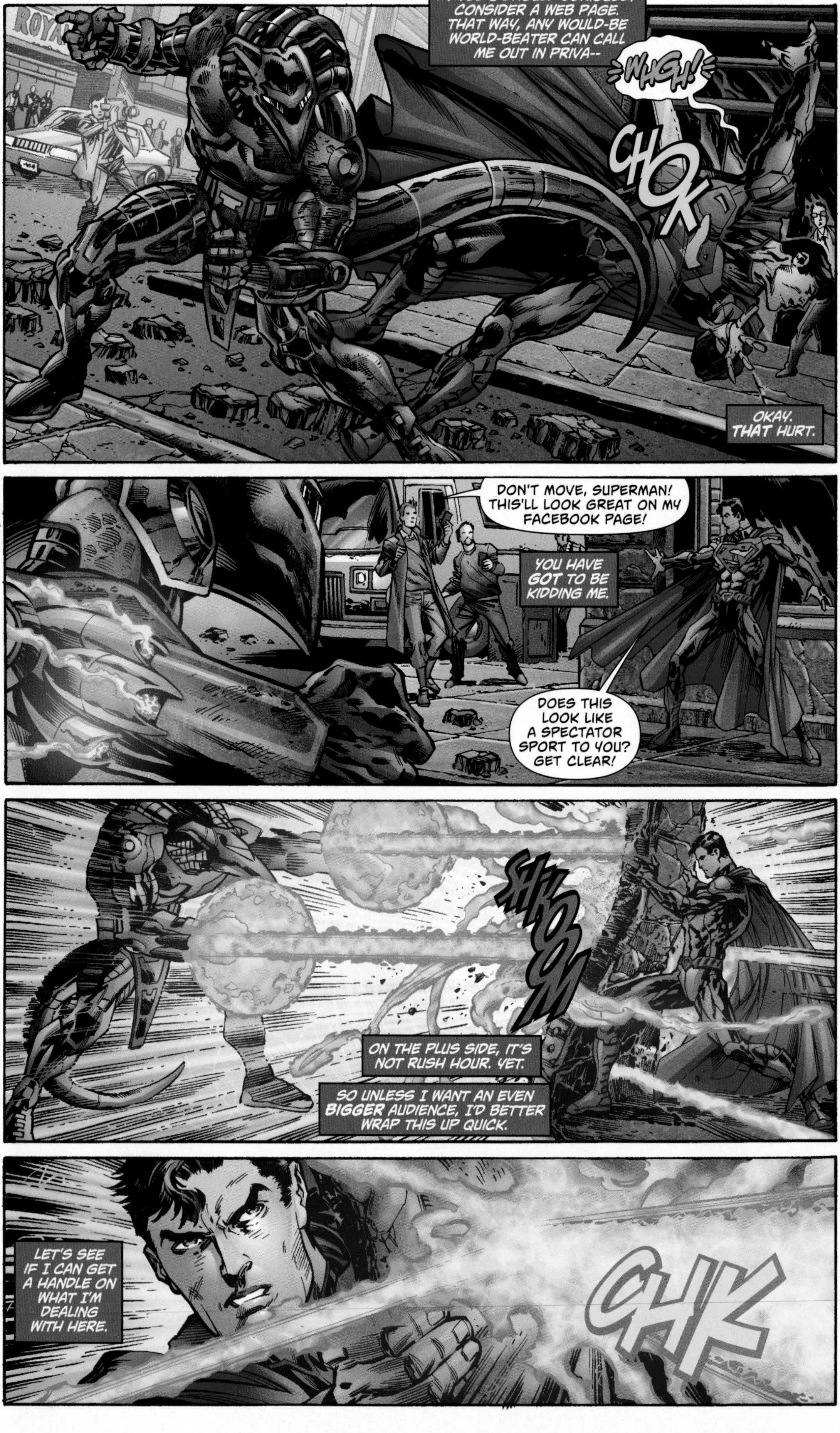
MAYBE I SHOULD SERIOUSLY CONSIDER A WEB PAGE. THAT WAY, ANY WOULD-BE WORLD-BEATER CAN CALL ME OUT IN PRIVA--
WHGH!
CHOK
OKAY. THAT HURT.
DON'T MOVE, SUPERMAN! THIS'LL LOOK GREAT ON MY FACEBOOK PAGE!
YOU HAVE GOT TO BE KIDDING ME.
DOES THIS LOOK LIKE A SPECTATOR SPORT TO YOU? GET CLEAR!
SHROOM
ON THE PLUS SIDE, IT'S NOT RUSH HOUR. YET.
SO UNLESS I WANT AN EVEN BIGGER AUDIENCE, I'D BETTER WRAP THIS UP QUICK.
LET'S SEE IF I CAN GET A HANDLE ON WHAT I'M DEALING WITH HERE.
CHK

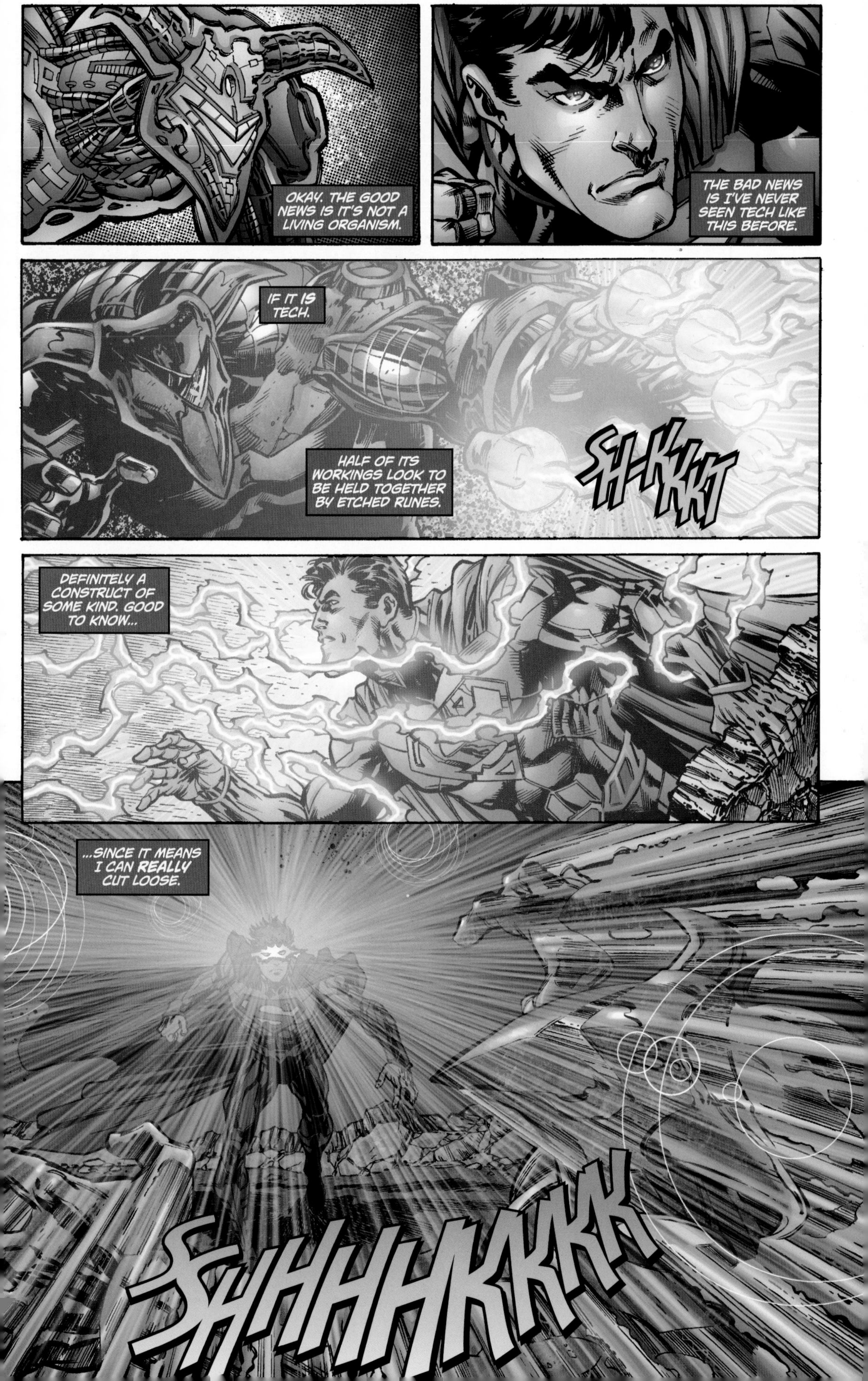
OKAY. THE GOOD NEWS IS IT'S NOT A LIVING ORGANISM.
THE BAD NEWS IS I'VE NEVER SEEN TECH LIKE THIS BEFORE.
IF IT IS TECH.
HALF OF ITS WORKINGS LOOK TO BE HELD TOGETHER BY ETCHED RUNES.
SH-KKKT
DEFINITELY A CONSTRUCT OF SOME KIND. GOOD TO KNOW...
...SINCE IT MEANS I CAN REALLY CUT LOOSE.
SHHHHKKKK

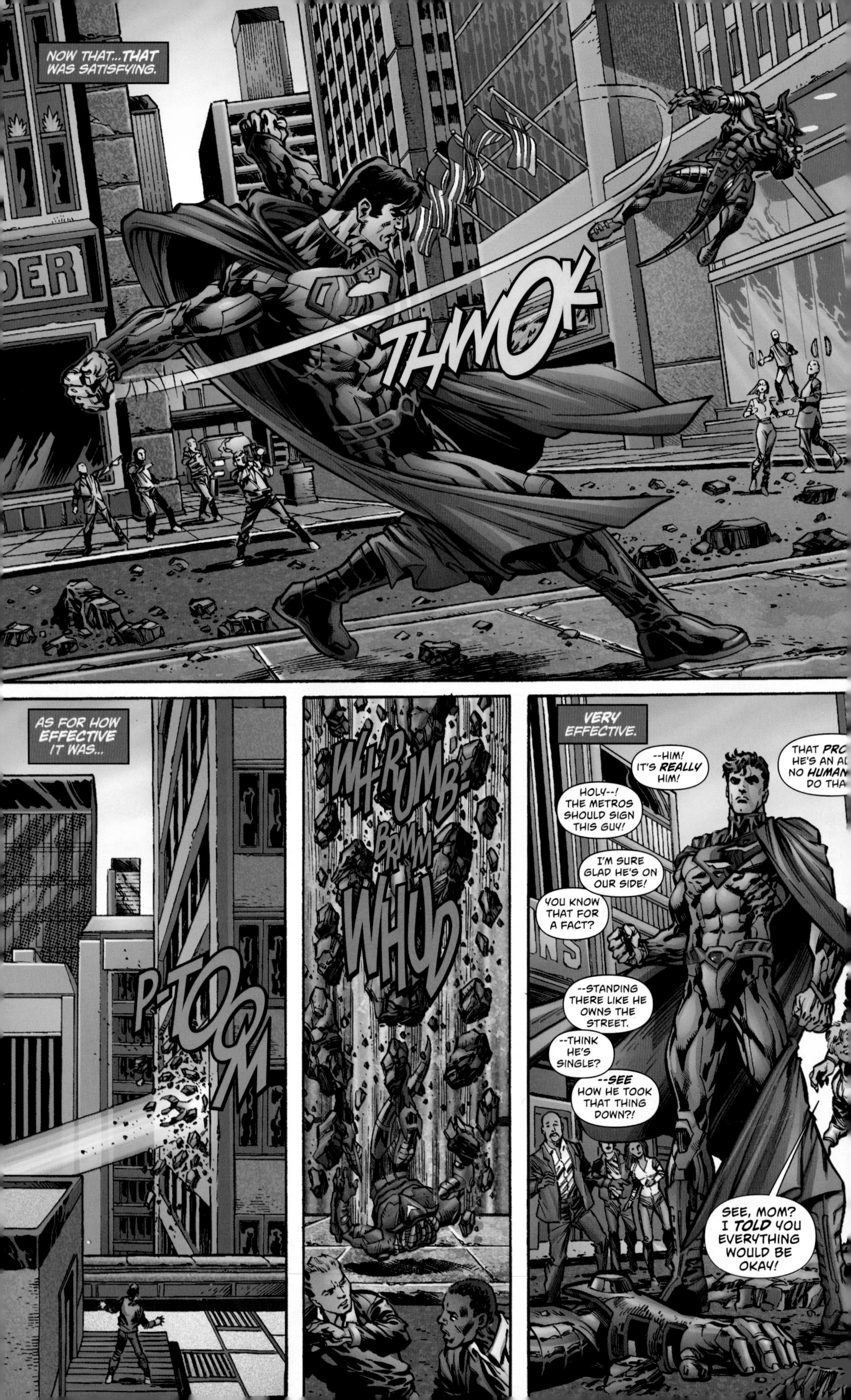
NOW THAT...THAT WAS SATISFYING.
THWOK
AS FOR HOW EFFECTIVE IT WAS...
P-TOOM
WH-RUMB-
BRMM-
WHUD
VERY EFFECTIVE.
--HIM! IT'S REALLY HIM!
HOLY--! THE METROS SHOULD SIGN THIS GUY!
I'M SURE GLAD HE'S ON OUR SIDE!
YOU KNOW THAT FOR A FACT?
--STANDING THERE LIKE HE OWNS THE STREET.
--THINK HE'S SINGLE?
--SEE HOW HE TOOK THAT THING DOWN?!
SEE, MOM? I TOLD YOU EVERYTHING WOULD BE OKAY!

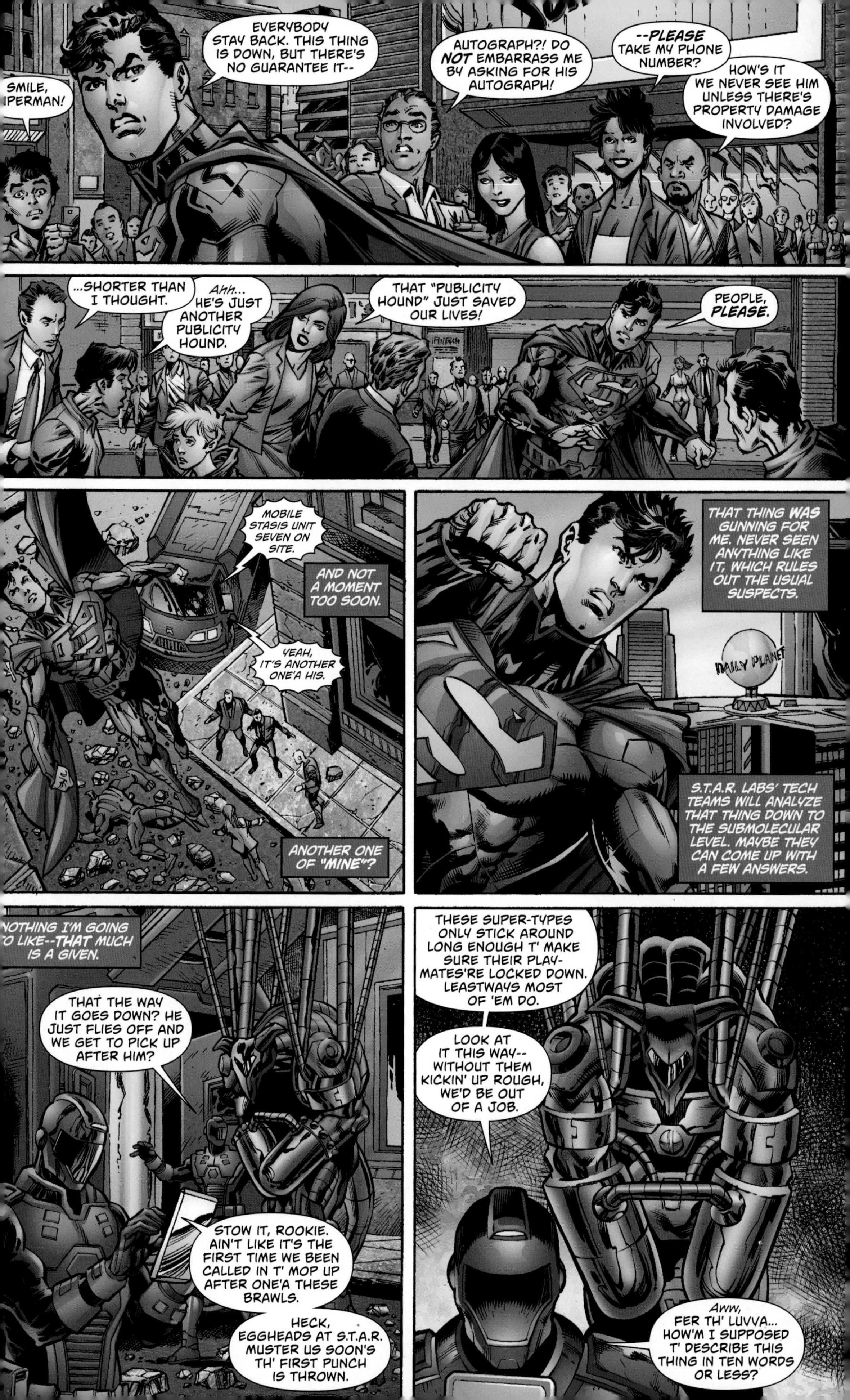
SMILE, IPERMAN!
EVERYBODY STAY BACK. THIS THING IS DOWN, BUT THERE'S NO GUARANTEE IT--
AUTOGRAPH?! DO NOT EMBARRASS ME BY ASKING FOR HIS AUTOGRAPH!
--PLEASE TAKE MY PHONE NUMBER?
HOW'S IT WE NEVER SEE HIM UNLESS THERE'S PROPERTY DAMAGE INVOLVED?
...SHORTER THAN I THOUGHT.
Ahh... HE'S JUST ANOTHER PUBLICITY HOUND.
THAT "PUBLICITY HOUND" JUST SAVED OUR LIVES!
PEOPLE, PLEASE.
MOBILE STASIS UNIT SEVEN ON SITE.
AND NOT A MOMENT TOO SOON.
YEAH, IT'S ANOTHER ONE'A HIS.
ANOTHER ONE OF "MINE"?
THAT THING WAS GUNNING FOR ME. NEVER SEEN ANYTHING LIKE IT, WHICH RULES OUT THE USUAL SUSPECTS.
DAILY PLANET
S.T.A.R. LABS' TECH TEAMS WILL ANALYZE THAT THING DOWN TO THE SUBMOLECULAR LEVEL. MAYBE THEY CAN COME UP WITH A FEW ANSWERS.
NOTHING I'M GOING O LIKE--THAT MUCH IS A GIVEN.
THAT THE WAY IT GOES DOWN? HE JUST FLIES OFF AND WE GET TO PICK UP AFTER HIM?
STOW IT, ROOKIE. AIN'T LIKE IT'S THE FIRST TIME WE BEEN CALLED IN T' MOP UP AFTER ONE'A THESE BRAWLS.
HECK, EGGHEADS AT S.T.A.R. MUSTER US SOON'S TH' FIRST PUNCH IS THROWN.
THESE SUPER-TYPES ONLY STICK AROUND LONG ENOUGH T' MAKE SURE THEIR PLAY-MATES'RE LOCKED DOWN. LEASTWAYS MOST OF 'EM DO.
LOOK AT IT THIS WAY-- WITHOUT THEM KICKIN' UP ROUGH, WE'D BE OUT OF A JOB.
AWW, FER TH' LUVVA... HOW'M I SUPPOSED T' DESCRIBE THIS THING IN TEN WORDS OR LESS?

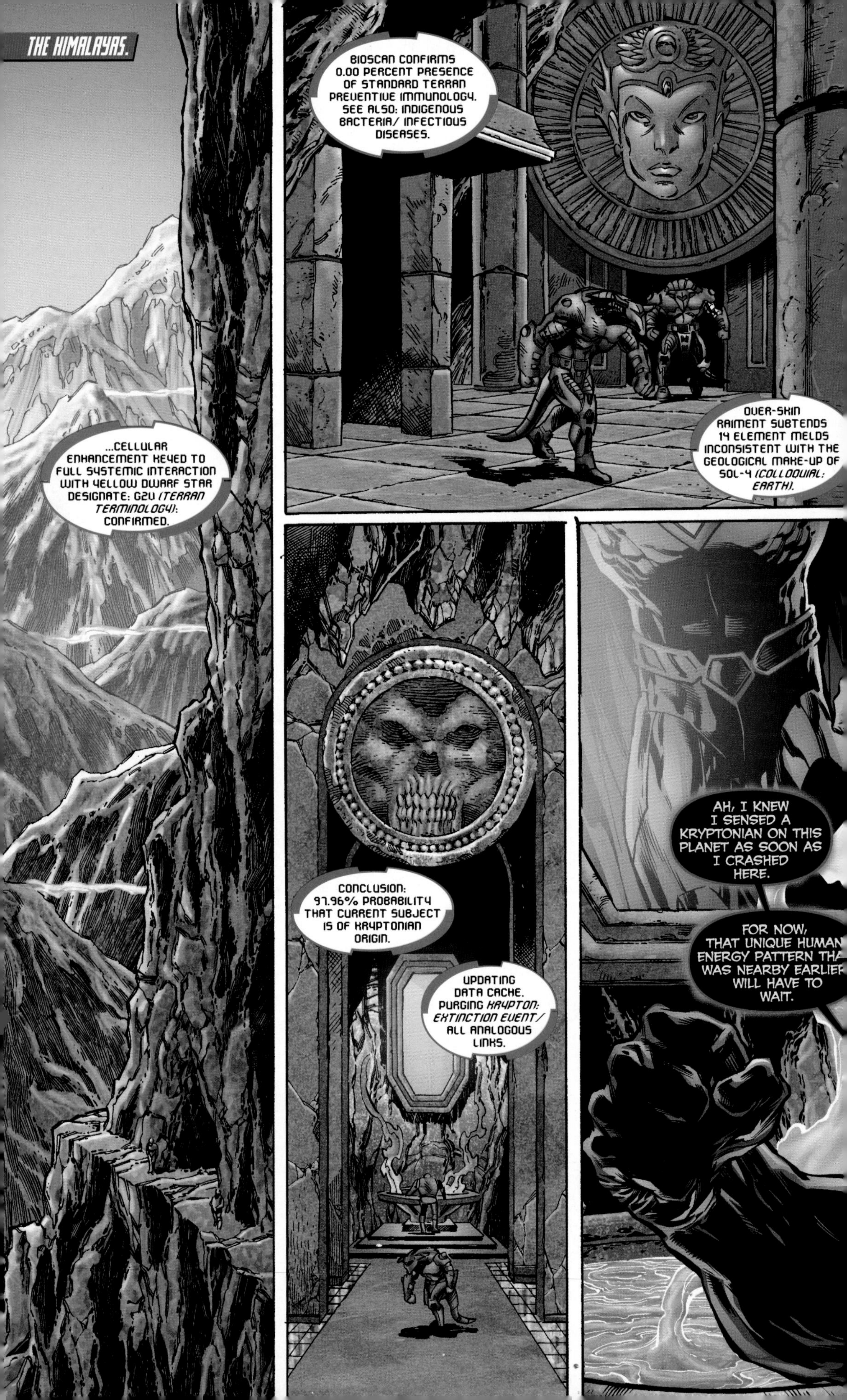
THE HIMALAYAS.
...CELLULAR ENHANCEMENT KEYED TO FULL SYSTEMIC INTERACTION WITH YELLOW DWARF STAR DESIGNATE: G2V (TERRAN TERMINOLOGY): CONFIRMED.
BIOSCAN CONFIRMS 0.00 PERCENT PRESENCE OF STANDARD TERRAN PREVENTIVE IMMUNOLOGY. SEE ALSO: INDIGENOUS BACTERIA/ INFECTIOUS DISEASES.
OVER-SKIN RAIMENT SUBTENDS 14 ELEMENT MELDS INCONSISTENT WITH THE GEOLOGICAL MAKE-UP OF SOL-4 (COLLOQUIAL: EARTH).
CONCLUSION: 97.96% PROBABILITY THAT CURRENT SUBJECT IS OF KRYPTONIAN ORIGIN.
UPDATING DATA CACHE. PURGING KRYPTON: EXTINCTION EVENT/ ALL ANALOGOUS LINKS.
AH, I KNEW I SENSED A KRYPTONIAN ON THIS PLANET AS SOON AS I CRASHED HERE.
FOR NOW, THAT UNIQUE HUMAN ENERGY PATTERN THA WAS NEARBY EARLIEF WILL HAVE TO WAIT.

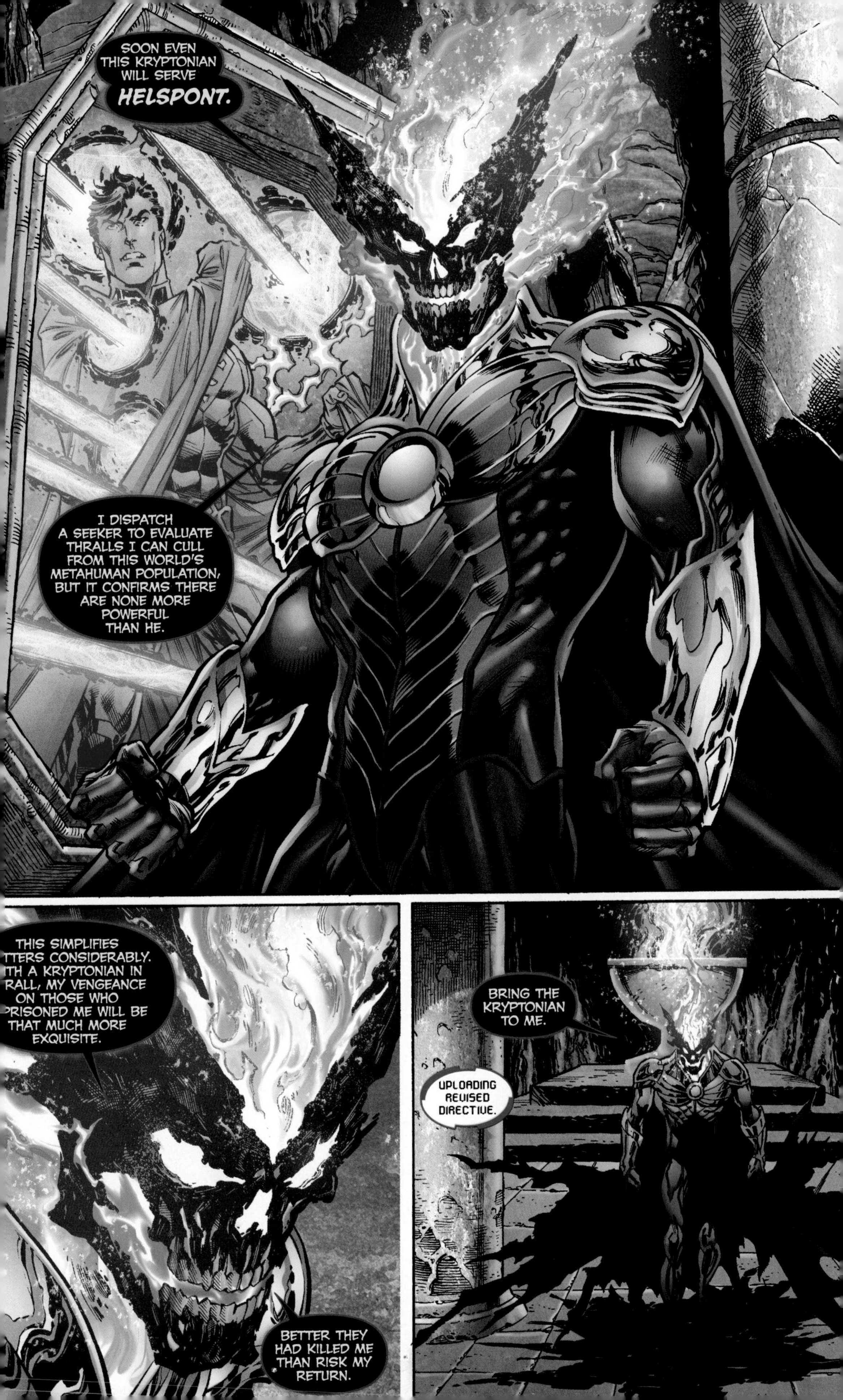
SOON EVEN THIS KRYPTONIAN WILL SERVE HELSPONT.
I DISPATCH A SEEKER TO EVALUATE THRALLS I CAN CULL FROM THIS WORLD'S METAHUMAN POPULATION, BUT IT CONFIRMS THERE ARE NONE MORE POWERFUL THAN HE.
THIS SIMPLIFIES TTERS CONSIDERABLY. ITH A KRYPTONIAN IN RALL, MY VENGEANCE ON THOSE WHO PRISONED ME WILL BE THAT MUCH MORE EXQUISITE.
BETTER THEY HAD KILLED ME THAN RISK MY RETURN.
BRING THE KRYPTONIAN TO ME.
UPLOADING REVISED DIRECTIVE.

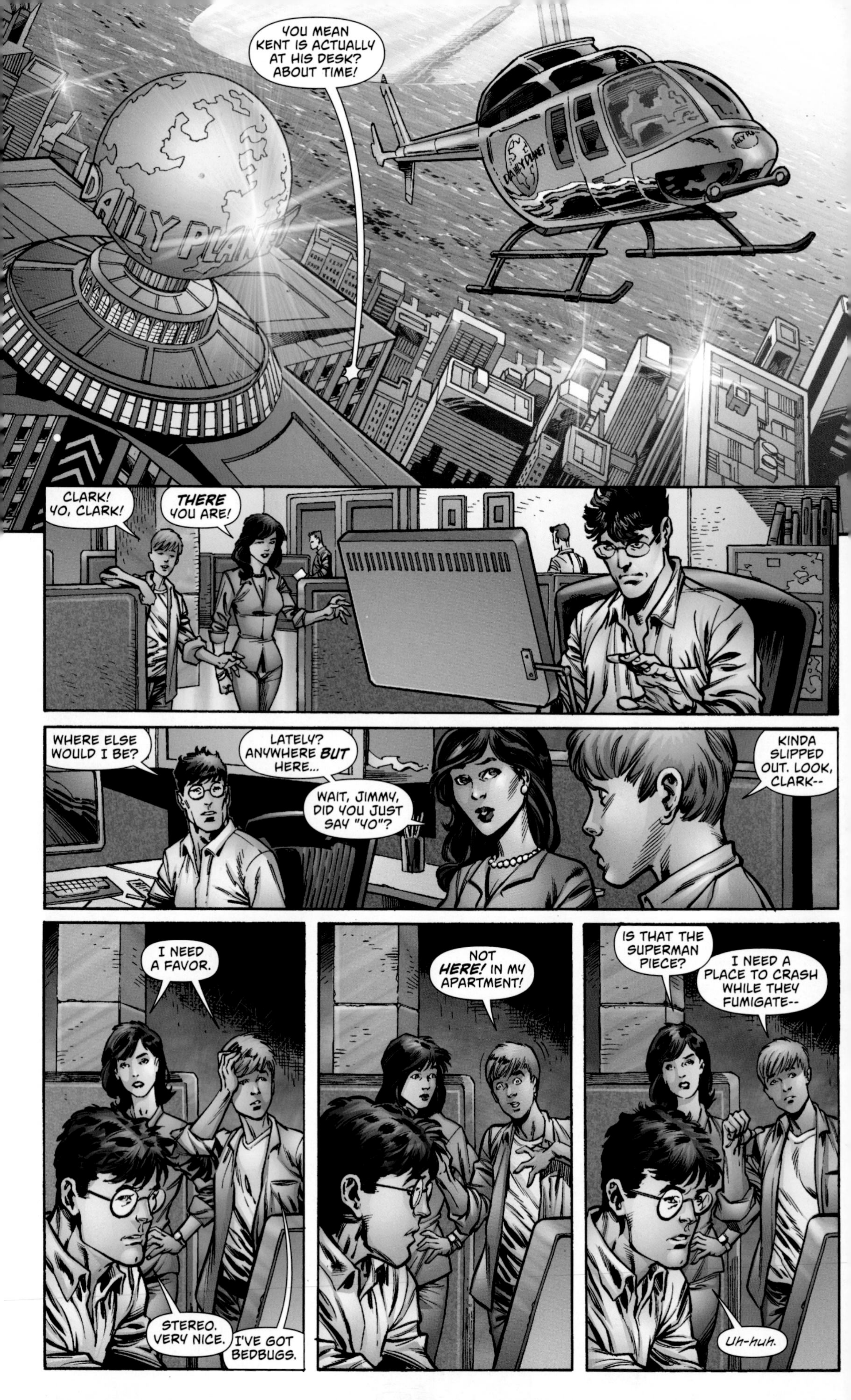
YOU MEAN KENT IS ACTUALLY AT HIS DESK? ABOUT TIME!
DAILY PLANET
CLARK! YO, CLARK!
THERE YOU ARE!
WHERE ELSE WOULD I BE?
LATELY? ANYWHERE BUT HERE...
WAIT, JIMMY, DID YOU JUST SAY "YO"?
KINDA SLIPPED OUT. LOOK, CLARK--
I NEED A FAVOR.
STEREO. VERY NICE.
I'VE GOT BEDBUGS.
NOT HERE! IN MY APARTMENT!
IS THAT THE SUPERMAN PIECE?
I NEED A PLACE TO CRASH WHILE THEY FUMIGATE--
Uh-huh.

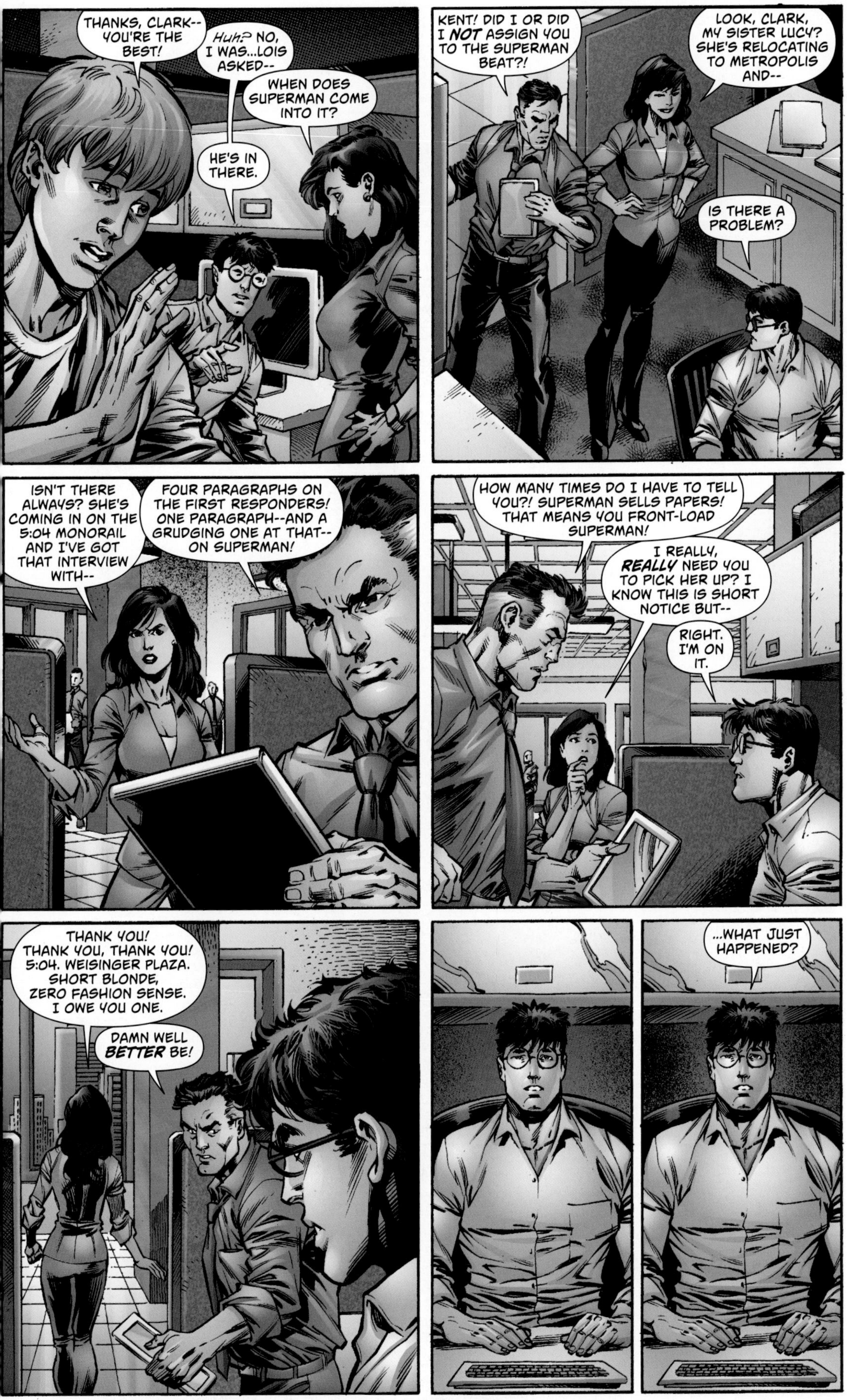
THANKS, CLARK-- YOU'RE THE BEST!
Huh? NO, I WAS...LOIS ASKED--
WHEN DOES SUPERMAN COME INTO IT?
HE'S IN THERE.
KENT! DID I OR DID I NOT ASSIGN YOU TO THE SUPERMAN BEAT?!
LOOK, CLARK, MY SISTER LUCY? SHE'S RELOCATING TO METROPOLIS AND--
IS THERE A PROBLEM?
ISN'T THERE ALWAYS? SHE'S COMING IN ON THE 5:04 MONORAIL AND I'VE GOT THAT INTERVIEW WITH--
FOUR PARAGRAPHS ON THE FIRST RESPONDERS! ONE PARAGRAPH--AND A GRUDGING ONE AT THAT--ON SUPERMAN!
HOW MANY TIMES DO I HAVE TO TELL YOU?! SUPERMAN SELLS PAPERS! THAT MEANS YOU FRONT-LOAD SUPERMAN!
I REALLY, REALLY NEED YOU TO PICK HER UP? I KNOW THIS IS SHORT NOTICE BUT--
RIGHT. I'M ON IT.
THANK YOU! THANK YOU, THANK YOU! 5:04. WEISINGER PLAZA. SHORT BLONDE, ZERO FASHION SENSE. I OWE YOU ONE.
DAMN WELL BETTER BE!
...WHAT JUST HAPPENED?

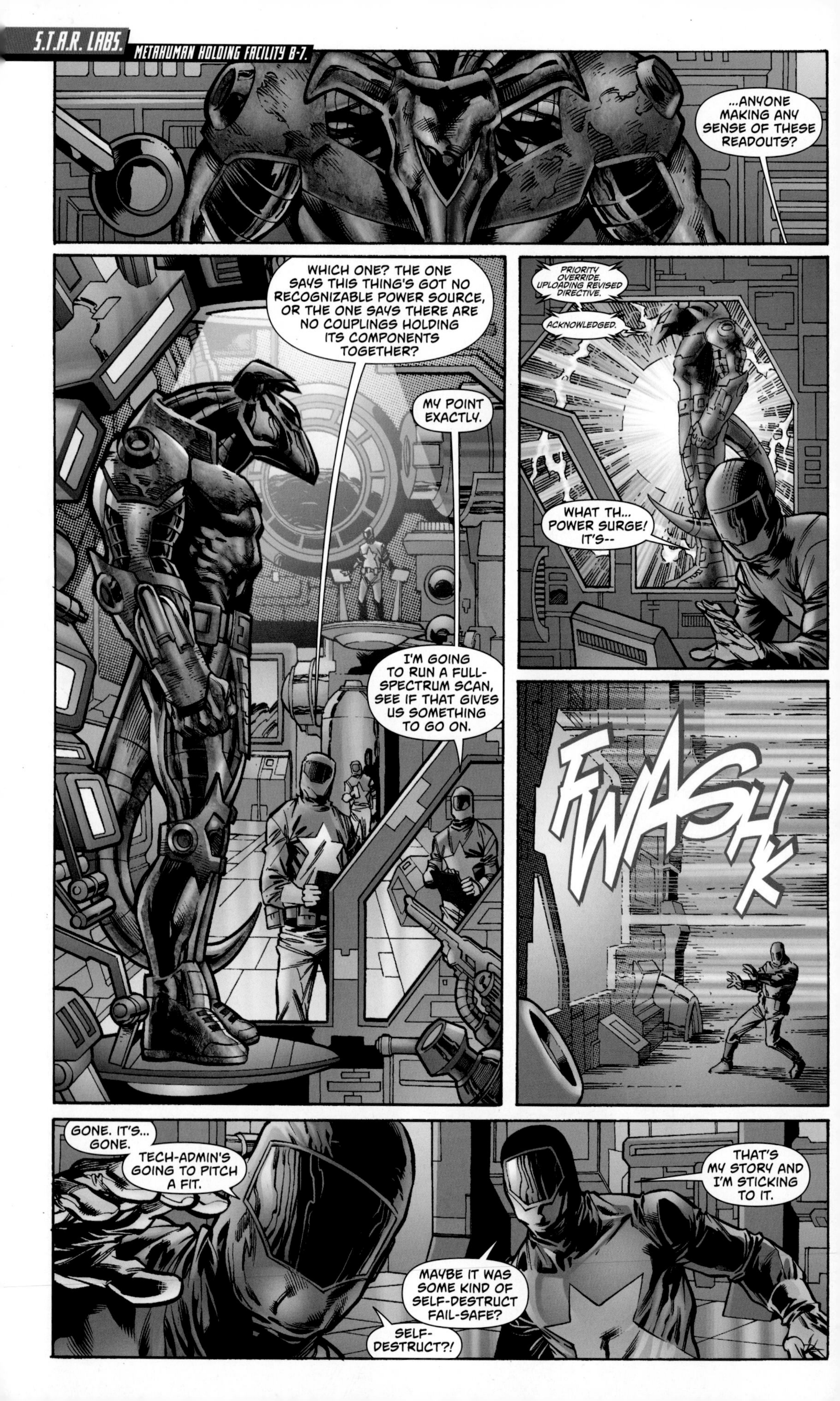

S.T.A.R. LABS.
METAHUMAN HOLDING FACILITY 8-7.
...ANYONE MAKING ANY SENSE OF THESE READOUTS?
WHICH ONE? THE ONE SAYS THIS THING'S GOT NO RECOGNIZABLE POWER SOURCE, OR THE ONE SAYS THERE ARE NO COUPLINGS HOLDING ITS COMPONENTS TOGETHER?
MY POINT EXACTLY.
I'M GOING TO RUN A FULL-SPECTRUM SCAN, SEE IF THAT GIVES US SOMETHING TO GO ON.
PRIORITY OVERRIDE. UPLOADING REVISED DIRECTIVE.
ACKNOWLEDGED.
WHAT TH... POWER SURGE! IT'S--
FWASHK
GONE. IT'S... GONE.
TECH-ADMIN'S GOING TO PITCH A FIT.
MAYBE IT WAS SOME KIND OF SELF-DESTRUCT FAIL-SAFE?
SELF-DESTRUCT?!
THAT'S MY STORY AND I'M STICKING TO IT.

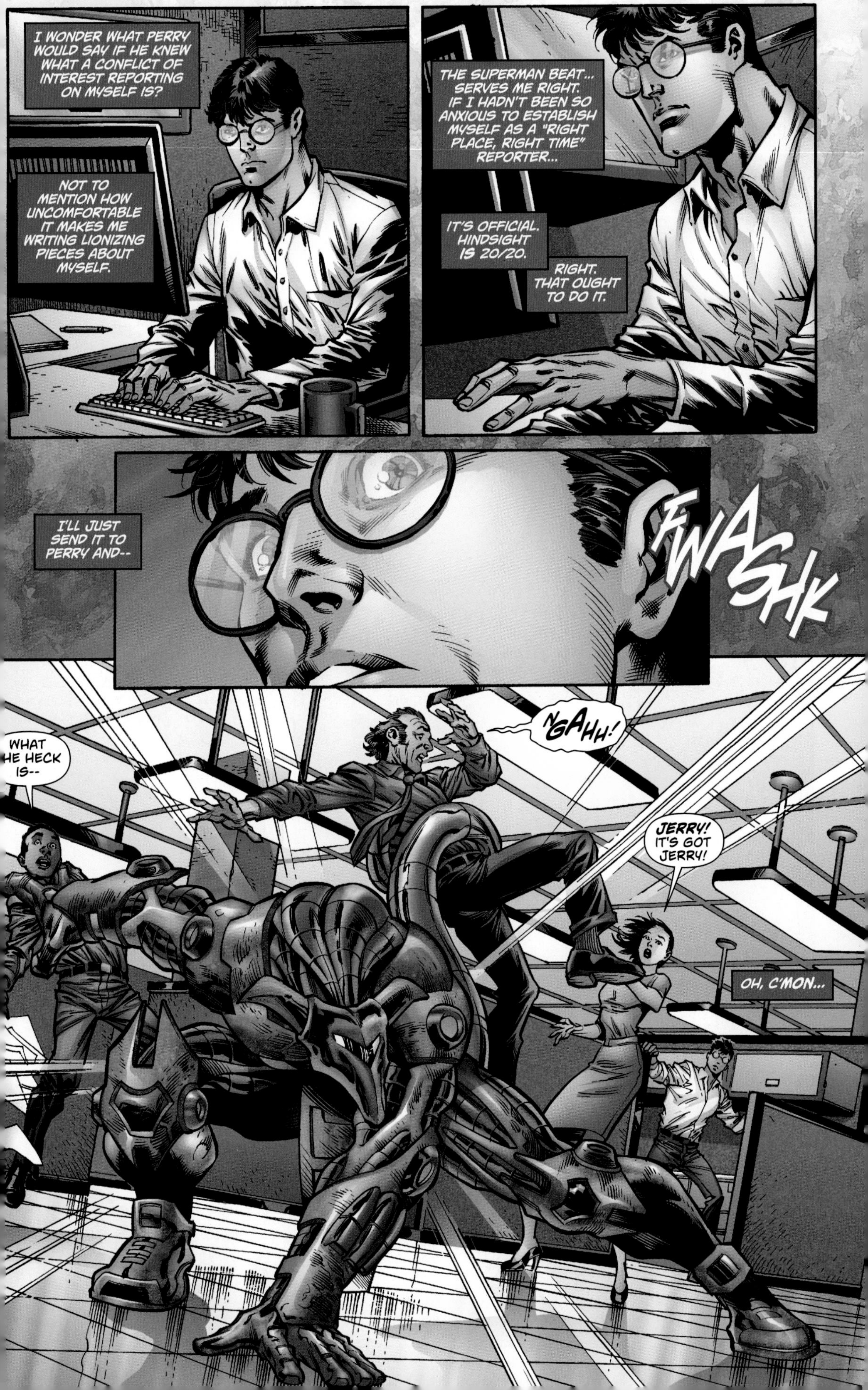
I WONDER WHAT PERRY WOULD SAY IF HE KNEW WHAT A CONFLICT OF INTEREST REPORTING ON MYSELF IS?
NOT TO MENTION HOW UNCOMFORTABLE IT MAKES ME WRITING LIONIZING PIECES ABOUT MYSELF.
THE SUPERMAN BEAT... SERVES ME RIGHT. IF I HADN'T BEEN SO ANXIOUS TO ESTABLISH MYSELF AS A "RIGHT PLACE, RIGHT TIME" REPORTER...
IT'S OFFICIAL. HINDSIGHT IS 20/20.
RIGHT. THAT OUGHT TO DO IT.
I'LL JUST SEND IT TO PERRY AND--
FWASHK
WHAT HE HECK IS--
NGAHH!
JERRY! IT'S GOT JERRY!
OH, C'MON...

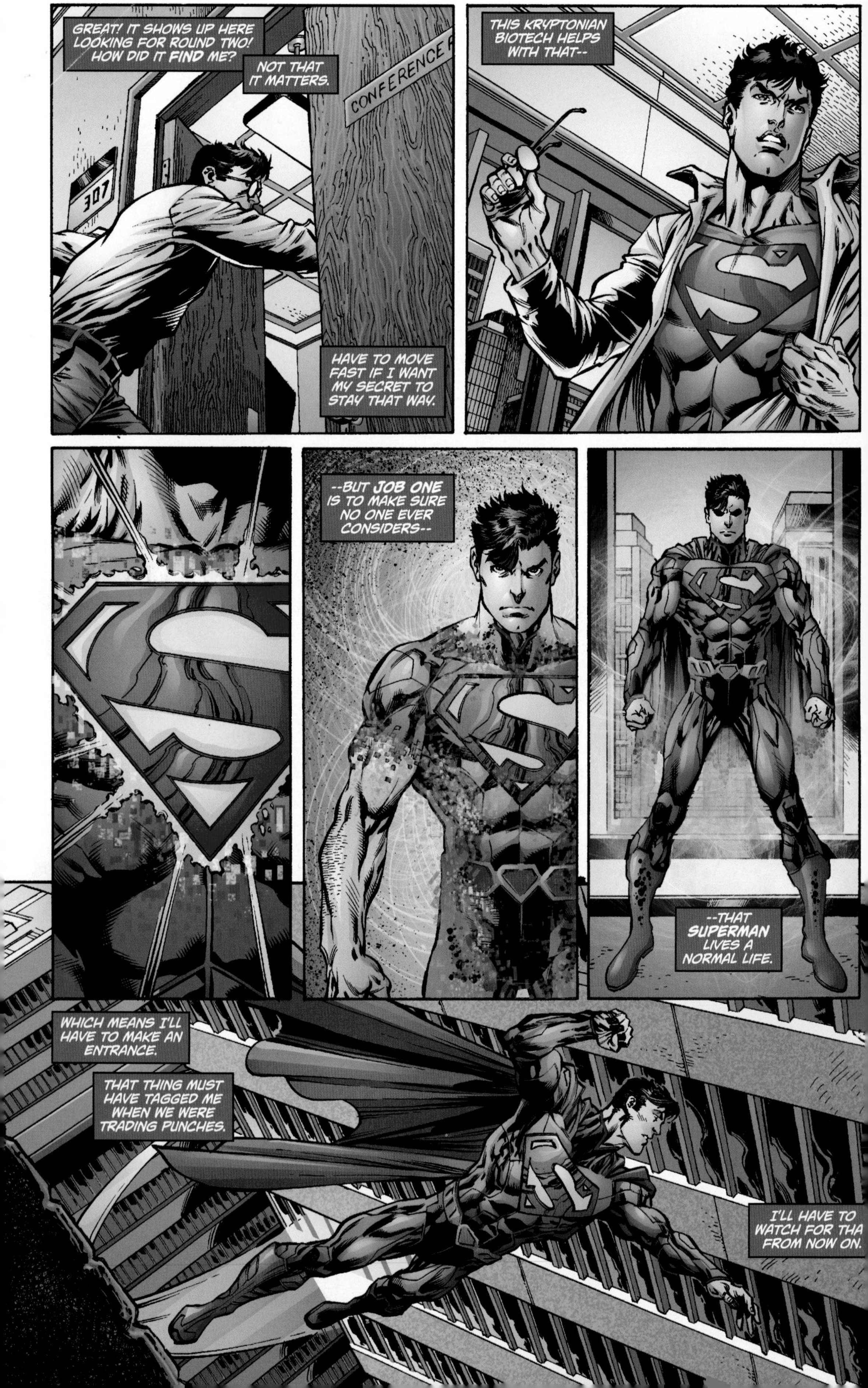
GREAT! IT SHOWS UP HERE LOOKING FOR ROUND TWO! HOW DID IT FIND ME?
NOT THAT IT MATTERS.
CONFERENCE
307
HAVE TO MOVE FAST IF I WANT MY SECRET TO STAY THAT WAY.
THIS KRYPTONIAN BIOTECH HELPS WITH THAT--
--BUT JOB ONE IS TO MAKE SURE NO ONE EVER CONSIDERS--
--THAT SUPERMAN LIVES A NORMAL LIFE.
WHICH MEANS I'LL HAVE TO MAKE AN ENTRANCE.
THAT THING MUST HAVE TAGGED ME WHEN WE WERE TRADING PUNCHES.
I'LL HAVE TO WATCH FOR THA FROM NOW ON.

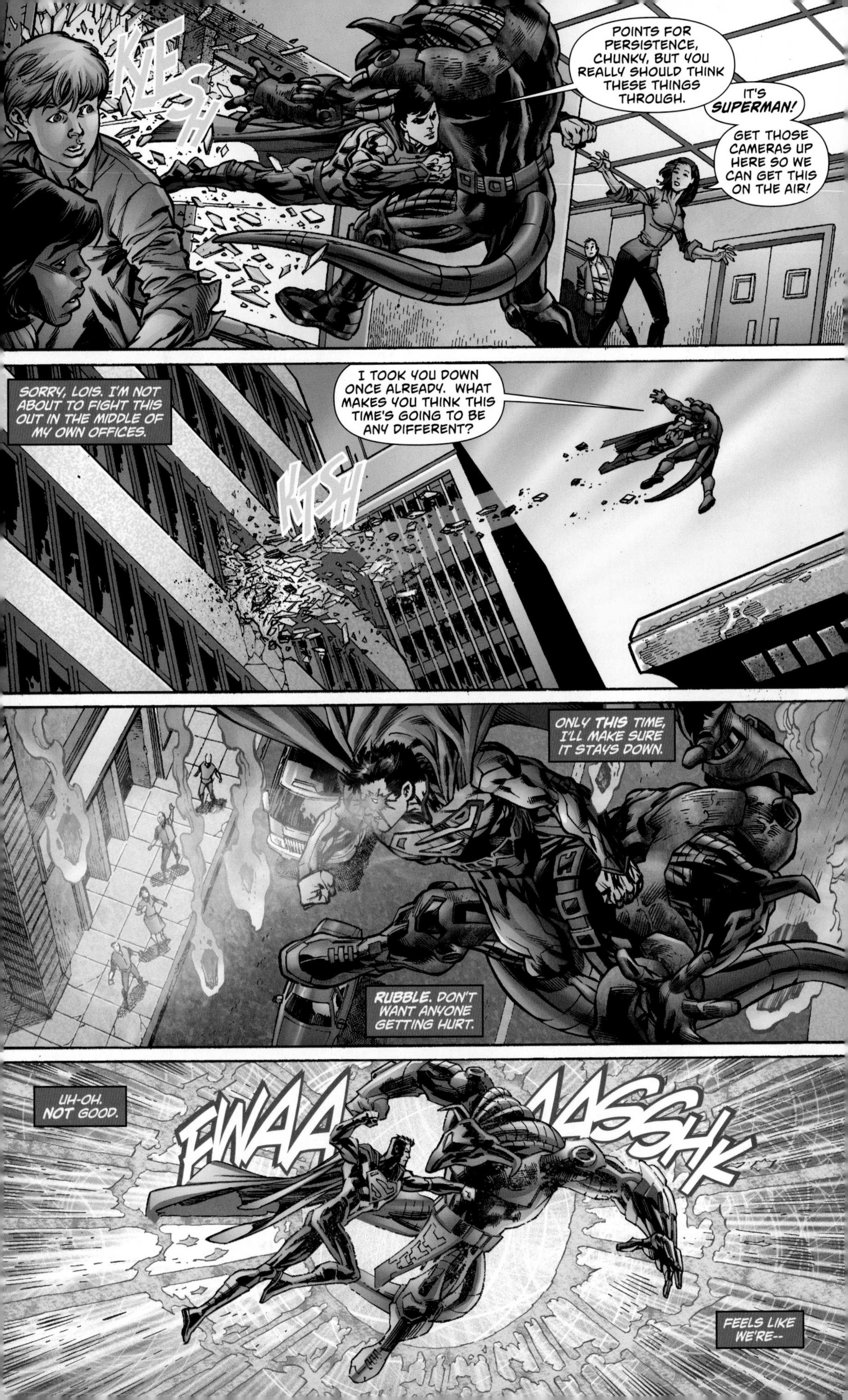
KLESH
POINTS FOR PERSISTENCE, CHUNKY, BUT YOU REALLY SHOULD THINK THESE THINGS THROUGH.
IT'S SUPERMAN!
GET THOSE CAMERAS UP HERE SO WE CAN GET THIS ON THE AIR!
SORRY, LOIS. I'M NOT ABOUT TO FIGHT THIS OUT IN THE MIDDLE OF MY OWN OFFICES.
I TOOK YOU DOWN ONCE ALREADY. WHAT MAKES YOU THINK THIS TIME'S GOING TO BE ANY DIFFERENT?
KTSH
ONLY THIS TIME, I'LL MAKE SURE IT STAYS DOWN.
RUBBLE. DON'T WANT ANYONE GETTING HURT.
UH-OH. NOT GOOD.
FWAAAASSHK
FEELS LIKE WE'RE--

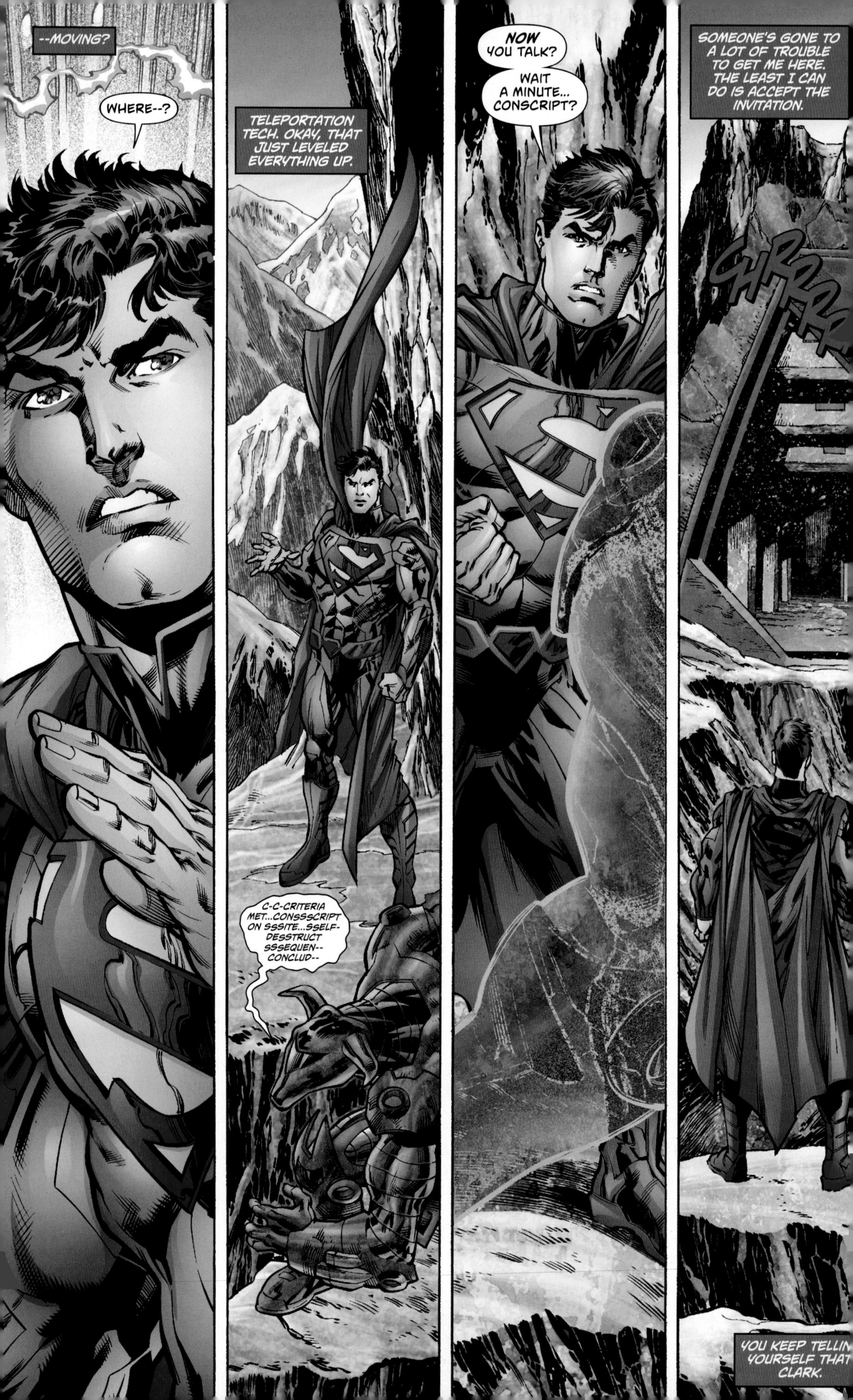

--MOVING?
WHERE--?
TELEPORTATION TECH. OKAY, THAT JUST LEVELED EVERYTHING UP.
C-C-CRITERIA MET...CONSSSCRIPT ON SSSITE...SSELF-DESSTRUCT SSSEQUEN-- CONCLUD--
NOW YOU TALK?
WAIT A MINUTE... CONSCRIPT?
SOMEONE'S GONE TO A LOT OF TROUBLE TO GET ME HERE. THE LEAST I CAN DO IS ACCEPT THE INVITATION.
YOU KEEP TELLIN YOURSELF THAT CLARK.

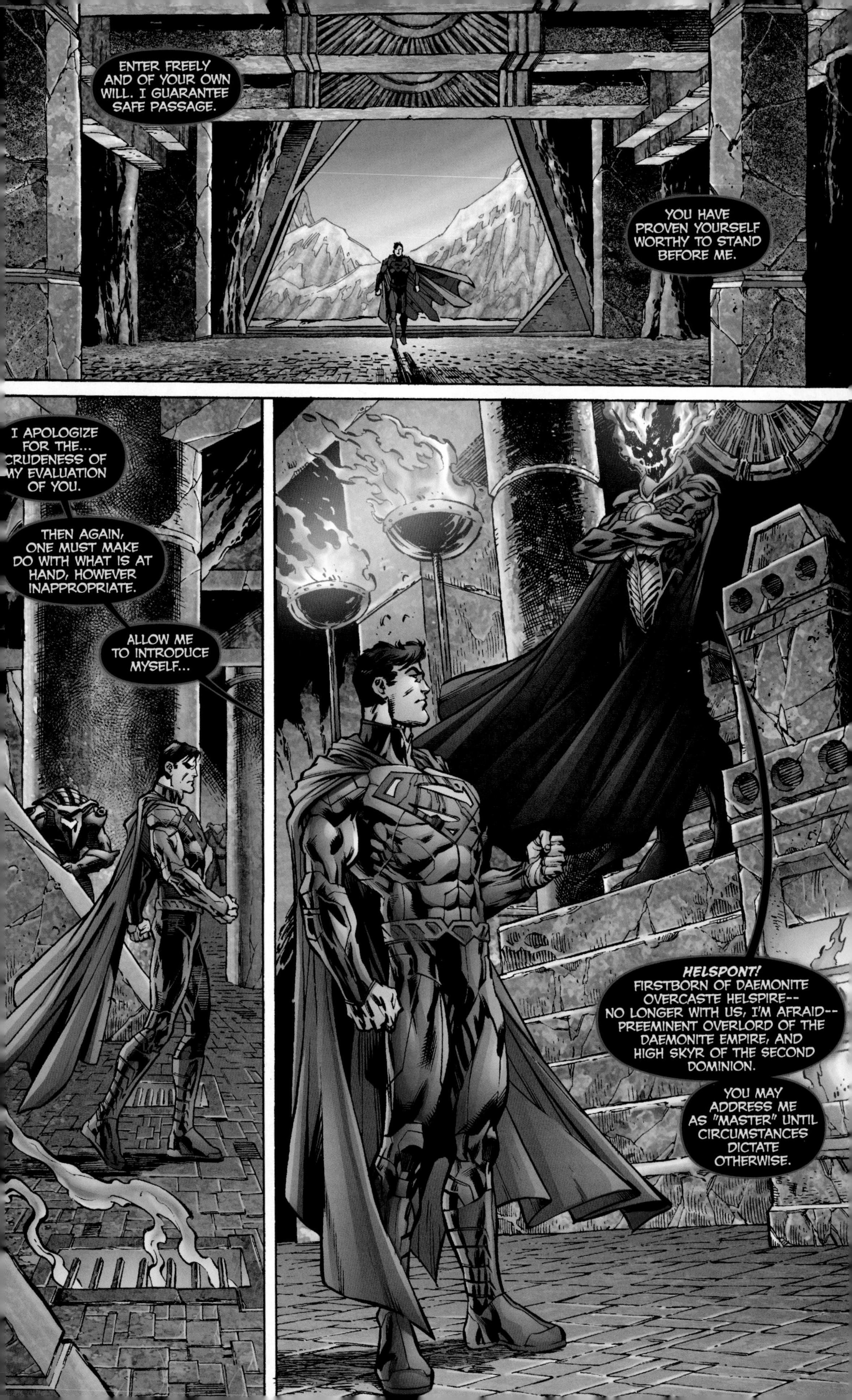
ENTER FREELY AND OF YOUR OWN WILL. I GUARANTEE SAFE PASSAGE.
YOU HAVE PROVEN YOURSELF WORTHY TO STAND BEFORE ME.
I APOLOGIZE FOR THE... CRUDENESS OF MY EVALUATION OF YOU.
THEN AGAIN, ONE MUST MAKE DO WITH WHAT IS AT HAND, HOWEVER INAPPROPRIATE.
ALLOW ME TO INTRODUCE MYSELF...
HELSPONT! FIRSTBORN OF DAEMONITE OVERCASTE HELSPIRE-- NO LONGER WITH US, I'M AFRAID-- PREEMINENT OVERLORD OF THE DAEMONITE EMPIRE, AND HIGH SKYR OF THE SECOND DOMINION.
YOU MAY ADDRESS ME AS "MASTER" UNTIL CIRCUMSTANCES DICTATE OTHERWISE.

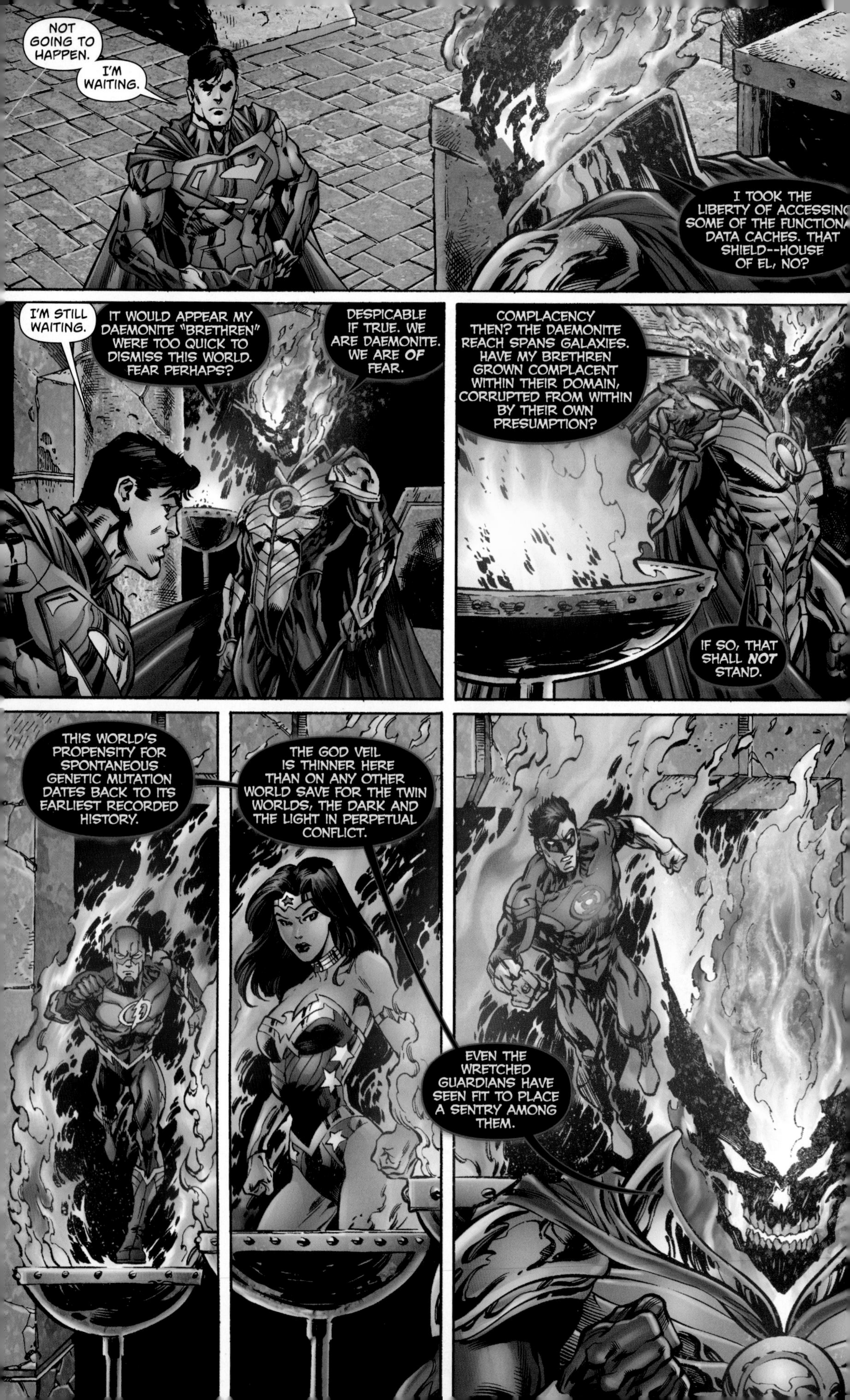

NOT GOING TO HAPPEN.
I'M WAITING.
I TOOK THE LIBERTY OF ACCESSING SOME OF THE FUNCTIONAL DATA CACHES. THAT SHIELD--HOUSE OF EL, NO?
I'M STILL WAITING.
IT WOULD APPEAR MY DAEMONITE "BRETHREN" WERE TOO QUICK TO DISMISS THIS WORLD. FEAR PERHAPS?
DESPICABLE IF TRUE. WE ARE DAEMONITE. WE ARE OF FEAR.
COMPLACENCY THEN? THE DAEMONITE REACH SPANS GALAXIES. HAVE MY BRETHREN GROWN COMPLACENT WITHIN THEIR DOMAIN, CORRUPTED FROM WITHIN BY THEIR OWN PRESUMPTION?
IF SO, THAT SHALL NOT STAND.
THIS WORLD'S PROPENSITY FOR SPONTANEOUS GENETIC MUTATION DATES BACK TO ITS EARLIEST RECORDED HISTORY.
THE GOD VEIL IS THINNER HERE THAN ON ANY OTHER WORLD SAVE FOR THE TWIN WORLDS, THE DARK AND THE LIGHT IN PERPETUAL CONFLICT.
EVEN THE WRETCHED GUARDIANS HAVE SEEN FIT TO PLACE A SENTRY AMONG THEM.

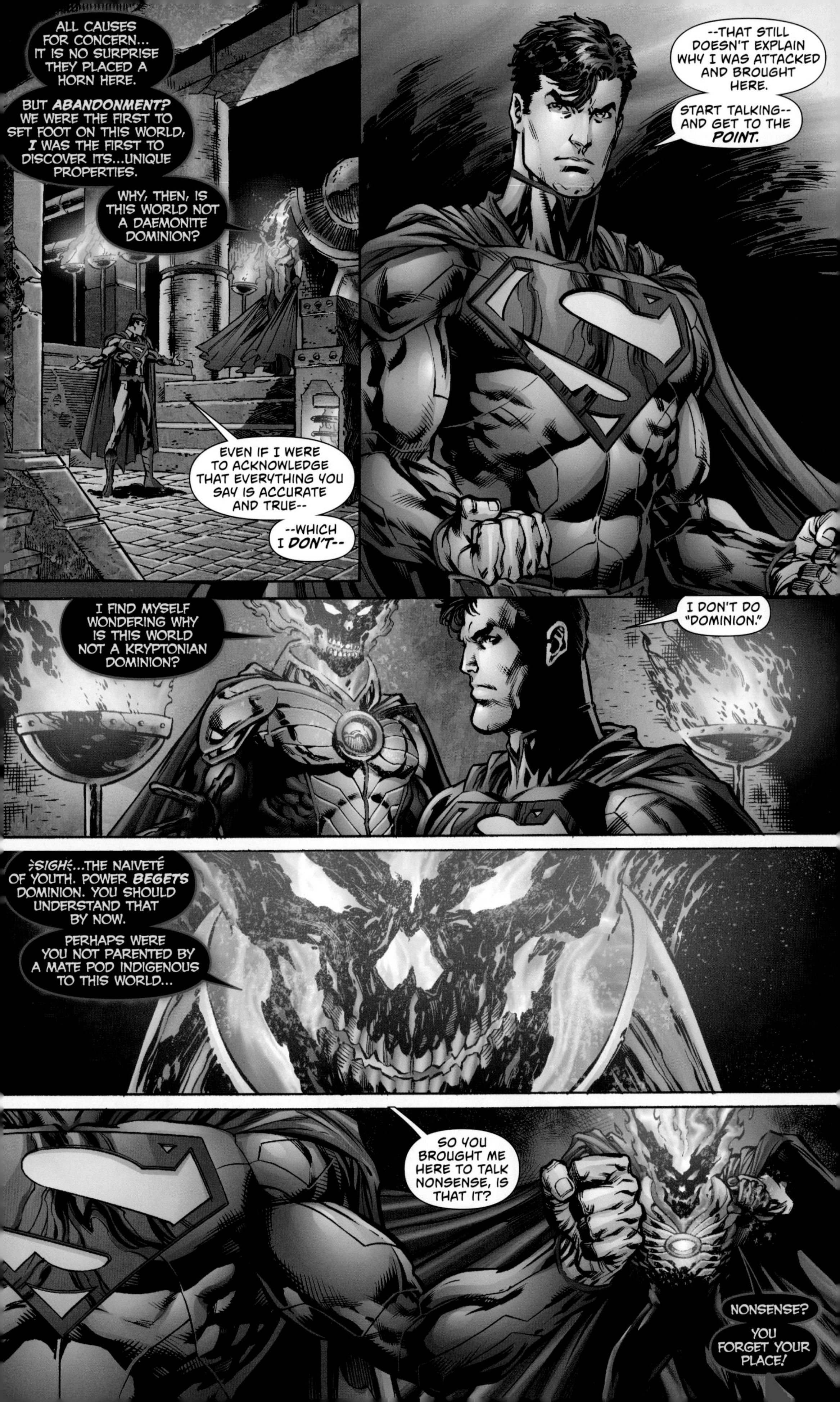

ALL CAUSES FOR CONCERN... IT IS NO SURPRISE THEY PLACED A HORN HERE.
BUT *ABANDONMENT?* WE WERE THE FIRST TO SET FOOT ON THIS WORLD, *I* WAS THE FIRST TO DISCOVER ITS...UNIQUE PROPERTIES.
WHY, THEN, IS THIS WORLD NOT A DAEMONITE DOMINION?
EVEN IF I WERE TO ACKNOWLEDGE THAT EVERYTHING YOU SAY IS ACCURATE AND TRUE--
--WHICH I *DON'T*--
--THAT STILL DOESN'T EXPLAIN WHY I WAS ATTACKED AND BROUGHT HERE.
START TALKING-- AND GET TO THE *POINT.*
I FIND MYSELF WONDERING WHY IS THIS WORLD NOT A KRYPTONIAN DOMINION?
I DON'T DO "DOMINION."
SIGH...THE NAIVETÉ OF YOUTH. POWER *BEGETS* DOMINION. YOU SHOULD UNDERSTAND THAT BY NOW.
PERHAPS WERE YOU NOT PARENTED BY A MATE POD INDIGENOUS TO THIS WORLD...
SO YOU BROUGHT ME HERE TO TALK NONSENSE, IS THAT IT?
NONSENSE?
YOU FORGET YOUR PLACE!

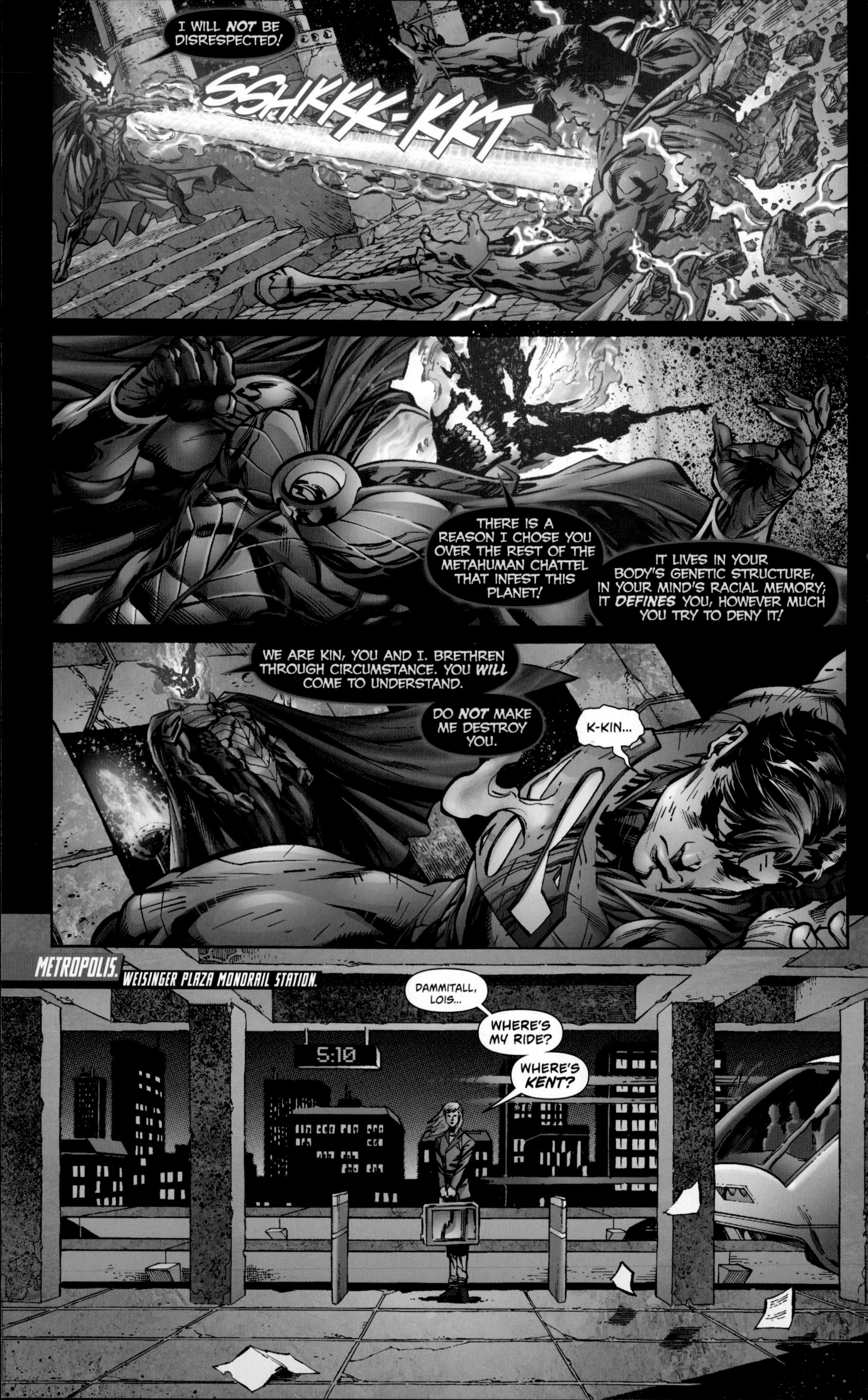

I WILL **NOT** BE DISRESPECTED!
SSHKKK-KKT
THERE IS A REASON I CHOSE YOU OVER THE REST OF THE METAHUMAN CHATTEL THAT INFEST THIS PLANET!
IT LIVES IN YOUR BODY'S GENETIC STRUCTURE, IN YOUR MIND'S RACIAL MEMORY; IT **DEFINES** YOU, HOWEVER MUCH YOU TRY TO DENY IT!
WE ARE KIN, YOU AND I. BRETHREN THROUGH CIRCUMSTANCE. YOU **WILL** COME TO UNDERSTAND.
DO **NOT** MAKE ME DESTROY YOU.
K-KIN...
METROPOLIS.
WEISINGER PLAZA MONORAIL STATION.
5:10
DAMMITALL, LOIS...
WHERE'S MY RIDE?
WHERE'S **KENT?**

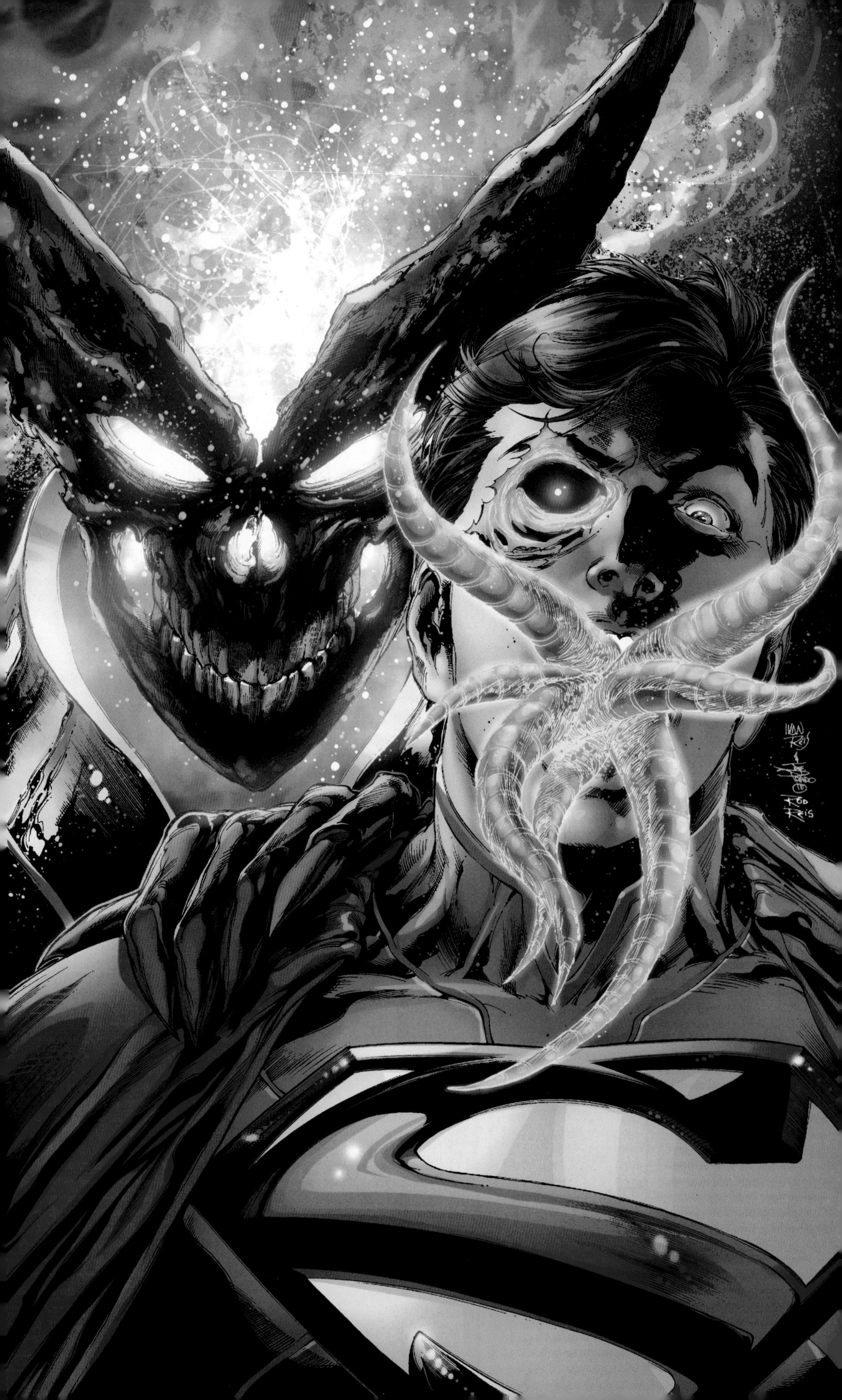

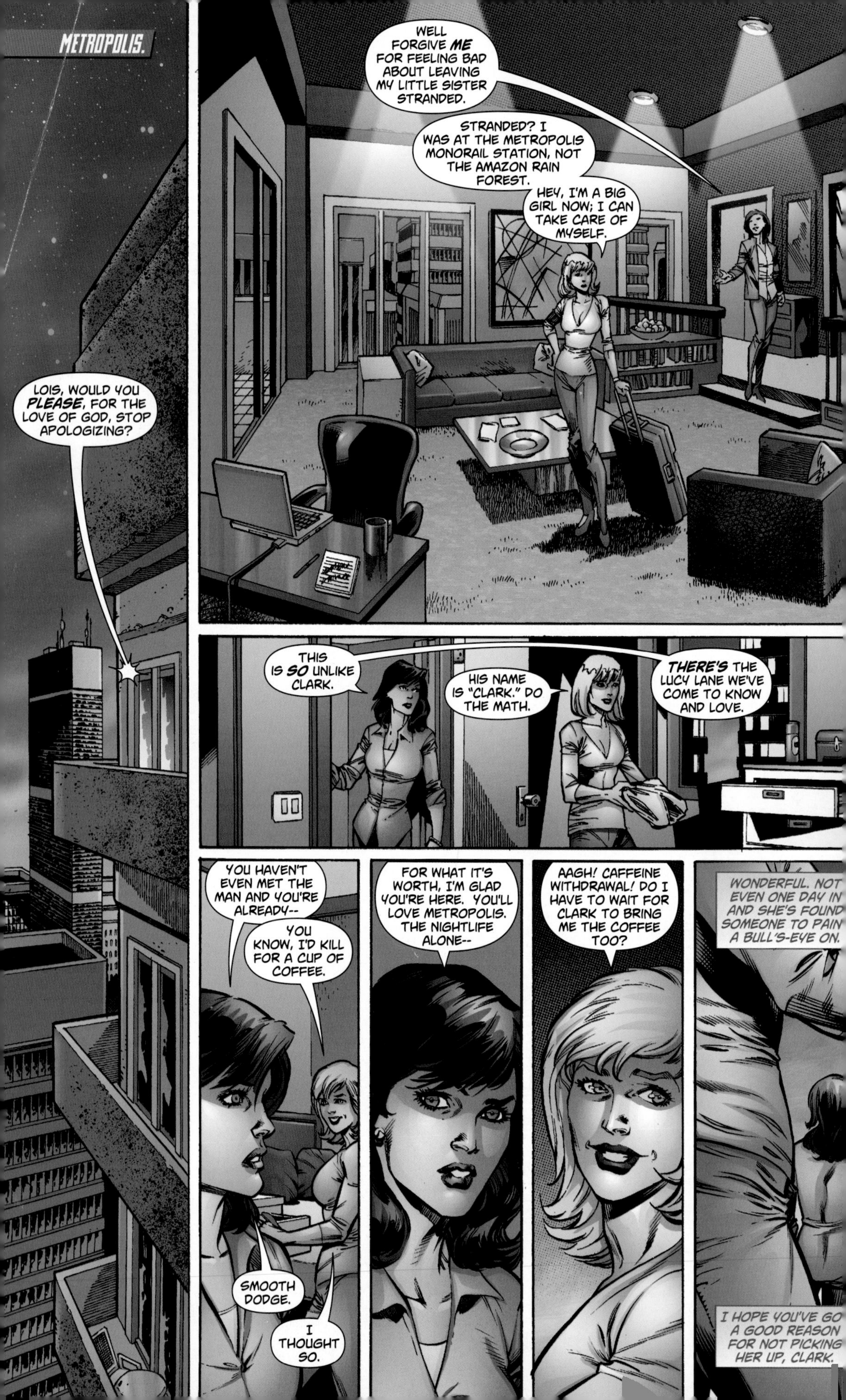
METROPOLIS.
WELL FORGIVE ME FOR FEELING BAD ABOUT LEAVING MY LITTLE SISTER STRANDED.
STRANDED? I WAS AT THE METROPOLIS MONORAIL STATION, NOT THE AMAZON RAIN FOREST.
HEY, I'M A BIG GIRL NOW; I CAN TAKE CARE OF MYSELF.
LOIS, WOULD YOU PLEASE, FOR THE LOVE OF GOD, STOP APOLOGIZING?
THIS IS SO UNLIKE CLARK.
HIS NAME IS "CLARK." DO THE MATH.
THERE'S THE LUCY LANE WE'VE COME TO KNOW AND LOVE.
YOU HAVEN'T EVEN MET THE MAN AND YOU'RE ALREADY--
YOU KNOW, I'D KILL FOR A CUP OF COFFEE.
SMOOTH DODGE.
I THOUGHT SO.
FOR WHAT IT'S WORTH, I'M GLAD YOU'RE HERE. YOU'LL LOVE METROPOLIS. THE NIGHTLIFE ALONE--
AAGH! CAFFEINE WITHDRAWAL! DO I HAVE TO WAIT FOR CLARK TO BRING ME THE COFFEE TOO?
WONDERFUL. NOT EVEN ONE DAY IN AND SHE'S FOUND SOMEONE TO PAIN A BULL'S-EYE ON.
I HOPE YOU'VE GO A GOOD REASON FOR NOT PICKING HER UP, CLARK.

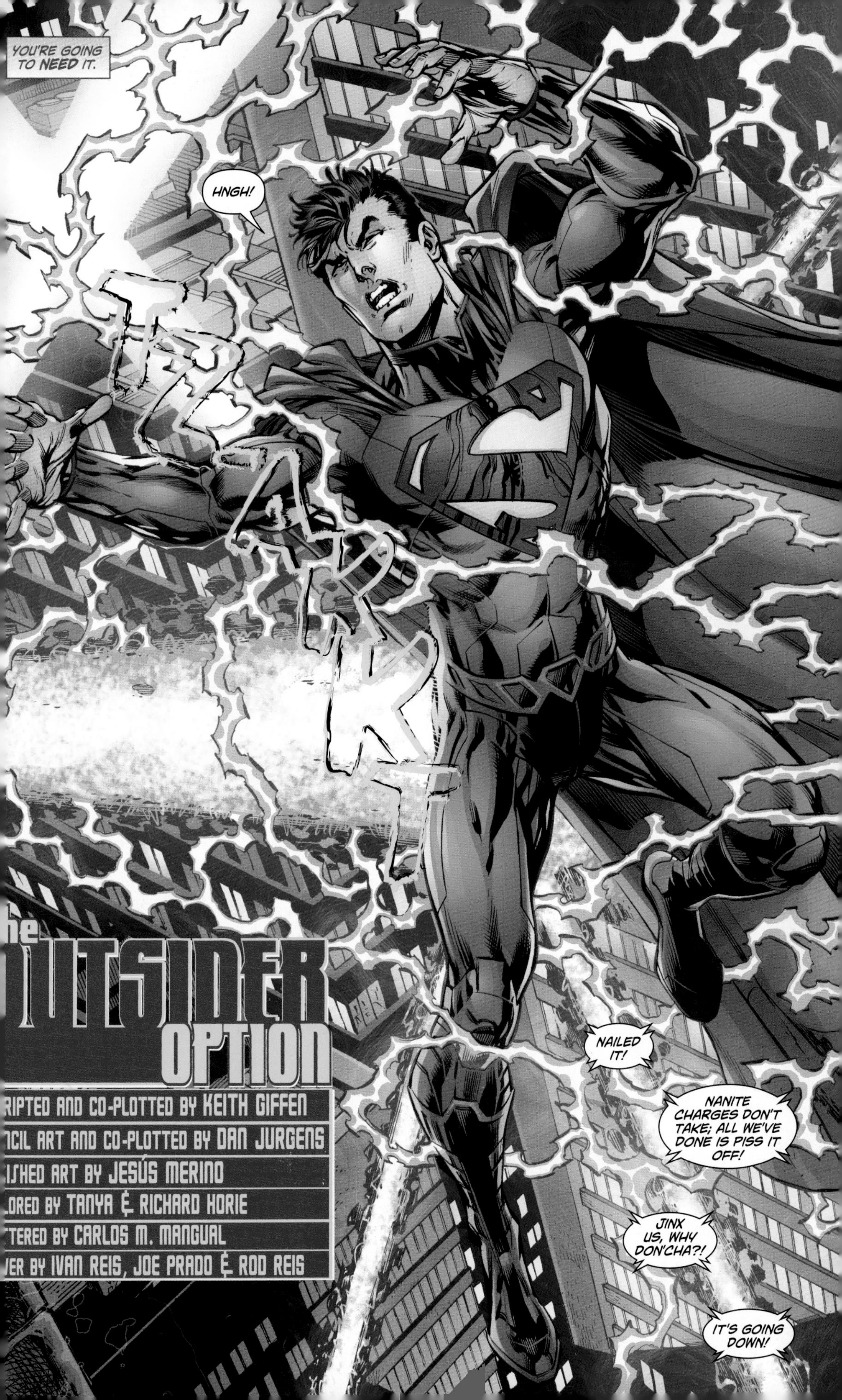
YOU'RE GOING TO NEED IT.
HNGH!
NAILED IT!
NANITE CHARGES DON'T TAKE; ALL WE'VE DONE IS PISS IT OFF!
JINX US, WHY DON'CHA?!
IT'S GOING DOWN!
HE
UTSIDER
OPTION
RIPTED AND CO-PLOTTED BY KEITH GIFFEN
NCIL ART AND CO-PLOTTED BY DAN JURGENS
ISHED ART BY JESÚS MERINO
LORED BY TANYA & RICHARD HORIE
TTERED BY CARLOS M. MANGUAL
VER BY IVAN REIS, JOE PRADO & ROD REIS

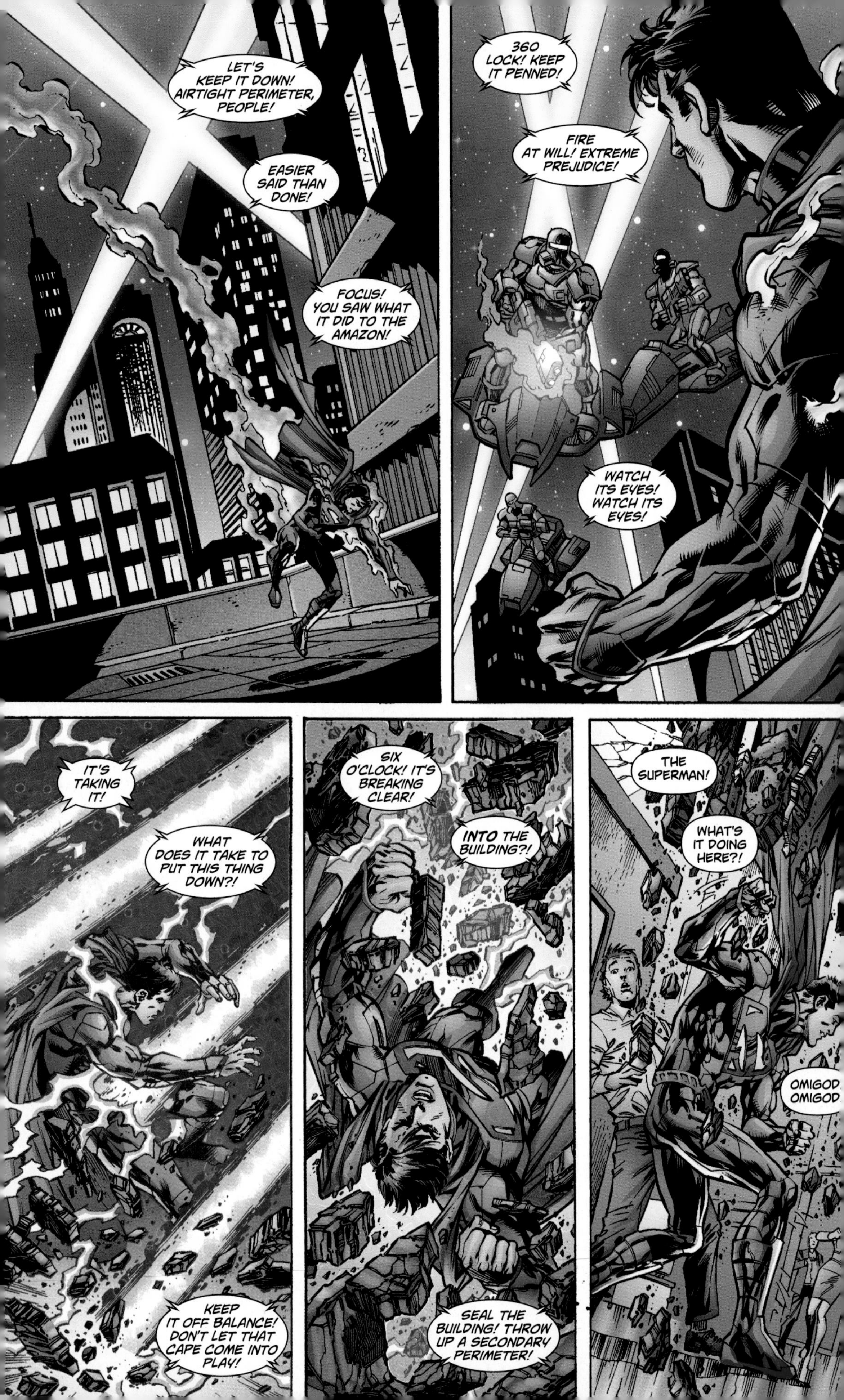
LET'S KEEP IT DOWN! AIRTIGHT PERIMETER, PEOPLE!
EASIER SAID THAN DONE!
FOCUS! YOU SAW WHAT IT DID TO THE AMAZON!
360 LOCK! KEEP IT PENNED!
FIRE AT WILL! EXTREME PREJUDICE!
WATCH ITS EYES! WATCH ITS EYES!
IT'S TAKING IT!
WHAT DOES IT TAKE TO PUT THIS THING DOWN?!
KEEP IT OFF BALANCE! DON'T LET THAT CAPE COME INTO PLAY!
SIX O'CLOCK! IT'S BREAKING CLEAR!
INTO THE BUILDING?!
SEAL THE BUILDING! THROW UP A SECONDARY PERIMETER!
THE SUPERMAN!
WHAT'S IT DOING HERE?!
OMIGOD OMIGOD

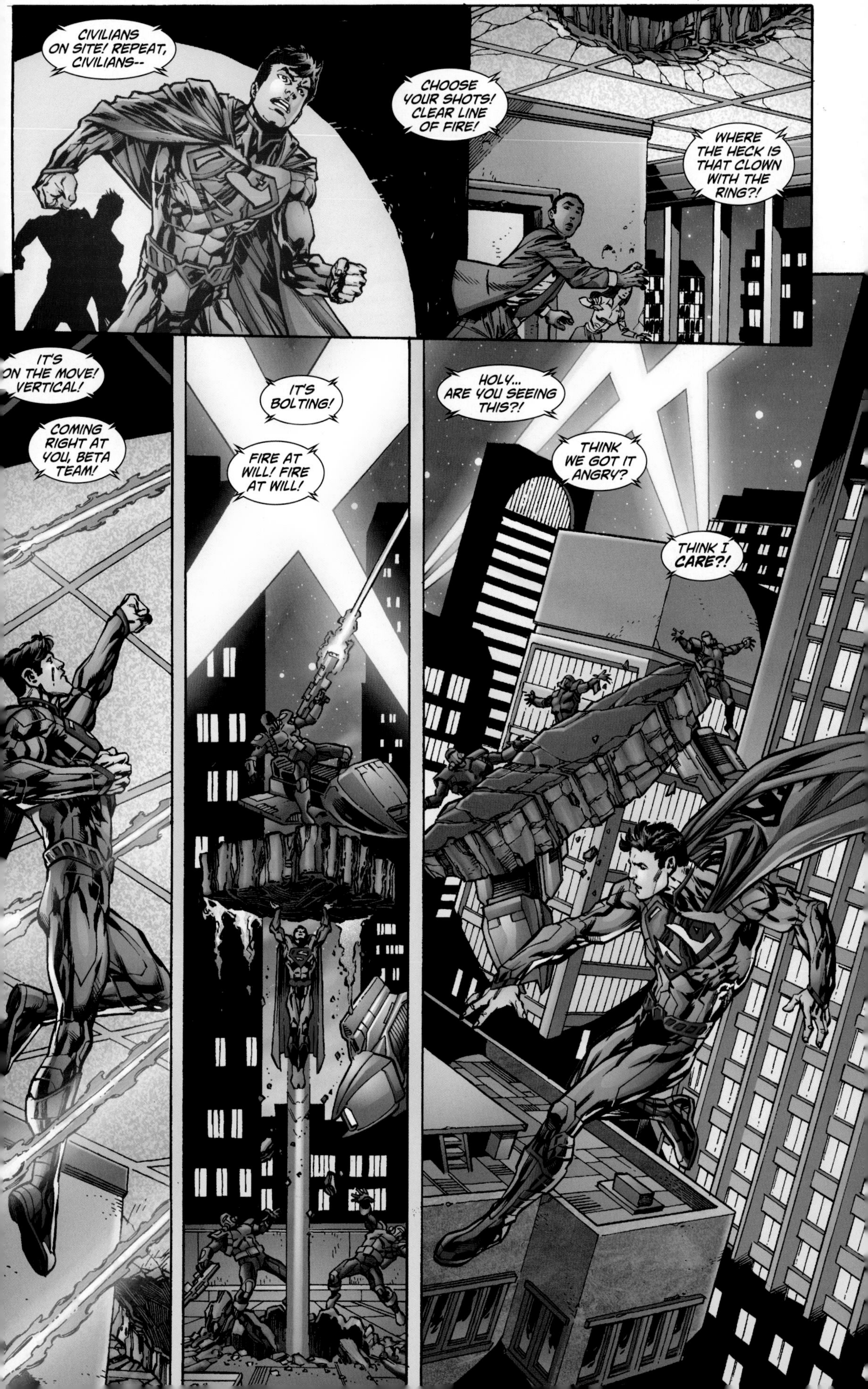

CIVILIANS ON SITE! REPEAT, CIVILIANS--
CHOOSE YOUR SHOTS! CLEAR LINE OF FIRE!
WHERE THE HECK IS THAT CLOWN WITH THE RING?!
IT'S ON THE MOVE! VERTICAL!
COMING RIGHT AT YOU, BETA TEAM!
IT'S BOLTING!
FIRE AT WILL! FIRE AT WILL!
HOLY... ARE YOU SEEING THIS?!
THINK WE GOT IT ANGRY?
THINK I CARE?!

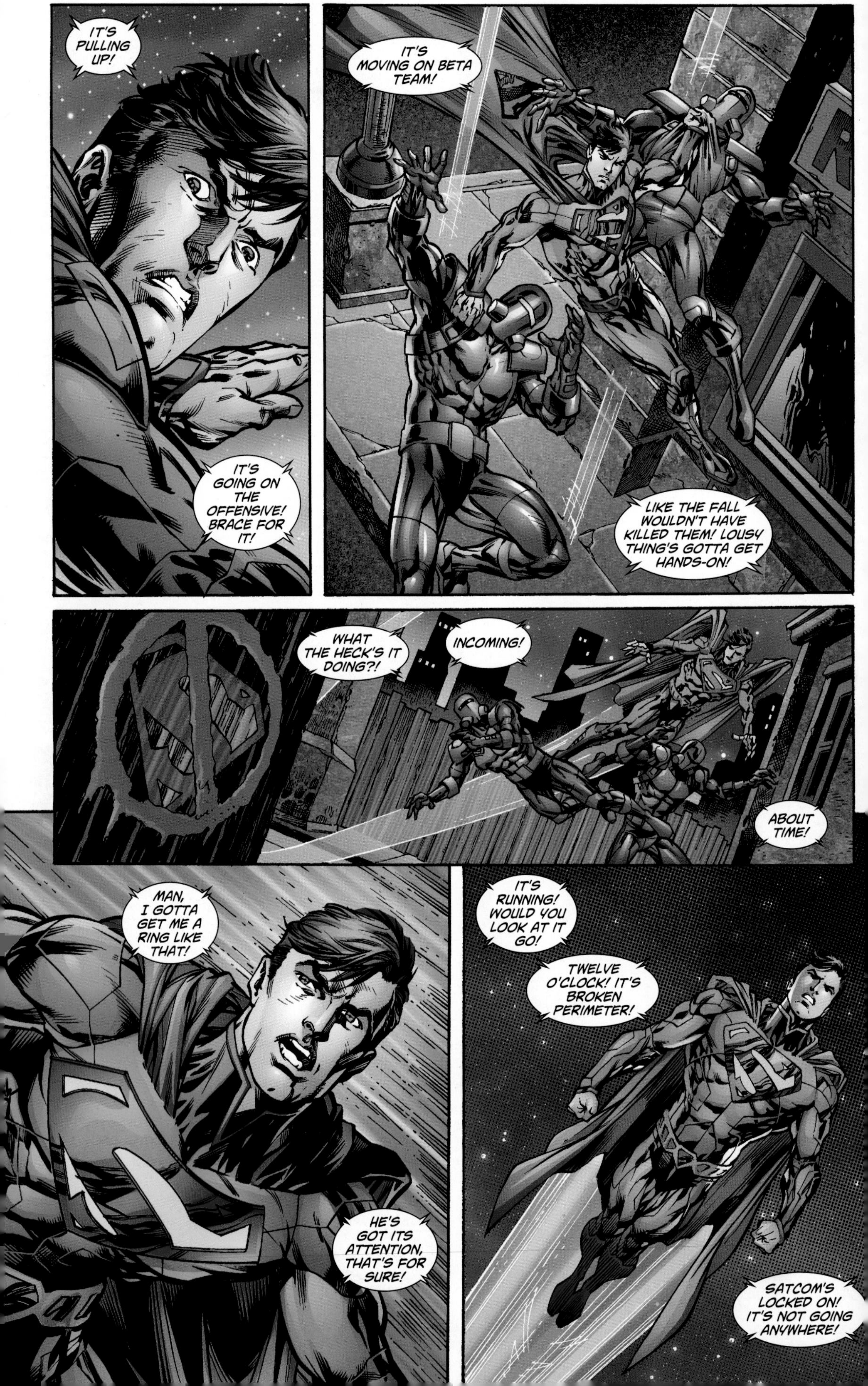
IT'S PULLING UP!
IT'S GOING ON THE OFFENSIVE! BRACE FOR IT!
IT'S MOVING ON BETA TEAM!
LIKE THE FALL WOULDN'T HAVE KILLED THEM! LOUSY THING'S GOTTA GET HANDS-ON!
WHAT THE HECK'S IT DOING?!
INCOMING!
ABOUT TIME!
MAN, I GOTTA GET ME A RING LIKE THAT!
HE'S GOT ITS ATTENTION, THAT'S FOR SURE!
IT'S RUNNING! WOULD YOU LOOK AT IT GO!
TWELVE O'CLOCK! IT'S BROKEN PERIMETER!
SATCOM'S LOCKED ON! IT'S NOT GOING ANYWHERE!

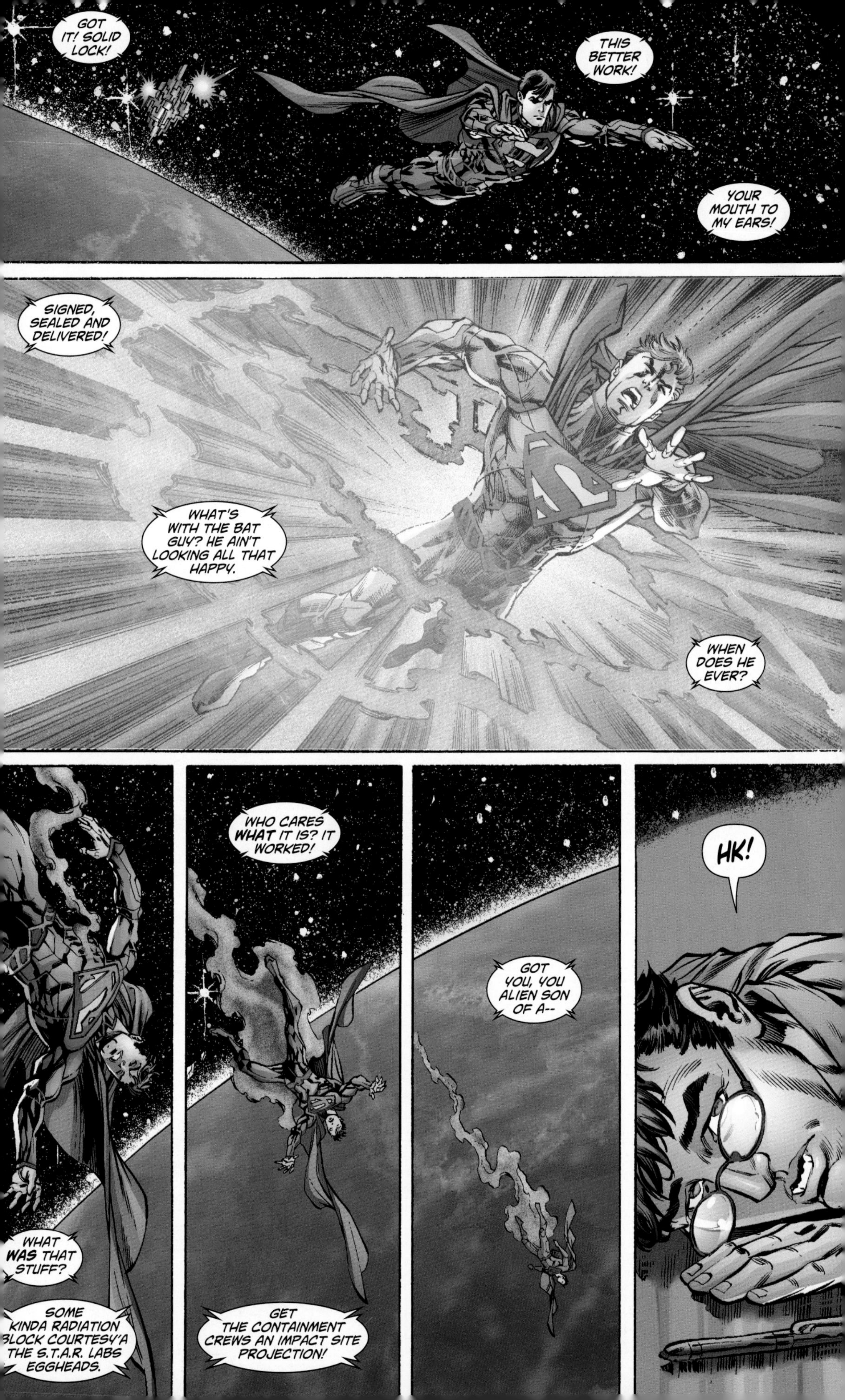
GOT IT! SOLID LOCK!
THIS BETTER WORK!
YOUR MOUTH TO MY EARS!
SIGNED, SEALED AND DELIVERED!
WHAT'S WITH THE BAT GUY? HE AIN'T LOOKING ALL THAT HAPPY.
WHEN DOES HE EVER?
WHAT WAS THAT STUFF?
SOME KINDA RADIATION BLOCK COURTESY'A THE S.T.A.R. LABS EGGHEADS.
WHO CARES WHAT IT IS? IT WORKED!
GET THE CONTAINMENT CREWS AN IMPACT SITE PROJECTION!
GOT YOU, YOU ALIEN SON OF A--
HK!

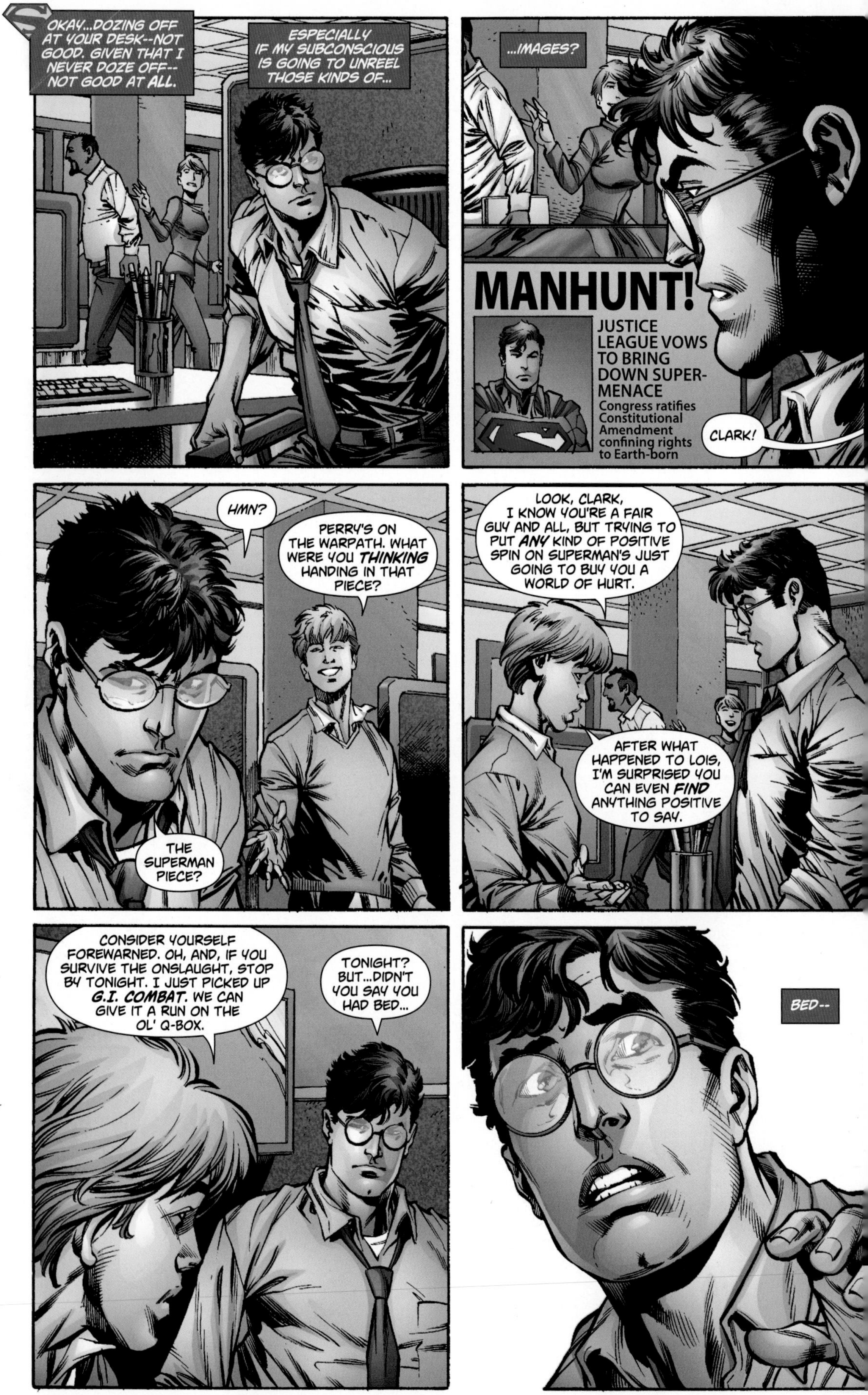
OKAY...DOZING OFF AT YOUR DESK--NOT GOOD. GIVEN THAT I NEVER DOZE OFF--NOT GOOD AT ALL.
ESPECIALLY IF MY SUBCONSCIOUS IS GOING TO UNREEL THOSE KINDS OF...
...IMAGES?
MANHUNT!
JUSTICE LEAGUE VOWS TO BRING DOWN SUPER-MENACE
Congress ratifies Constitutional Amendment confining rights to Earth-born
CLARK!
HMN?
PERRY'S ON THE WARPATH. WHAT WERE YOU THINKING HANDING IN THAT PIECE?
THE SUPERMAN PIECE?
LOOK, CLARK, I KNOW YOU'RE A FAIR GUY AND ALL, BUT TRYING TO PUT ANY KIND OF POSITIVE SPIN ON SUPERMAN'S JUST GOING TO BUY YOU A WORLD OF HURT.
AFTER WHAT HAPPENED TO LOIS, I'M SURPRISED YOU CAN EVEN FIND ANYTHING POSITIVE TO SAY.
CONSIDER YOURSELF FOREWARNED. OH, AND, IF YOU SURVIVE THE ONSLAUGHT, STOP BY TONIGHT. I JUST PICKED UP G.I. COMBAT. WE CAN GIVE IT A RUN ON THE OL' Q-BOX.
TONIGHT? BUT...DIDN'T YOU SAY YOU HAD BED...
BED--

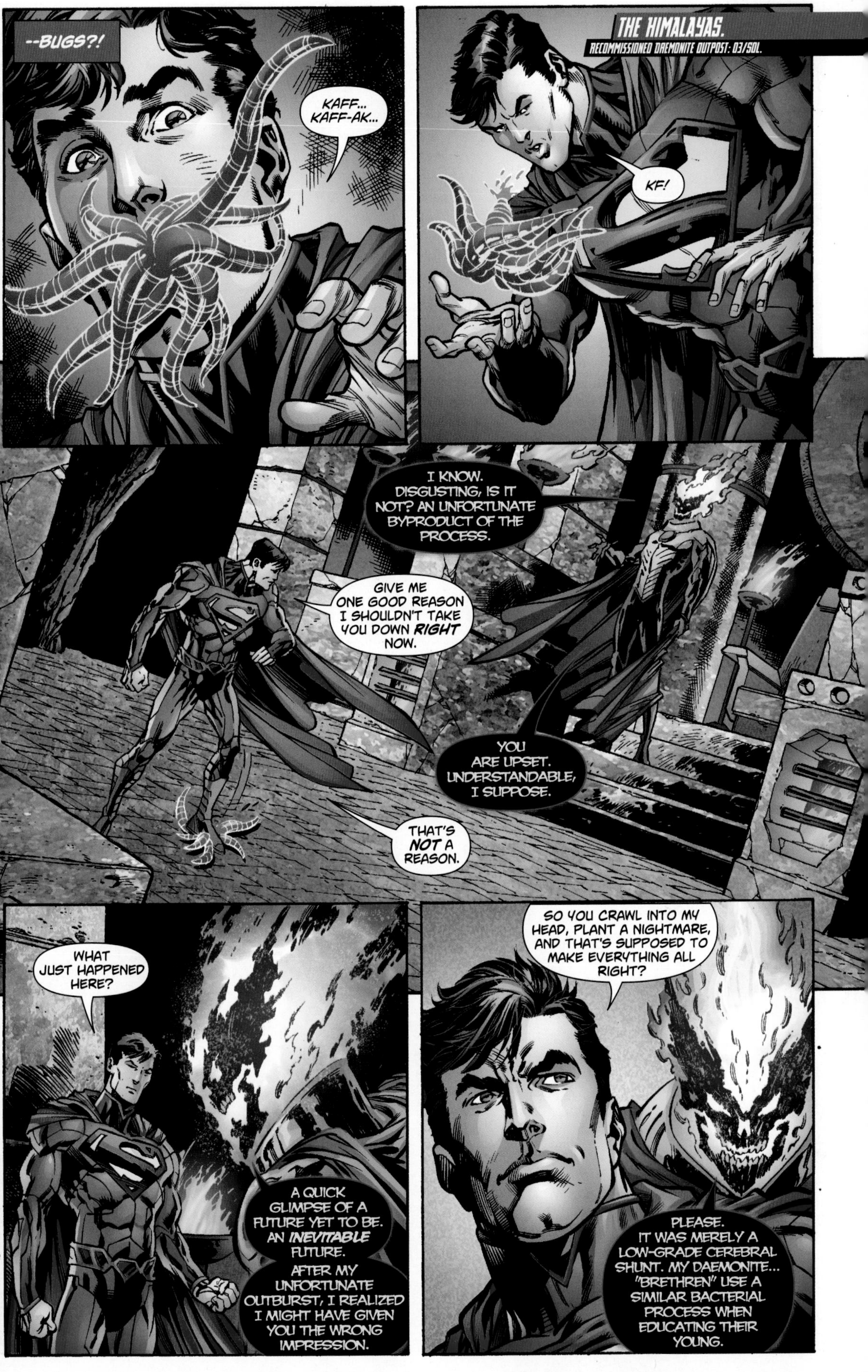
--BUGS?!
KAFF... KAFF-AK...
THE HIMALAYAS.
RECOMMISSIONED DAEMONITE OUTPOST: 03/SOL.
KF!
I KNOW. DISGUSTING, IS IT NOT? AN UNFORTUNATE BYPRODUCT OF THE PROCESS.
GIVE ME ONE GOOD REASON I SHOULDN'T TAKE YOU DOWN RIGHT NOW.
YOU ARE UPSET. UNDERSTANDABLE, I SUPPOSE.
THAT'S NOT A REASON.
WHAT JUST HAPPENED HERE?
A QUICK GLIMPSE OF A FUTURE YET TO BE. AN INEVITABLE FUTURE.
AFTER MY UNFORTUNATE OUTBURST, I REALIZED I MIGHT HAVE GIVEN YOU THE WRONG IMPRESSION.
SO YOU CRAWL INTO MY HEAD, PLANT A NIGHTMARE, AND THAT'S SUPPOSED TO MAKE EVERYTHING ALL RIGHT?
PLEASE. IT WAS MERELY A LOW-GRADE CEREBRAL SHUNT. MY DAEMONITE... "BRETHREN" USE A SIMILAR BACTERIAL PROCESS WHEN EDUCATING THEIR YOUNG.

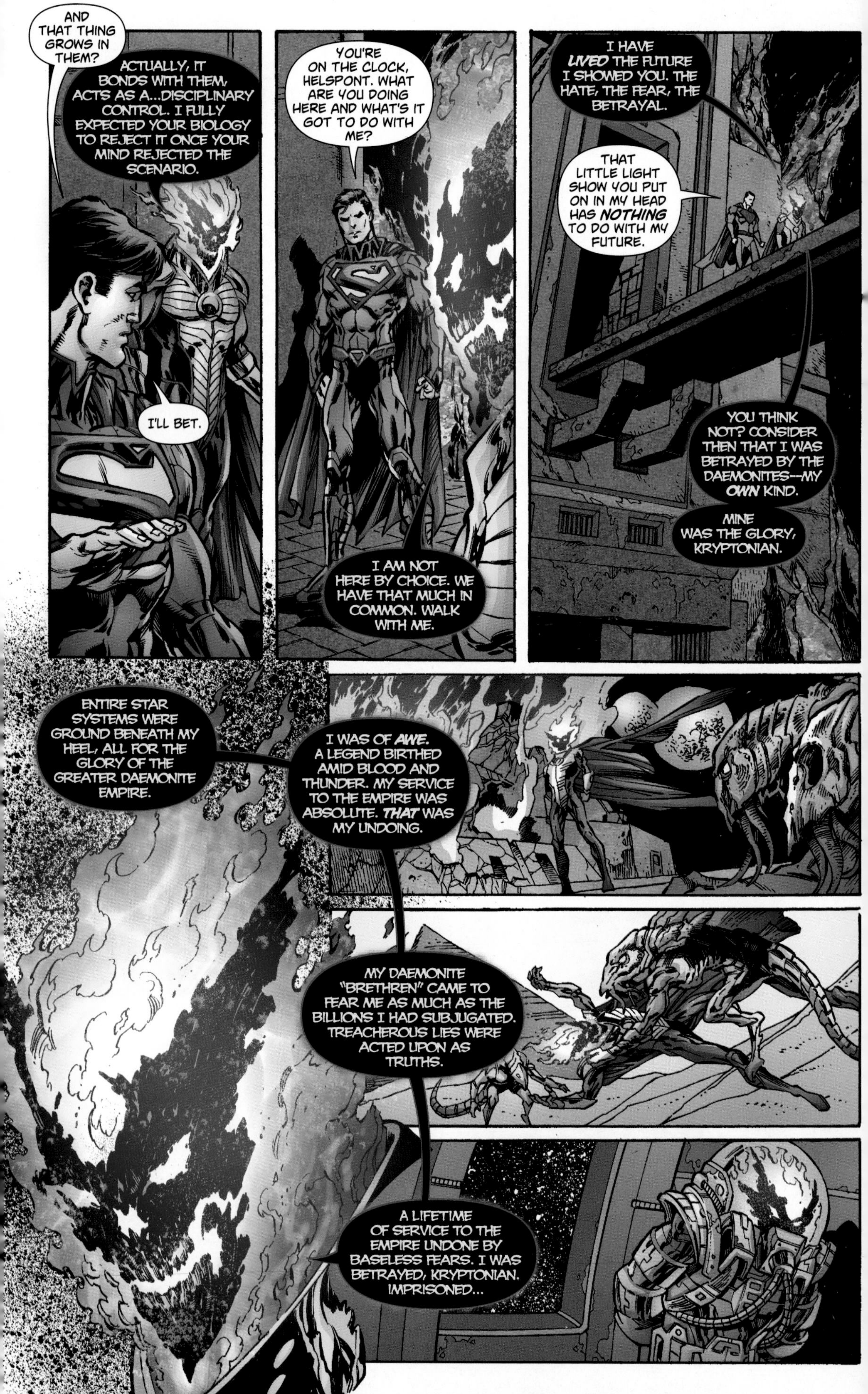
AND THAT THING GROWS IN THEM?
ACTUALLY, IT BONDS WITH THEM, ACTS AS A...DISCIPLINARY CONTROL. I FULLY EXPECTED YOUR BIOLOGY TO REJECT IT ONCE YOUR MIND REJECTED THE SCENARIO.
I'LL BET.
YOU'RE ON THE CLOCK, HELSPONT. WHAT ARE YOU DOING HERE AND WHAT'S IT GOT TO DO WITH ME?
I AM NOT HERE BY CHOICE. WE HAVE THAT MUCH IN COMMON. WALK WITH ME.
I HAVE *LIVED* THE FUTURE I SHOWED YOU. THE HATE, THE FEAR, THE BETRAYAL.
THAT LITTLE LIGHT SHOW YOU PUT ON IN MY HEAD HAS **NOTHING** TO DO WITH MY FUTURE.
YOU THINK NOT? CONSIDER THEN THAT I WAS BETRAYED BY THE DAEMONITES--MY *OWN* KIND.
MINE WAS THE GLORY, KRYPTONIAN.
ENTIRE STAR SYSTEMS WERE GROUND BENEATH MY HEEL, ALL FOR THE GLORY OF THE GREATER DAEMONITE EMPIRE.
I WAS OF ***AWE.*** A LEGEND BIRTHED AMID BLOOD AND THUNDER. MY SERVICE TO THE EMPIRE WAS ABSOLUTE. ***THAT*** WAS MY UNDOING.
MY DAEMONITE "BRETHREN" CAME TO FEAR ME AS MUCH AS THE BILLIONS I HAD SUBJUGATED. TREACHEROUS LIES WERE ACTED UPON AS TRUTHS.
A LIFETIME OF SERVICE TO THE EMPIRE UNDONE BY BASELESS FEARS. I WAS BETRAYED, KRYPTONIAN. IMPRISONED...

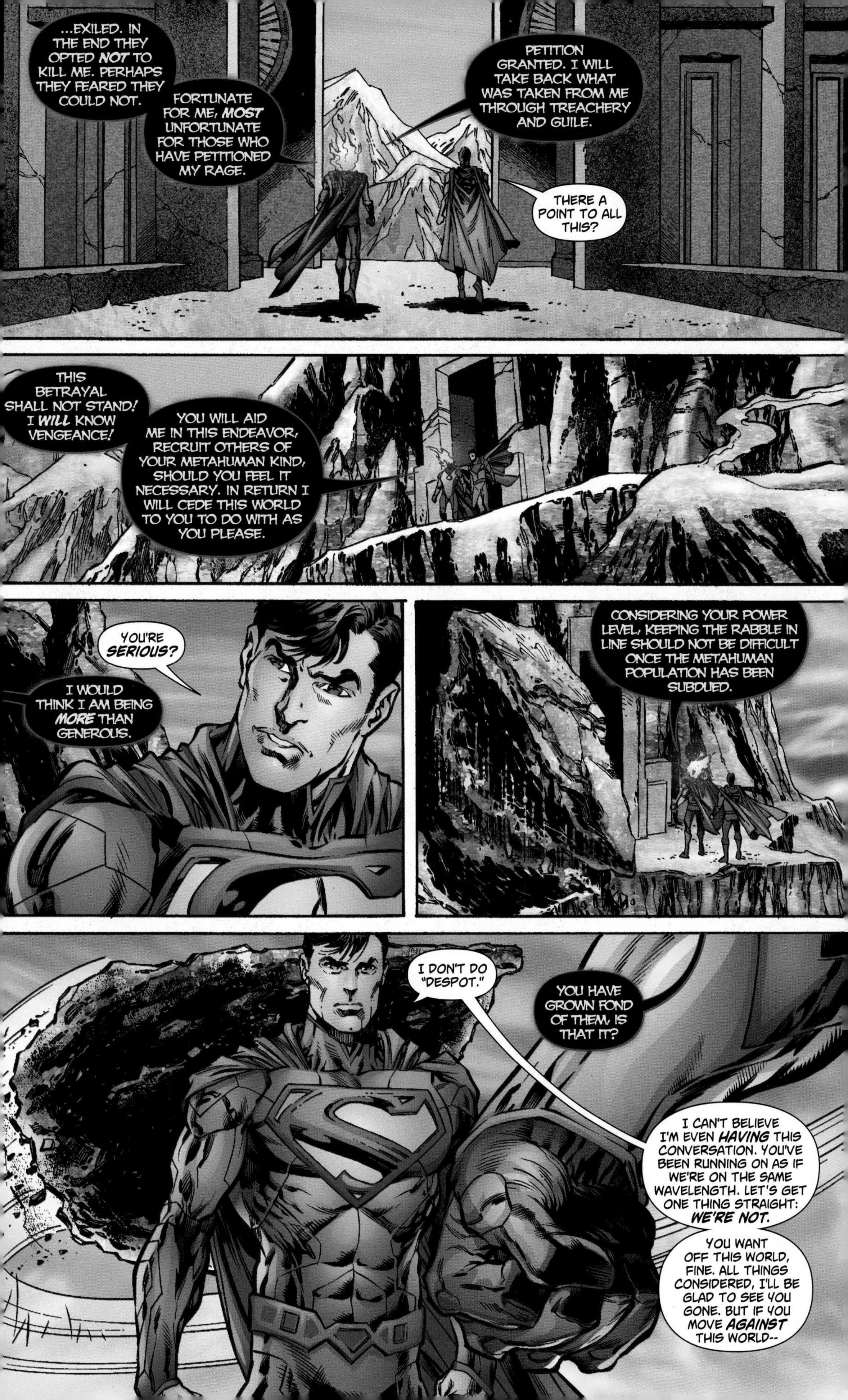
...EXILED. IN THE END THEY OPTED NOT TO KILL ME. PERHAPS THEY FEARED THEY COULD NOT.
FORTUNATE FOR ME, MOST UNFORTUNATE FOR THOSE WHO HAVE PETITIONED MY RAGE.
PETITION GRANTED. I WILL TAKE BACK WHAT WAS TAKEN FROM ME THROUGH TREACHERY AND GUILE.
THERE A POINT TO ALL THIS?
THIS BETRAYAL SHALL NOT STAND! I WILL KNOW VENGEANCE!
YOU WILL AID ME IN THIS ENDEAVOR, RECRUIT OTHERS OF YOUR METAHUMAN KIND, SHOULD YOU FEEL IT NECESSARY. IN RETURN I WILL CEDE THIS WORLD TO YOU TO DO WITH AS YOU PLEASE.
YOU'RE SERIOUS?
I WOULD THINK I AM BEING MORE THAN GENEROUS.
CONSIDERING YOUR POWER LEVEL, KEEPING THE RABBLE IN LINE SHOULD NOT BE DIFFICULT ONCE THE METAHUMAN POPULATION HAS BEEN SUBDUED.
I DON'T DO "DESPOT."
YOU HAVE GROWN FOND OF THEM, IS THAT IT?
I CAN'T BELIEVE I'M EVEN HAVING THIS CONVERSATION. YOU'VE BEEN RUNNING ON AS IF WE'RE ON THE SAME WAVELENGTH. LET'S GET ONE THING STRAIGHT: WE'RE NOT.
YOU WANT OFF THIS WORLD, FINE. ALL THINGS CONSIDERED, I'LL BE GLAD TO SEE YOU GONE. BUT IF YOU MOVE AGAINST THIS WORLD--

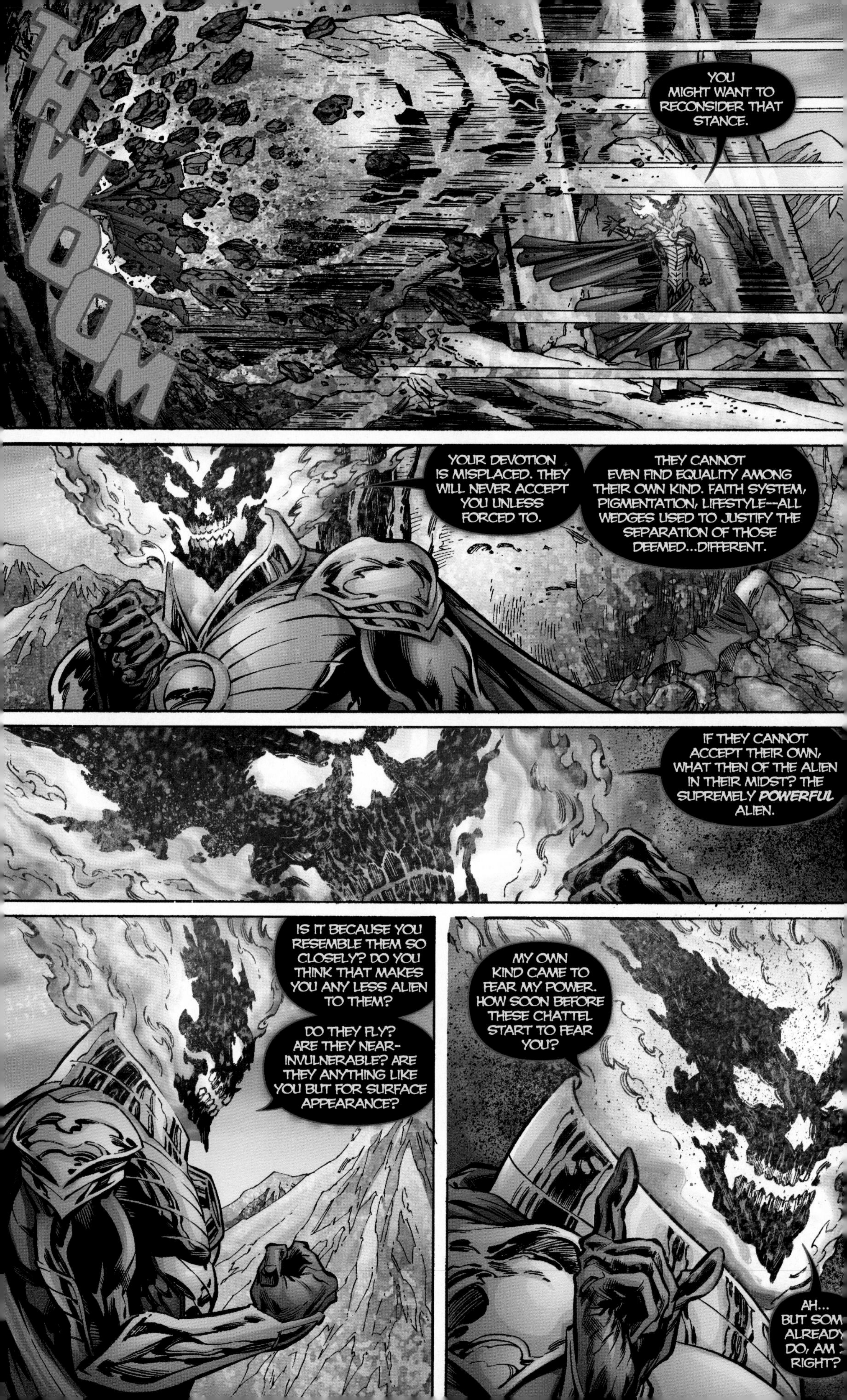
THWOOM
YOU MIGHT WANT TO RECONSIDER THAT STANCE.
YOUR DEVOTION IS MISPLACED. THEY WILL NEVER ACCEPT YOU UNLESS FORCED TO.
THEY CANNOT EVEN FIND EQUALITY AMONG THEIR OWN KIND. FAITH SYSTEM, PIGMENTATION, LIFESTYLE--ALL WEDGES USED TO JUSTIFY THE SEPARATION OF THOSE DEEMED...DIFFERENT.
IF THEY CANNOT ACCEPT THEIR OWN, WHAT THEN OF THE ALIEN IN THEIR MIDST? THE SUPREMELY *POWERFUL* ALIEN.
IS IT BECAUSE YOU RESEMBLE THEM SO CLOSELY? DO YOU THINK THAT MAKES YOU ANY LESS ALIEN TO THEM?
DO THEY FLY? ARE THEY NEAR-INVULNERABLE? ARE THEY ANYTHING LIKE YOU BUT FOR SURFACE APPEARANCE?
MY OWN KIND CAME TO FEAR MY POWER. HOW SOON BEFORE THESE CHATTEL START TO FEAR YOU?

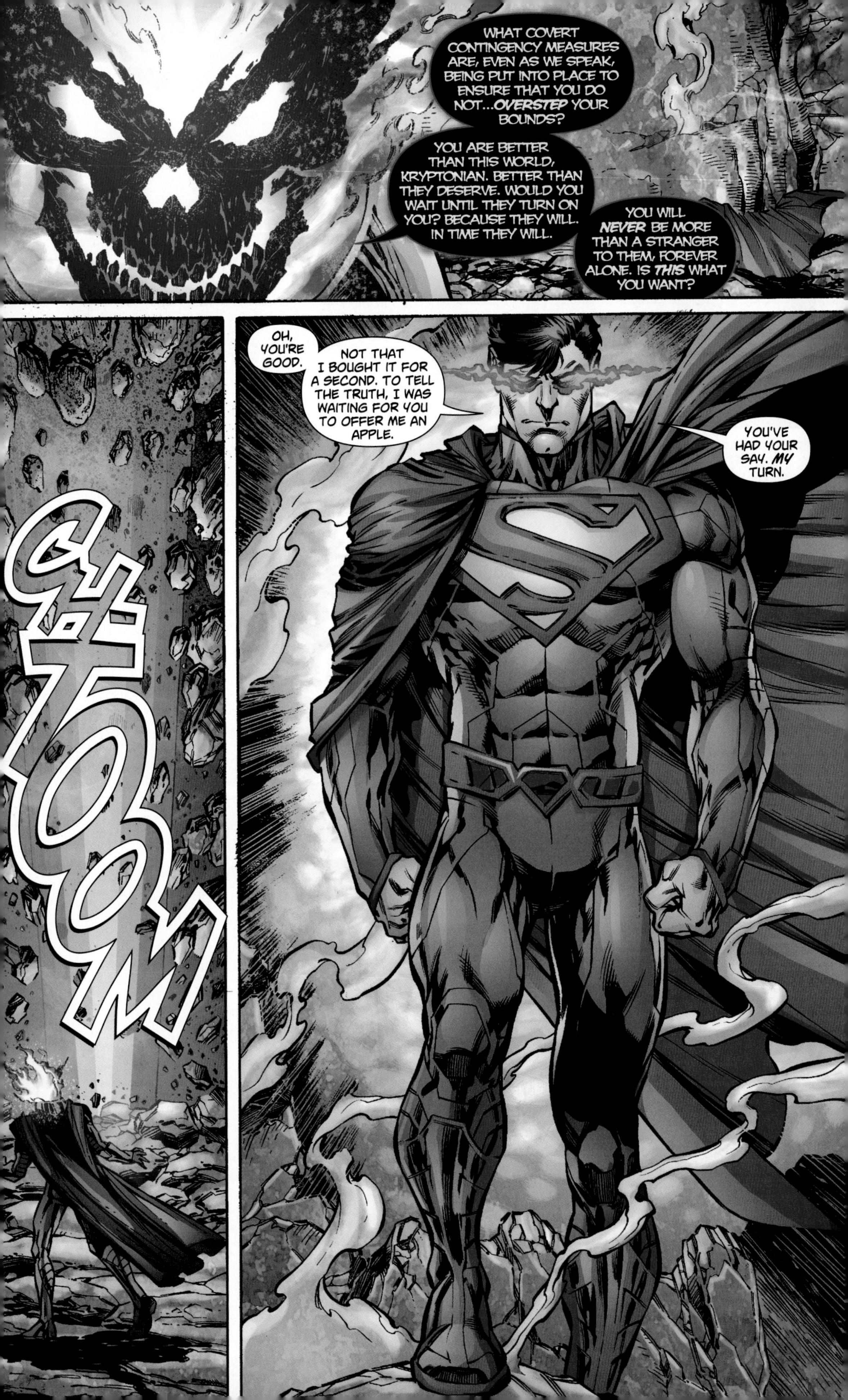
WHAT COVERT CONTINGENCY MEASURES ARE, EVEN AS WE SPEAK, BEING PUT INTO PLACE TO ENSURE THAT YOU DO NOT...OVERSTEP YOUR BOUNDS?
YOU ARE BETTER THAN THIS WORLD, KRYPTONIAN. BETTER THAN THEY DESERVE. WOULD YOU WAIT UNTIL THEY TURN ON YOU? BECAUSE THEY WILL. IN TIME THEY WILL.
YOU WILL NEVER BE MORE THAN A STRANGER TO THEM, FOREVER ALONE. IS THIS WHAT YOU WANT?
CHOOM
OH, YOU'RE GOOD.
NOT THAT I BOUGHT IT FOR A SECOND. TO TELL THE TRUTH, I WAS WAITING FOR YOU TO OFFER ME AN APPLE.
YOU'VE HAD YOUR SAY. MY TURN.

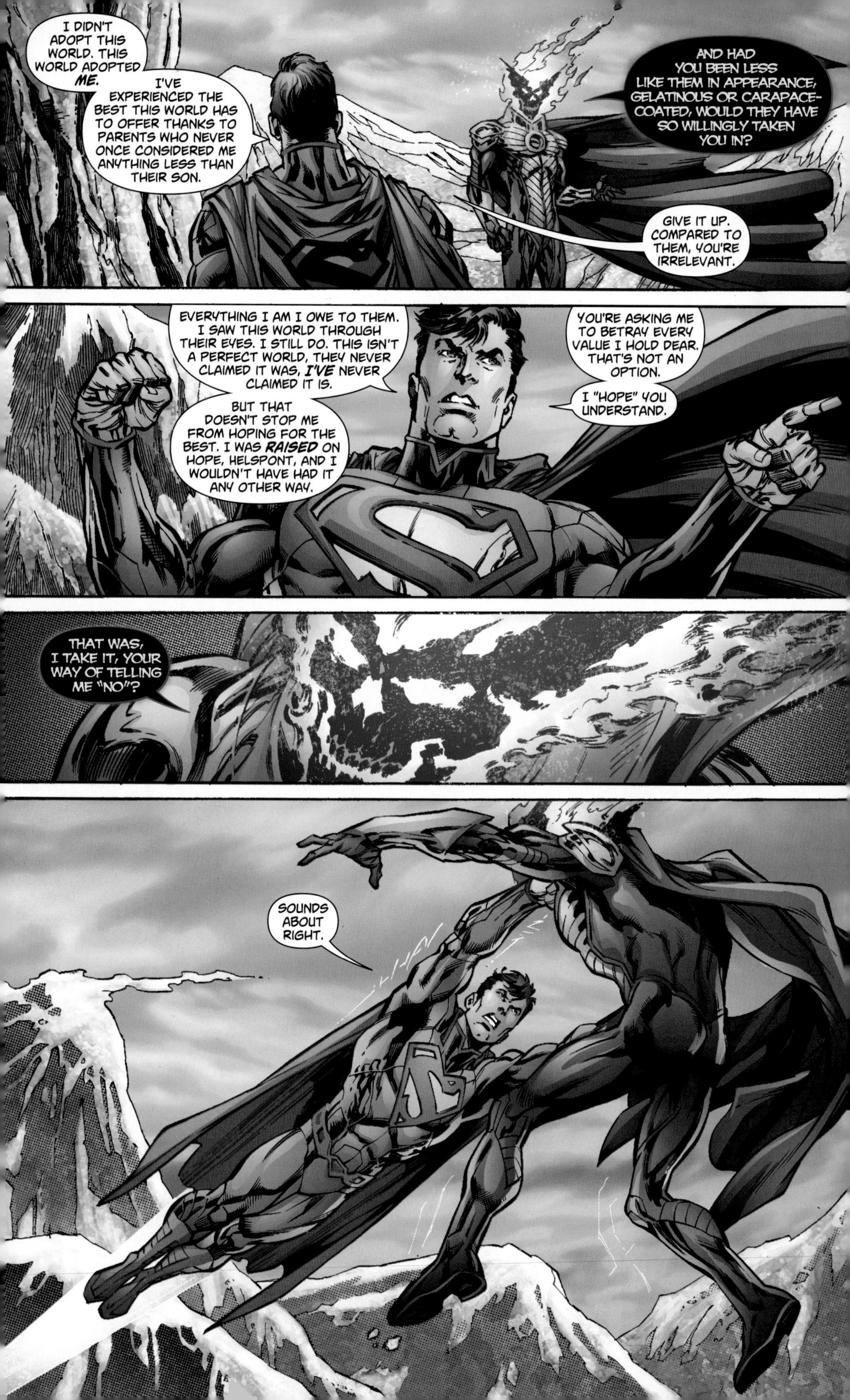
I DIDN'T ADOPT THIS WORLD. THIS WORLD ADOPTED ME.
I'VE EXPERIENCED THE BEST THIS WORLD HAS TO OFFER THANKS TO PARENTS WHO NEVER ONCE CONSIDERED ME ANYTHING LESS THAN THEIR SON.
AND HAD YOU BEEN LESS LIKE THEM IN APPEARANCE, GELATINOUS OR CARAPACE-COATED, WOULD THEY HAVE SO WILLINGLY TAKEN YOU IN?
GIVE IT UP. COMPARED TO THEM, YOU'RE IRRELEVANT.
EVERYTHING I AM I OWE TO THEM. I SAW THIS WORLD THROUGH THEIR EYES. I STILL DO. THIS ISN'T A PERFECT WORLD, THEY NEVER CLAIMED IT WAS, I'VE NEVER CLAIMED IT IS.
BUT THAT DOESN'T STOP ME FROM HOPING FOR THE BEST. I WAS RAISED ON HOPE, HELSPONT, AND I WOULDN'T HAVE HAD IT ANY OTHER WAY.
YOU'RE ASKING ME TO BETRAY EVERY VALUE I HOLD DEAR. THAT'S NOT AN OPTION.
I "HOPE" YOU UNDERSTAND.
THAT WAS, I TAKE IT, YOUR WAY OF TELLING ME "NO"?
SOUNDS ABOUT RIGHT.

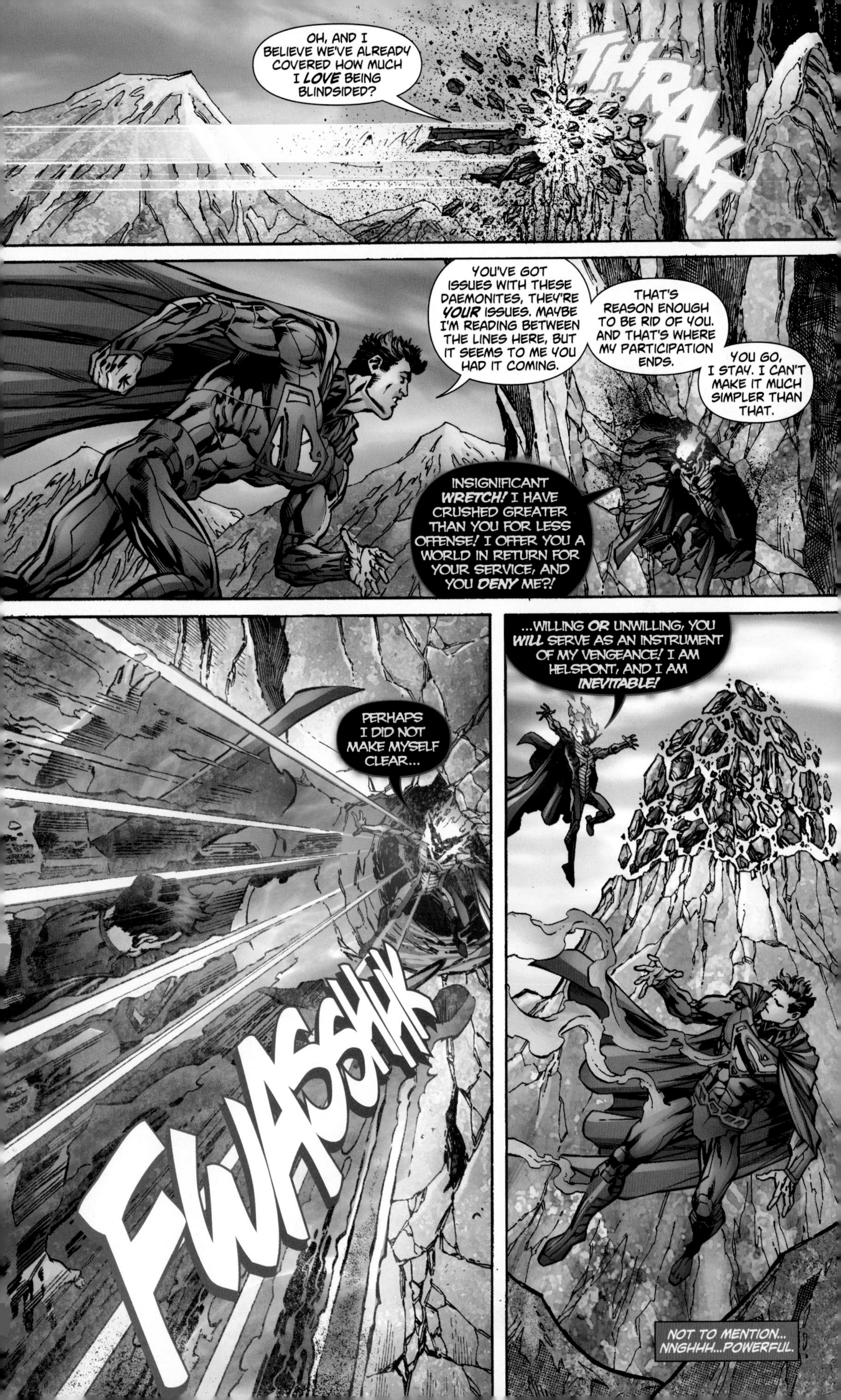
OH, AND I BELIEVE WE'VE ALREADY COVERED HOW MUCH I LOVE BEING BLINDSIDED?
THRAKT
YOU'VE GOT ISSUES WITH THESE DAEMONITES, THEY'RE YOUR ISSUES. MAYBE I'M READING BETWEEN THE LINES HERE, BUT IT SEEMS TO ME YOU HAD IT COMING.
THAT'S REASON ENOUGH TO BE RID OF YOU. AND THAT'S WHERE MY PARTICIPATION ENDS.
YOU GO, I STAY. I CAN'T MAKE IT MUCH SIMPLER THAN THAT.
INSIGNIFICANT WRETCH! I HAVE CRUSHED GREATER THAN YOU FOR LESS OFFENSE! I OFFER YOU A WORLD IN RETURN FOR YOUR SERVICE, AND YOU DENY ME?!
PERHAPS I DID NOT MAKE MYSELF CLEAR...
FWASHK
...WILLING OR UNWILLING, YOU WILL SERVE AS AN INSTRUMENT OF MY VENGEANCE! I AM HELSPONT, AND I AM INEVITABLE!
NOT TO MENTION... NNGHHH...POWERFUL.

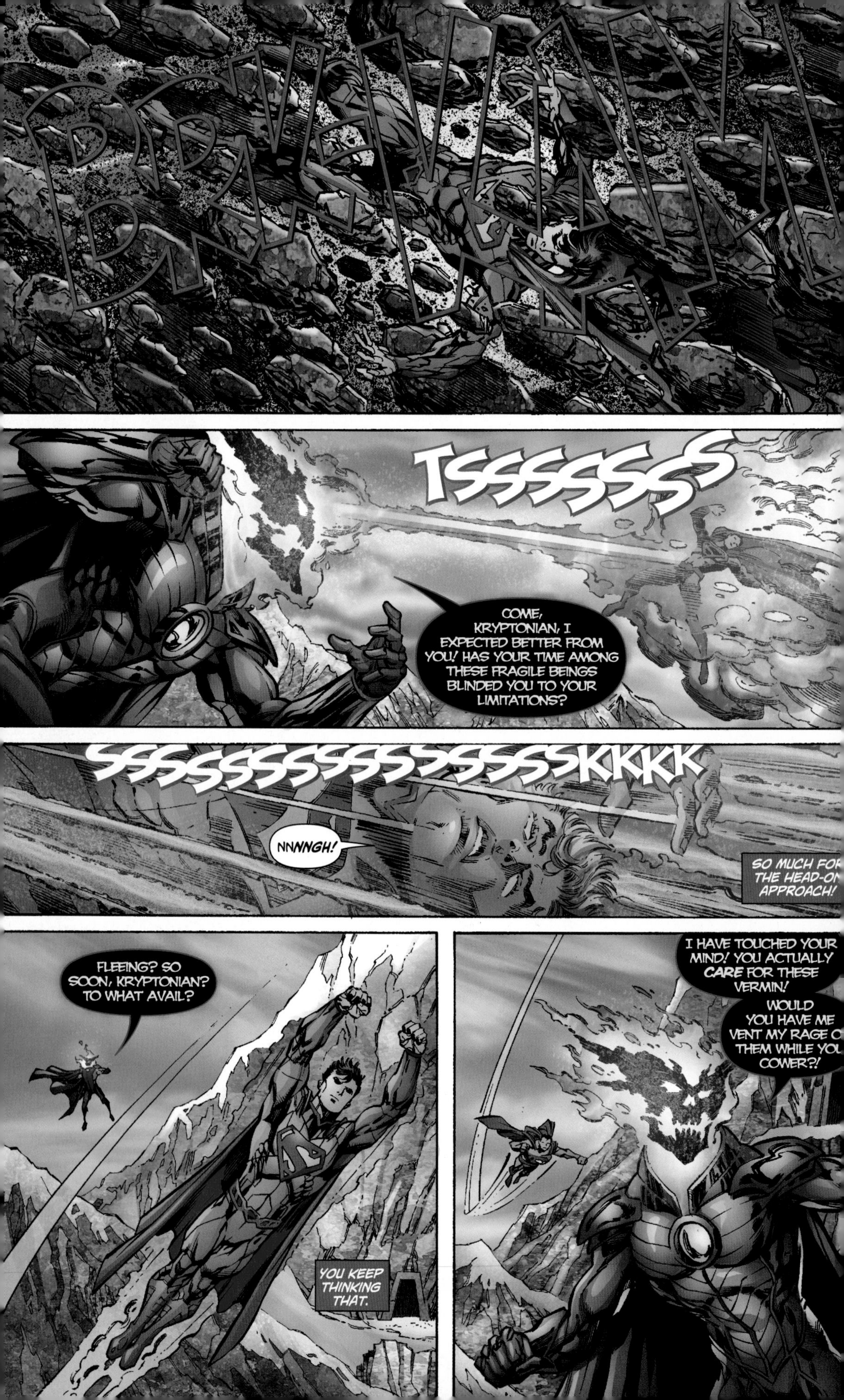
TSSSSSSS
COME, KRYPTONIAN; I EXPECTED BETTER FROM YOU! HAS YOUR TIME AMONG THESE FRAGILE BEINGS BLINDED YOU TO YOUR LIMITATIONS?
SSSSSSSSSSSSSSSSKKKK
NNNNGH!
SO MUCH FOR THE HEAD-ON APPROACH!
FLEEING? SO SOON, KRYPTONIAN? TO WHAT AVAIL?
YOU KEEP THINKING THAT.
I HAVE TOUCHED YOUR MIND! YOU ACTUALLY CARE FOR THESE VERMIN!
WOULD YOU HAVE ME VENT MY RAGE ON THEM WHILE YOU COWER?!

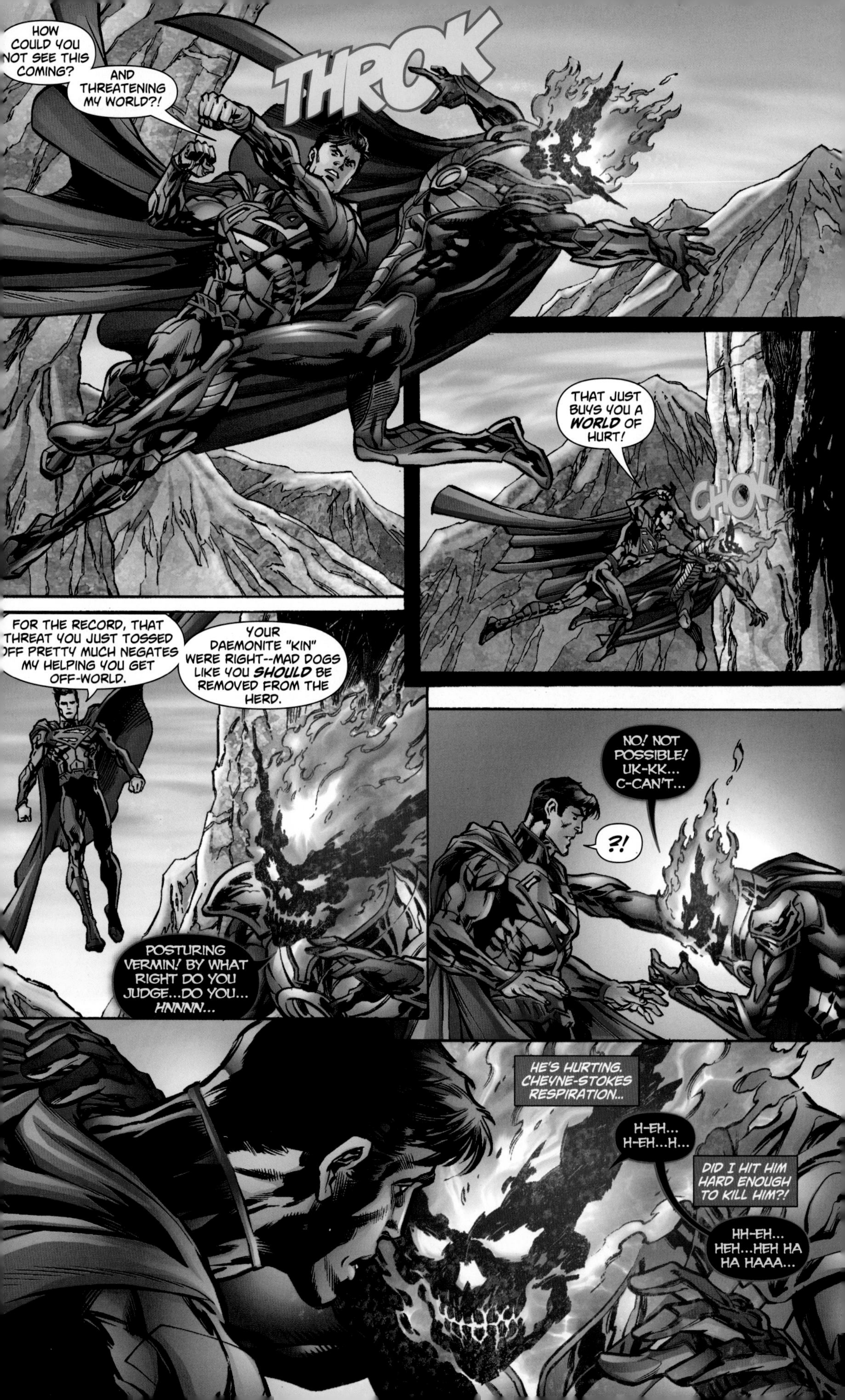
HOW COULD YOU NOT SEE THIS COMING?
AND THREATENING MY WORLD?!
THROCK
THAT JUST BUYS YOU A WORLD OF HURT!
CHOK
FOR THE RECORD, THAT THREAT YOU JUST TOSSED OFF PRETTY MUCH NEGATES MY HELPING YOU GET OFF-WORLD.
YOUR DAEMONITE "KIN" WERE RIGHT--MAD DOGS LIKE YOU SHOULD BE REMOVED FROM THE HERD.
POSTURING VERMIN! BY WHAT RIGHT DO YOU JUDGE...DO YOU... HNNNN...
NO! NOT POSSIBLE! UK-KK... C-CAN'T...
?!
HE'S HURTING. CHEYNE-STOKES RESPIRATION...
H-EH... H-EH...H...
DID I HIT HIM HARD ENOUGH TO KILL HIM?!
HH-EH... HEH...HEH HA HA HAAA...

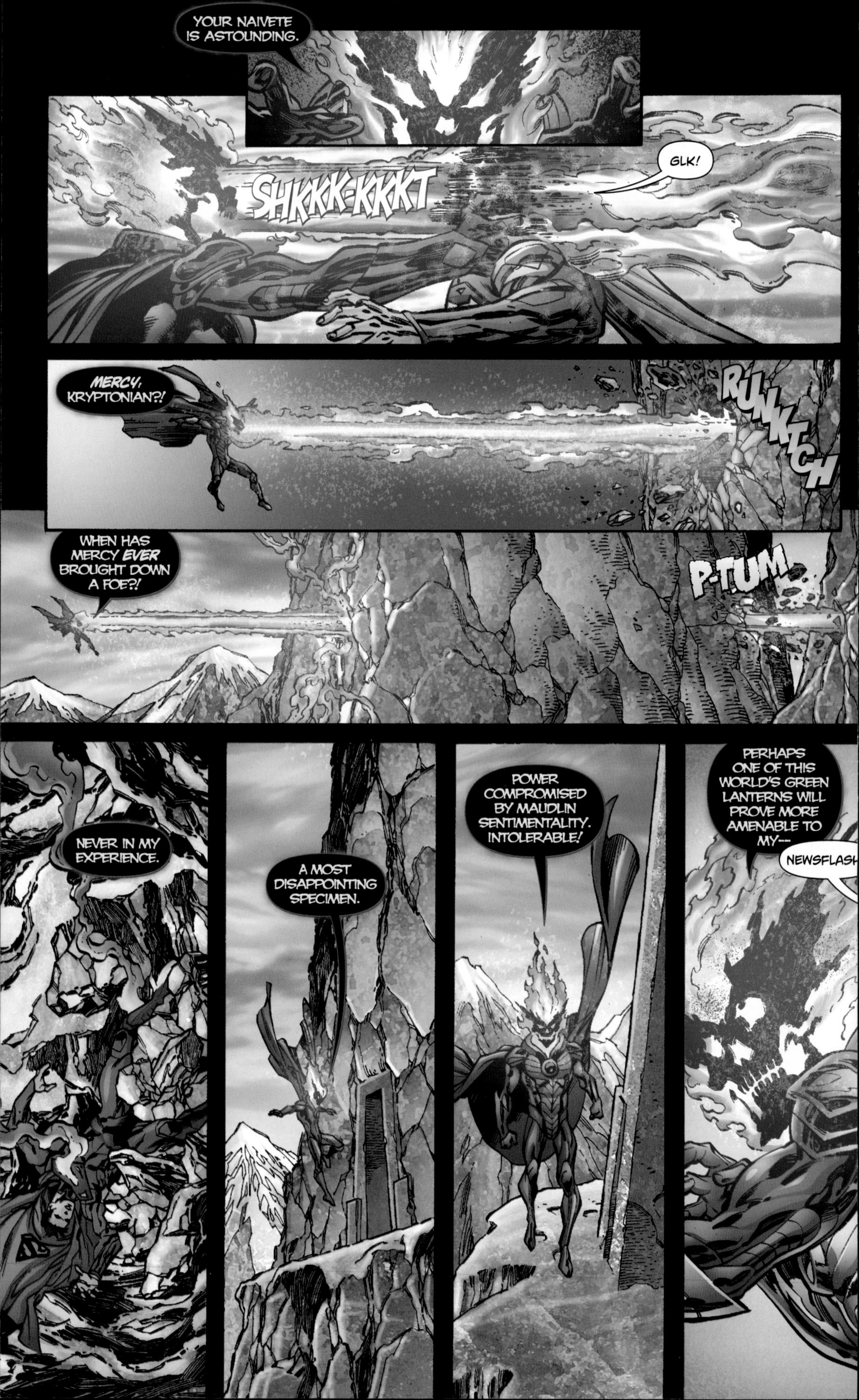
YOUR NAIVETE IS ASTOUNDING.
SHKKK-KKKT
GLK!
MERCY, KRYPTONIAN?!
RUNKTCH
WHEN HAS MERCY EVER BROUGHT DOWN A FOE?!
P-TUM
NEVER IN MY EXPERIENCE.
A MOST DISAPPOINTING SPECIMEN.
POWER COMPROMISED BY MAUDLIN SENTIMENTALITY. INTOLERABLE!
PERHAPS ONE OF THIS WORLD'S GREEN LANTERNS WILL PROVE MORE AMENABLE TO MY--
NEWSFLASH

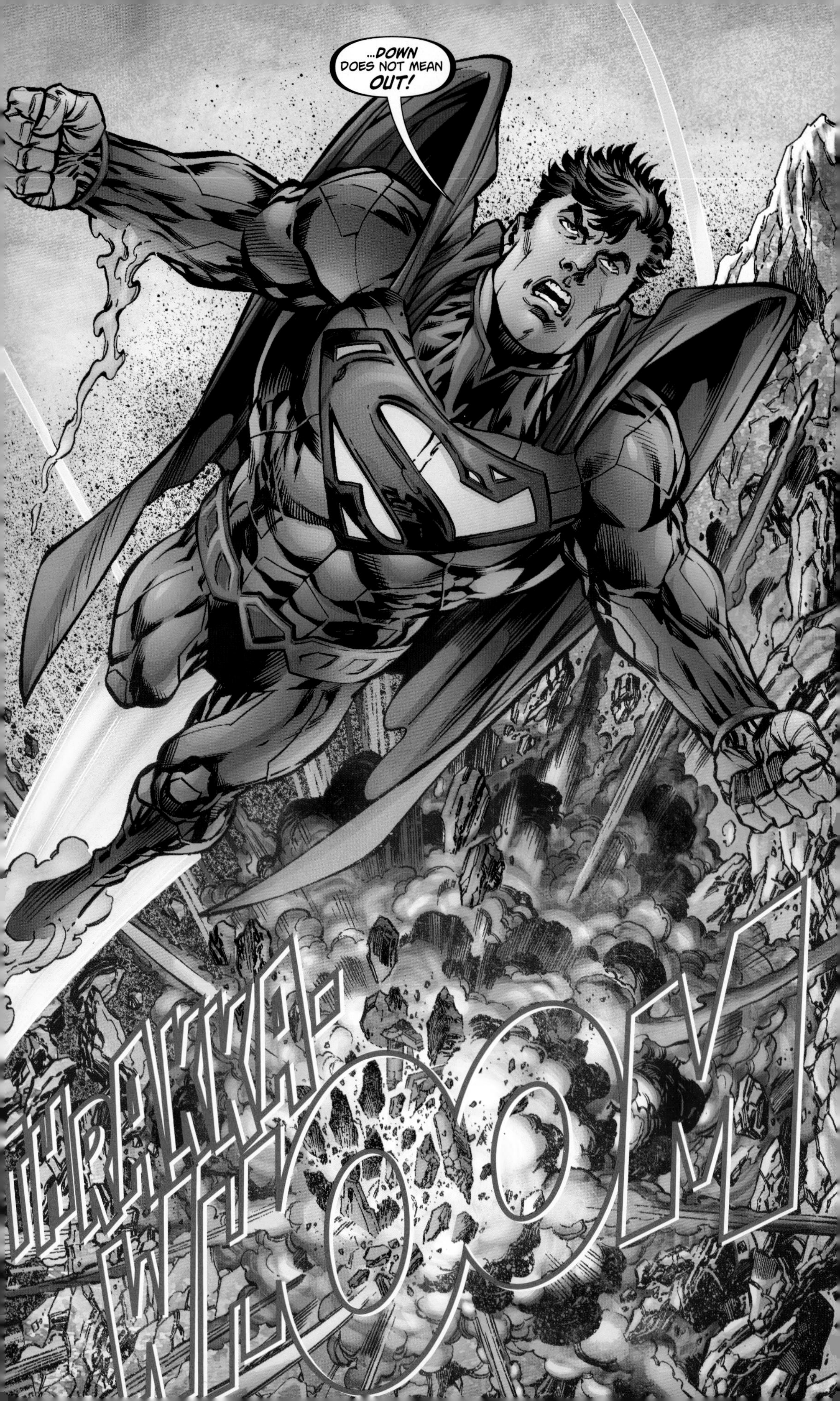

...DOWN DOES NOT MEAN OUT!
THRAKKA-WHOOOM!

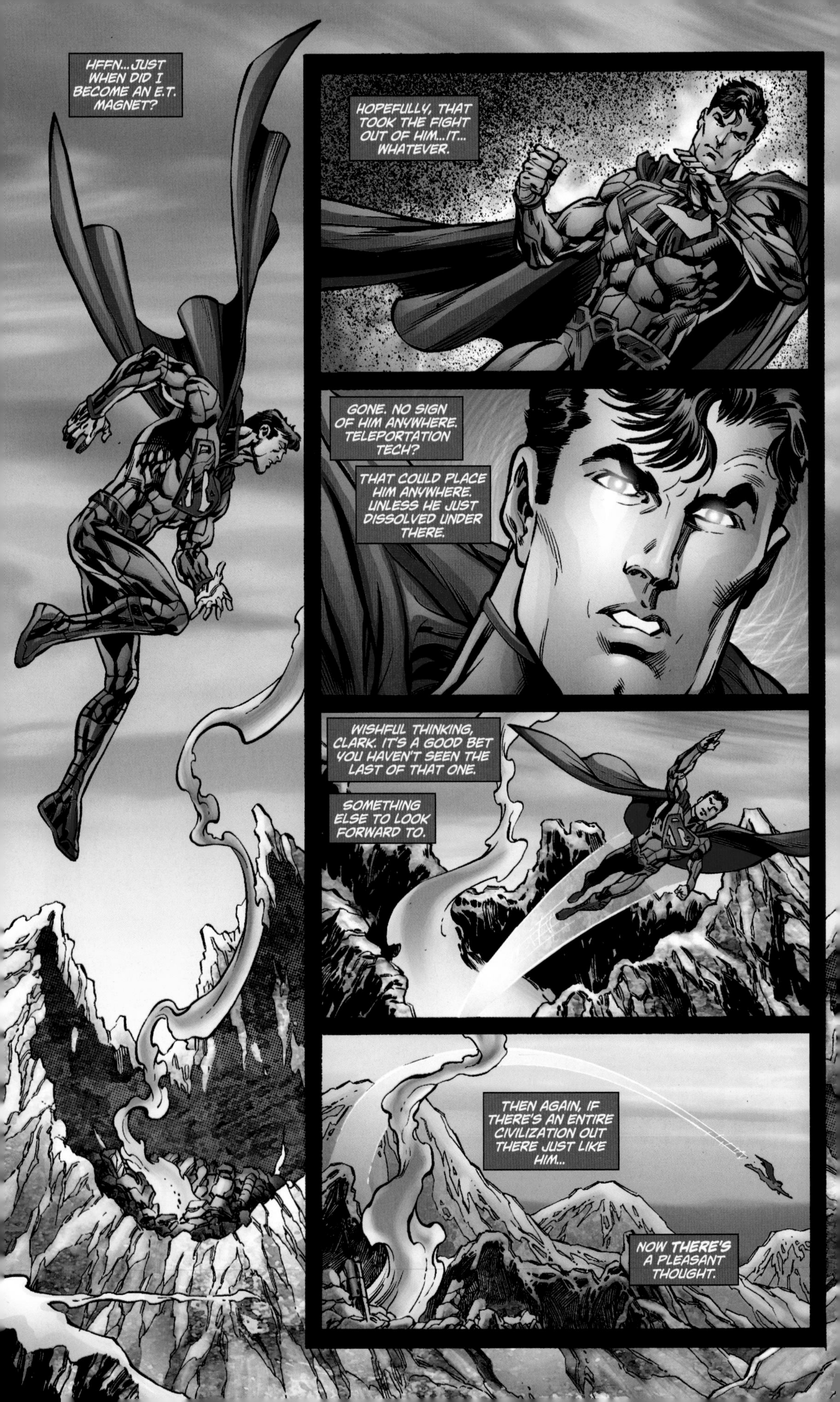
HFFN...JUST WHEN DID I BECOME AN E.T. MAGNET?
HOPEFULLY, THAT TOOK THE FIGHT OUT OF HIM...IT... WHATEVER.
GONE. NO SIGN OF HIM ANYWHERE. TELEPORTATION TECH?
THAT COULD PLACE HIM ANYWHERE. UNLESS HE JUST DISSOLVED UNDER THERE.
WISHFUL THINKING, CLARK. IT'S A GOOD BET YOU HAVEN'T SEEN THE LAST OF THAT ONE.
SOMETHING ELSE TO LOOK FORWARD TO.
THEN AGAIN, IF THERE'S AN ENTIRE CIVILIZATION OUT THERE JUST LIKE HIM...
NOW THERE'S A PLEASANT THOUGHT.

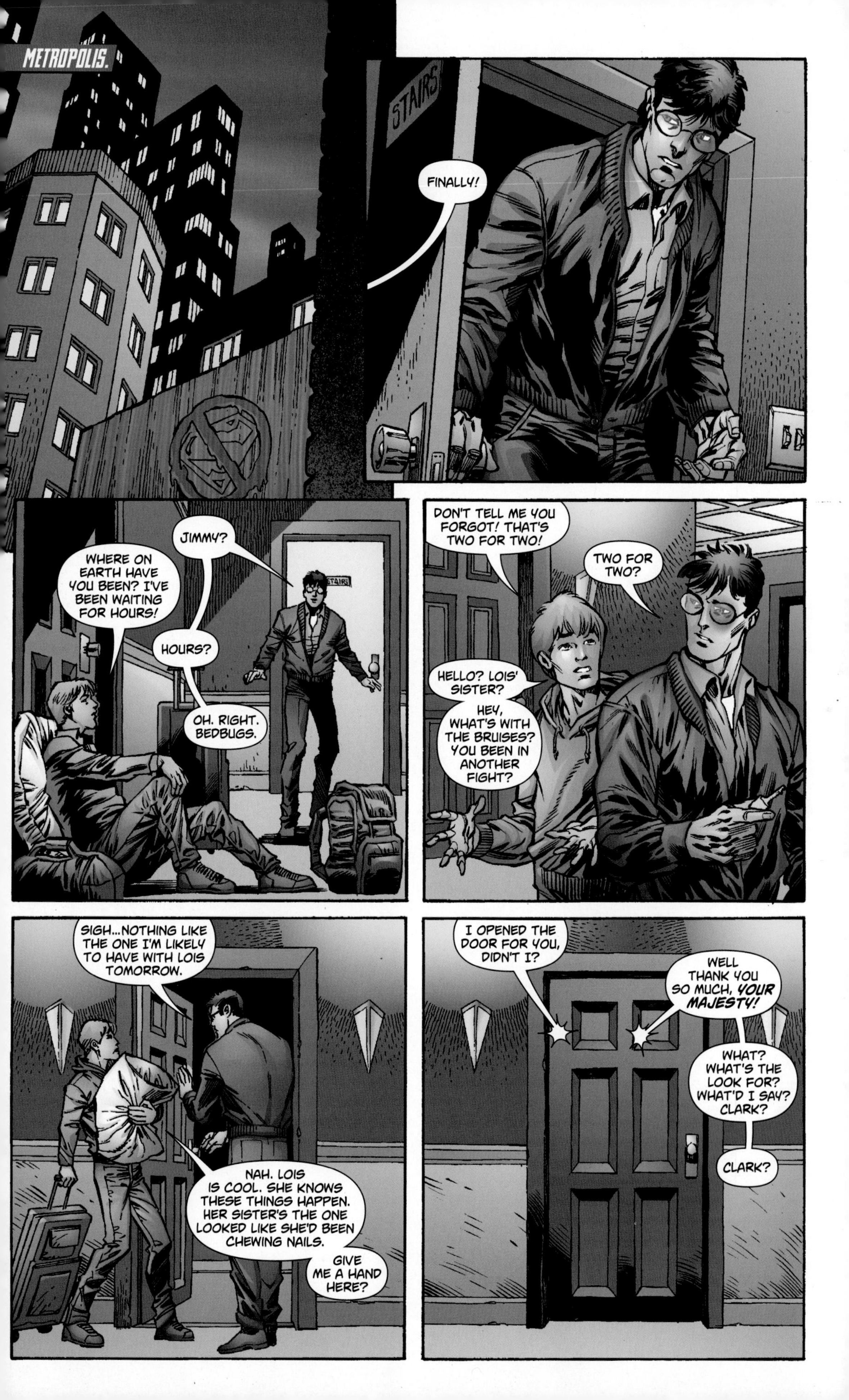
METROPOLIS.
FINALLY!
WHERE ON EARTH HAVE YOU BEEN? I'VE BEEN WAITING FOR HOURS!
JIMMY?
HOURS?
OH. RIGHT. BEDBUGS.
DON'T TELL ME YOU FORGOT! THAT'S TWO FOR TWO!
TWO FOR TWO?
HELLO? LOIS' SISTER?
HEY, WHAT'S WITH THE BRUISES? YOU BEEN IN ANOTHER FIGHT?
SIGH...NOTHING LIKE THE ONE I'M LIKELY TO HAVE WITH LOIS TOMORROW.
NAH. LOIS IS COOL. SHE KNOWS THESE THINGS HAPPEN. HER SISTER'S THE ONE LOOKED LIKE SHE'D BEEN CHEWING NAILS.
GIVE ME A HAND HERE?
I OPENED THE DOOR FOR YOU, DIDN'T I?
WELL THANK YOU SO MUCH, YOUR MAJESTY!
WHAT? WHAT'S THE LOOK FOR? WHAT'D I SAY? CLARK?
CLARK?

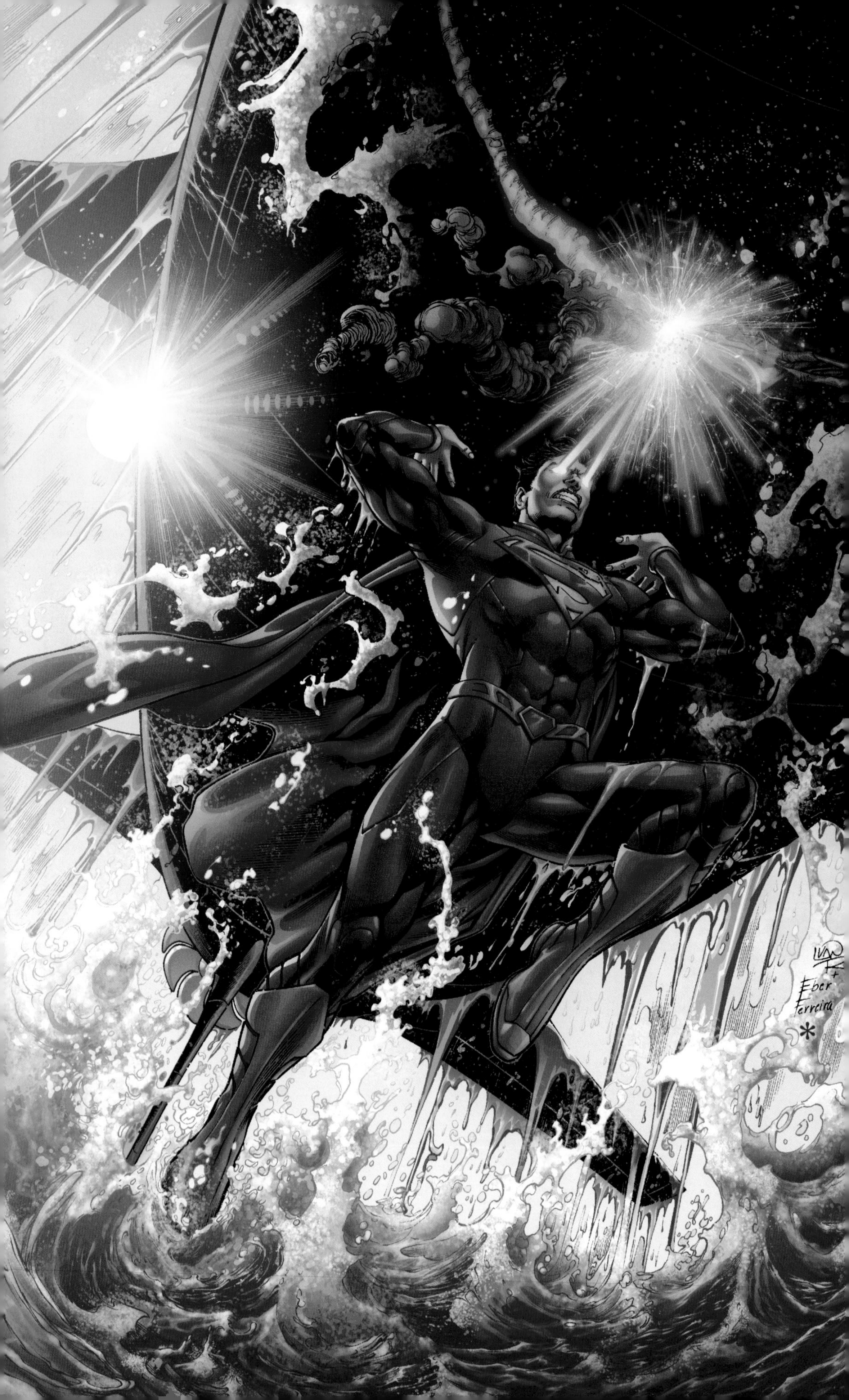
IVAN
+
Eber
Ferreira

THE BERING STRAIT.

LATITUDE, LONGITUDE...I SHOULD HAVE PAID MORE ATTENTION IN CLASS. IT'S ONE THING TO KNOW THE NUMBERS. NOW *APPLYING* THEM...

OKAY, ACCORDING TO THE NEWS FLASH--AND THANK YOU VERY MUCH, GALAXY BROADCASTING-- THERE'S A SUBMERSIBLE DOWN HERE SOUNDING "MAYDAY."

S e c r e t s

& LIES

SCRIPTED & CO-PLOTTED BY	PENCIL ART & CO-PLOTTED BY	FINISHED ART BY
KEITH GIFFEN	DAN JURGENS	JESÚS MERINO

COLORED BY	LETTERED BY	COVER BY
TANYA & RICHARD HORIE	ROB LEIGH	IVAN REIS, EBER FERREIRA & HI-FI

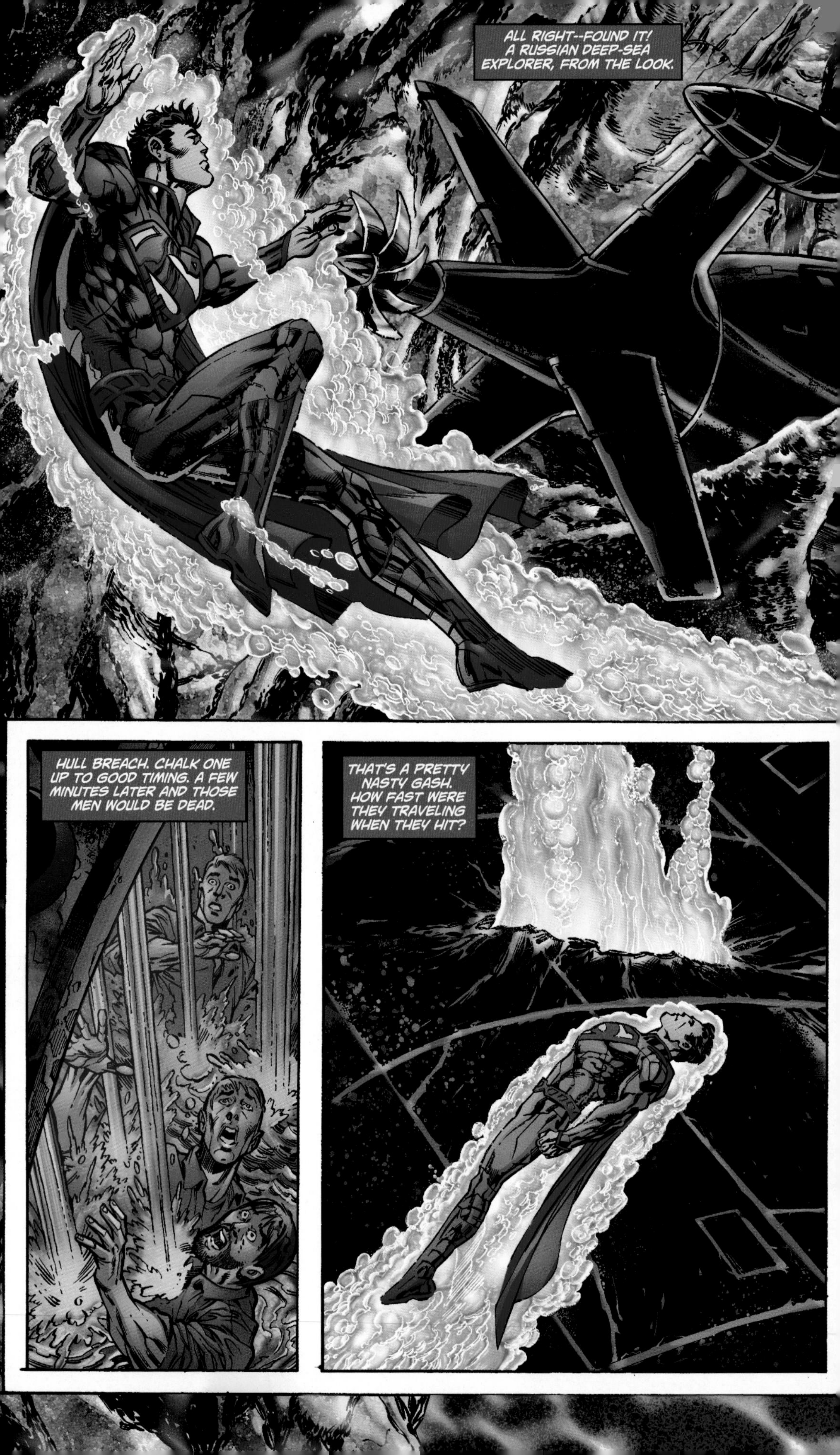
ALL RIGHT--FOUND IT! A RUSSIAN DEEP-SEA EXPLORER, FROM THE LOOK.
HULL BREACH. CHALK ONE UP TO GOOD TIMING. A FEW MINUTES LATER AND THOSE MEN WOULD BE DEAD.
THAT'S A PRETTY NASTY GASH. HOW FAST WERE THEY TRAVELING WHEN THEY HIT?

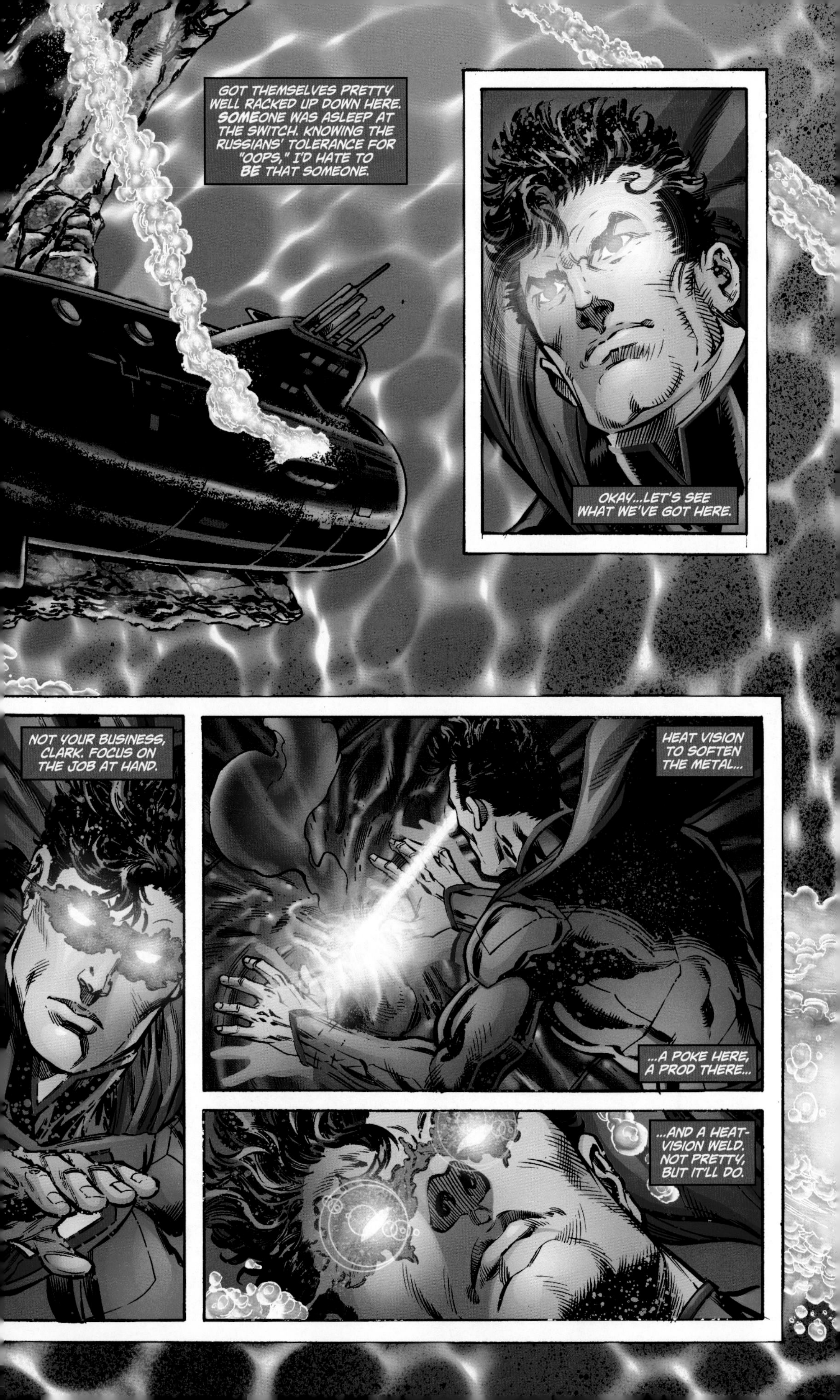
GOT THEMSELVES PRETTY WELL RACKED UP DOWN HERE. SOMEONE WAS ASLEEP AT THE SWITCH. KNOWING THE RUSSIANS' TOLERANCE FOR "OOPS," I'D HATE TO BE THAT SOMEONE.
OKAY...LET'S SEE WHAT WE'VE GOT HERE.
NOT YOUR BUSINESS, CLARK. FOCUS ON THE JOB AT HAND.
HEAT VISION TO SOFTEN THE METAL...
...A POKE HERE, A PROD THERE...
...AND A HEAT-VISION WELD. NOT PRETTY, BUT IT'LL DO.

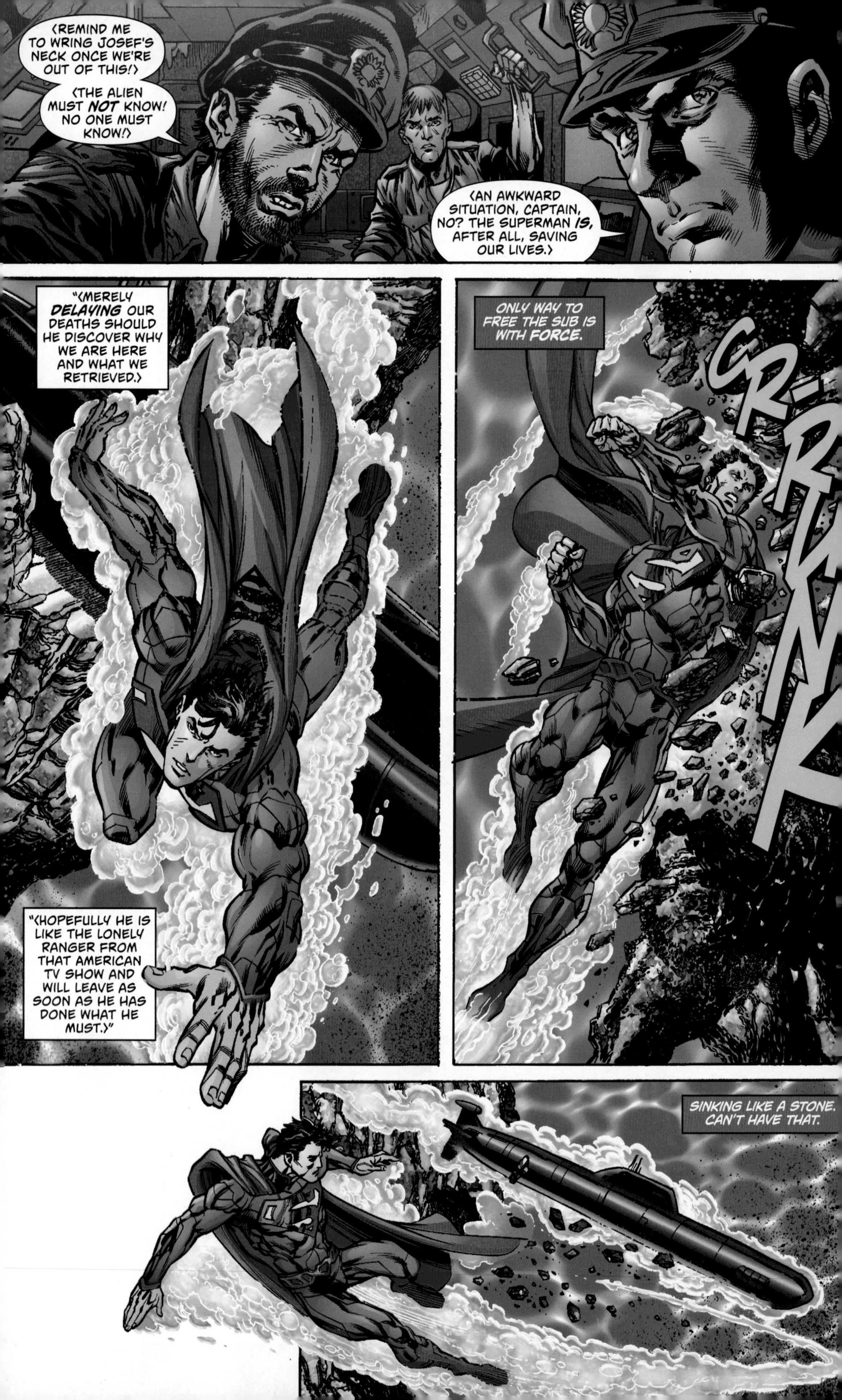

‹REMIND ME TO WRING JOSEF'S NECK ONCE WE'RE OUT OF THIS!›
‹THE ALIEN MUST NOT KNOW! NO ONE MUST KNOW!›
‹AN AWKWARD SITUATION, CAPTAIN, NO? THE SUPERMAN IS, AFTER ALL, SAVING OUR LIVES.›
"‹MERELY DELAYING OUR DEATHS SHOULD HE DISCOVER WHY WE ARE HERE AND WHAT WE RETRIEVED.›
"‹HOPEFULLY HE IS LIKE THE LONELY RANGER FROM THAT AMERICAN TV SHOW AND WILL LEAVE AS SOON AS HE HAS DONE WHAT HE MUST.›"
ONLY WAY TO FREE THE SUB IS WITH FORCE.
CR-RUNK
SINKING LIKE A STONE. CAN'T HAVE THAT.

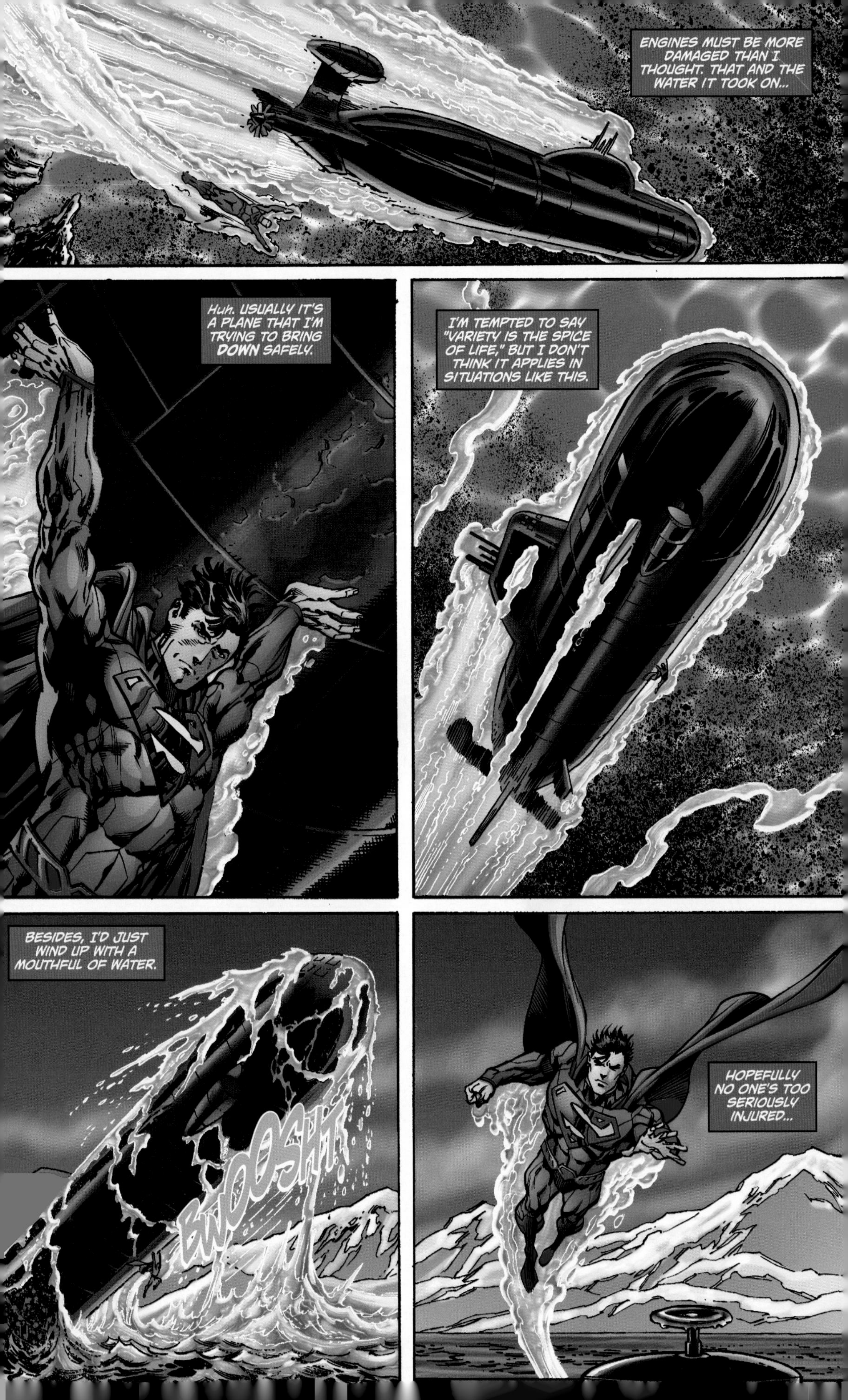
ENGINES MUST BE MORE DAMAGED THAN I THOUGHT. THAT AND THE WATER IT TOOK ON...
Huh. USUALLY IT'S A PLANE THAT I'M TRYING TO BRING DOWN SAFELY.
I'M TEMPTED TO SAY "VARIETY IS THE SPICE OF LIFE," BUT I DON'T THINK IT APPLIES IN SITUATIONS LIKE THIS.
BESIDES, I'D JUST WIND UP WITH A MOUTHFUL OF WATER.
BWOOSHH
HOPEFULLY NO ONE'S TOO SERIOUSLY INJURED...

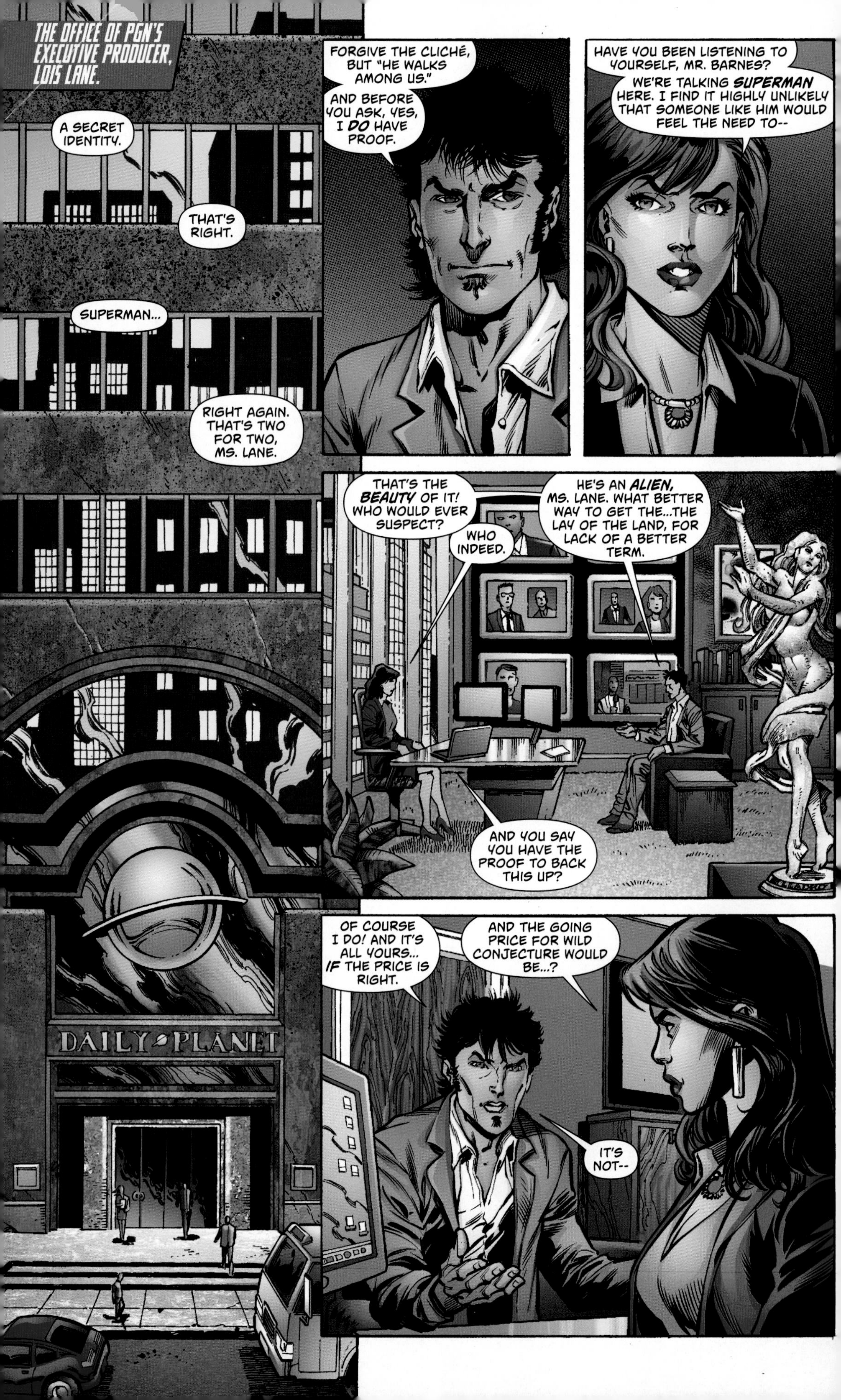
THE OFFICE OF PGN'S EXECUTIVE PRODUCER, LOIS LANE.
A SECRET IDENTITY.
THAT'S RIGHT.
SUPERMAN...
RIGHT AGAIN. THAT'S TWO FOR TWO, MS. LANE.
FORGIVE THE CLICHÉ, BUT "HE WALKS AMONG US."
AND BEFORE YOU ASK, YES, I DO HAVE PROOF.
HAVE YOU BEEN LISTENING TO YOURSELF, MR. BARNES?
WE'RE TALKING SUPERMAN HERE. I FIND IT HIGHLY UNLIKELY THAT SOMEONE LIKE HIM WOULD FEEL THE NEED TO--
THAT'S THE BEAUTY OF IT! WHO WOULD EVER SUSPECT?
WHO INDEED.
HE'S AN ALIEN, MS. LANE. WHAT BETTER WAY TO GET THE...THE LAY OF THE LAND, FOR LACK OF A BETTER TERM.
AND YOU SAY YOU HAVE THE PROOF TO BACK THIS UP?
OF COURSE I DO! AND IT'S ALL YOURS... IF THE PRICE IS RIGHT.
AND THE GOING PRICE FOR WILD CONJECTURE WOULD BE...?
IT'S NOT--
DAILY PLANET

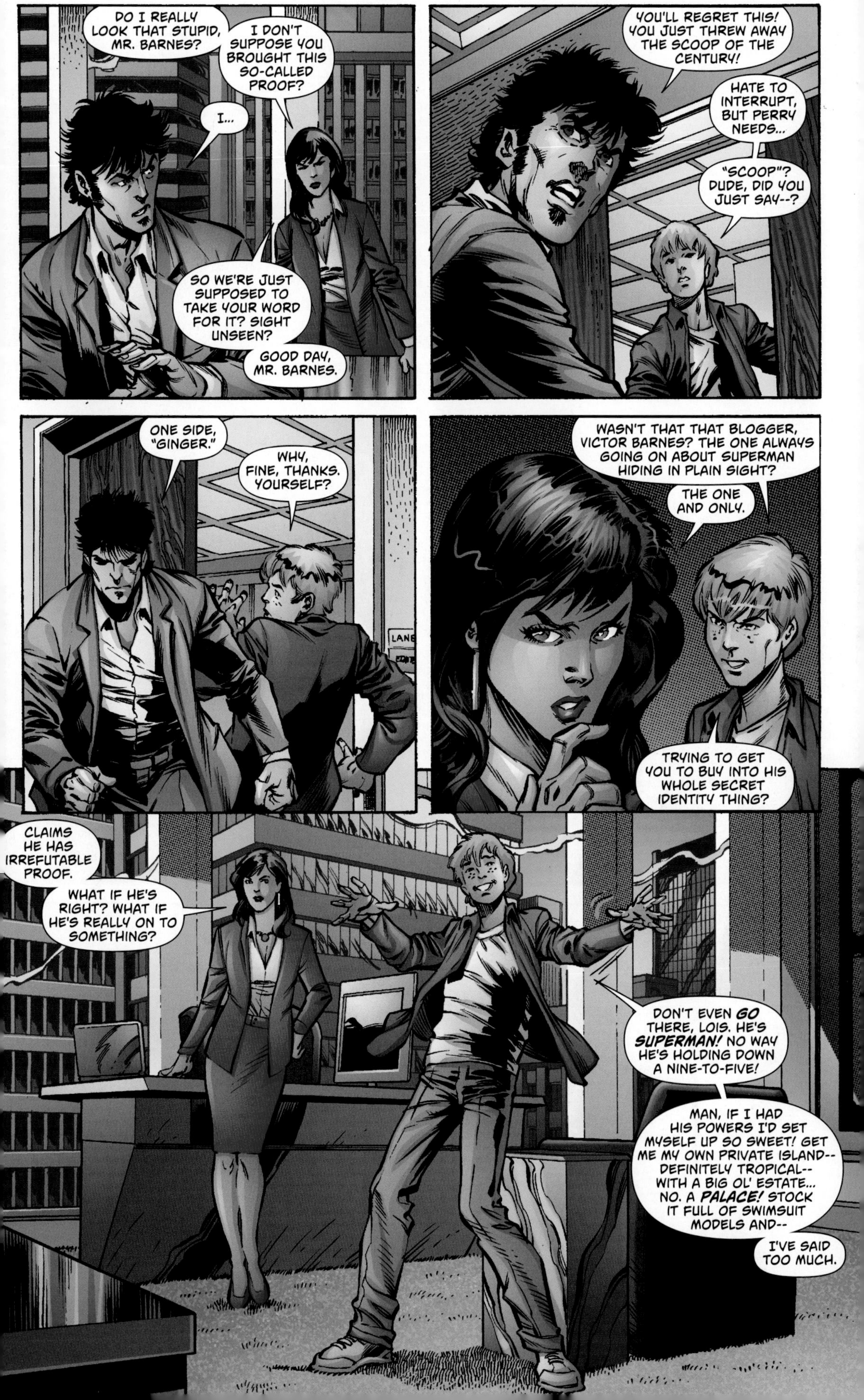

DO I REALLY LOOK THAT STUPID, MR. BARNES?
I DON'T SUPPOSE YOU BROUGHT THIS SO-CALLED PROOF?
I...
SO WE'RE JUST SUPPOSED TO TAKE YOUR WORD FOR IT? SIGHT UNSEEN?
GOOD DAY, MR. BARNES.
YOU'LL REGRET THIS! YOU JUST THREW AWAY THE SCOOP OF THE CENTURY!
HATE TO INTERRUPT, BUT PERRY NEEDS...
"SCOOP"? DUDE, DID YOU JUST SAY--?
ONE SIDE, "GINGER."
WHY, FINE, THANKS. YOURSELF?
LANE
WASN'T THAT THAT BLOGGER, VICTOR BARNES? THE ONE ALWAYS GOING ON ABOUT SUPERMAN HIDING IN PLAIN SIGHT?
THE ONE AND ONLY.
TRYING TO GET YOU TO BUY INTO HIS WHOLE SECRET IDENTITY THING?
CLAIMS HE HAS IRREFUTABLE PROOF.
WHAT IF HE'S RIGHT? WHAT IF HE'S REALLY ON TO SOMETHING?
DON'T EVEN ***GO*** THERE, LOIS. HE'S ***SUPERMAN!*** NO WAY HE'S HOLDING DOWN A NINE-TO-FIVE!
MAN, IF I HAD HIS POWERS I'D SET MYSELF UP SO SWEET! GET ME MY OWN PRIVATE ISLAND-- DEFINITELY TROPICAL-- WITH A BIG OL' ESTATE... NO. A ***PALACE!*** STOCK IT FULL OF SWIMSUIT MODELS AND--
I'VE SAID TOO MUCH.

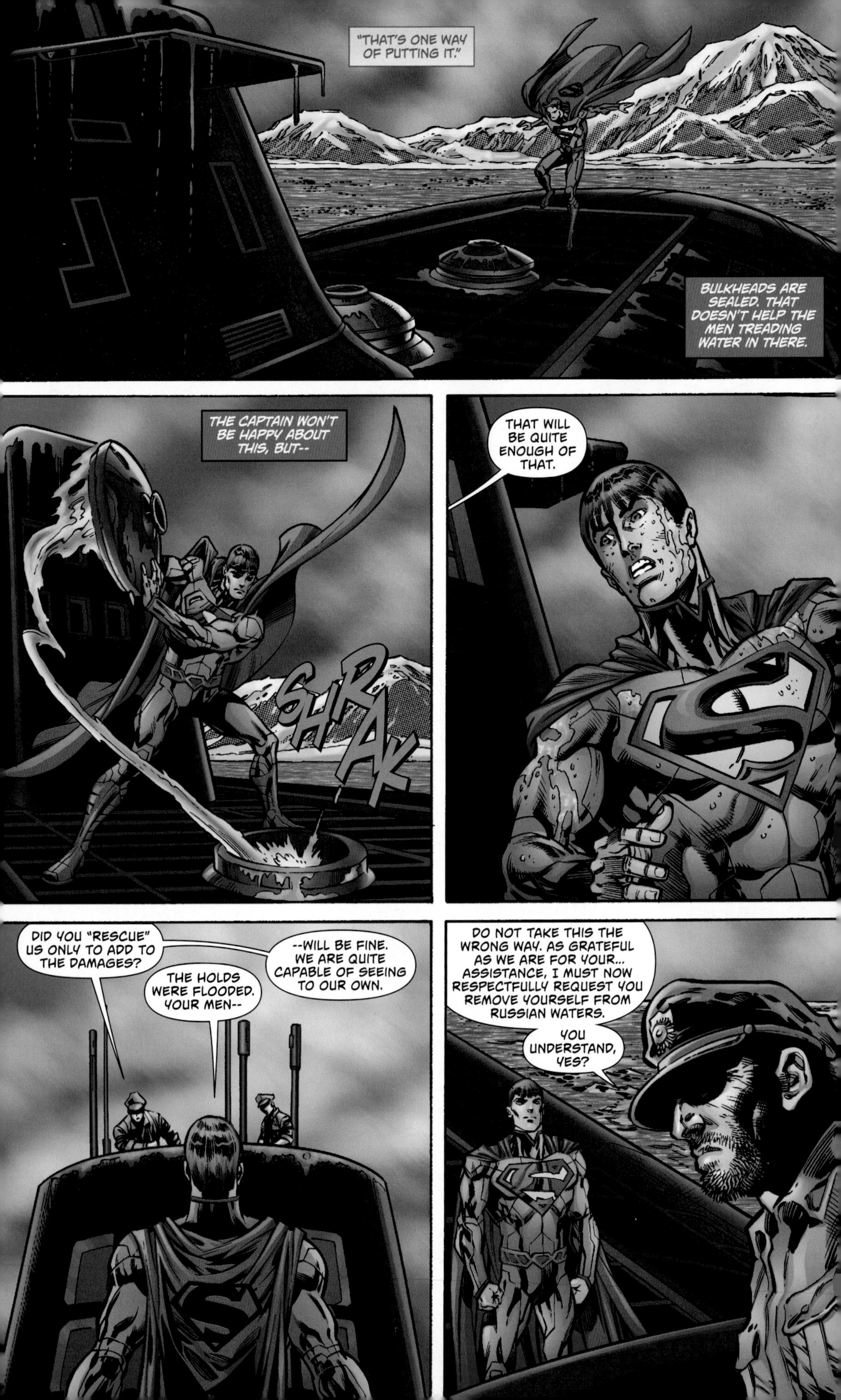
"THAT'S ONE WAY OF PUTTING IT."
BULKHEADS ARE SEALED. THAT DOESN'T HELP THE MEN TREADING WATER IN THERE.
THE CAPTAIN WON'T BE HAPPY ABOUT THIS, BUT--
SHRAK
THAT WILL BE QUITE ENOUGH OF THAT.
DID YOU "RESCUE" US ONLY TO ADD TO THE DAMAGES?
THE HOLDS WERE FLOODED. YOUR MEN--
--WILL BE FINE. WE ARE QUITE CAPABLE OF SEEING TO OUR OWN.
DO NOT TAKE THIS THE WRONG WAY. AS GRATEFUL AS WE ARE FOR YOUR... ASSISTANCE, I MUST NOW RESPECTFULLY REQUEST YOU REMOVE YOURSELF FROM RUSSIAN WATERS.
YOU UNDERSTAND, YES?

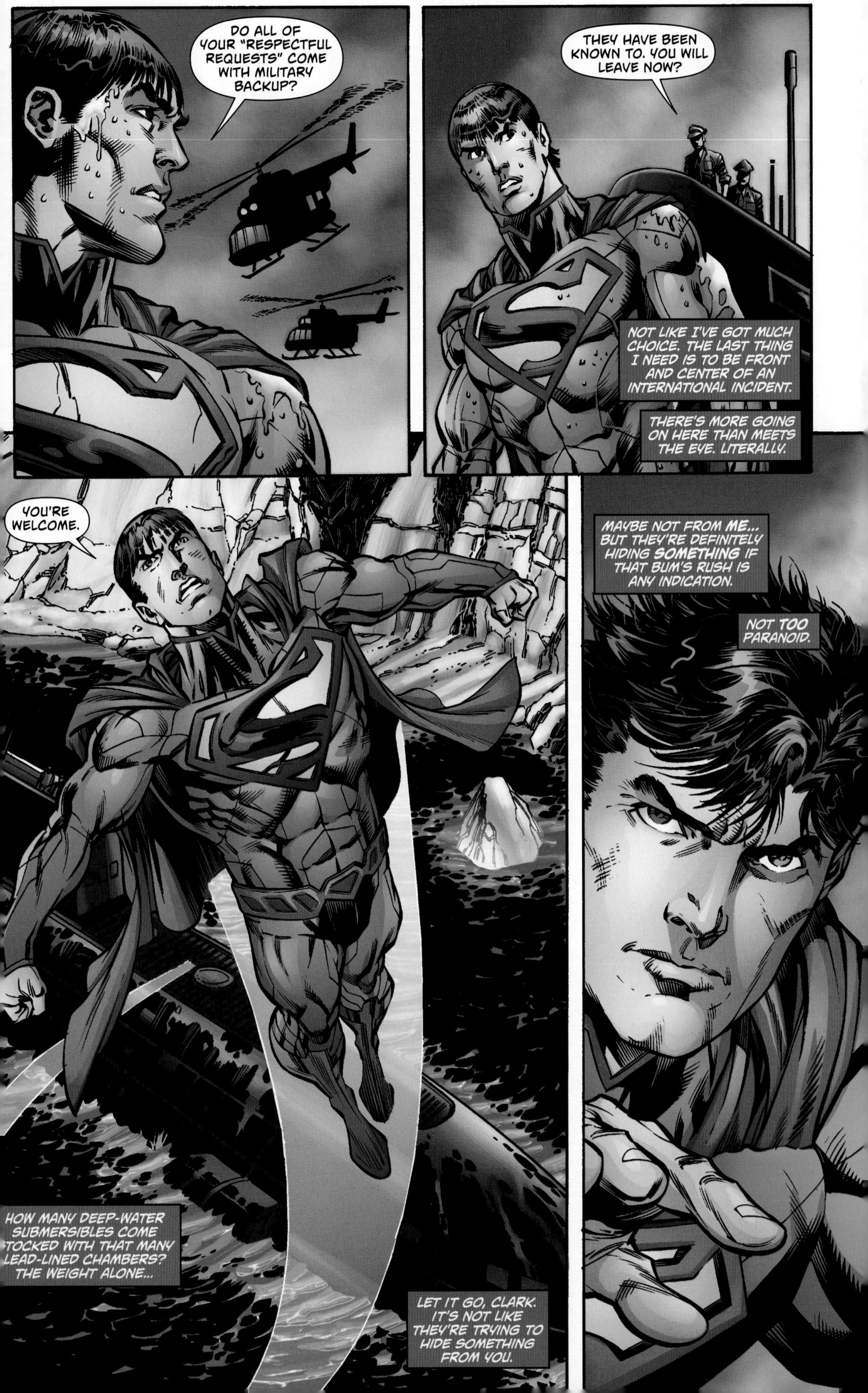
DO ALL OF YOUR "RESPECTFUL REQUESTS" COME WITH MILITARY BACKUP?
THEY HAVE BEEN KNOWN TO. YOU WILL LEAVE NOW?
NOT LIKE I'VE GOT MUCH CHOICE. THE LAST THING I NEED IS TO BE FRONT AND CENTER OF AN INTERNATIONAL INCIDENT.
THERE'S MORE GOING ON HERE THAN MEETS THE EYE. LITERALLY.
YOU'RE WELCOME.
HOW MANY DEEP-WATER SUBMERSIBLES COME STOCKED WITH THAT MANY LEAD-LINED CHAMBERS? THE WEIGHT ALONE...
LET IT GO, CLARK. IT'S NOT LIKE THEY'RE TRYING TO HIDE SOMETHING FROM YOU.
MAYBE NOT FROM ME... BUT THEY'RE DEFINITELY HIDING SOMETHING IF THAT BUM'S RUSH IS ANY INDICATION.
NOT TOO PARANOID.

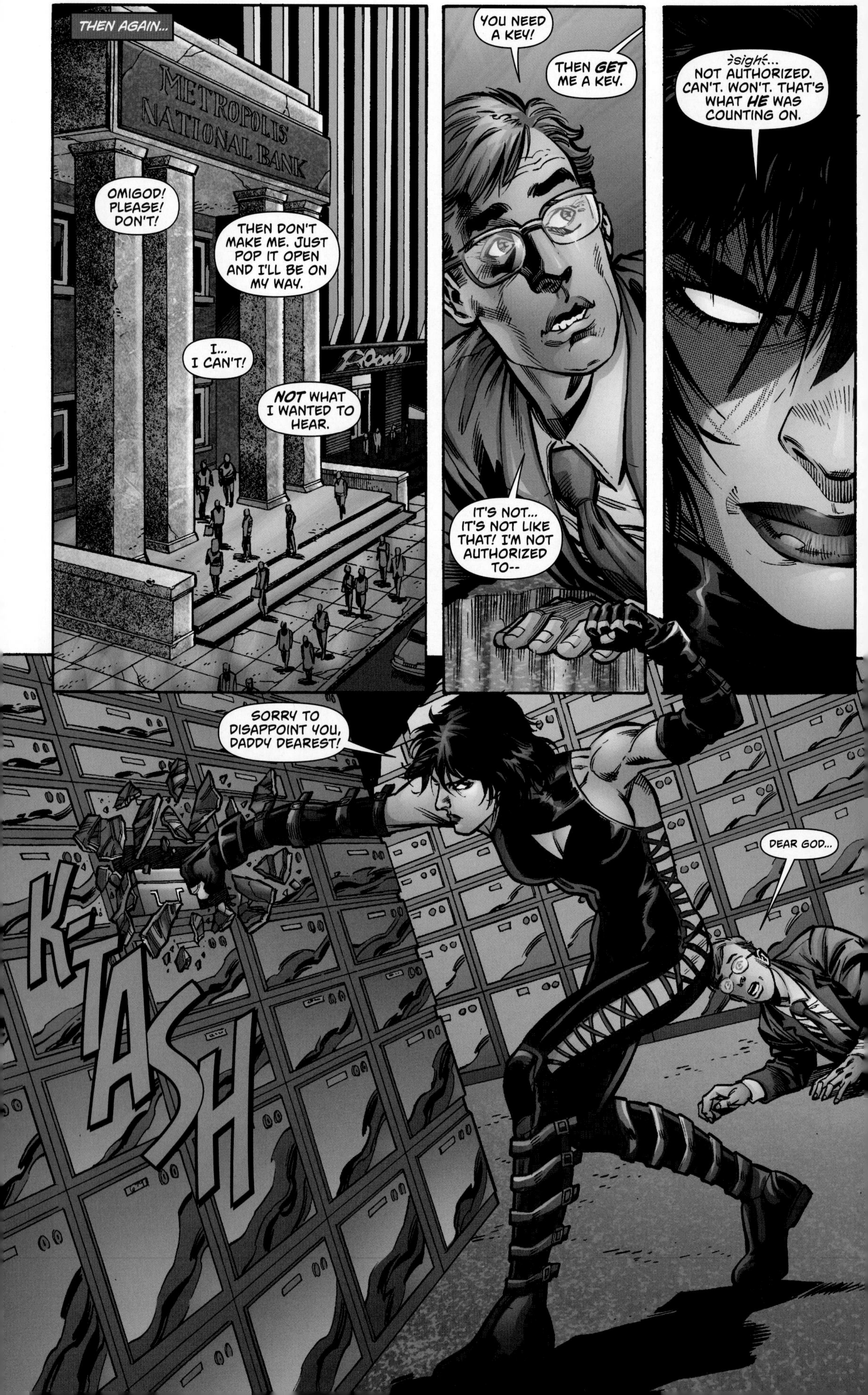
THEN AGAIN...
METROPOLIS NATIONAL BANK
OMIGOD! PLEASE! DON'T!
THEN DON'T MAKE ME. JUST POP IT OPEN AND I'LL BE ON MY WAY.
I... I CAN'T!
NOT WHAT I WANTED TO HEAR.
YOU NEED A KEY!
THEN GET ME A KEY.
IT'S NOT... IT'S NOT LIKE THAT! I'M NOT AUTHORIZED TO--
sigh... NOT AUTHORIZED. CAN'T. WON'T. THAT'S WHAT HE WAS COUNTING ON.
SORRY TO DISAPPOINT YOU, DADDY DEAREST!
K-TASH
DEAR GOD...

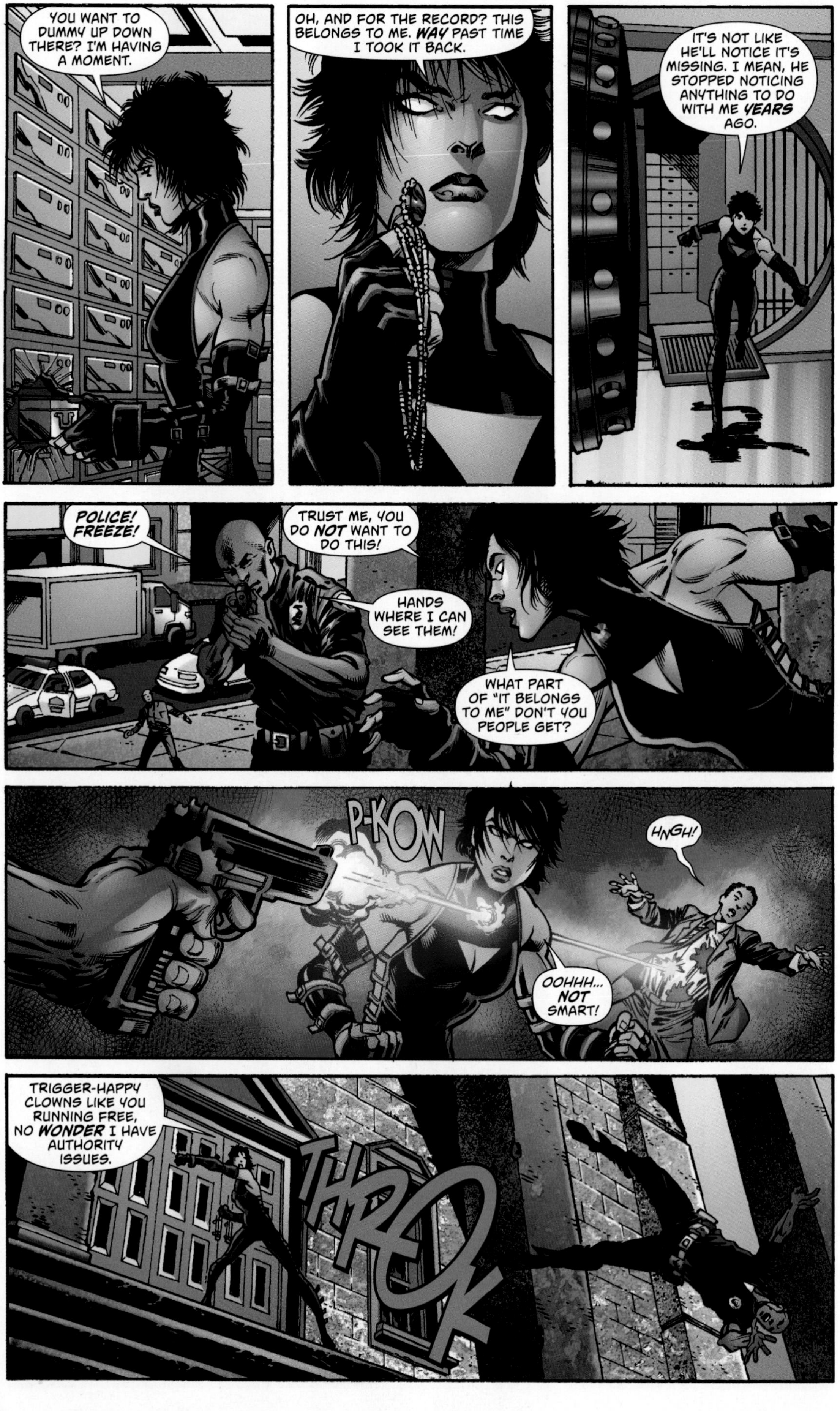
YOU WANT TO DUMMY UP DOWN THERE? I'M HAVING A MOMENT.
OH, AND FOR THE RECORD? THIS BELONGS TO ME. WAY PAST TIME I TOOK IT BACK.
IT'S NOT LIKE HE'LL NOTICE IT'S MISSING. I MEAN, HE STOPPED NOTICING ANYTHING TO DO WITH ME YEARS AGO.
POLICE! FREEZE!
TRUST ME, YOU DO NOT WANT TO DO THIS!
HANDS WHERE I CAN SEE THEM!
WHAT PART OF "IT BELONGS TO ME" DON'T YOU PEOPLE GET?
P-KOW
HNGH!
OOHHH... NOT SMART!
TRIGGER-HAPPY CLOWNS LIKE YOU RUNNING FREE, NO WONDER I HAVE AUTHORITY ISSUES.
THROK

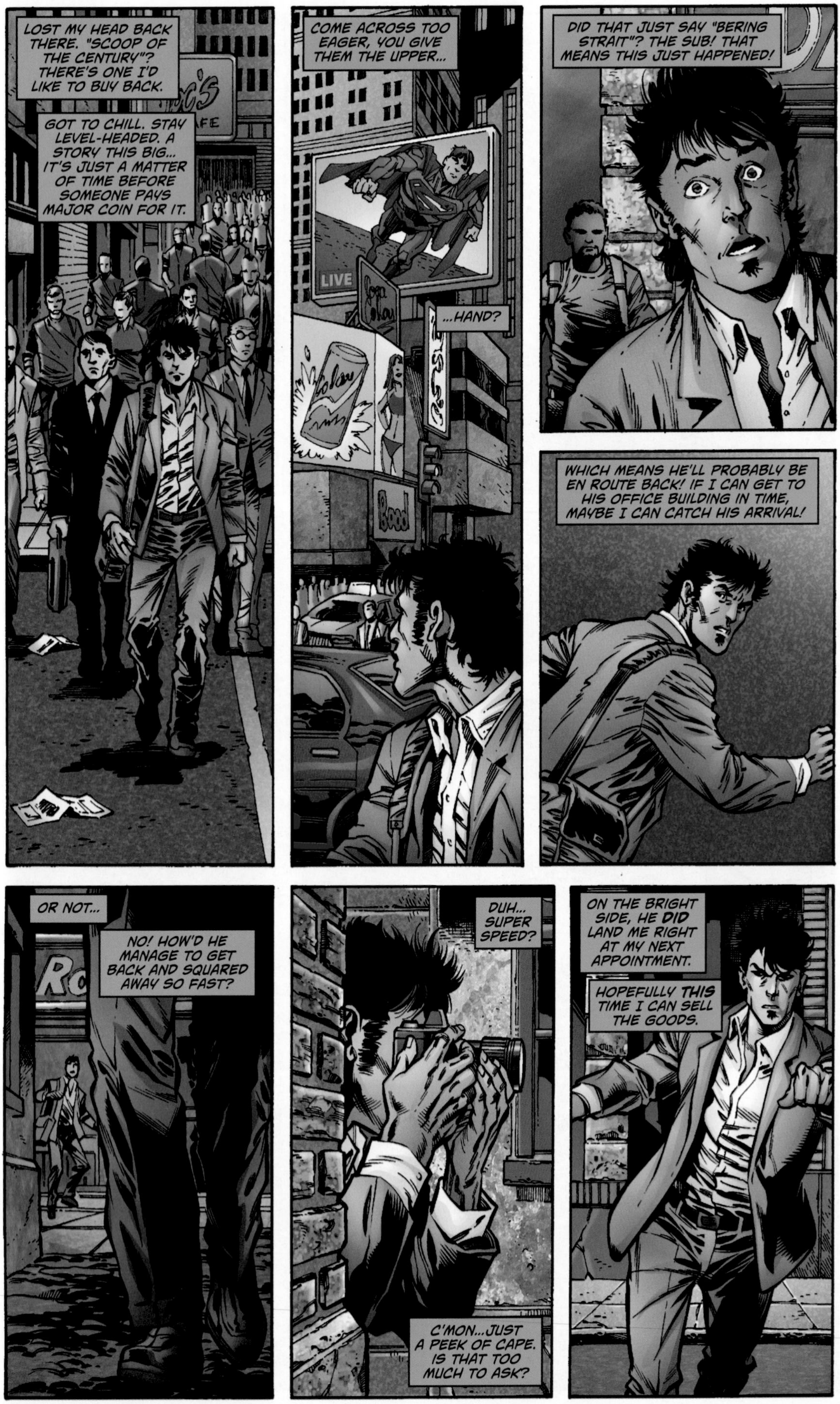
LOST MY HEAD BACK THERE. "SCOOP OF THE CENTURY"? THERE'S ONE I'D LIKE TO BUY BACK.
GOT TO CHILL. STAY LEVEL-HEADED. A STORY THIS BIG... IT'S JUST A MATTER OF TIME BEFORE SOMEONE PAYS MAJOR COIN FOR IT.
COME ACROSS TOO EAGER, YOU GIVE THEM THE UPPER...
LIVE
...HAND?
DID THAT JUST SAY "BERING STRAIT"? THE SUB! THAT MEANS THIS JUST HAPPENED!
WHICH MEANS HE'LL PROBABLY BE EN ROUTE BACK! IF I CAN GET TO HIS OFFICE BUILDING IN TIME, MAYBE I CAN CATCH HIS ARRIVAL!
OR NOT...
NO! HOW'D HE MANAGE TO GET BACK AND SQUARED AWAY SO FAST?
DUH... SUPER SPEED?
C'MON...JUST A PEEK OF CAPE. IS THAT TOO MUCH TO ASK?
ON THE BRIGHT SIDE, HE DID LAND ME RIGHT AT MY NEXT APPOINTMENT.
HOPEFULLY THIS TIME I CAN SELL THE GOODS.

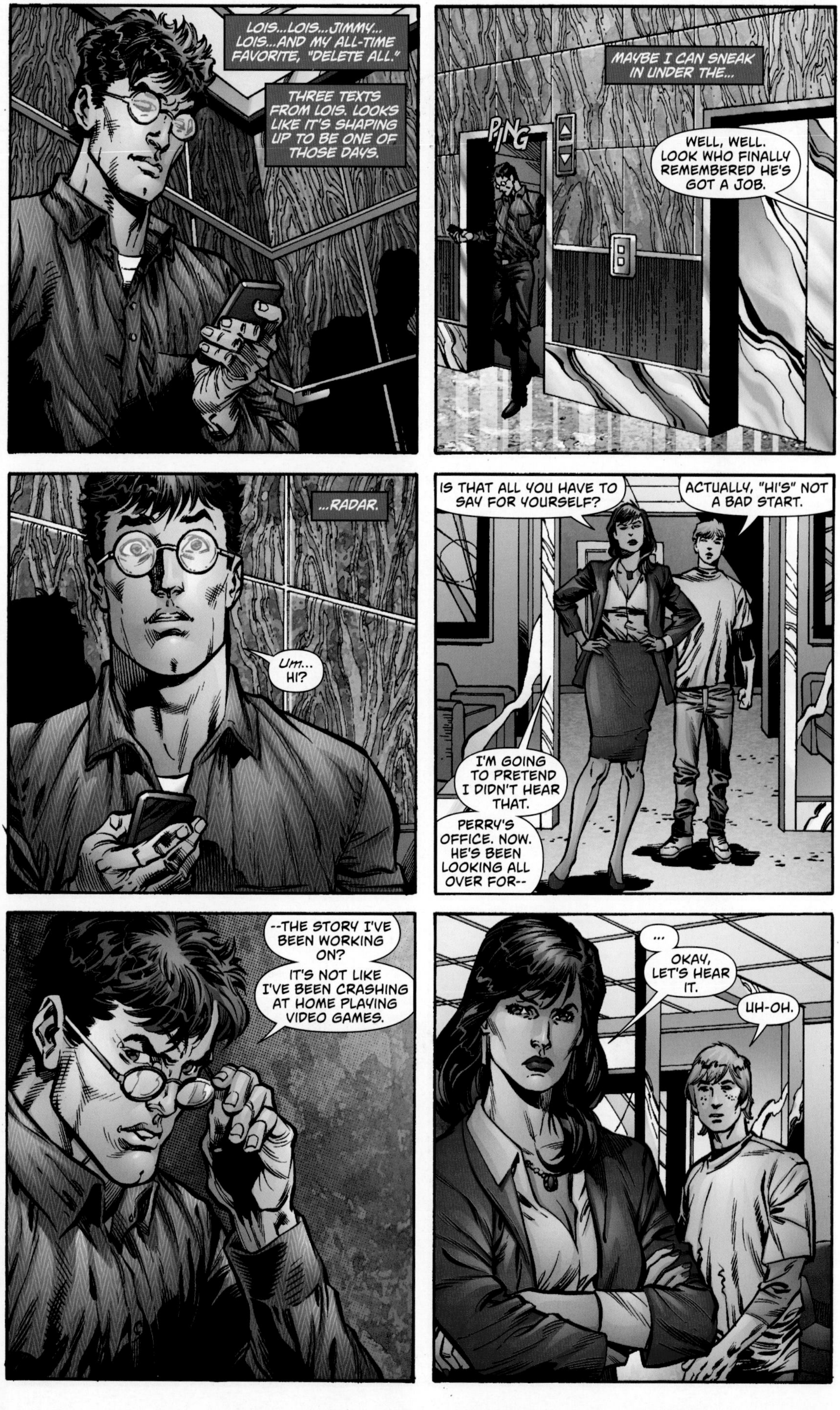
LOIS...LOIS...JIMMY... LOIS...AND MY ALL-TIME FAVORITE, "DELETE ALL."
THREE TEXTS FROM LOIS. LOOKS LIKE IT'S SHAPING UP TO BE ONE OF THOSE DAYS.
MAYBE I CAN SNEAK IN UNDER THE...
PING
WELL, WELL. LOOK WHO FINALLY REMEMBERED HE'S GOT A JOB.
...RADAR.
UM... HI?
IS THAT ALL YOU HAVE TO SAY FOR YOURSELF?
ACTUALLY, "HI'S" NOT A BAD START.
I'M GOING TO PRETEND I DIDN'T HEAR THAT.
PERRY'S OFFICE. NOW. HE'S BEEN LOOKING ALL OVER FOR--
--THE STORY I'VE BEEN WORKING ON?
IT'S NOT LIKE I'VE BEEN CRASHING AT HOME PLAYING VIDEO GAMES.
...
OKAY, LET'S HEAR IT.
UH-OH.

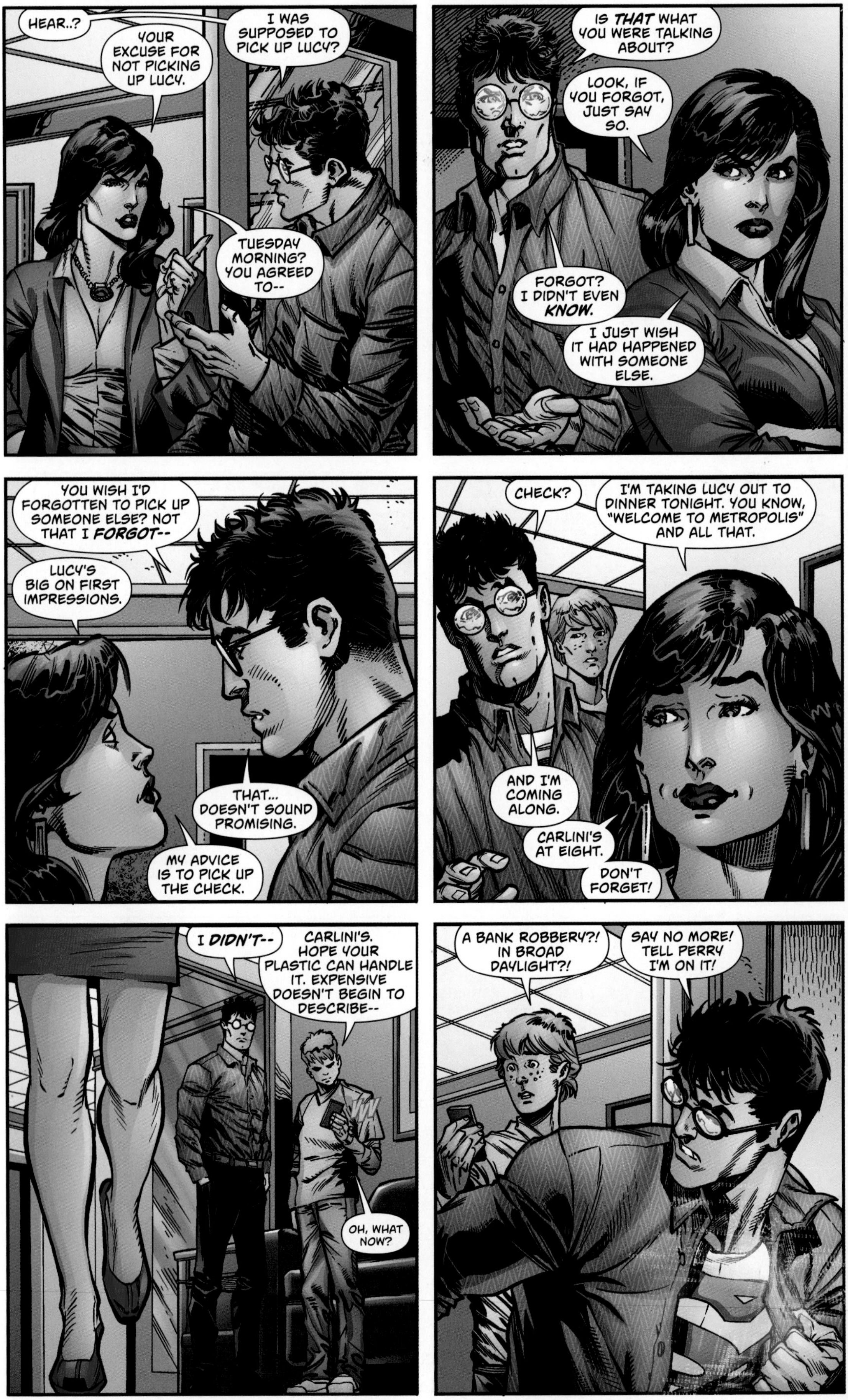
HEAR..?
I WAS SUPPOSED TO PICK UP LUCY?
YOUR EXCUSE FOR NOT PICKING UP LUCY.
TUESDAY MORNING? YOU AGREED TO--
IS *THAT* WHAT YOU WERE TALKING ABOUT?
LOOK, IF YOU FORGOT, JUST SAY SO.
FORGOT? I DIDN'T EVEN ***KNOW***.
I JUST WISH IT HAD HAPPENED WITH SOMEONE ELSE.
YOU WISH I'D FORGOTTEN TO PICK UP SOMEONE ELSE? NOT THAT I *FORGOT*--
LUCY'S BIG ON FIRST IMPRESSIONS.
THAT... DOESN'T SOUND PROMISING.
MY ADVICE IS TO PICK UP THE CHECK.
CHECK?
I'M TAKING LUCY OUT TO DINNER TONIGHT. YOU KNOW, "WELCOME TO METROPOLIS" AND ALL THAT.
AND I'M COMING ALONG.
CARLINI'S AT EIGHT.
DON'T FORGET!
I *DIDN'T*--
CARLINI'S. HOPE YOUR PLASTIC CAN HANDLE IT. EXPENSIVE DOESN'T BEGIN TO DESCRIBE--
OH, WHAT NOW?
A BANK ROBBERY?! IN BROAD DAYLIGHT?!
SAY NO MORE! TELL PERRY I'M ON IT!

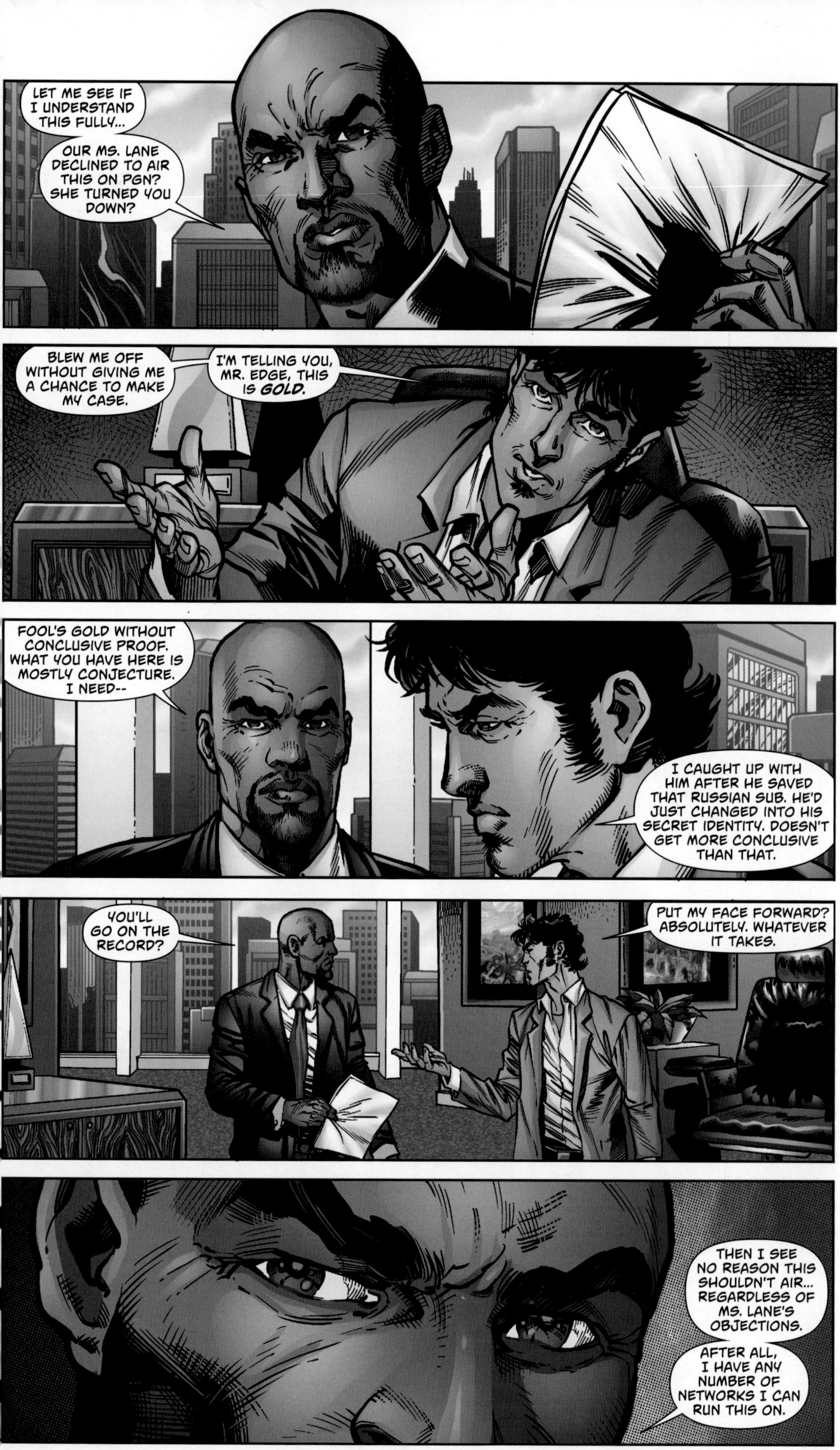
LET ME SEE IF I UNDERSTAND THIS FULLY...
OUR MS. LANE DECLINED TO AIR THIS ON PGN? SHE TURNED YOU DOWN?
BLEW ME OFF WITHOUT GIVING ME A CHANCE TO MAKE MY CASE.
I'M TELLING YOU, MR. EDGE, THIS IS GOLD.
FOOL'S GOLD WITHOUT CONCLUSIVE PROOF. WHAT YOU HAVE HERE IS MOSTLY CONJECTURE. I NEED--
I CAUGHT UP WITH HIM AFTER HE SAVED THAT RUSSIAN SUB. HE'D JUST CHANGED INTO HIS SECRET IDENTITY. DOESN'T GET MORE CONCLUSIVE THAN THAT.
YOU'LL GO ON THE RECORD?
PUT MY FACE FORWARD? ABSOLUTELY. WHATEVER IT TAKES.
THEN I SEE NO REASON THIS SHOULDN'T AIR... REGARDLESS OF MS. LANE'S OBJECTIONS.
AFTER ALL, I HAVE ANY NUMBER OF NETWORKS I CAN RUN THIS ON.

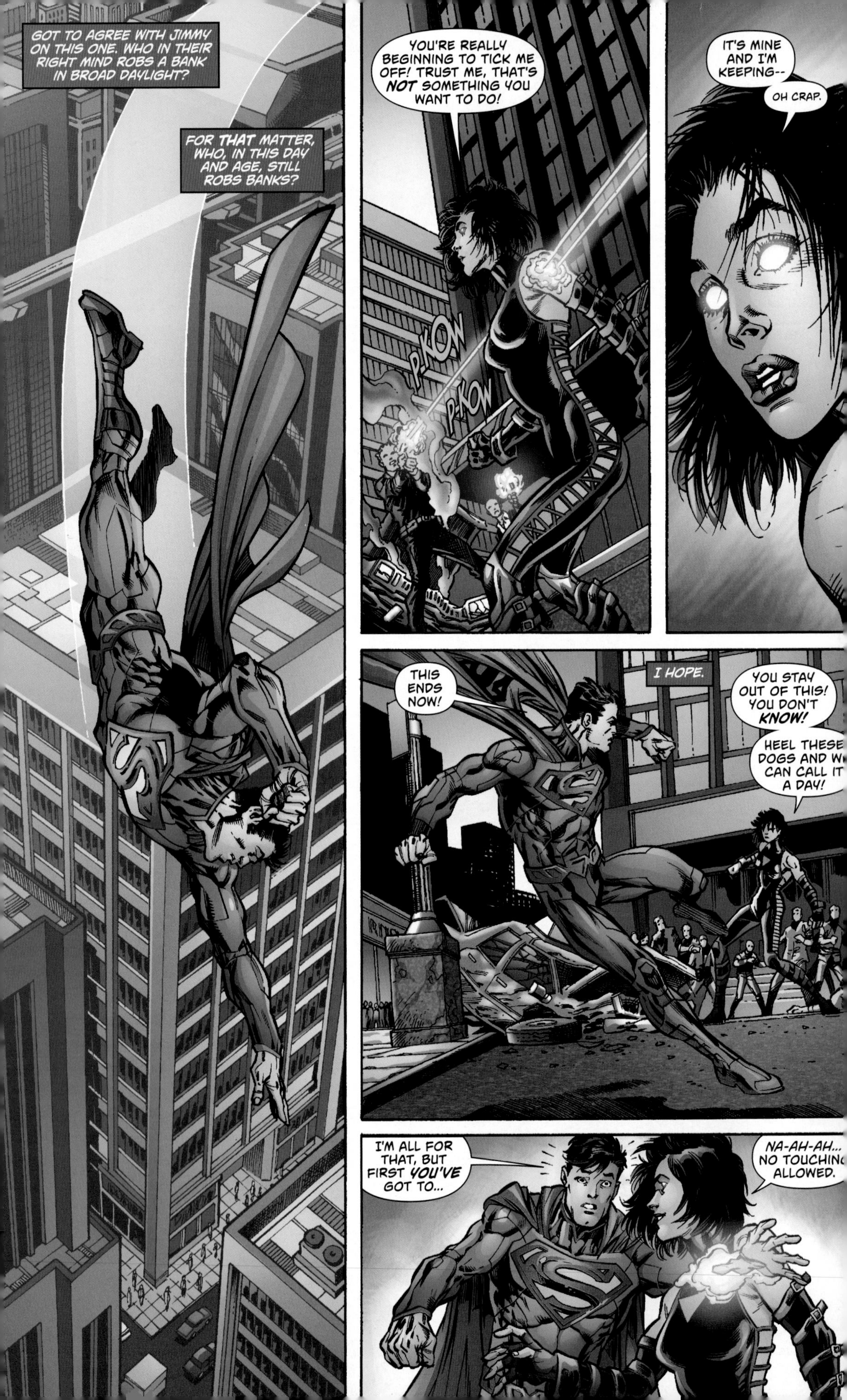
GOT TO AGREE WITH JIMMY ON THIS ONE. WHO IN THEIR RIGHT MIND ROBS A BANK IN BROAD DAYLIGHT?
FOR THAT MATTER, WHO, IN THIS DAY AND AGE, STILL ROBS BANKS?
YOU'RE REALLY BEGINNING TO TICK ME OFF! TRUST ME, THAT'S NOT SOMETHING YOU WANT TO DO!
P-KOW
P-KOW
IT'S MINE AND I'M KEEPING--
OH CRAP.
THIS ENDS NOW!
I HOPE.
YOU STAY OUT OF THIS! YOU DON'T KNOW!
HEEL THESE DOGS AND W CAN CALL IT A DAY!
I'M ALL FOR THAT, BUT FIRST YOU'VE GOT TO...
NA-AH-AH... NO TOUCHING ALLOWED.

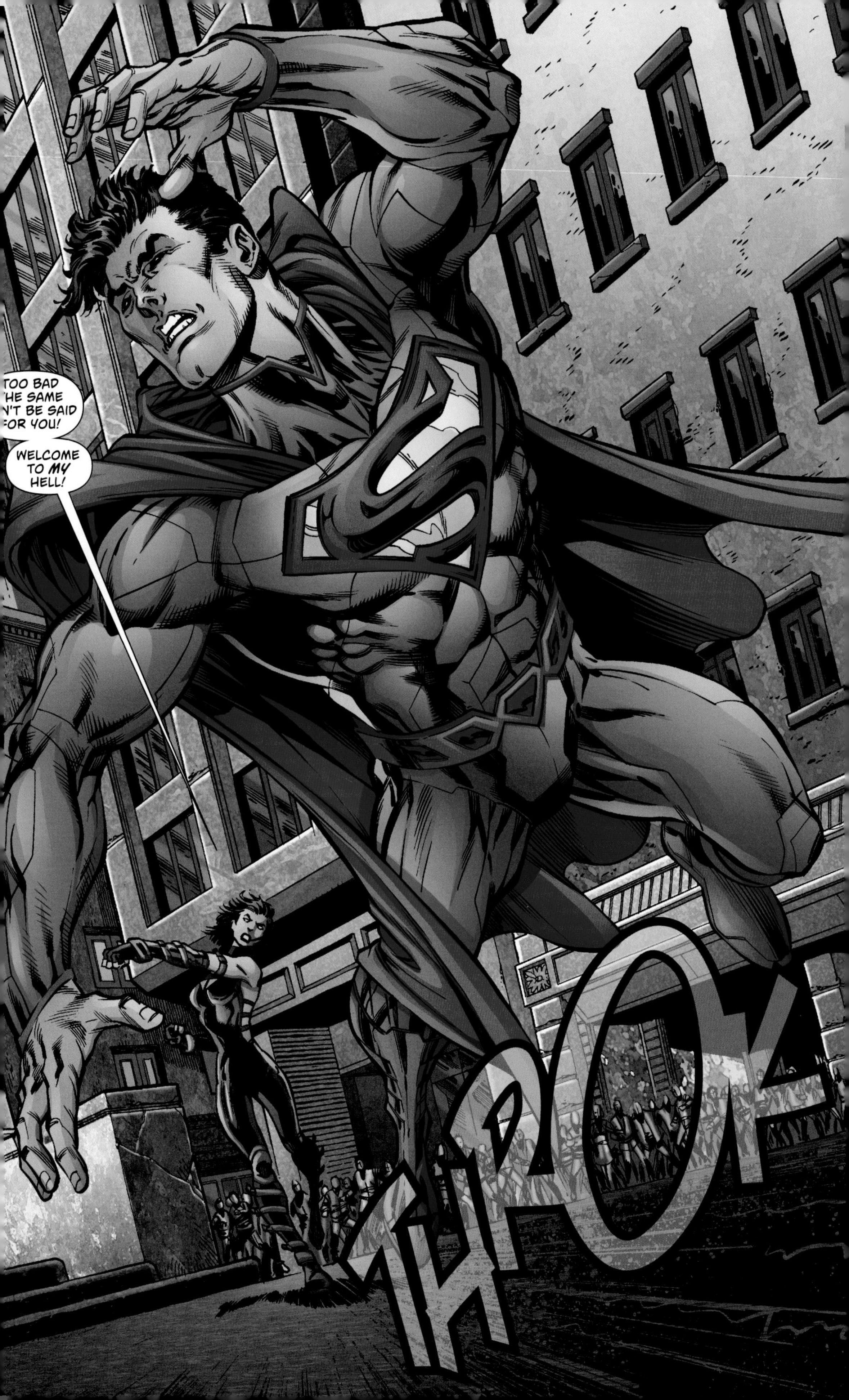
TOO BAD
HE SAME
'T BE SAID
OR YOU!
WELCOME TO *MY* HELL!

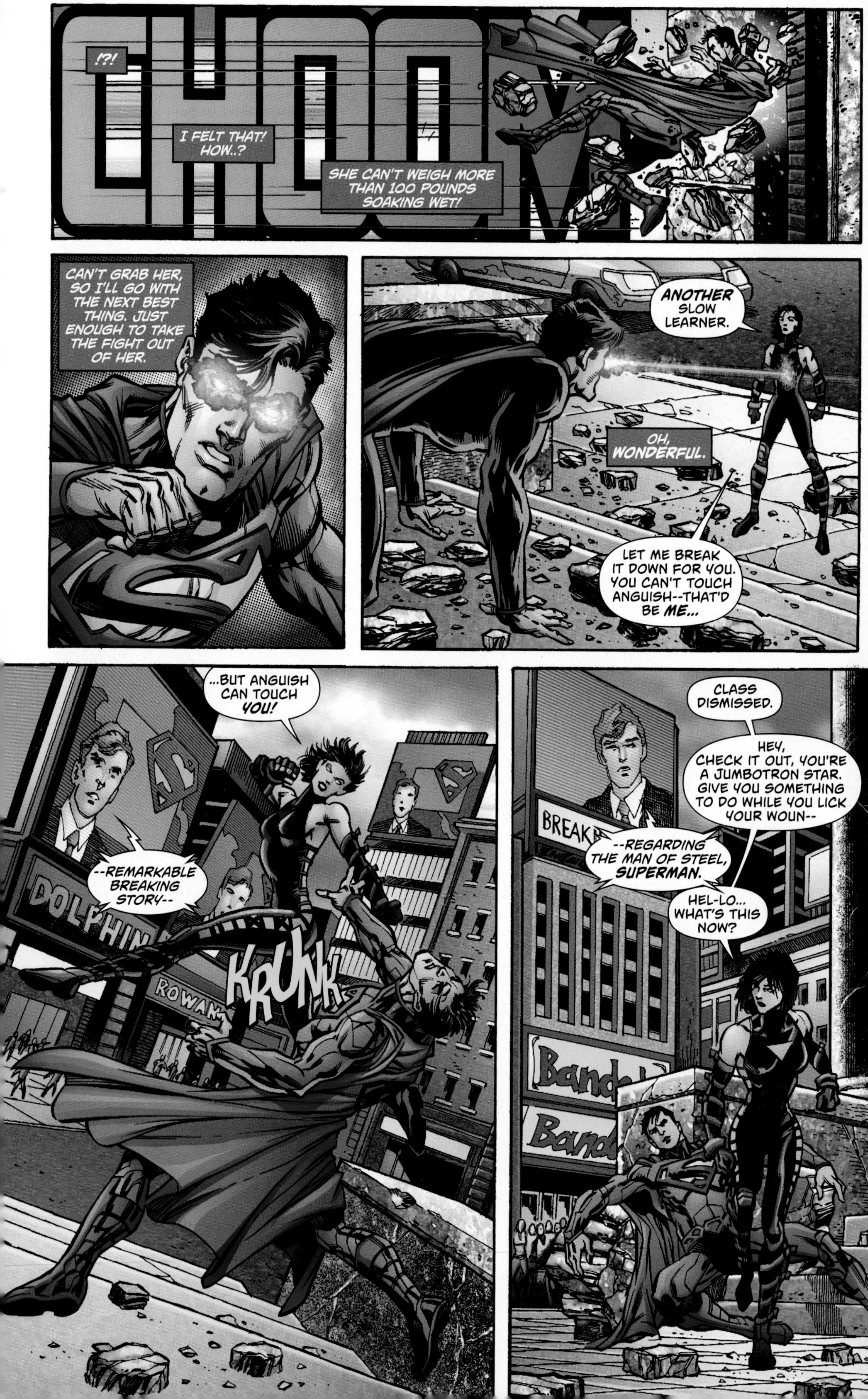
CHOOM
!?!
I FELT THAT! HOW..?
SHE CAN'T WEIGH MORE THAN 100 POUNDS SOAKING WET!
CAN'T GRAB HER, SO I'LL GO WITH THE NEXT BEST THING. JUST ENOUGH TO TAKE THE FIGHT OUT OF HER.
ANOTHER SLOW LEARNER.
OH, WONDERFUL.
LET ME BREAK IT DOWN FOR YOU. YOU CAN'T TOUCH ANGUISH--THAT'D BE ME...
...BUT ANGUISH CAN TOUCH YOU!
--REMARKABLE BREAKING STORY--
DOLPHIN
ROWAN
KRUNK
CLASS DISMISSED.
HEY, CHECK IT OUT, YOU'RE A JUMBOTRON STAR. GIVE YOU SOMETHING TO DO WHILE YOU LICK YOUR WOUN--
--REGARDING THE MAN OF STEEL, SUPERMAN.
HEL-LO... WHAT'S THIS NOW?

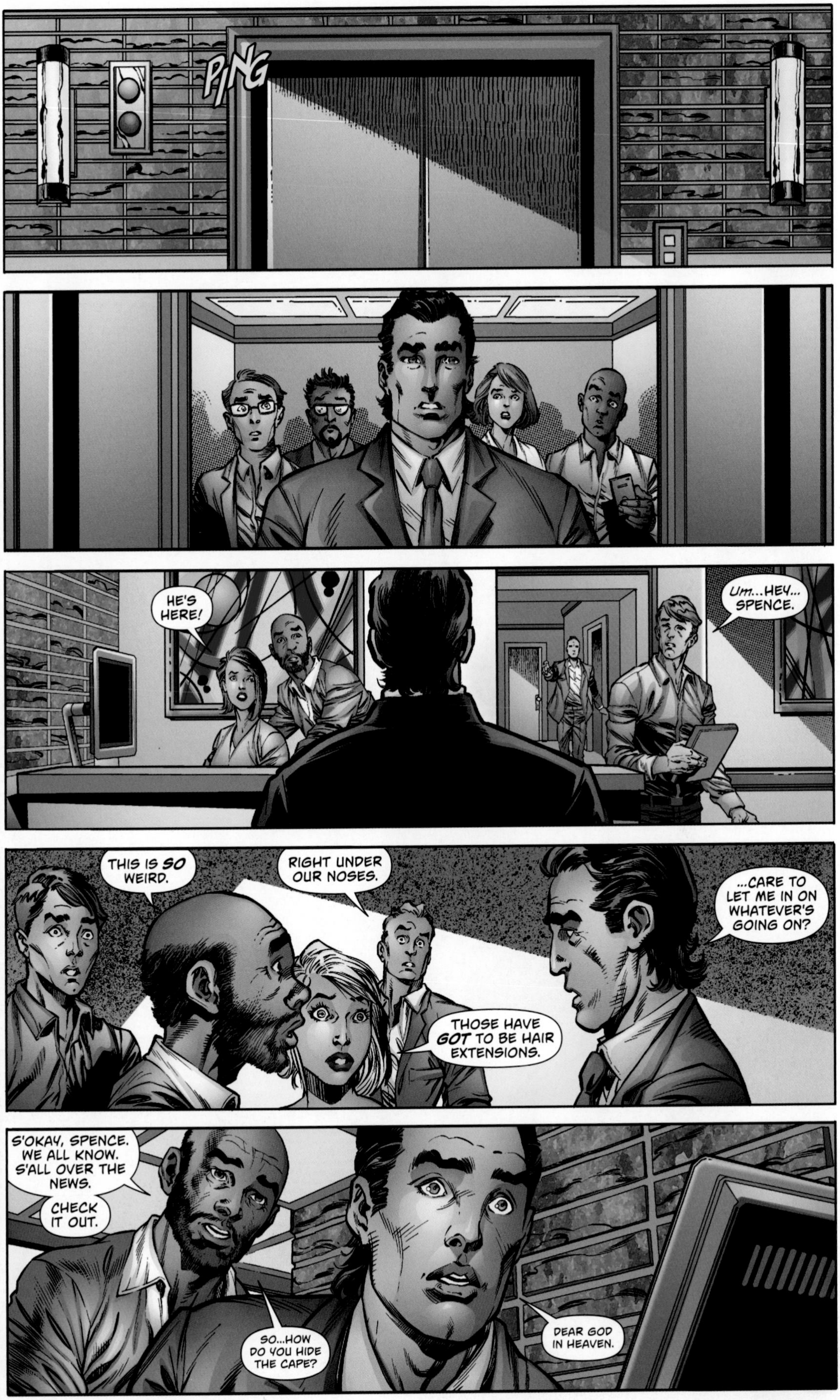
PING
HE'S HERE!
Um...HEY... SPENCE.
THIS IS SO WEIRD.
RIGHT UNDER OUR NOSES.
...CARE TO LET ME IN ON WHATEVER'S GOING ON?
THOSE HAVE GOT TO BE HAIR EXTENSIONS.
S'OKAY, SPENCE. WE ALL KNOW. S'ALL OVER THE NEWS.
CHECK IT OUT.
SO...HOW DO YOU HIDE THE CAPE?
DEAR GOD IN HEAVEN.

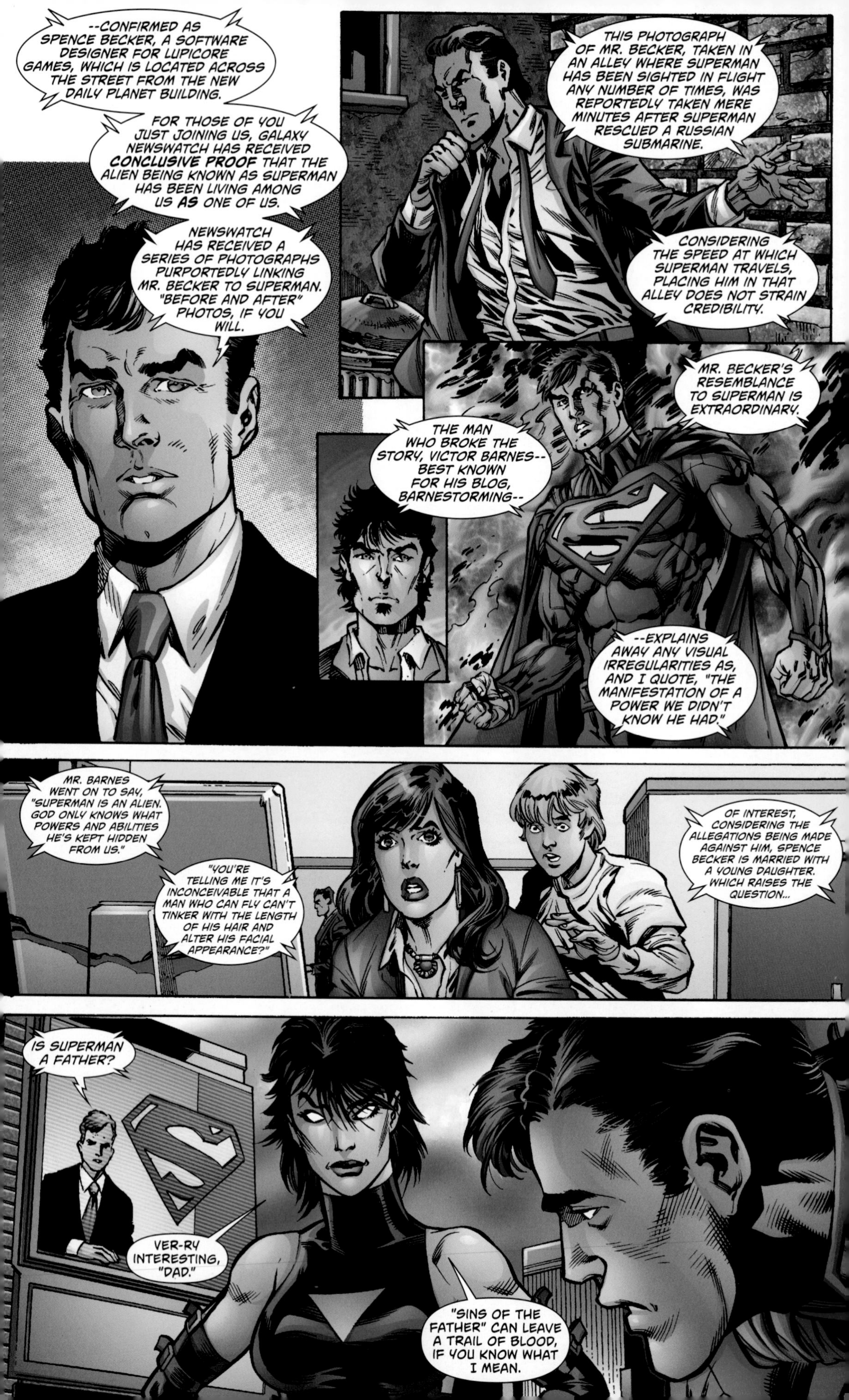
--CONFIRMED AS SPENCE BECKER, A SOFTWARE DESIGNER FOR LUPICORE GAMES, WHICH IS LOCATED ACROSS THE STREET FROM THE NEW DAILY PLANET BUILDING.
FOR THOSE OF YOU JUST JOINING US, GALAXY NEWSWATCH HAS RECEIVED **CONCLUSIVE PROOF** THAT THE ALIEN BEING KNOWN AS SUPERMAN HAS BEEN LIVING AMONG US **AS** ONE OF US.
NEWSWATCH HAS RECEIVED A SERIES OF PHOTOGRAPHS PURPORTEDLY LINKING MR. BECKER TO SUPERMAN. "BEFORE AND AFTER" PHOTOS, IF YOU WILL.
THIS PHOTOGRAPH OF MR. BECKER, TAKEN IN AN ALLEY WHERE SUPERMAN HAS BEEN SIGHTED IN FLIGHT ANY NUMBER OF TIMES, WAS REPORTEDLY TAKEN MERE MINUTES AFTER SUPERMAN RESCUED A RUSSIAN SUBMARINE.
CONSIDERING THE SPEED AT WHICH SUPERMAN TRAVELS, PLACING HIM IN THAT ALLEY DOES NOT STRAIN CREDIBILITY.
MR. BECKER'S RESEMBLANCE TO SUPERMAN IS EXTRAORDINARY.
THE MAN WHO BROKE THE STORY, VICTOR BARNES--BEST KNOWN FOR HIS BLOG, BARNESTORMING--
--EXPLAINS AWAY ANY VISUAL IRREGULARITIES AS, AND I QUOTE, "THE MANIFESTATION OF A POWER WE DIDN'T KNOW HE HAD."
MR. BARNES WENT ON TO SAY, "SUPERMAN IS AN ALIEN. GOD ONLY KNOWS WHAT POWERS AND ABILITIES HE'S KEPT HIDDEN FROM US."
"YOU'RE TELLING ME IT'S INCONCEIVABLE THAT A MAN WHO CAN FLY CAN'T TINKER WITH THE LENGTH OF HIS HAIR AND ALTER HIS FACIAL APPEARANCE?"
OF INTEREST, CONSIDERING THE ALLEGATIONS BEING MADE AGAINST HIM, SPENCE BECKER IS MARRIED WITH A YOUNG DAUGHTER. WHICH RAISES THE QUESTION...
IS SUPERMAN A FATHER?
VER-RY INTERESTING, "DAD."
"SINS OF THE FATHER" CAN LEAVE A TRAIL OF BLOOD, IF YOU KNOW WHAT I MEAN.

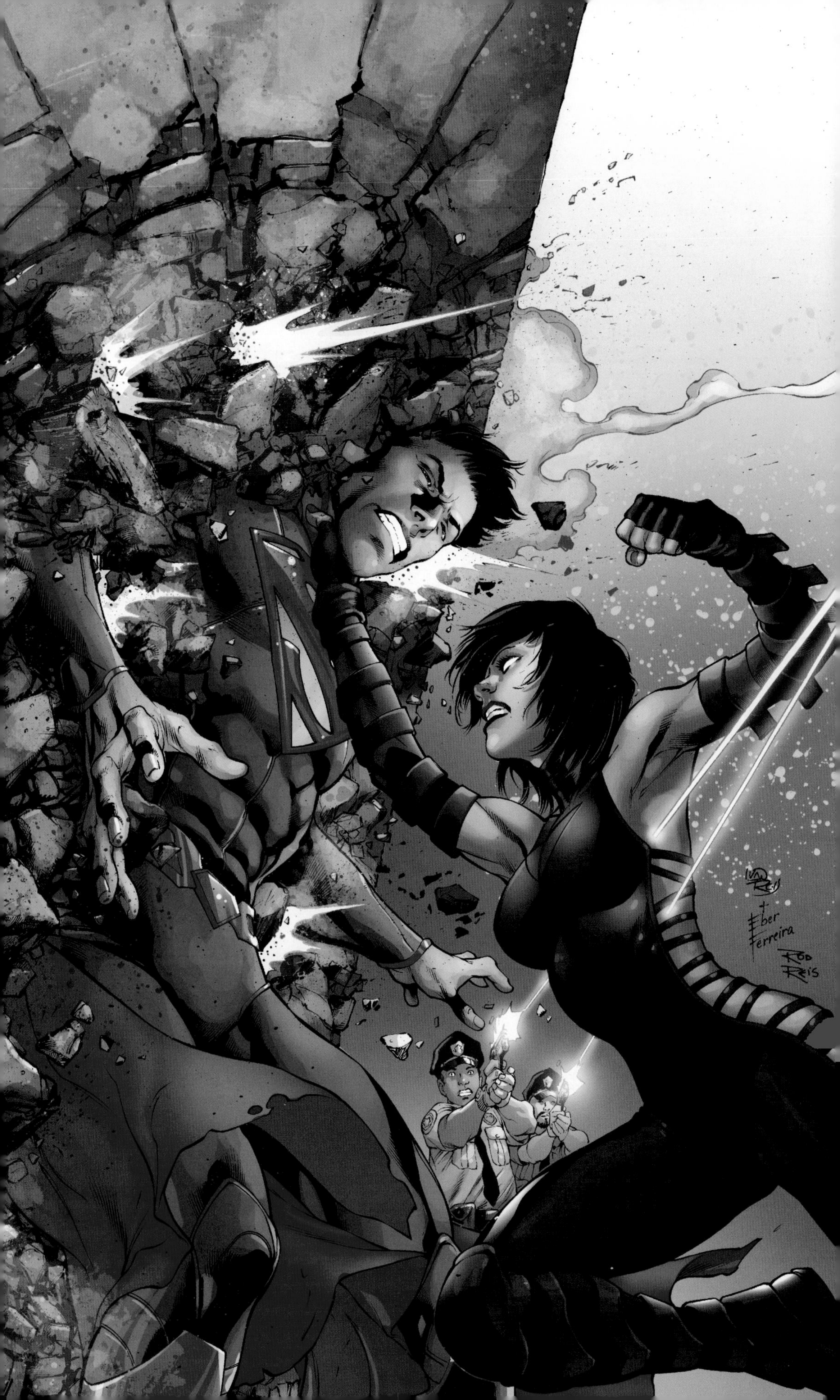

Eber
Ferreira
Rod
Reis

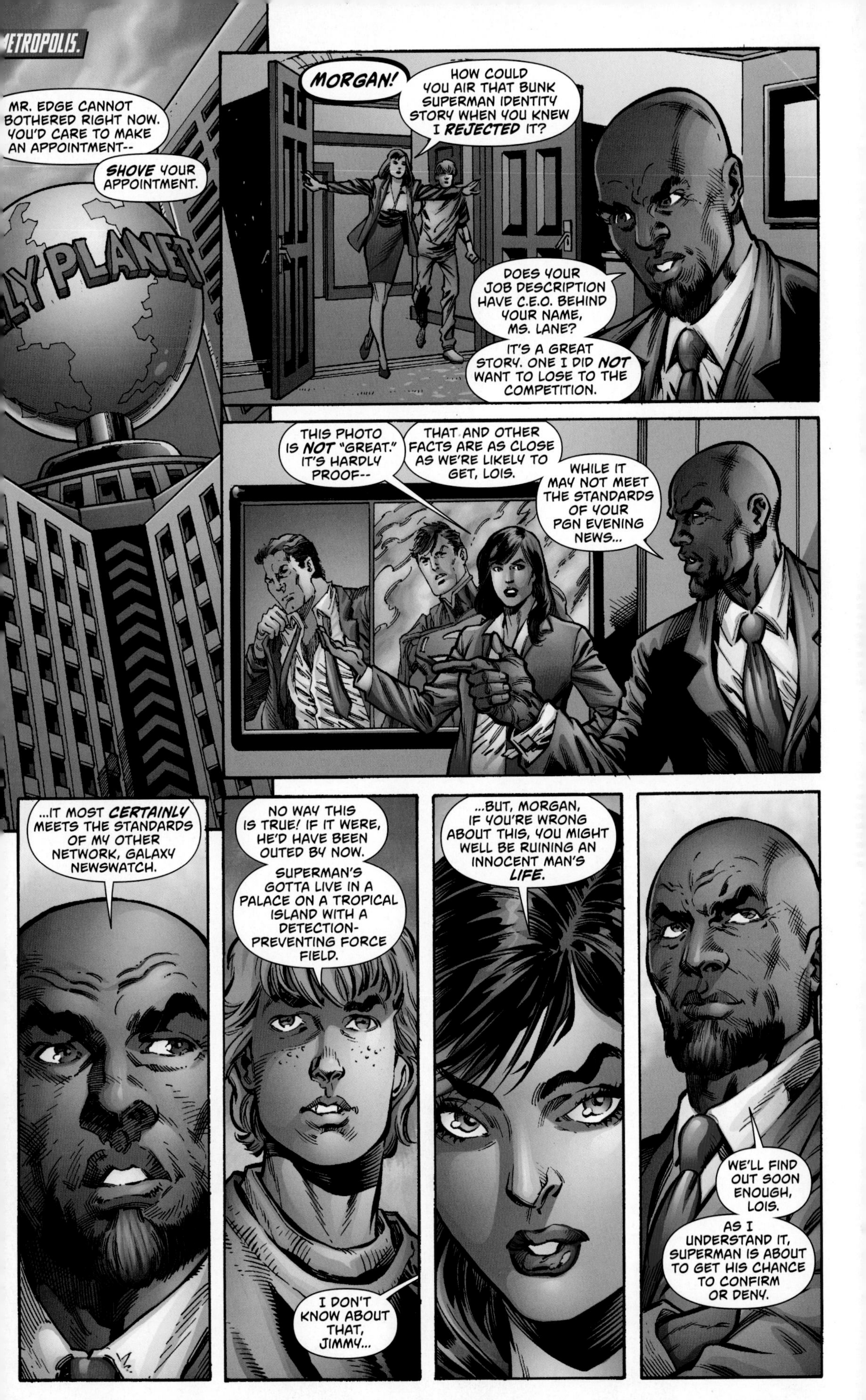
METROPOLIS.
MR. EDGE CANNOT BOTHERED RIGHT NOW. YOU'D CARE TO MAKE AN APPOINTMENT--
SHOVE YOUR APPOINTMENT.
LY PLANET
MORGAN!
HOW COULD YOU AIR THAT BUNK SUPERMAN IDENTITY STORY WHEN YOU KNEW I REJECTED IT?
DOES YOUR JOB DESCRIPTION HAVE C.E.O. BEHIND YOUR NAME, MS. LANE?
IT'S A GREAT STORY. ONE I DID NOT WANT TO LOSE TO THE COMPETITION.
THIS PHOTO IS NOT "GREAT." IT'S HARDLY PROOF--
THAT AND OTHER FACTS ARE AS CLOSE AS WE'RE LIKELY TO GET, LOIS.
WHILE IT MAY NOT MEET THE STANDARDS OF YOUR PGN EVENING NEWS...
...IT MOST CERTAINLY MEETS THE STANDARDS OF MY OTHER NETWORK, GALAXY NEWSWATCH.
NO WAY THIS IS TRUE! IF IT WERE, HE'D HAVE BEEN OUTED BY NOW.
SUPERMAN'S GOTTA LIVE IN A PALACE ON A TROPICAL ISLAND WITH A DETECTION-PREVENTING FORCE FIELD.
I DON'T KNOW ABOUT THAT, JIMMY...
...BUT, MORGAN, IF YOU'RE WRONG ABOUT THIS, YOU MIGHT WELL BE RUINING AN INNOCENT MAN'S LIFE.
WE'LL FIND OUT SOON ENOUGH, LOIS.
AS I UNDERSTAND IT, SUPERMAN IS ABOUT TO GET HIS CHANCE TO CONFIRM OR DENY.

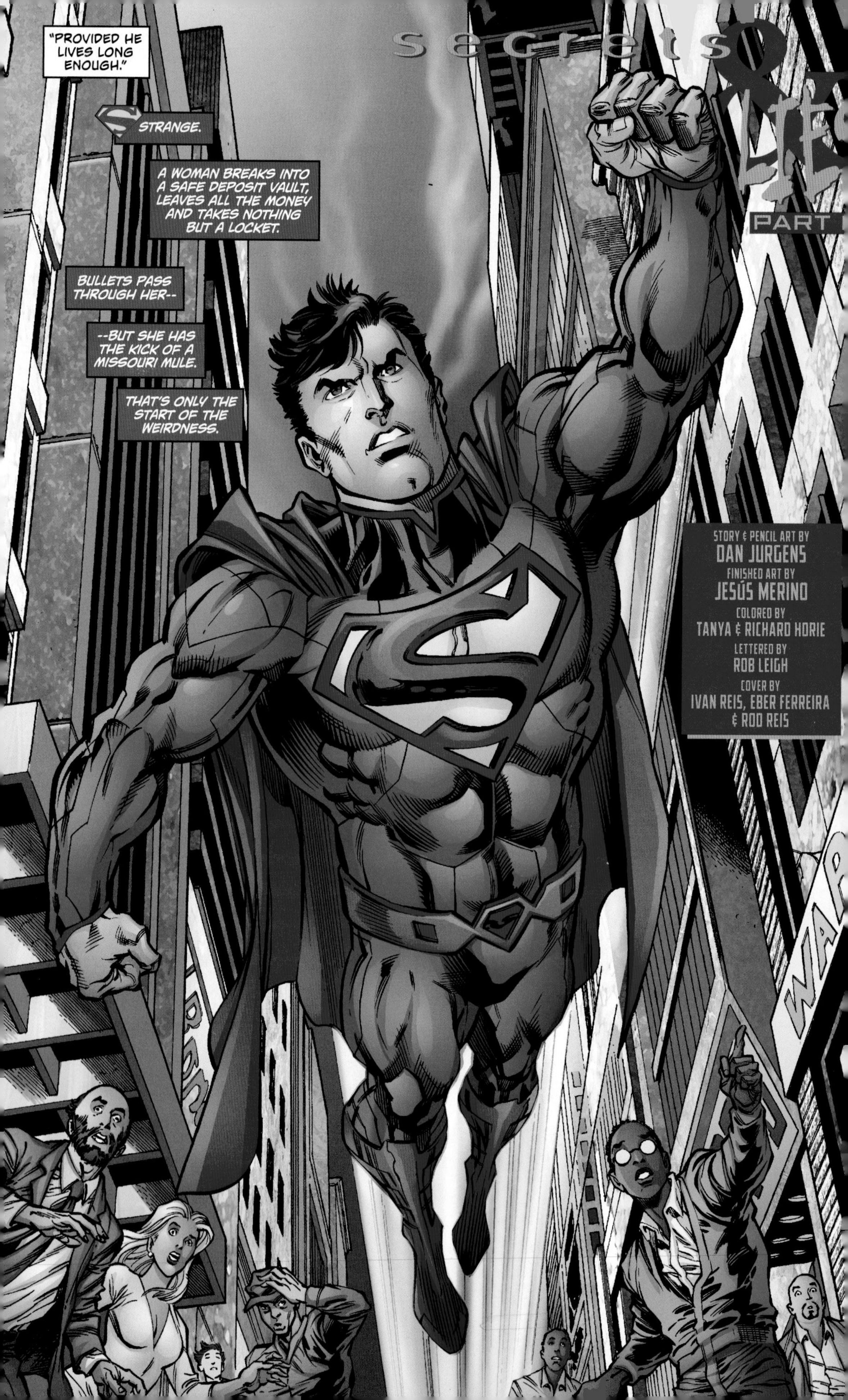
"PROVIDED HE LIVES LONG ENOUGH."
SECRETS & LIES
PART
STRANGE.
A WOMAN BREAKS INTO A SAFE DEPOSIT VAULT, LEAVES ALL THE MONEY AND TAKES NOTHING BUT A LOCKET.
BULLETS PASS THROUGH HER--
--BUT SHE HAS THE KICK OF A MISSOURI MULE.
THAT'S ONLY THE START OF THE WEIRDNESS.
STORY & PENCIL ART BY DAN JURGENS
FINISHED ART BY JESÚS MERINO
COLORED BY TANYA & RICHARD HORIE
LETTERED BY ROB LEIGH
COVER BY IVAN REIS, EBER FERREIRA & ROD REIS

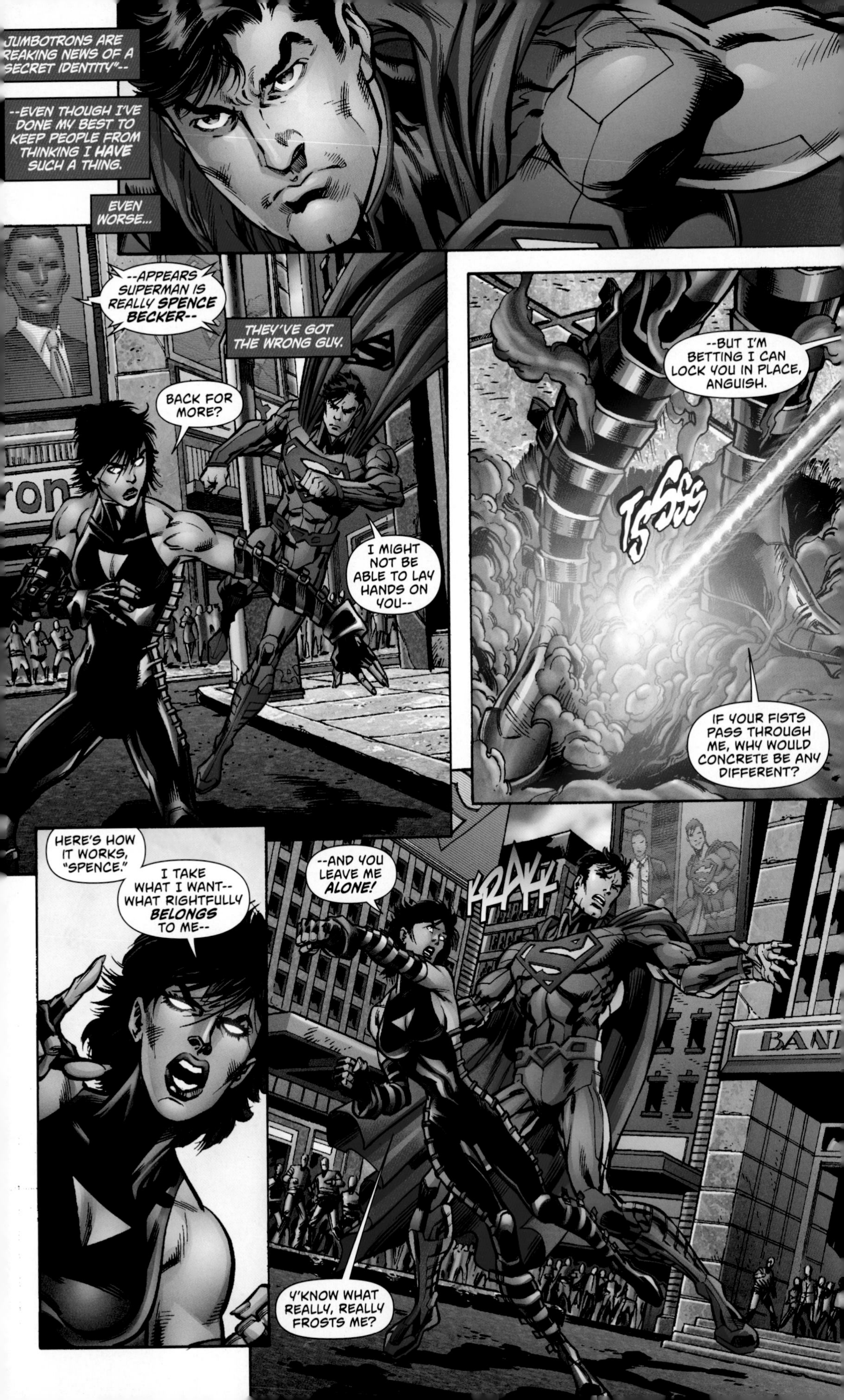
JUMBOTRONS ARE
REAKING NEWS OF A
SECRET IDENTITY"--
--EVEN THOUGH I'VE DONE MY BEST TO KEEP PEOPLE FROM THINKING I HAVE SUCH A THING.
EVEN WORSE...
--APPEARS SUPERMAN IS REALLY SPENCE BECKER--
THEY'VE GOT THE WRONG GUY.
BACK FOR MORE?
I MIGHT NOT BE ABLE TO LAY HANDS ON YOU--
--BUT I'M BETTING I CAN LOCK YOU IN PLACE, ANGUISH.
TSSSS
IF YOUR FISTS PASS THROUGH ME, WHY WOULD CONCRETE BE ANY DIFFERENT?
HERE'S HOW IT WORKS, "SPENCE."
I TAKE WHAT I WANT-- WHAT RIGHTFULLY BELONGS TO ME--
--AND YOU LEAVE ME ALONE!
KRAKK
Y'KNOW WHAT REALLY, REALLY FROSTS ME?

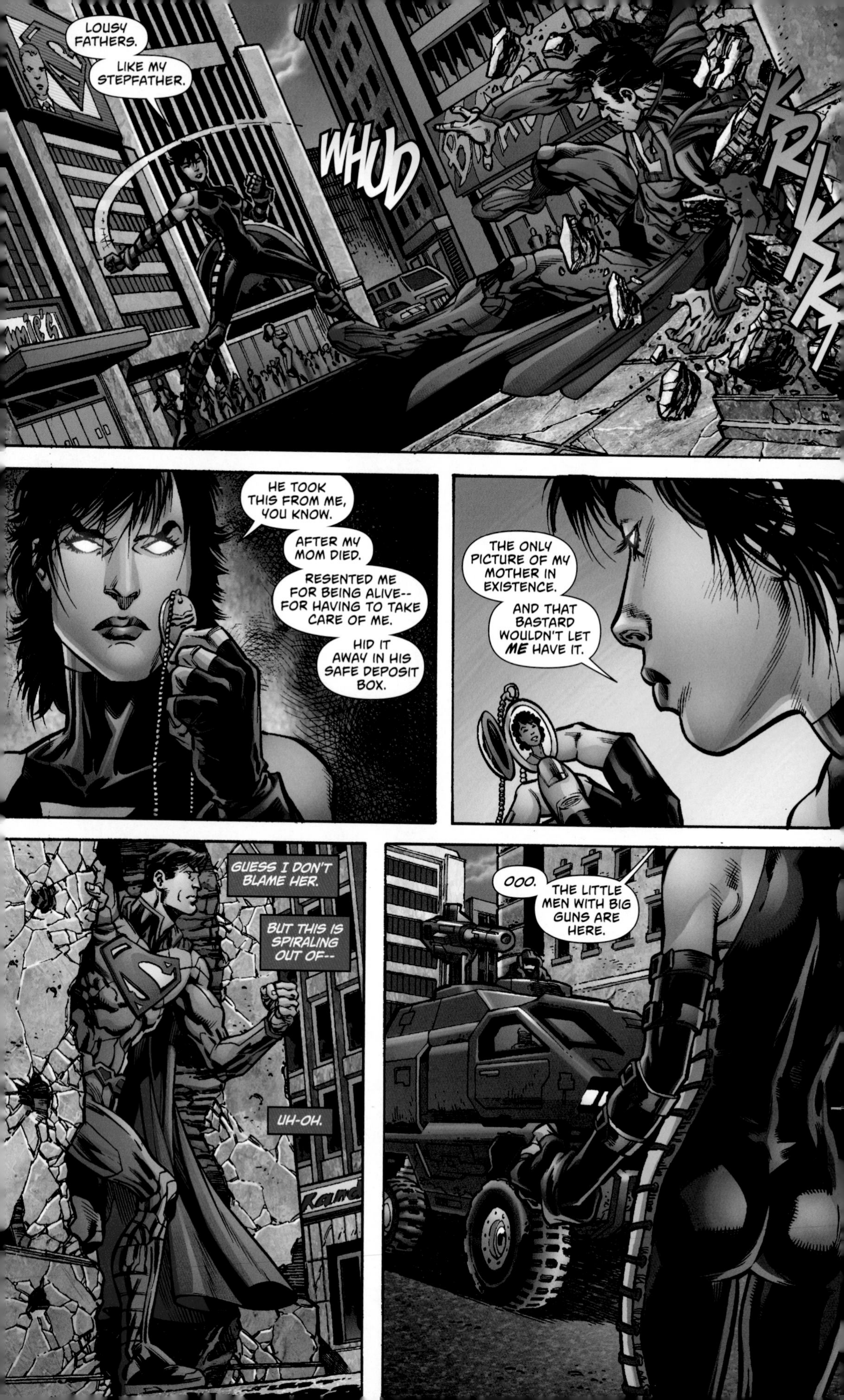
LOUSY FATHERS.
LIKE MY STEPFATHER.
WHUD
KRKKK
HE TOOK THIS FROM ME, YOU KNOW.
AFTER MY MOM DIED.
RESENTED ME FOR BEING ALIVE-- FOR HAVING TO TAKE CARE OF ME.
HID IT AWAY IN HIS SAFE DEPOSIT BOX.
THE ONLY PICTURE OF MY MOTHER IN EXISTENCE.
AND THAT BASTARD WOULDN'T LET ME HAVE IT.
GUESS I DON'T BLAME HER.
BUT THIS IS SPIRALING OUT OF--
UH-OH.
OOO.
THE LITTLE MEN WITH BIG GUNS ARE HERE.

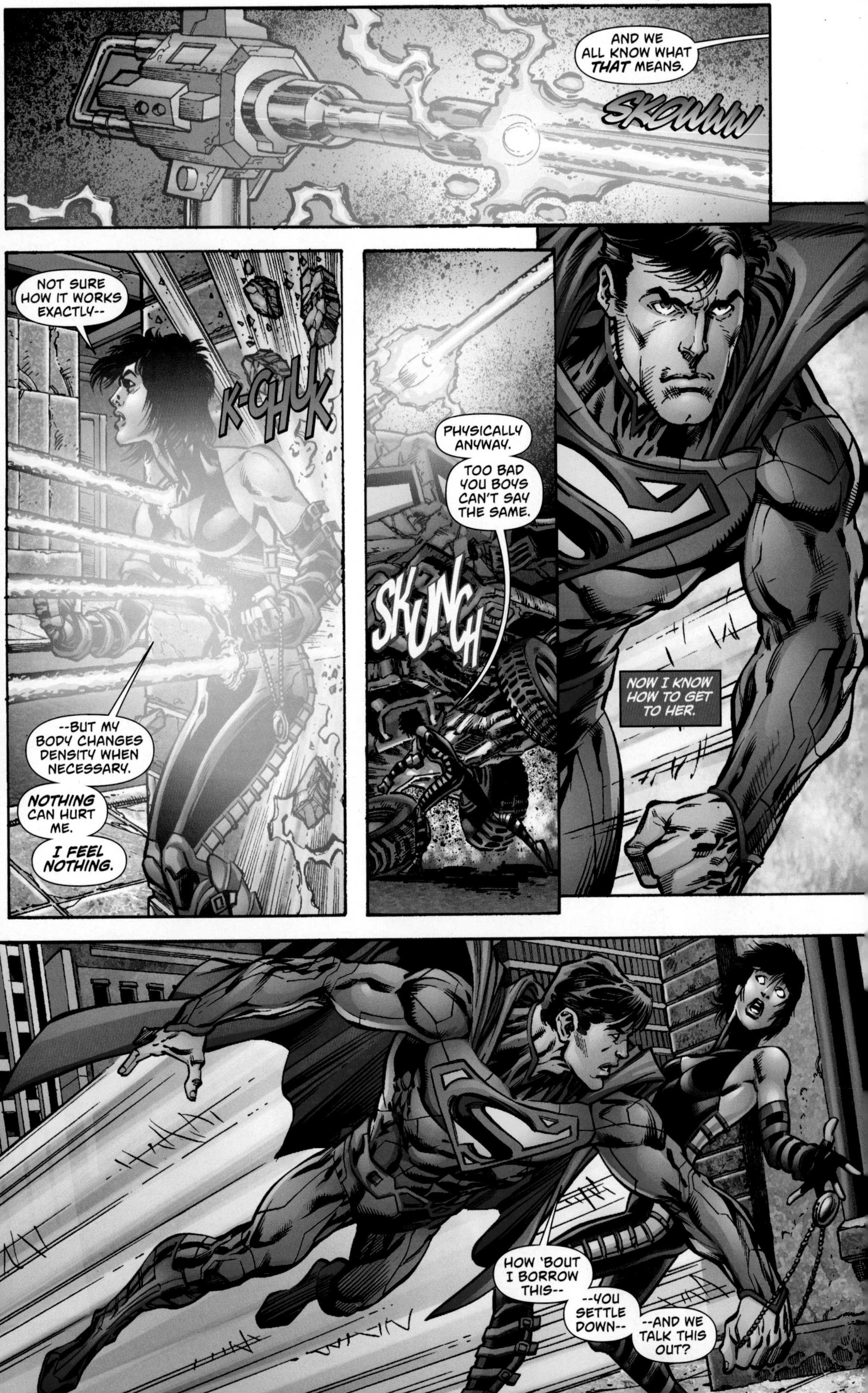
AND WE ALL KNOW WHAT *THAT* MEANS.
SKOWWW
NOT SURE HOW IT WORKS EXACTLY--
K-CHUK
--BUT MY BODY CHANGES DENSITY WHEN NECESSARY.
NOTHING CAN HURT ME.
I FEEL NOTHING.
PHYSICALLY ANYWAY.
TOO BAD YOU BOYS CAN'T SAY THE SAME.
SKUNCH
NOW I KNOW HOW TO GET TO HER.
HOW 'BOUT I BORROW THIS--
--YOU SETTLE DOWN--
--AND WE TALK THIS OUT?

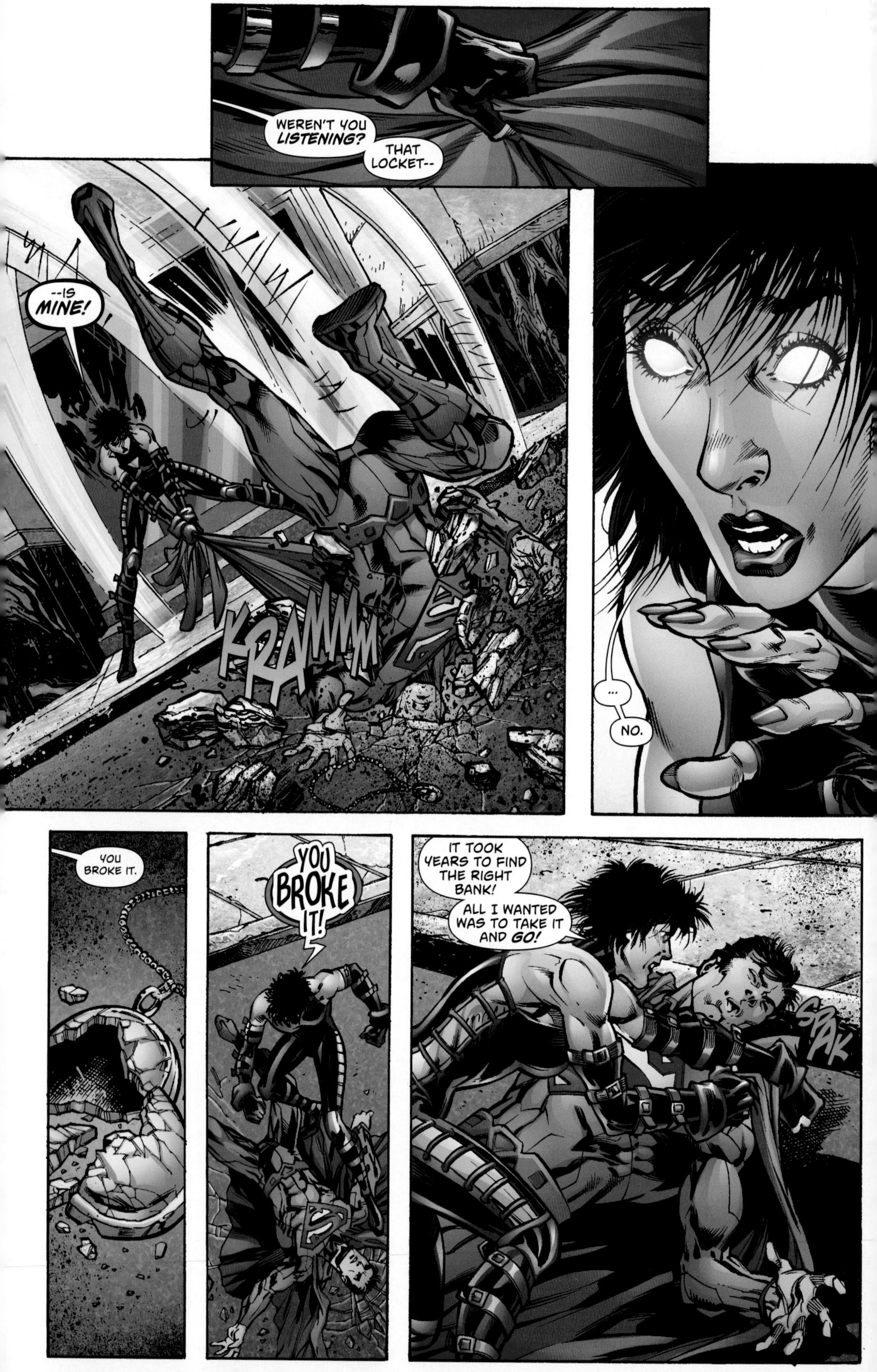
WEREN'T YOU LISTENING?
THAT LOCKET--
--IS MINE!
KRAMMM
...
NO.
YOU BROKE IT.
YOU BROKE IT!
IT TOOK YEARS TO FIND THE RIGHT BANK!
ALL I WANTED WAS TO TAKE IT AND GO!
SPAK

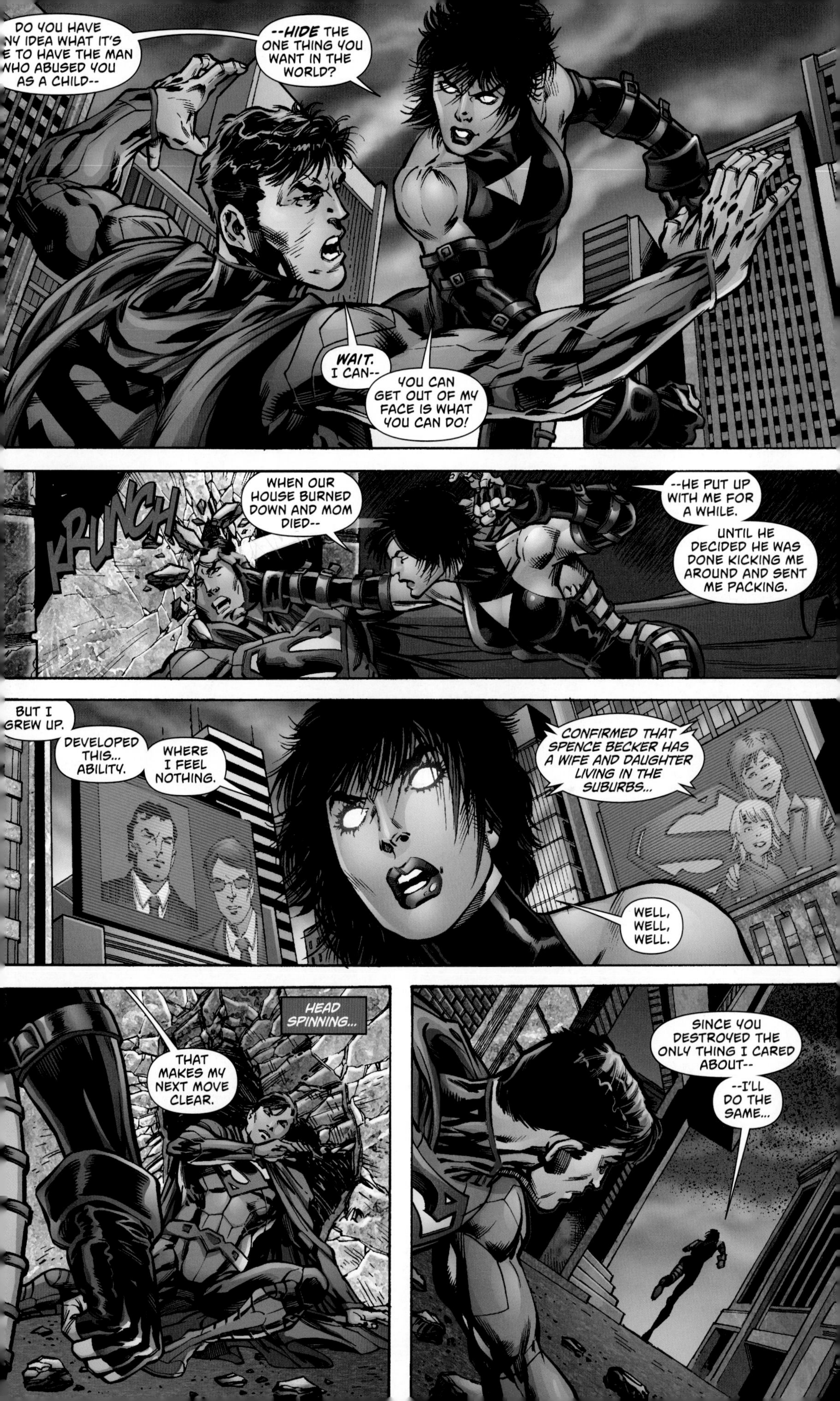
DO YOU HAVE
NY IDEA WHAT IT'S
E TO HAVE THE MAN
WHO ABUSED YOU
AS A CHILD--
--HIDE THE ONE THING YOU WANT IN THE WORLD?
WAIT. I CAN--
YOU CAN GET OUT OF MY FACE IS WHAT YOU CAN DO!
KRUNCH
WHEN OUR HOUSE BURNED DOWN AND MOM DIED--
--HE PUT UP WITH ME FOR A WHILE.
UNTIL HE DECIDED HE WAS DONE KICKING ME AROUND AND SENT ME PACKING.
BUT I GREW UP.
DEVELOPED THIS... ABILITY.
WHERE I FEEL NOTHING.
CONFIRMED THAT SPENCE BECKER HAS A WIFE AND DAUGHTER LIVING IN THE SUBURBS...
WELL, WELL, WELL.
HEAD SPINNING...
THAT MAKES MY NEXT MOVE CLEAR.
SINCE YOU DESTROYED THE ONLY THING I CARED ABOUT--
--I'LL DO THE SAME...

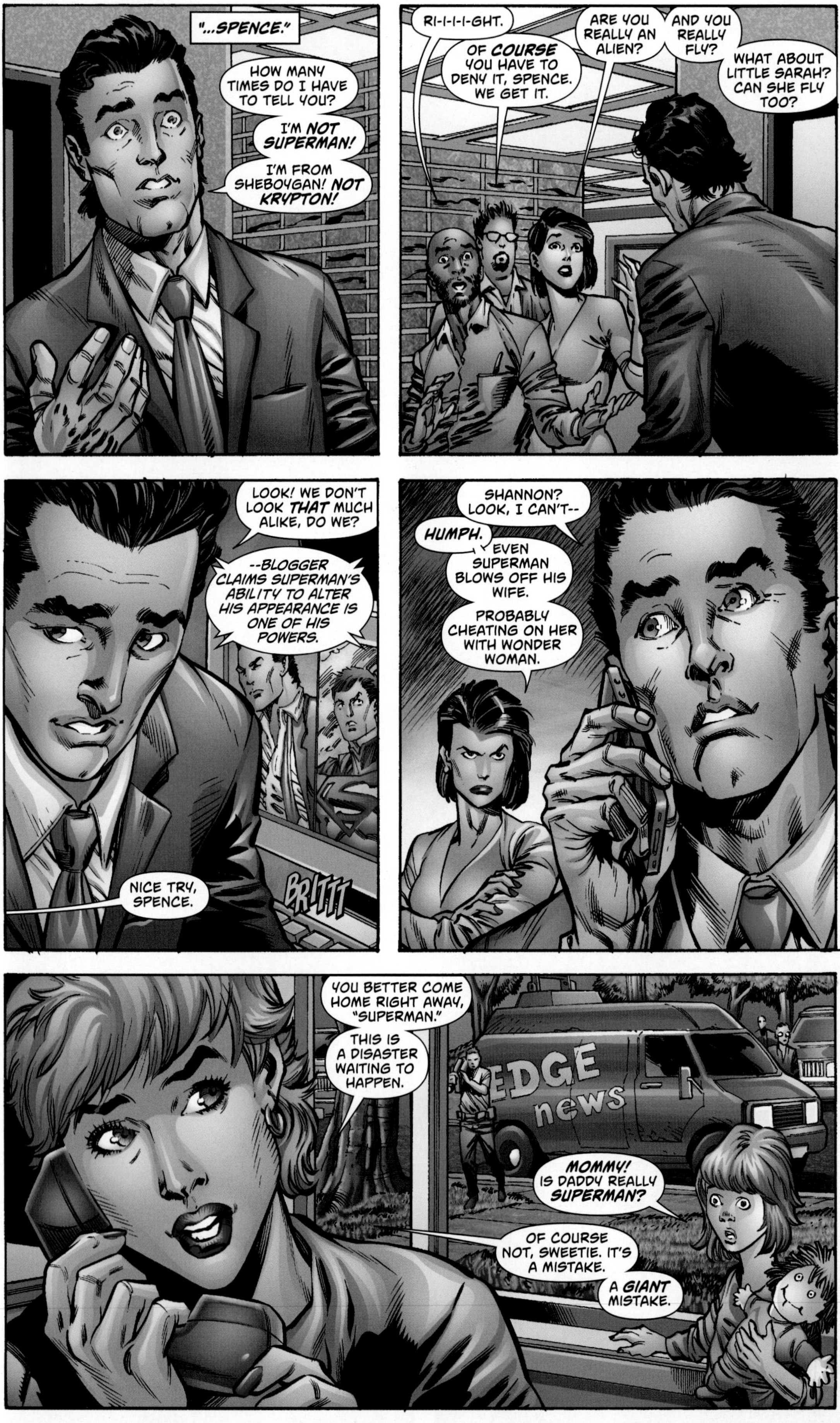
"...SPENCE."
HOW MANY TIMES DO I HAVE TO TELL YOU?
I'M NOT SUPERMAN!
I'M FROM SHEBOYGAN! NOT KRYPTON!
RI-I-I-I-GHT.
OF COURSE YOU HAVE TO DENY IT, SPENCE. WE GET IT.
ARE YOU REALLY AN ALIEN?
AND YOU REALLY FLY?
WHAT ABOUT LITTLE SARAH? CAN SHE FLY TOO?
LOOK! WE DON'T LOOK THAT MUCH ALIKE, DO WE?
--BLOGGER CLAIMS SUPERMAN'S ABILITY TO ALTER HIS APPEARANCE IS ONE OF HIS POWERS.
NICE TRY, SPENCE.
BRITTT
SHANNON? LOOK, I CAN'T--
HUMPH.
EVEN SUPERMAN BLOWS OFF HIS WIFE.
PROBABLY CHEATING ON HER WITH WONDER WOMAN.
YOU BETTER COME HOME RIGHT AWAY, "SUPERMAN."
THIS IS A DISASTER WAITING TO HAPPEN.
EDGE news
MOMMY! IS DADDY REALLY SUPERMAN?
OF COURSE NOT, SWEETIE. IT'S A MISTAKE.
A GIANT MISTAKE.

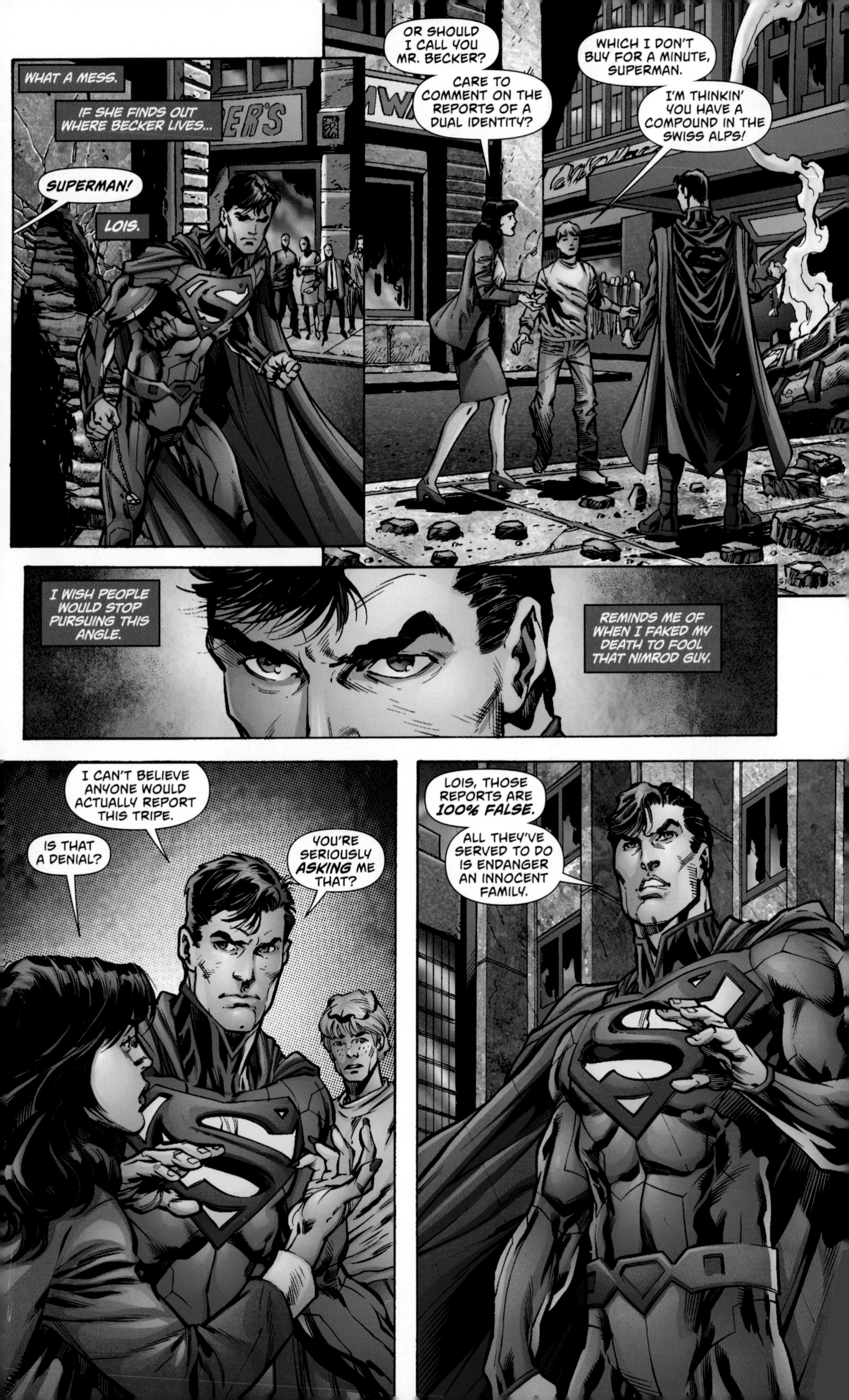
WHAT A MESS.
IF SHE FINDS OUT WHERE BECKER LIVES...
SUPERMAN!
LOIS.
OR SHOULD I CALL YOU MR. BECKER?
CARE TO COMMENT ON THE REPORTS OF A DUAL IDENTITY?
WHICH I DON'T BUY FOR A MINUTE, SUPERMAN.
I'M THINKIN' YOU HAVE A COMPOUND IN THE SWISS ALPS!
I WISH PEOPLE WOULD STOP PURSUING THIS ANGLE.
REMINDS ME OF WHEN I FAKED MY DEATH TO FOOL THAT NIMROD GUY.
I CAN'T BELIEVE ANYONE WOULD ACTUALLY REPORT THIS TRIPE.
IS THAT A DENIAL?
YOU'RE SERIOUSLY ASKING ME THAT?
LOIS, THOSE REPORTS ARE 100% FALSE.
ALL THEY'VE SERVED TO DO IS ENDANGER AN INNOCENT FAMILY.

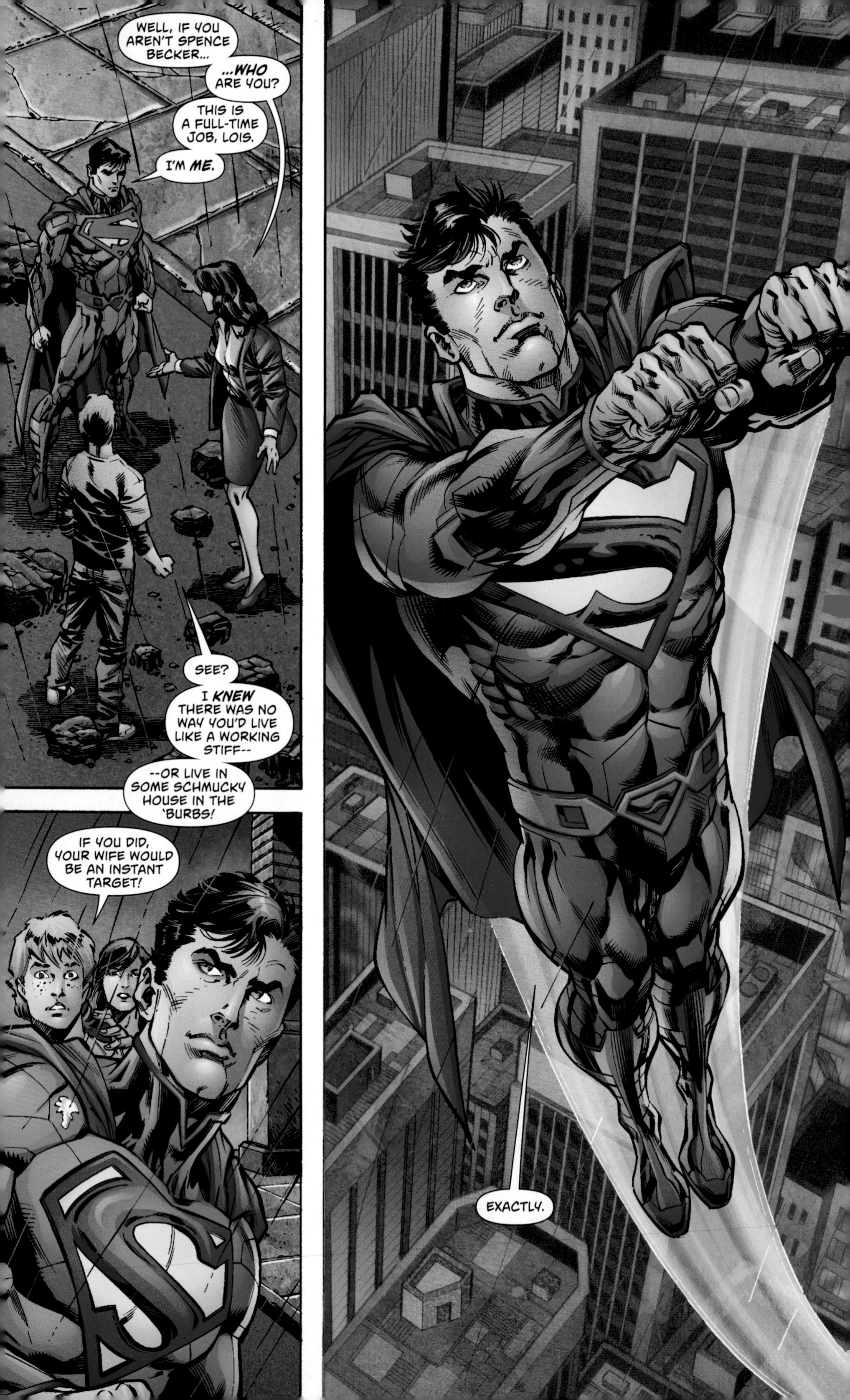
WELL, IF YOU AREN'T SPENCE BECKER...
...WHO ARE YOU?
THIS IS A FULL-TIME JOB, LOIS.
I'M ME.
SEE?
I KNEW THERE WAS NO WAY YOU'D LIVE LIKE A WORKING STIFF--
--OR LIVE IN SOME SCHMUCKY HOUSE IN THE 'BURBS!
IF YOU DID, YOUR WIFE WOULD BE AN INSTANT TARGET!
EXACTLY.

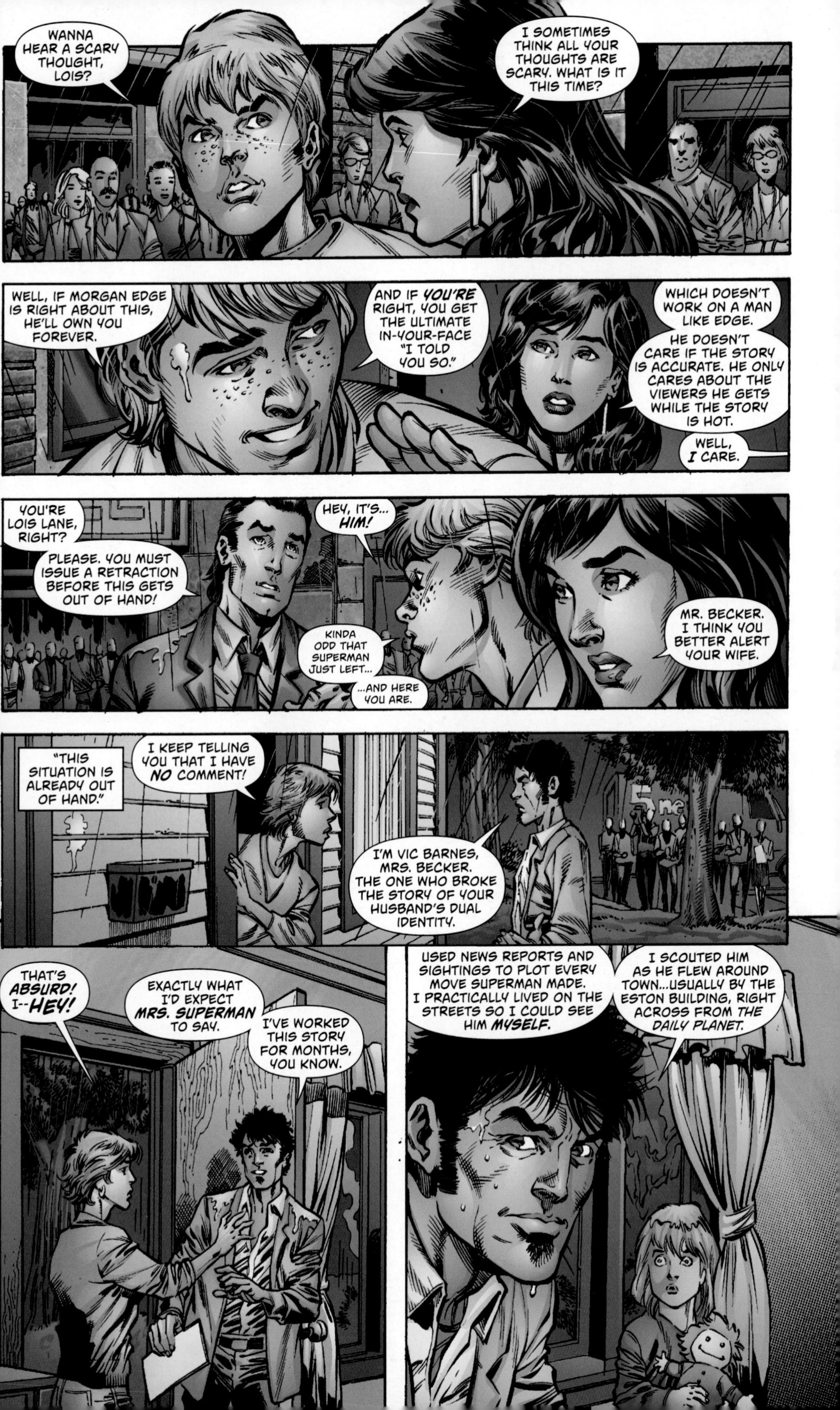

WANNA HEAR A SCARY THOUGHT, LOIS?
I SOMETIMES THINK ALL YOUR THOUGHTS ARE SCARY. WHAT IS IT THIS TIME?
WELL, IF MORGAN EDGE IS RIGHT ABOUT THIS, HE'LL OWN YOU FOREVER.
AND IF YOU'RE RIGHT, YOU GET THE ULTIMATE IN-YOUR-FACE "I TOLD YOU SO."
WHICH DOESN'T WORK ON A MAN LIKE EDGE.
HE DOESN'T CARE IF THE STORY IS ACCURATE. HE ONLY CARES ABOUT THE VIEWERS HE GETS WHILE THE STORY IS HOT.
WELL, I CARE.
YOU'RE LOIS LANE, RIGHT?
PLEASE. YOU MUST ISSUE A RETRACTION BEFORE THIS GETS OUT OF HAND!
HEY, IT'S... HIM!
KINDA ODD THAT SUPERMAN JUST LEFT...
...AND HERE YOU ARE.
MR. BECKER. I THINK YOU BETTER ALERT YOUR WIFE.
"THIS SITUATION IS ALREADY OUT OF HAND."
I KEEP TELLING YOU THAT I HAVE NO COMMENT!
I'M VIC BARNES, MRS. BECKER. THE ONE WHO BROKE THE STORY OF YOUR HUSBAND'S DUAL IDENTITY.
THAT'S ABSURD! I--HEY!
EXACTLY WHAT I'D EXPECT MRS. SUPERMAN TO SAY.
I'VE WORKED THIS STORY FOR MONTHS, YOU KNOW.
USED NEWS REPORTS AND SIGHTINGS TO PLOT EVERY MOVE SUPERMAN MADE. I PRACTICALLY LIVED ON THE STREETS SO I COULD SEE HIM MYSELF.
I SCOUTED HIM AS HE FLEW AROUND TOWN...USUALLY BY THE ESTON BUILDING, RIGHT ACROSS FROM THE DAILY PLANET.

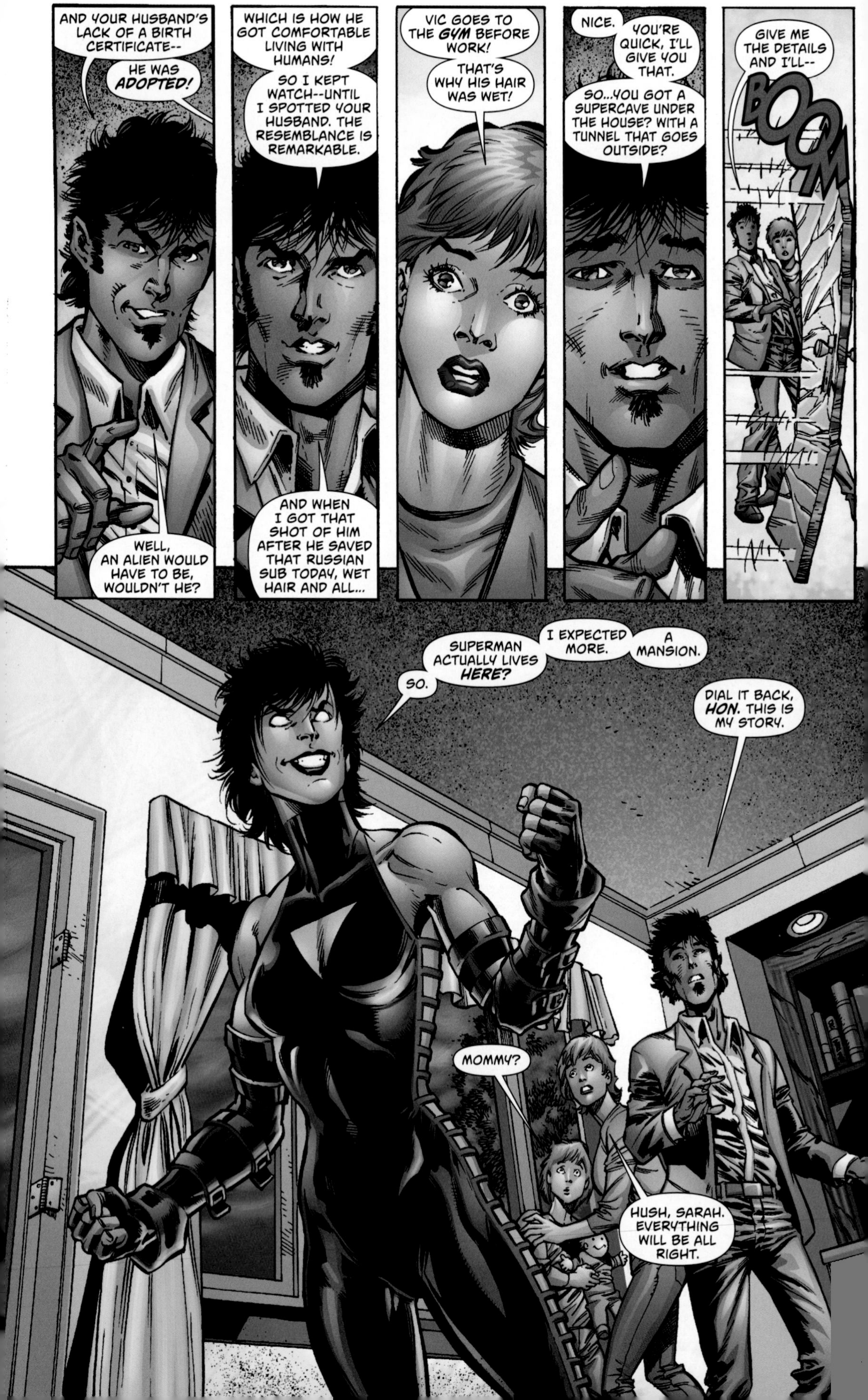

AND YOUR HUSBAND'S LACK OF A BIRTH CERTIFICATE--
HE WAS *ADOPTED!*
WELL, AN ALIEN WOULD HAVE TO BE, WOULDN'T HE?
WHICH IS HOW HE GOT COMFORTABLE LIVING WITH HUMANS!
SO I KEPT WATCH--UNTIL I SPOTTED YOUR HUSBAND. THE RESEMBLANCE IS REMARKABLE.
AND WHEN I GOT THAT SHOT OF HIM AFTER HE SAVED THAT RUSSIAN SUB TODAY, WET HAIR AND ALL...
VIC GOES TO THE *GYM* BEFORE WORK!
THAT'S WHY HIS HAIR WAS WET!
NICE.
YOU'RE QUICK, I'LL GIVE YOU THAT.
SO...YOU GOT A SUPERCAVE UNDER THE HOUSE? WITH A TUNNEL THAT GOES OUTSIDE?
GIVE ME THE DETAILS AND I'LL--
BOOM
SO.
SUPERMAN ACTUALLY LIVES *HERE?*
I EXPECTED MORE.
A MANSION.
DIAL IT BACK, *HON.* THIS IS MY STORY.
MOMMY?
HUSH, SARAH. EVERYTHING WILL BE ALL RIGHT.

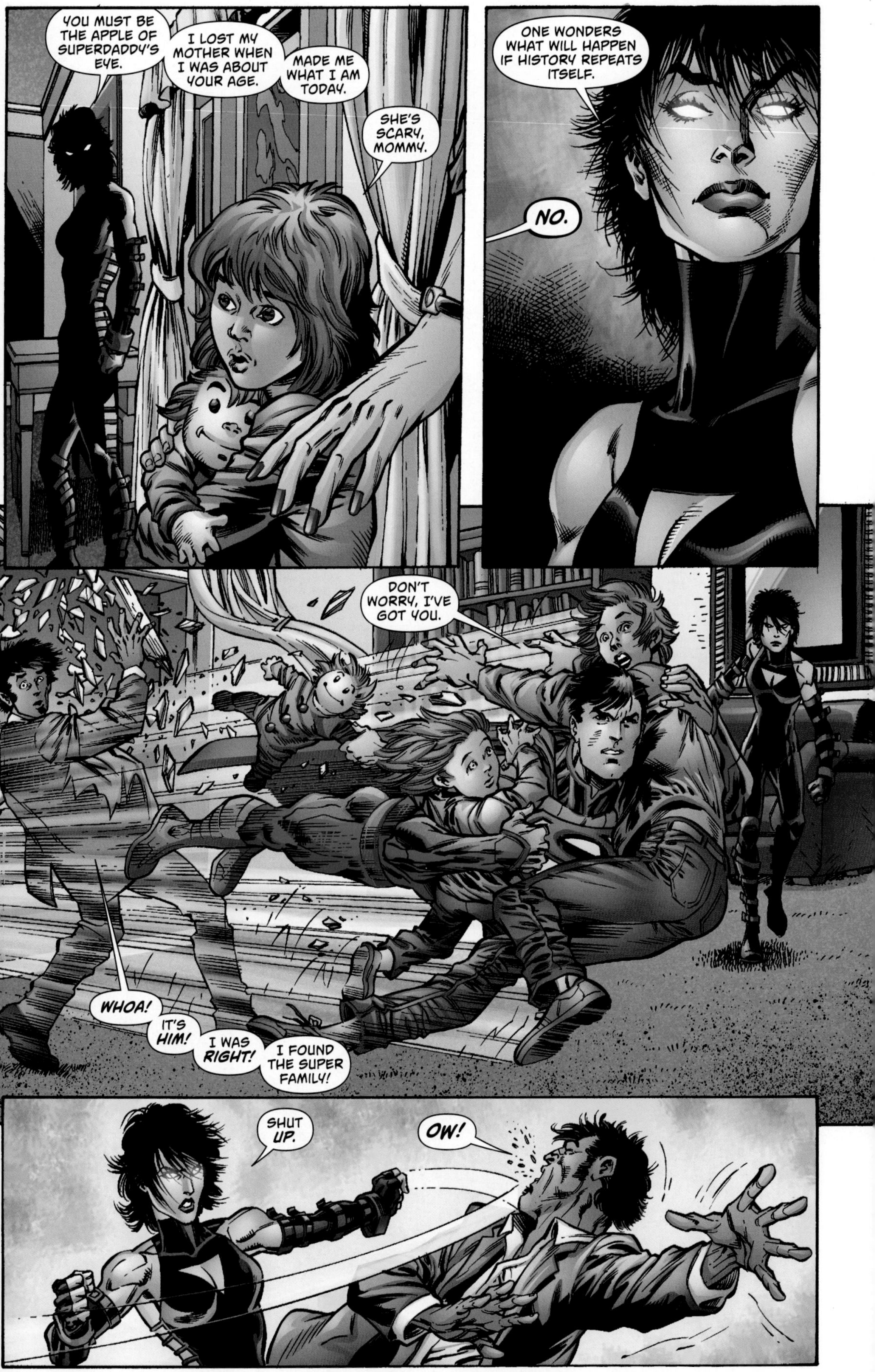
YOU MUST BE THE APPLE OF SUPERDADDY'S EYE.
I LOST MY MOTHER WHEN I WAS ABOUT YOUR AGE.
MADE ME WHAT I AM TODAY.
SHE'S SCARY, MOMMY.
ONE WONDERS WHAT WILL HAPPEN IF HISTORY REPEATS ITSELF.
NO.
DON'T WORRY, I'VE GOT YOU.
WHOA!
IT'S HIM!
I WAS RIGHT!
I FOUND THE SUPER FAMILY!
SHUT UP.
OW!

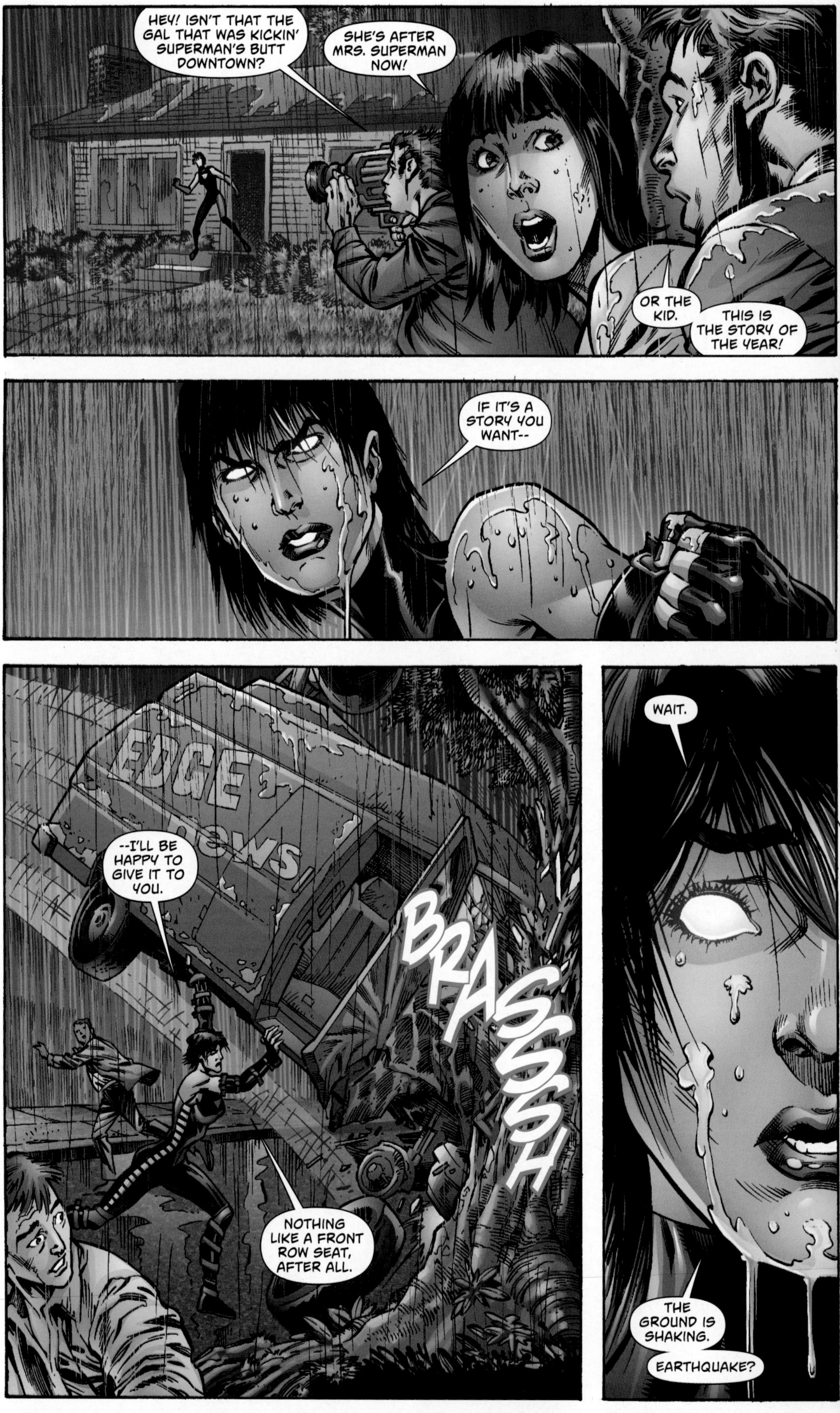
HEY! ISN'T THAT THE GAL THAT WAS KICKIN' SUPERMAN'S BUTT DOWNTOWN?
SHE'S AFTER MRS. SUPERMAN NOW!
OR THE KID.
THIS IS THE STORY OF THE YEAR!
IF IT'S A STORY YOU WANT--
EDGE NEWS
--I'LL BE HAPPY TO GIVE IT TO YOU.
BRASSSH
NOTHING LIKE A FRONT ROW SEAT, AFTER ALL.
WAIT.
THE GROUND IS SHAKING.
EARTHQUAKE?

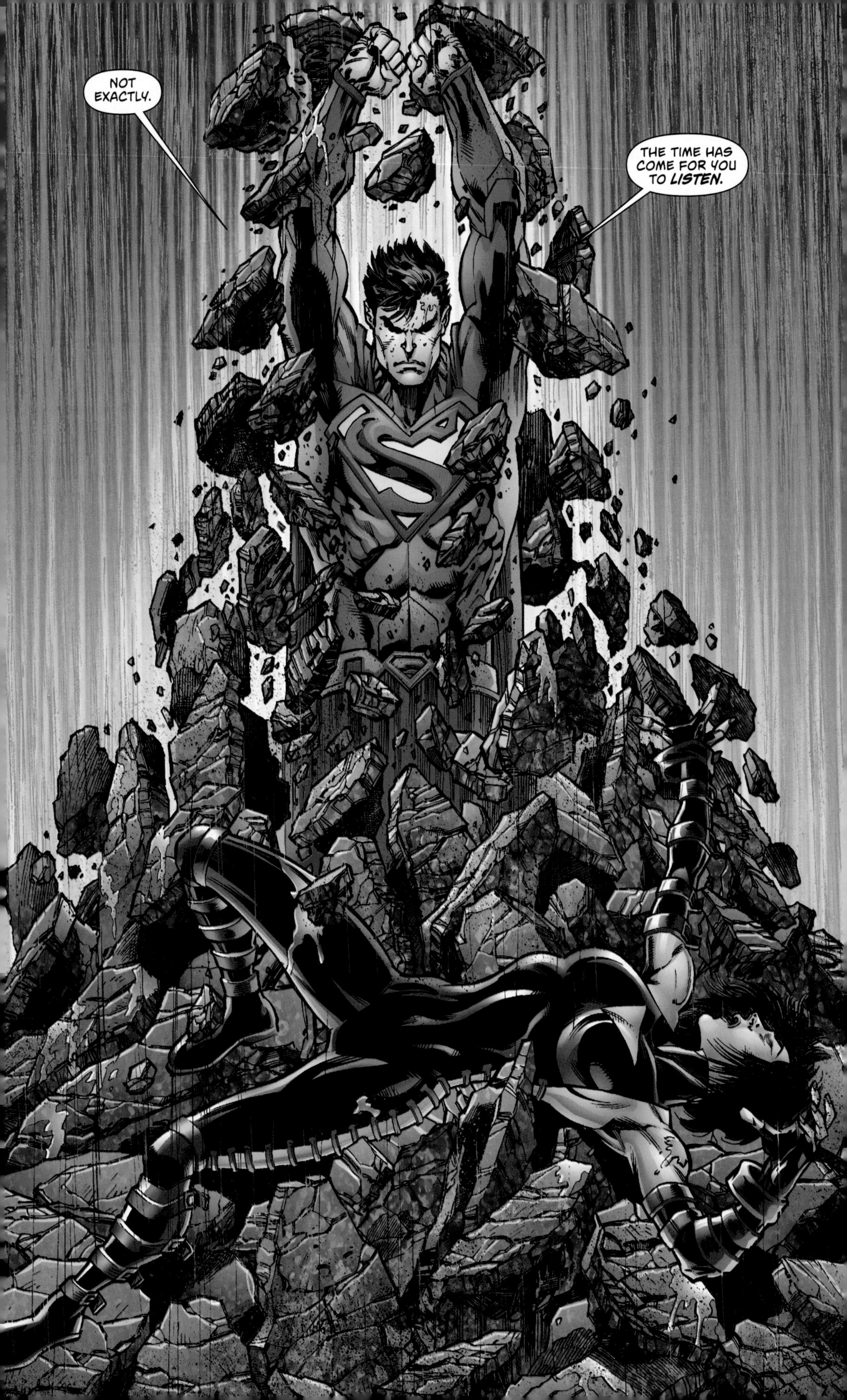
NOT EXACTLY.
THE TIME HAS COME FOR YOU TO LISTEN.

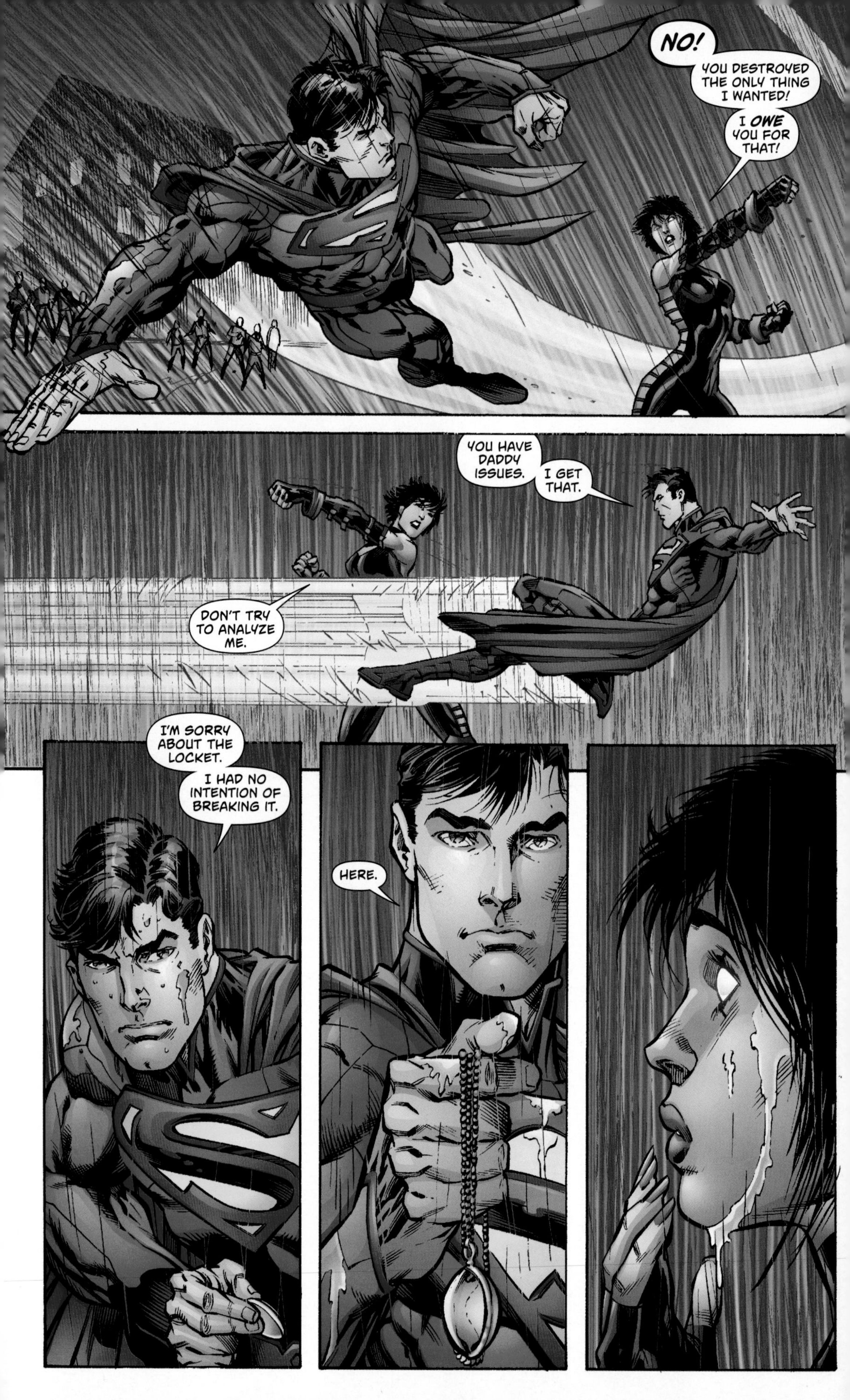
NO!
YOU DESTROYED THE ONLY THING I WANTED!
I OWE YOU FOR THAT!
YOU HAVE DADDY ISSUES.
I GET THAT.
DON'T TRY TO ANALYZE ME.
I'M SORRY ABOUT THE LOCKET.
I HAD NO INTENTION OF BREAKING IT.
HERE.

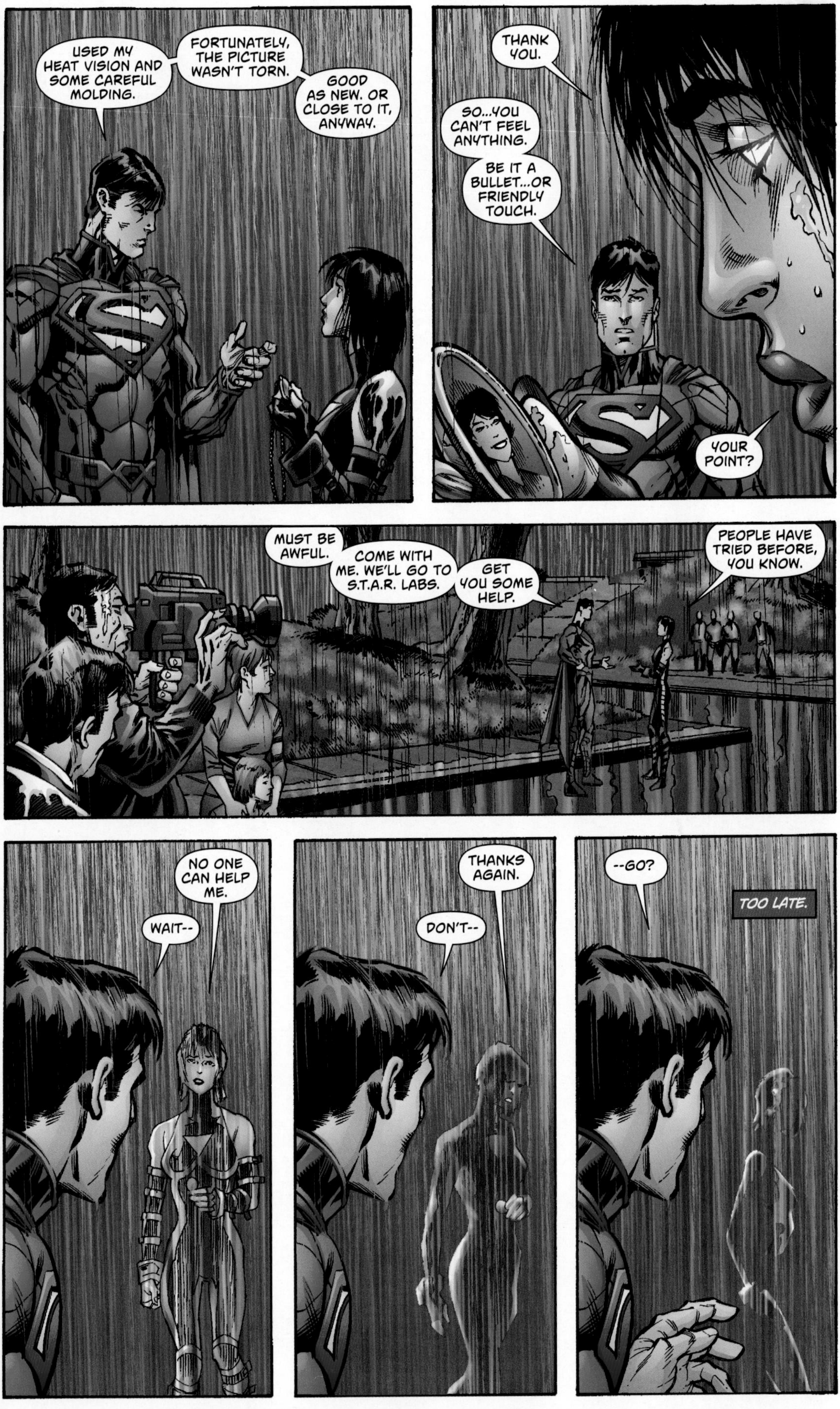
USED MY HEAT VISION AND SOME CAREFUL MOLDING.
FORTUNATELY, THE PICTURE WASN'T TORN.
GOOD AS NEW. OR CLOSE TO IT, ANYWAY.
THANK YOU.
SO...YOU CAN'T FEEL ANYTHING.
BE IT A BULLET...OR FRIENDLY TOUCH.
YOUR POINT?
MUST BE AWFUL.
COME WITH ME. WE'LL GO TO S.T.A.R. LABS.
GET YOU SOME HELP.
PEOPLE HAVE TRIED BEFORE, YOU KNOW.
NO ONE CAN HELP ME.
WAIT--
THANKS AGAIN.
DON'T--
--GO?
TOO LATE.

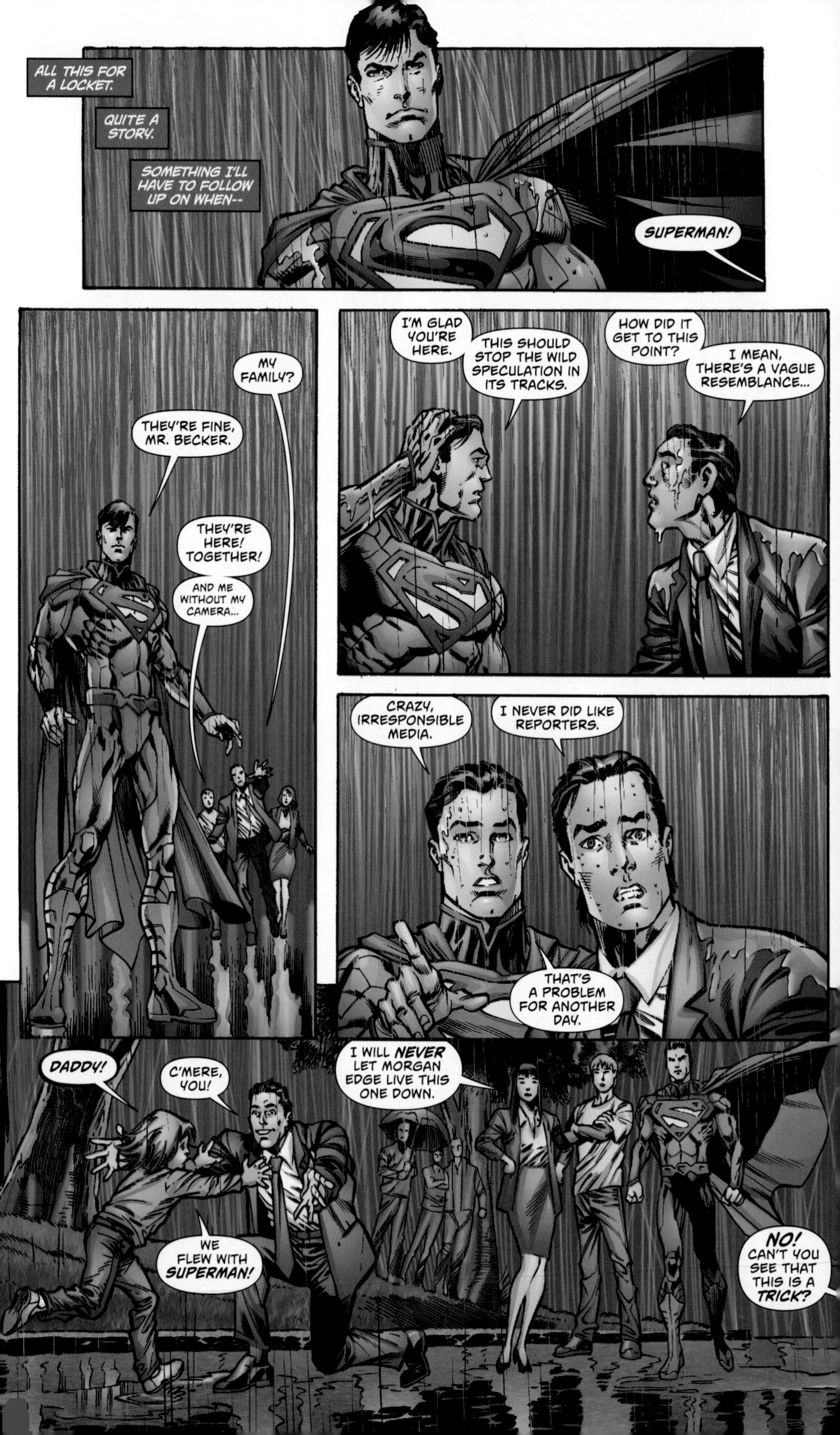
ALL THIS FOR A LOCKET.
QUITE A STORY.
SOMETHING I'LL HAVE TO FOLLOW UP ON WHEN--
SUPERMAN!
MY FAMILY?
THEY'RE FINE, MR. BECKER.
THEY'RE HERE! TOGETHER!
AND ME WITHOUT MY CAMERA...
I'M GLAD YOU'RE HERE.
THIS SHOULD STOP THE WILD SPECULATION IN ITS TRACKS.
HOW DID IT GET TO THIS POINT?
I MEAN, THERE'S A VAGUE RESEMBLANCE...
CRAZY, IRRESPONSIBLE MEDIA.
I NEVER DID LIKE REPORTERS.
THAT'S A PROBLEM FOR ANOTHER DAY.
DADDY!
C'MERE, YOU!
I WILL NEVER LET MORGAN EDGE LIVE THIS ONE DOWN.
WE FLEW WITH SUPERMAN!
NO! CAN'T YOU SEE THAT THIS IS A TRICK?

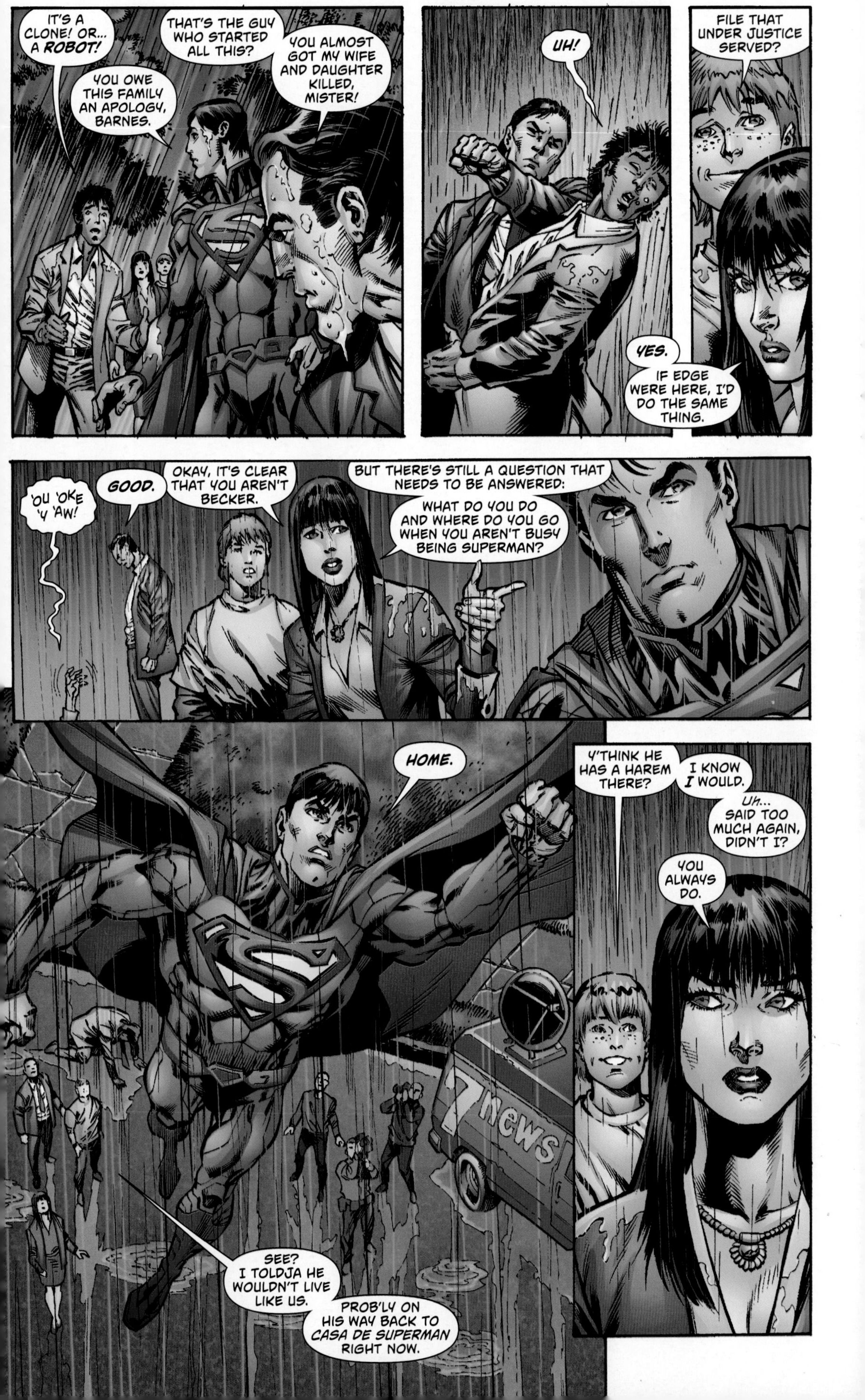

IT'S A CLONE! OR... A *ROBOT!*
THAT'S THE GUY WHO STARTED ALL THIS?
YOU ALMOST GOT MY WIFE AND DAUGHTER KILLED, MISTER!
YOU OWE THIS FAMILY AN APOLOGY, BARNES.
UH!
FILE THAT UNDER JUSTICE SERVED?
YES.
IF EDGE WERE HERE, I'D DO THE SAME THING.
'OU 'OKE 'Y 'AW!
GOOD.
OKAY, IT'S CLEAR THAT YOU AREN'T BECKER.
BUT THERE'S STILL A QUESTION THAT NEEDS TO BE ANSWERED:
WHAT DO YOU DO AND WHERE DO YOU GO WHEN YOU AREN'T BUSY BEING SUPERMAN?
HOME.
SEE? I TOLDJA HE WOULDN'T LIVE LIKE US.
PROB'LY ON HIS WAY BACK TO *CASA DE SUPERMAN* RIGHT NOW.
Y'THINK HE HAS A HAREM THERE?
I KNOW *I* WOULD.
Uh... SAID TOO MUCH AGAIN, DIDN'T I?
YOU ALWAYS DO.
7news

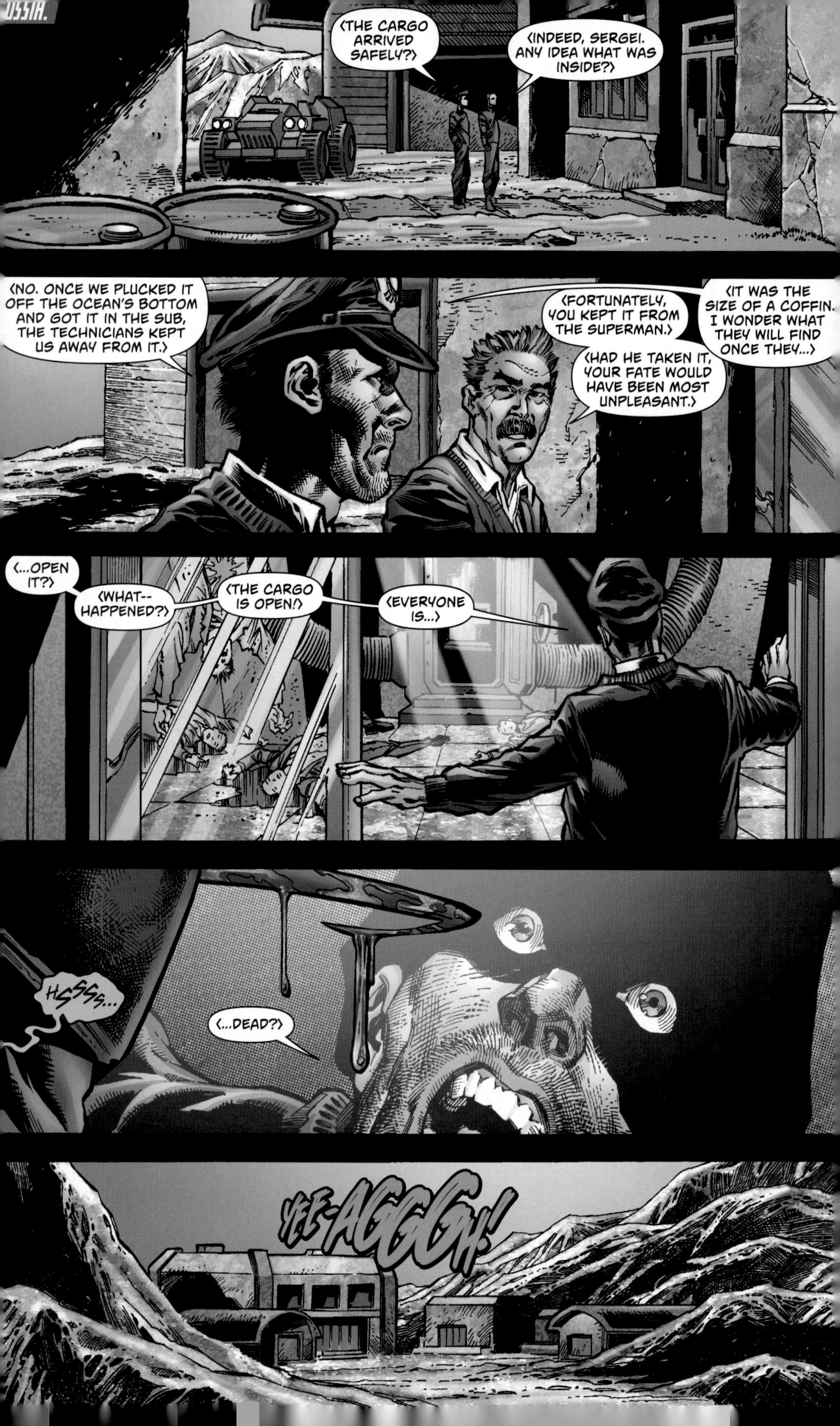
USSIA.
‹THE CARGO ARRIVED SAFELY?›
‹INDEED, SERGEI. ANY IDEA WHAT WAS INSIDE?›
‹NO. ONCE WE PLUCKED IT OFF THE OCEAN'S BOTTOM AND GOT IT IN THE SUB, THE TECHNICIANS KEPT US AWAY FROM IT.›
‹FORTUNATELY, YOU KEPT IT FROM THE SUPERMAN.›
‹HAD HE TAKEN IT, YOUR FATE WOULD HAVE BEEN MOST UNPLEASANT.›
‹IT WAS THE SIZE OF A COFFIN. I WONDER WHAT THEY WILL FIND ONCE THEY...›
‹...OPEN IT?›
‹WHAT--HAPPENED?›
‹THE CARGO IS OPEN!›
‹EVERYONE IS...›
HSSSS...
‹...DEAD?›
YEE-AGGGH!

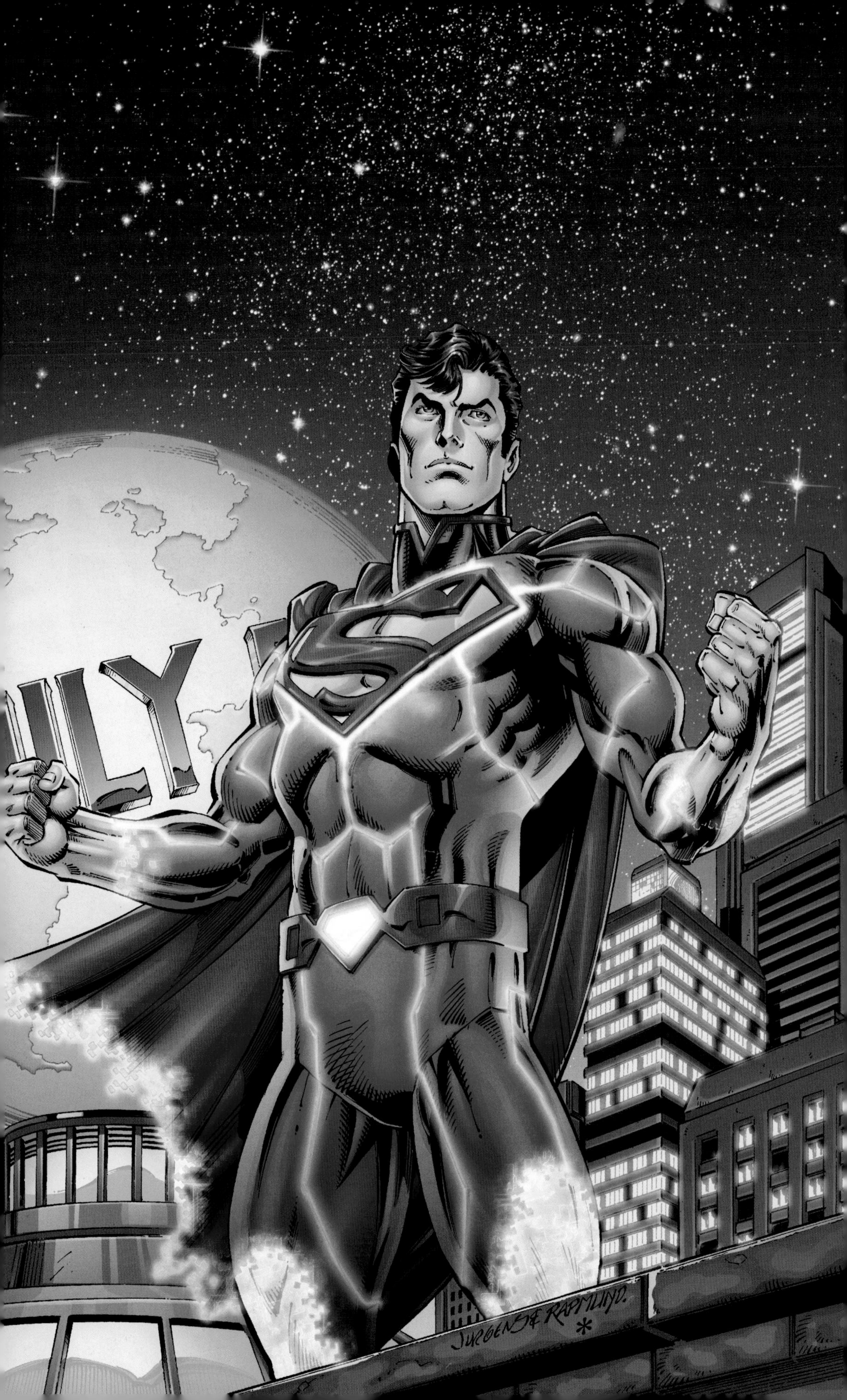
JURGENS & RAPMUND.

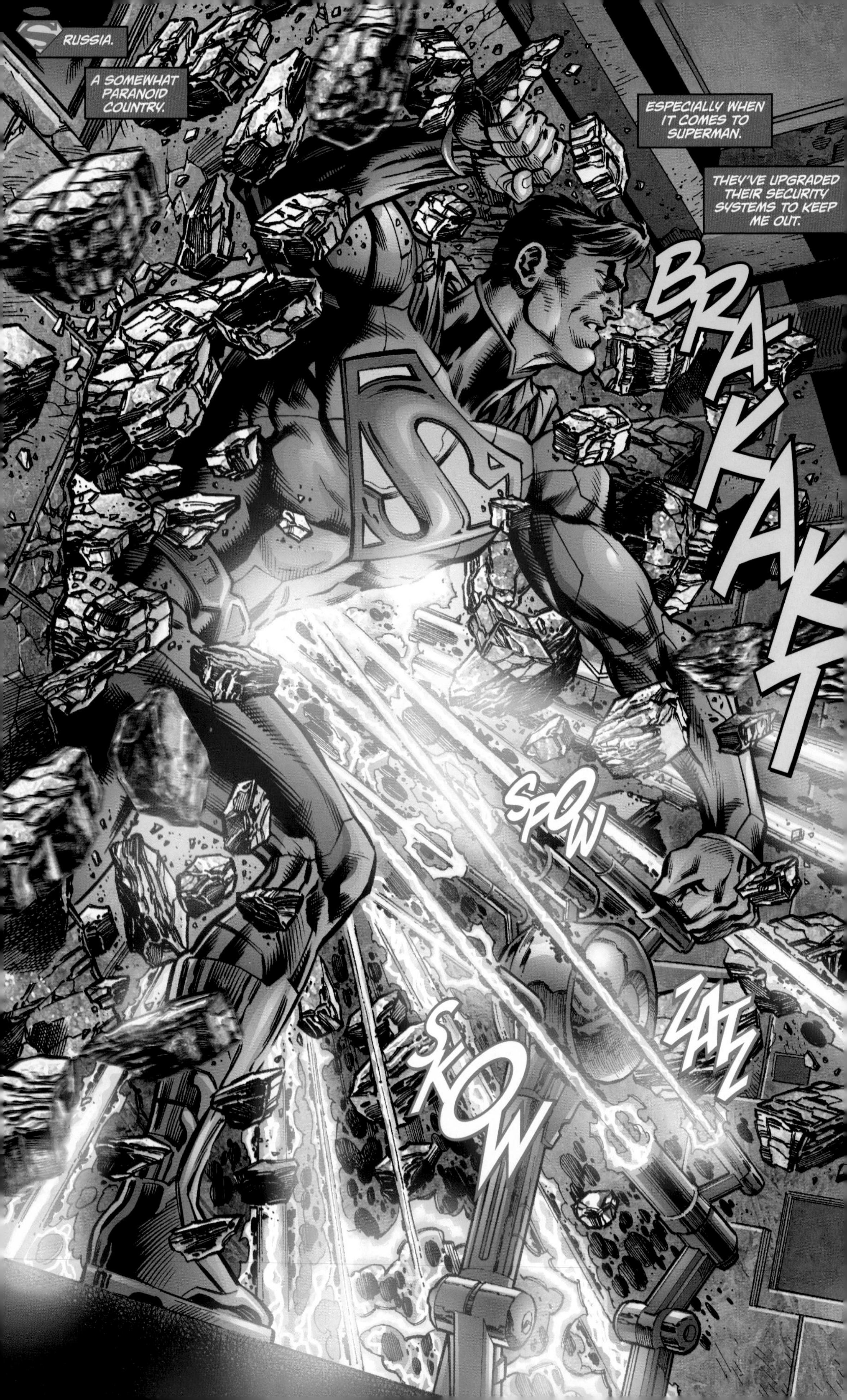
RUSSIA.
A SOMEWHAT PARANOID COUNTRY.
ESPECIALLY WHEN IT COMES TO SUPERMAN.
THEY'VE UPGRADED THEIR SECURITY SYSTEMS TO KEEP ME OUT.
BRAKAKT
SPOW
ZAZZ
SKOW

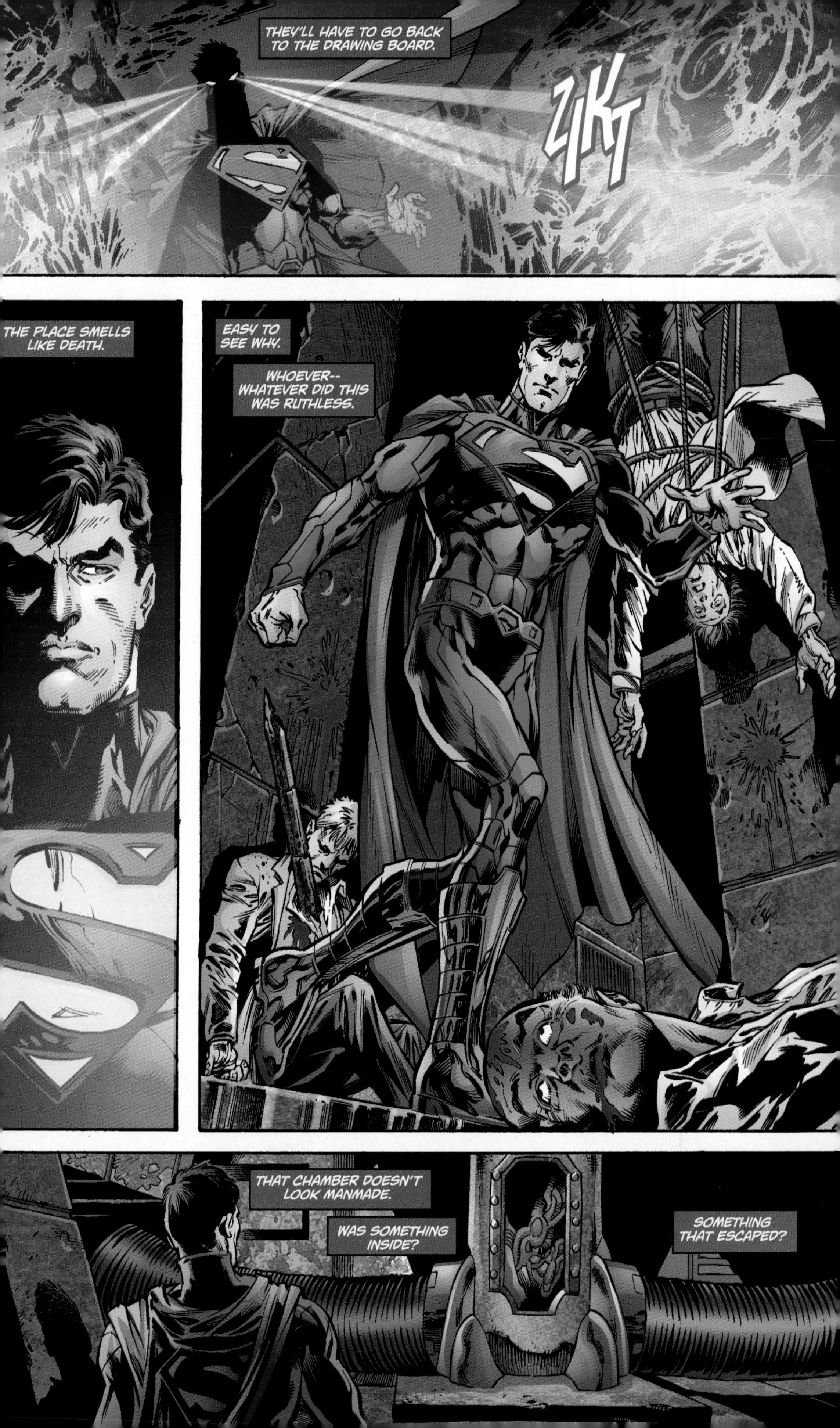
THEY'LL HAVE TO GO BACK TO THE DRAWING BOARD.
ZIKT
THE PLACE SMELLS LIKE DEATH.
EASY TO SEE WHY.
WHOEVER-- WHATEVER DID THIS WAS RUTHLESS.
THAT CHAMBER DOESN'T LOOK MANMADE.
WAS SOMETHING INSIDE?
SOMETHING THAT ESCAPED?

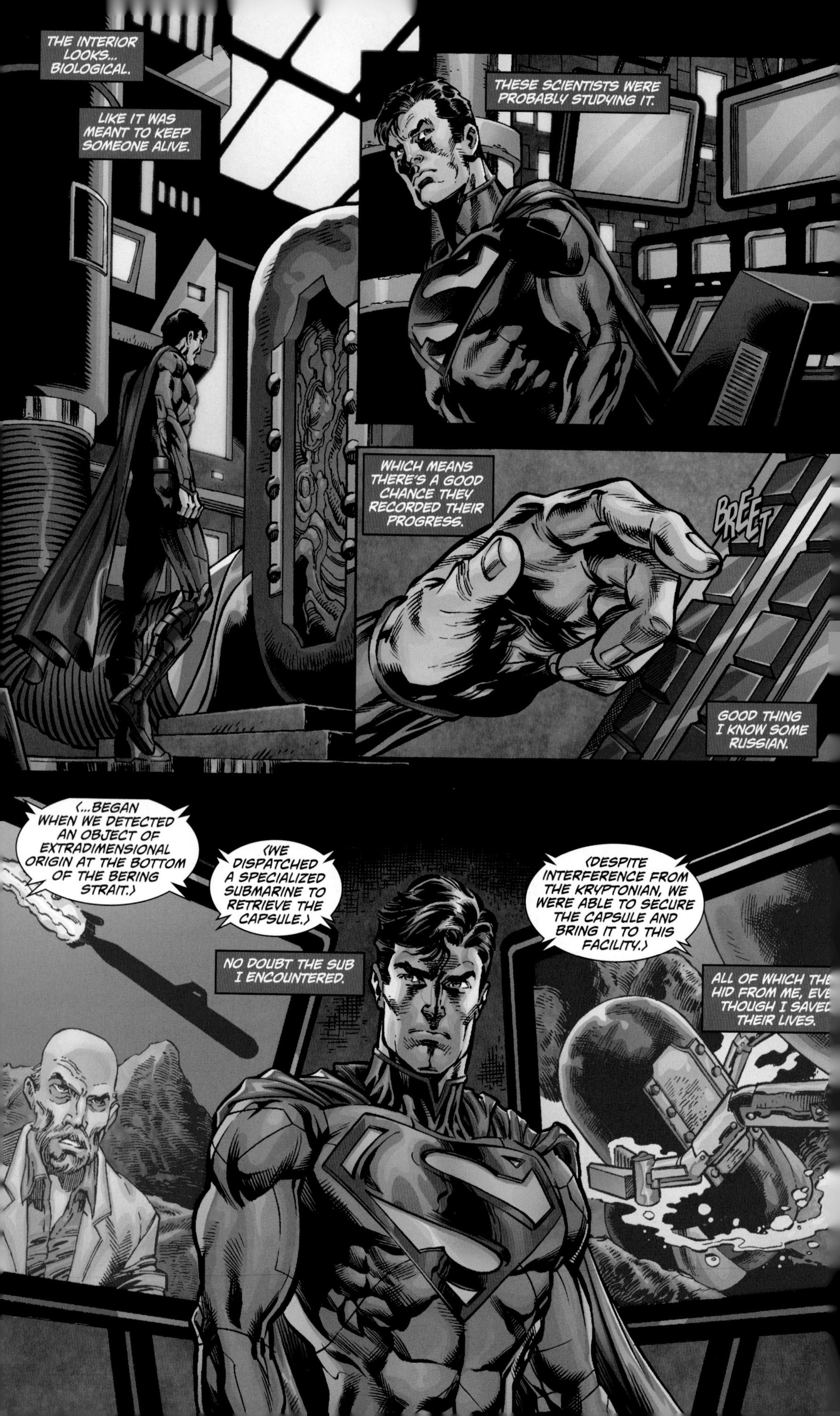
THE INTERIOR LOOKS... BIOLOGICAL.
LIKE IT WAS MEANT TO KEEP SOMEONE ALIVE.
THESE SCIENTISTS WERE PROBABLY STUDYING IT.
WHICH MEANS THERE'S A GOOD CHANCE THEY RECORDED THEIR PROGRESS.
BREET
GOOD THING I KNOW SOME RUSSIAN.
(...BEGAN WHEN WE DETECTED AN OBJECT OF EXTRADIMENSIONAL ORIGIN AT THE BOTTOM OF THE BERING STRAIT.)
(WE DISPATCHED A SPECIALIZED SUBMARINE TO RETRIEVE THE CAPSULE.)
NO DOUBT THE SUB I ENCOUNTERED.
(DESPITE INTERFERENCE FROM THE KRYPTONIAN, WE WERE ABLE TO SECURE THE CAPSULE AND BRING IT TO THIS FACILITY.)
ALL OF WHICH THE HID FROM ME, EVE THOUGH I SAVED THEIR LIVES.

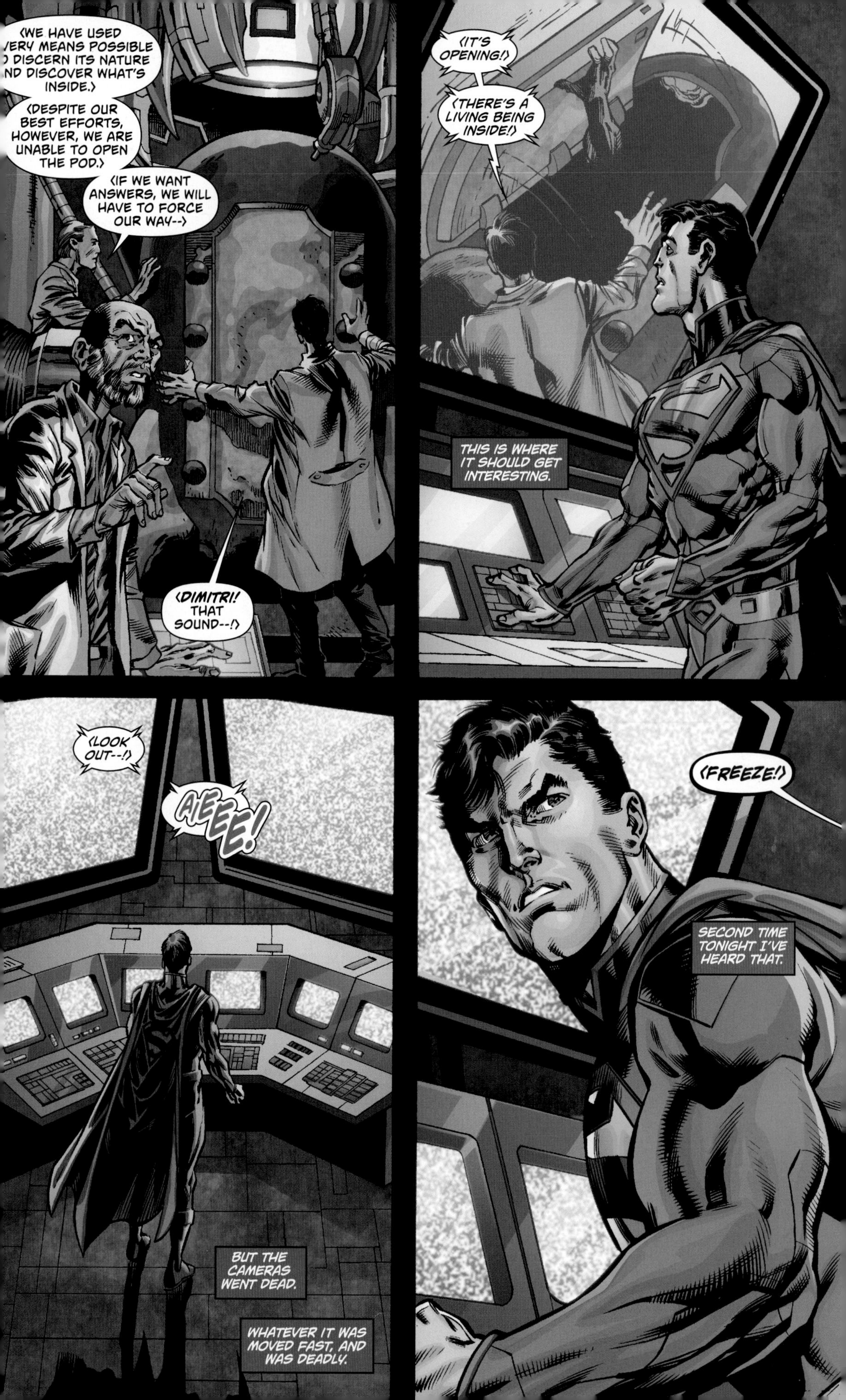
‹WE HAVE USED
VERY MEANS POSSIBLE
O DISCERN ITS NATURE
ND DISCOVER WHAT'S
INSIDE.›
‹DESPITE OUR BEST EFFORTS, HOWEVER, WE ARE UNABLE TO OPEN THE POD.›
‹IF WE WANT ANSWERS, WE WILL HAVE TO FORCE OUR WAY--›
‹DIMITRI! THAT SOUND--!›
‹IT'S OPENING!›
‹THERE'S A LIVING BEING INSIDE!›
THIS IS WHERE IT SHOULD GET INTERESTING.
‹LOOK OUT--!›
AIEEE!
BUT THE CAMERAS WENT DEAD.
WHATEVER IT WAS MOVED FAST, AND WAS DEADLY.
‹FREEZE!›
SECOND TIME TONIGHT I'VE HEARD THAT.

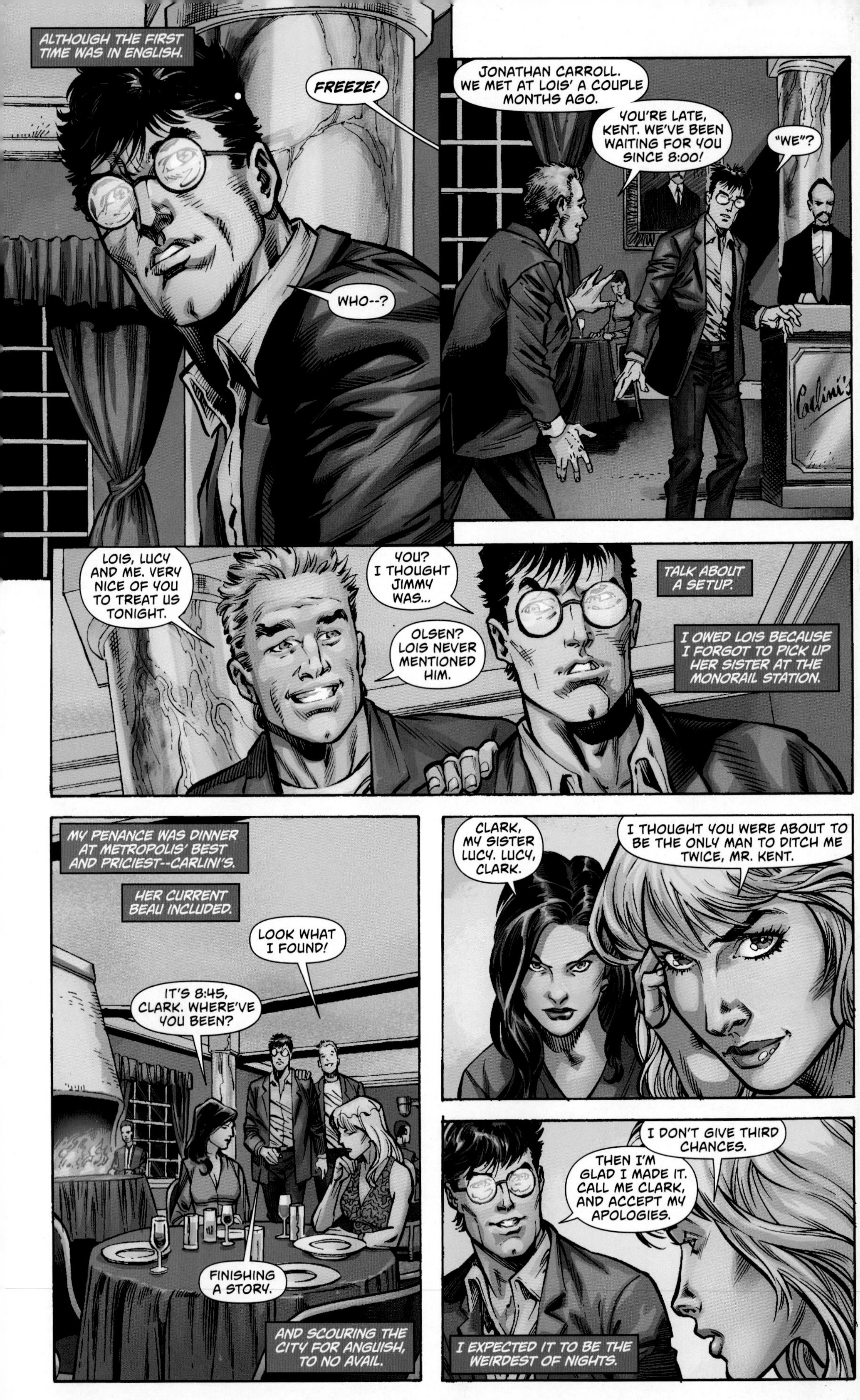
ALTHOUGH THE FIRST TIME WAS IN ENGLISH.
FREEZE!
WHO--?
JONATHAN CARROLL. WE MET AT LOIS' A COUPLE MONTHS AGO.
YOU'RE LATE, KENT. WE'VE BEEN WAITING FOR YOU SINCE 8:00!
"WE"?
Carlini's
LOIS, LUCY AND ME. VERY NICE OF YOU TO TREAT US TONIGHT.
YOU? I THOUGHT JIMMY WAS...
OLSEN? LOIS NEVER MENTIONED HIM.
TALK ABOUT A SETUP.
I OWED LOIS BECAUSE I FORGOT TO PICK UP HER SISTER AT THE MONORAIL STATION.
MY PENANCE WAS DINNER AT METROPOLIS' BEST AND PRICIEST--CARLINI'S.
HER CURRENT BEAU INCLUDED.
LOOK WHAT I FOUND!
IT'S 8:45, CLARK. WHERE'VE YOU BEEN?
FINISHING A STORY.
AND SCOURING THE CITY FOR ANGUISH, TO NO AVAIL.
CLARK, MY SISTER LUCY. LUCY, CLARK.
I THOUGHT YOU WERE ABOUT TO BE THE ONLY MAN TO DITCH ME TWICE, MR. KENT.
I DON'T GIVE THIRD CHANCES.
THEN I'M GLAD I MADE IT. CALL ME CLARK, AND ACCEPT MY APOLOGIES.
I EXPECTED IT TO BE THE WEIRDEST OF NIGHTS.

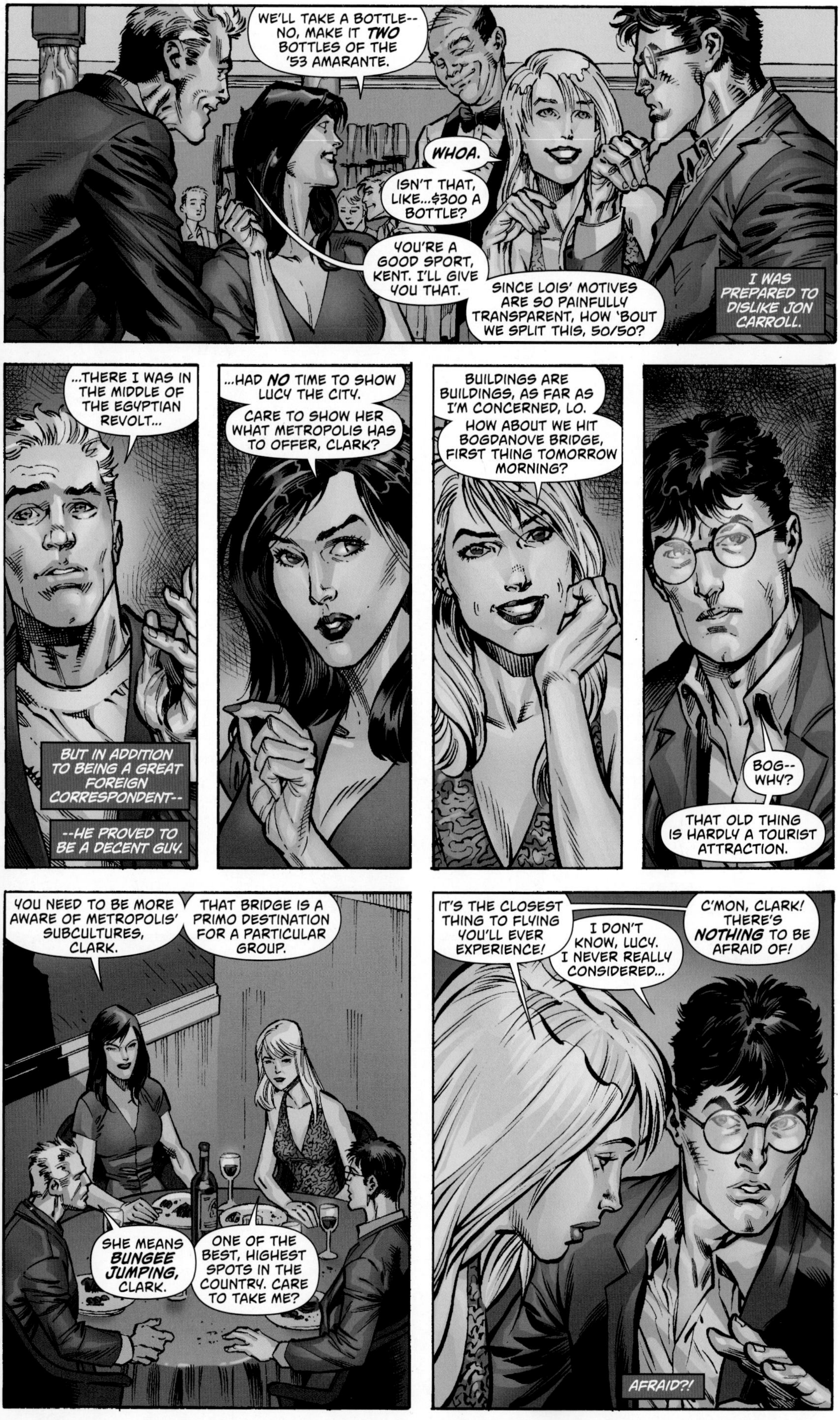

WE'LL TAKE A BOTTLE-- NO, MAKE IT TWO BOTTLES OF THE '53 AMARANTE.
WHOA.
ISN'T THAT, LIKE...$300 A BOTTLE?
YOU'RE A GOOD SPORT, KENT. I'LL GIVE YOU THAT.
SINCE LOIS' MOTIVES ARE SO PAINFULLY TRANSPARENT, HOW 'BOUT WE SPLIT THIS, 50/50?
I WAS PREPARED TO DISLIKE JON CARROLL.
...THERE I WAS IN THE MIDDLE OF THE EGYPTIAN REVOLT...
BUT IN ADDITION TO BEING A GREAT FOREIGN CORRESPONDENT--
--HE PROVED TO BE A DECENT GUY.
...HAD NO TIME TO SHOW LUCY THE CITY.
CARE TO SHOW HER WHAT METROPOLIS HAS TO OFFER, CLARK?
BUILDINGS ARE BUILDINGS, AS FAR AS I'M CONCERNED, LO.
HOW ABOUT WE HIT BOGDANOVE BRIDGE, FIRST THING TOMORROW MORNING?
BOG-- WHY?
THAT OLD THING IS HARDLY A TOURIST ATTRACTION.
YOU NEED TO BE MORE AWARE OF METROPOLIS' SUBCULTURES, CLARK.
THAT BRIDGE IS A PRIMO DESTINATION FOR A PARTICULAR GROUP.
SHE MEANS BUNGEE JUMPING, CLARK.
ONE OF THE BEST, HIGHEST SPOTS IN THE COUNTRY. CARE TO TAKE ME?
IT'S THE CLOSEST THING TO FLYING YOU'LL EVER EXPERIENCE!
I DON'T KNOW, LUCY. I NEVER REALLY CONSIDERED...
C'MON, CLARK! THERE'S NOTHING TO BE AFRAID OF!
AFRAID?!

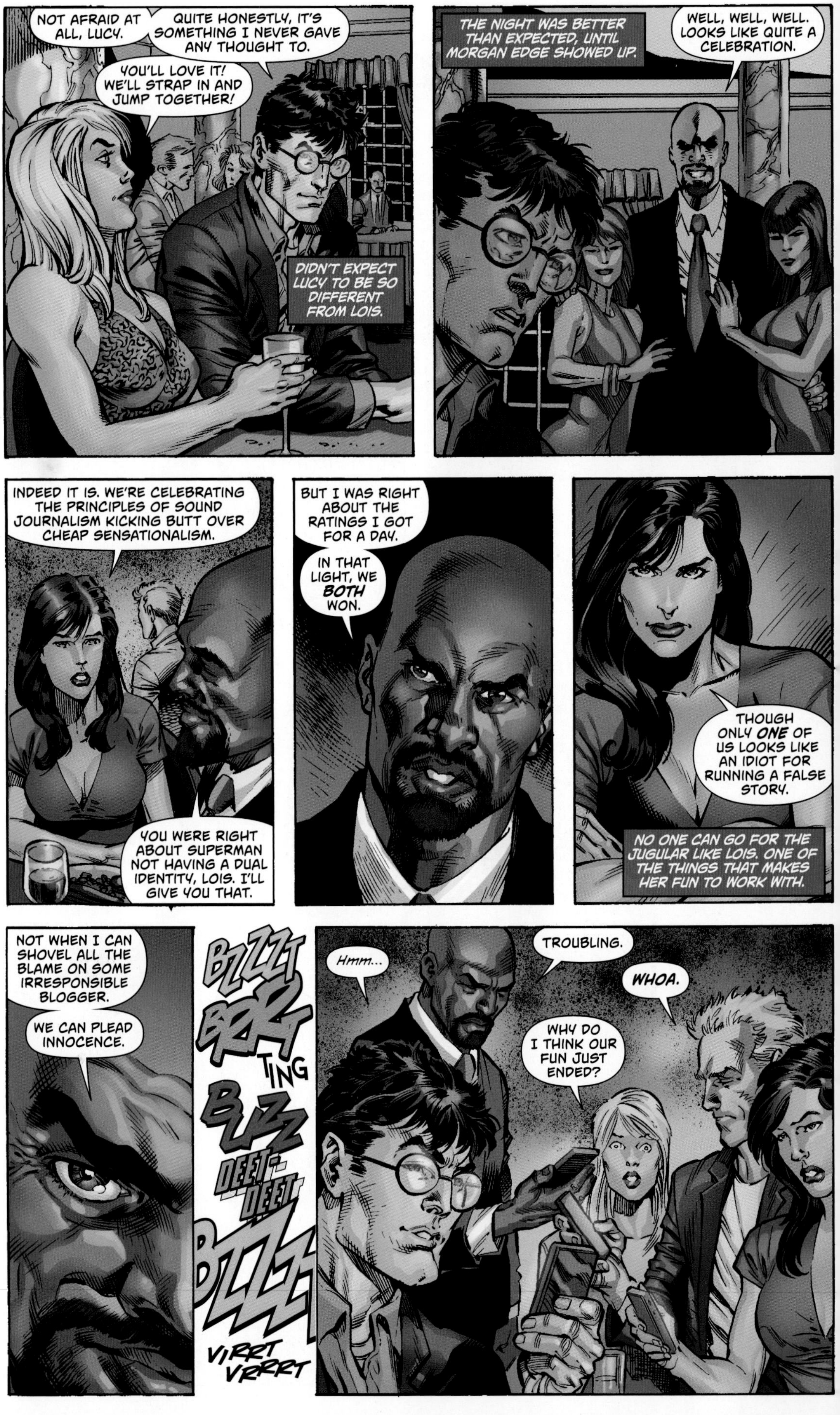

NOT AFRAID AT ALL, LUCY.
QUITE HONESTLY, IT'S SOMETHING I NEVER GAVE ANY THOUGHT TO.
YOU'LL LOVE IT! WE'LL STRAP IN AND JUMP TOGETHER!
DIDN'T EXPECT LUCY TO BE SO DIFFERENT FROM LOIS.
THE NIGHT WAS BETTER THAN EXPECTED, UNTIL MORGAN EDGE SHOWED UP.
WELL, WELL, WELL. LOOKS LIKE QUITE A CELEBRATION.
INDEED IT IS. WE'RE CELEBRATING THE PRINCIPLES OF SOUND JOURNALISM KICKING BUTT OVER CHEAP SENSATIONALISM.
YOU WERE RIGHT ABOUT SUPERMAN NOT HAVING A DUAL IDENTITY, LOIS. I'LL GIVE YOU THAT.
BUT I WAS RIGHT ABOUT THE RATINGS I GOT FOR A DAY.
IN THAT LIGHT, WE BOTH WON.
THOUGH ONLY ONE OF US LOOKS LIKE AN IDIOT FOR RUNNING A FALSE STORY.
NO ONE CAN GO FOR THE JUGULAR LIKE LOIS. ONE OF THE THINGS THAT MAKES HER FUN TO WORK WITH.
NOT WHEN I CAN SHOVEL ALL THE BLAME ON SOME IRRESPONSIBLE BLOGGER.
WE CAN PLEAD INNOCENCE.
BZZZT
BRRT
TING
BUZZ
DEET-DEET
BZZZ
VIRRT VRRRT
Hmm...
TROUBLING.
WHOA.
WHY DO I THINK OUR FUN JUST ENDED?

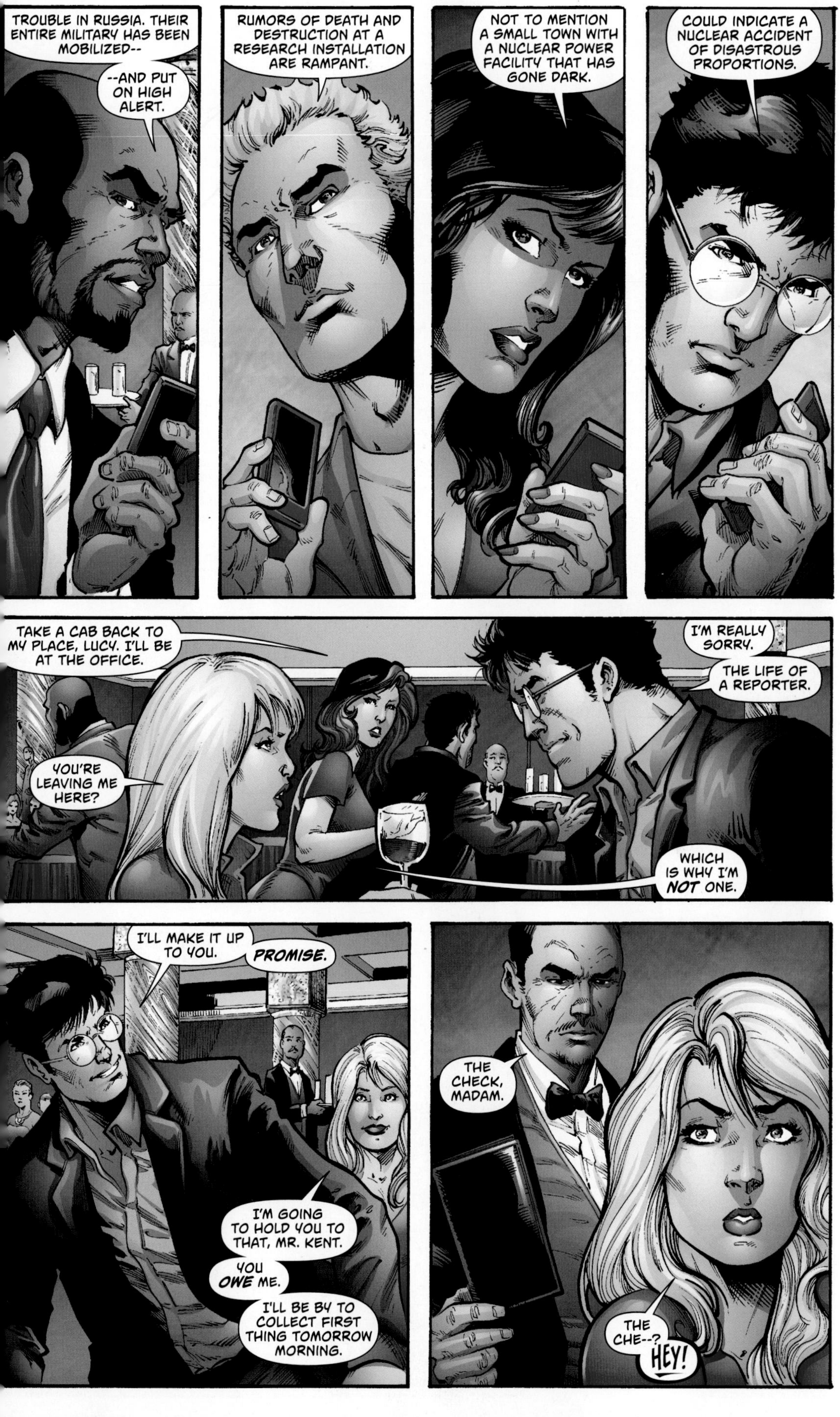
TROUBLE IN RUSSIA. THEIR ENTIRE MILITARY HAS BEEN MOBILIZED--
--AND PUT ON HIGH ALERT.
RUMORS OF DEATH AND DESTRUCTION AT A RESEARCH INSTALLATION ARE RAMPANT.
NOT TO MENTION A SMALL TOWN WITH A NUCLEAR POWER FACILITY THAT HAS GONE DARK.
COULD INDICATE A NUCLEAR ACCIDENT OF DISASTROUS PROPORTIONS.
TAKE A CAB BACK TO MY PLACE, LUCY. I'LL BE AT THE OFFICE.
I'M REALLY SORRY.
THE LIFE OF A REPORTER.
YOU'RE LEAVING ME HERE?
WHICH IS WHY I'M NOT ONE.
I'LL MAKE IT UP TO YOU.
PROMISE.
I'M GOING TO HOLD YOU TO THAT, MR. KENT.
YOU OWE ME.
I'LL BE BY TO COLLECT FIRST THING TOMORROW MORNING.
THE CHECK, MADAM.
THE CHE--? HEY!

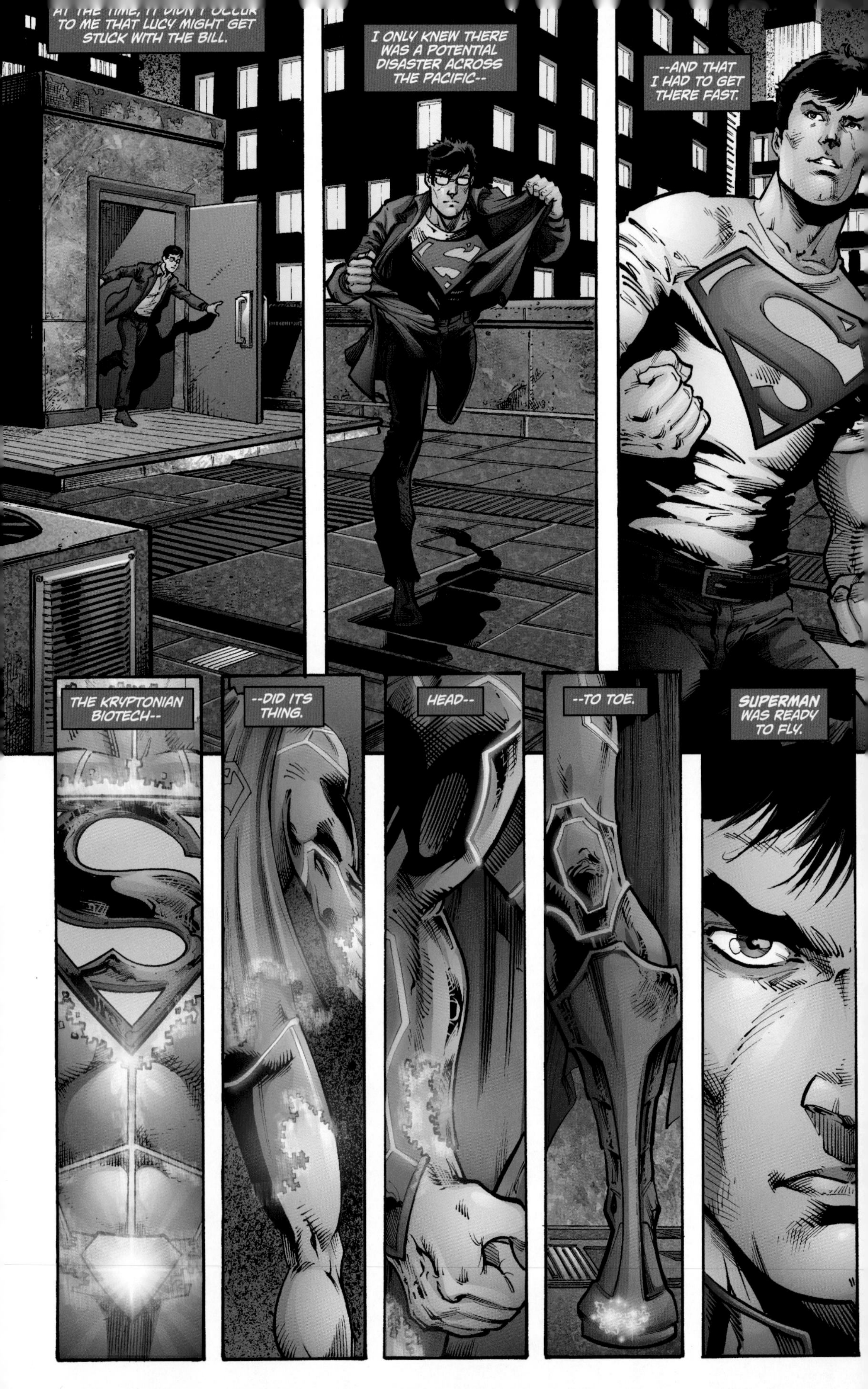
AT THE TIME, IT DIDN'T OCCUR TO ME THAT LUCY MIGHT GET STUCK WITH THE BILL.
I ONLY KNEW THERE WAS A POTENTIAL DISASTER ACROSS THE PACIFIC--
--AND THAT I HAD TO GET THERE FAST.
THE KRYPTONIAN BIOTECH--
--DID ITS THING.
HEAD--
--TO TOE.
SUPERMAN WAS READY TO FLY.

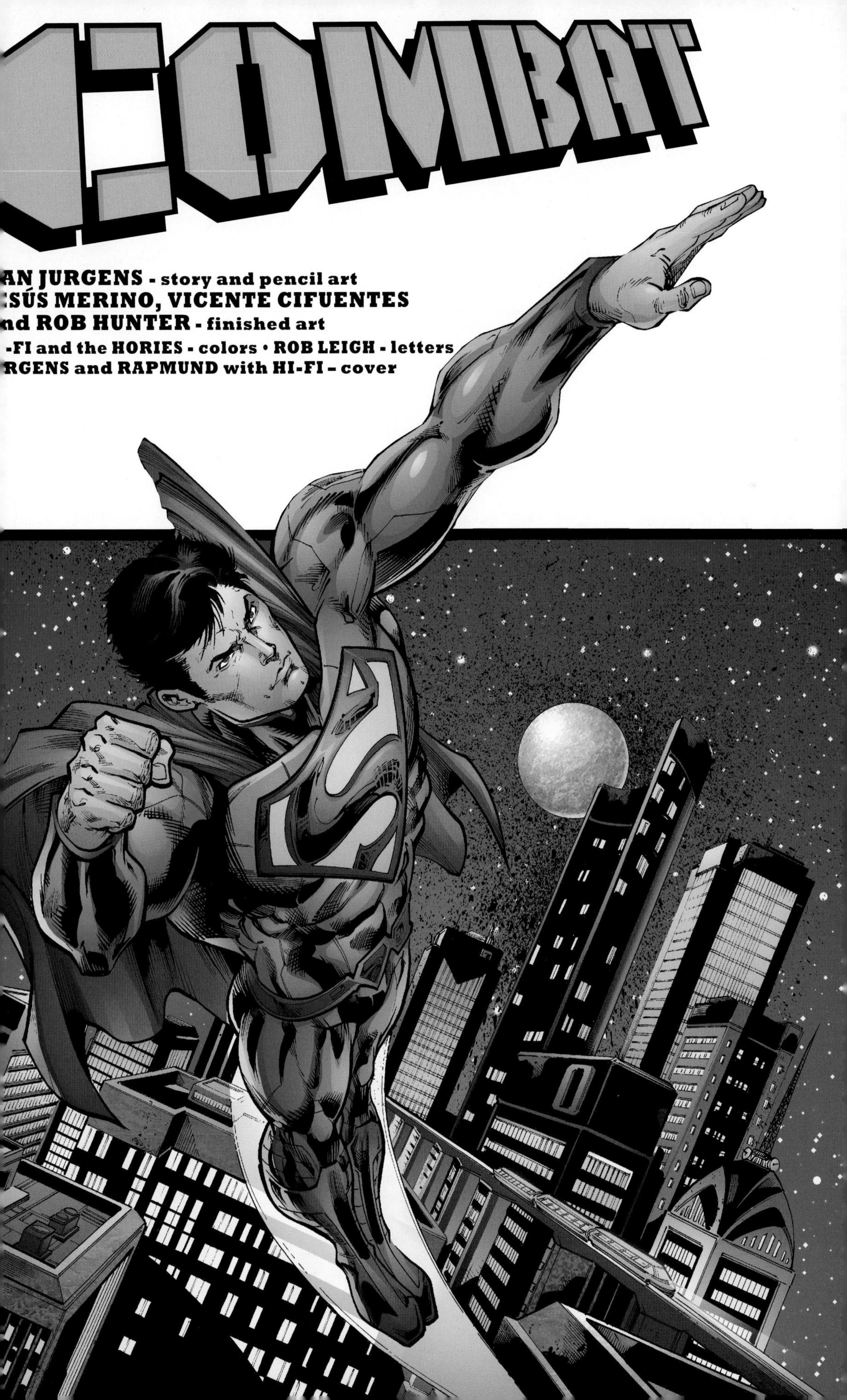

COMBAT
AN JURGENS - story and pencil art
:SÚS MERINO, VICENTE CIFUENTES
nd ROB HUNTER - finished art
-FI and the HORIES - colors • ROB LEIGH - letters
RGENS and RAPMUND with HI-FI - cover

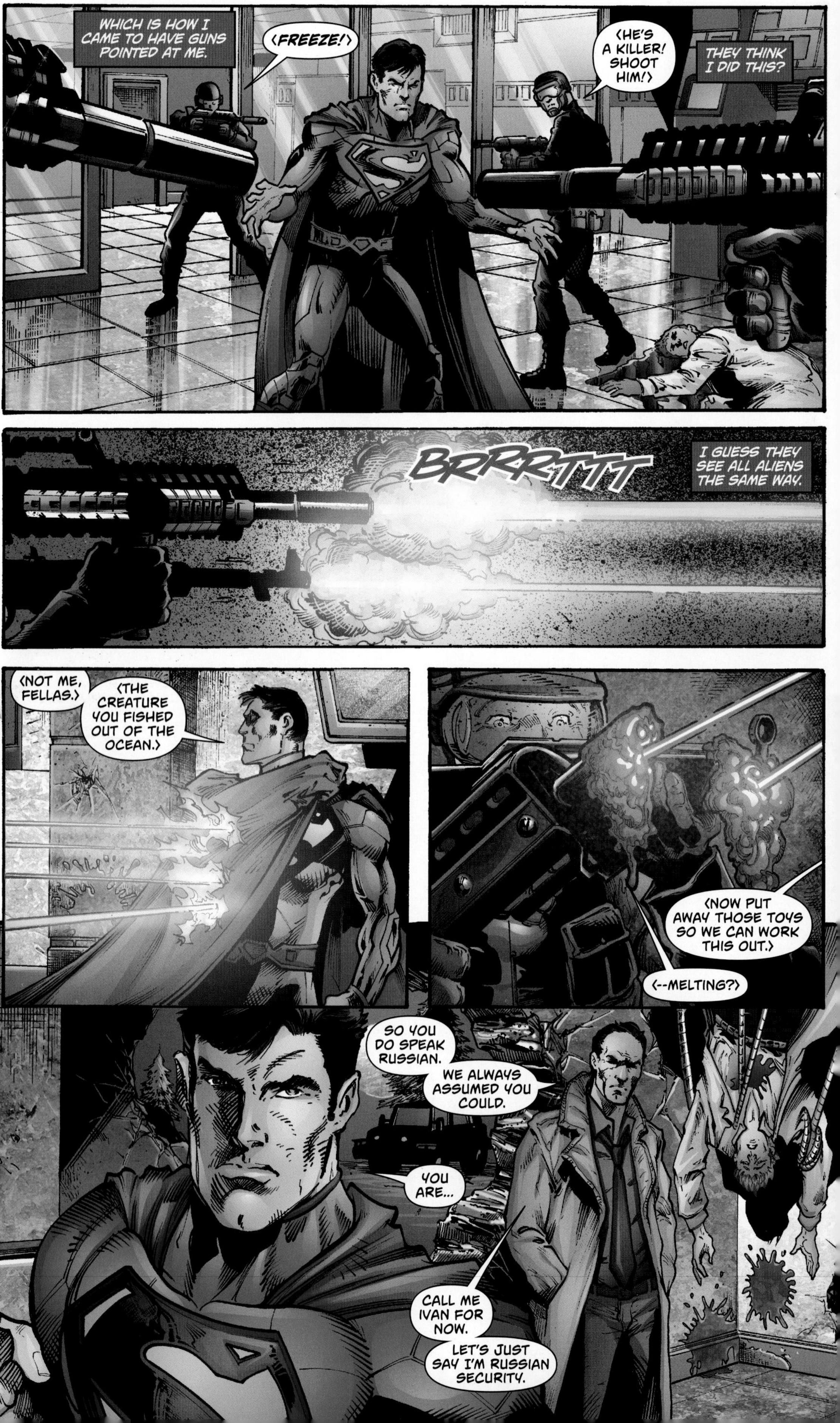
WHICH IS HOW I CAME TO HAVE GUNS POINTED AT ME.
‹FREEZE!›
‹HE'S A KILLER! SHOOT HIM!›
THEY THINK I DID THIS?
BRRRTTT
I GUESS THEY SEE ALL ALIENS THE SAME WAY.
‹NOT ME, FELLAS.›
‹THE CREATURE YOU FISHED OUT OF THE OCEAN.›
‹NOW PUT AWAY THOSE TOYS SO WE CAN WORK THIS OUT.›
‹--MELTING?›
SO YOU DO SPEAK RUSSIAN.
WE ALWAYS ASSUMED YOU COULD.
YOU ARE...
CALL ME IVAN FOR NOW.
LET'S JUST SAY I'M RUSSIAN SECURITY.

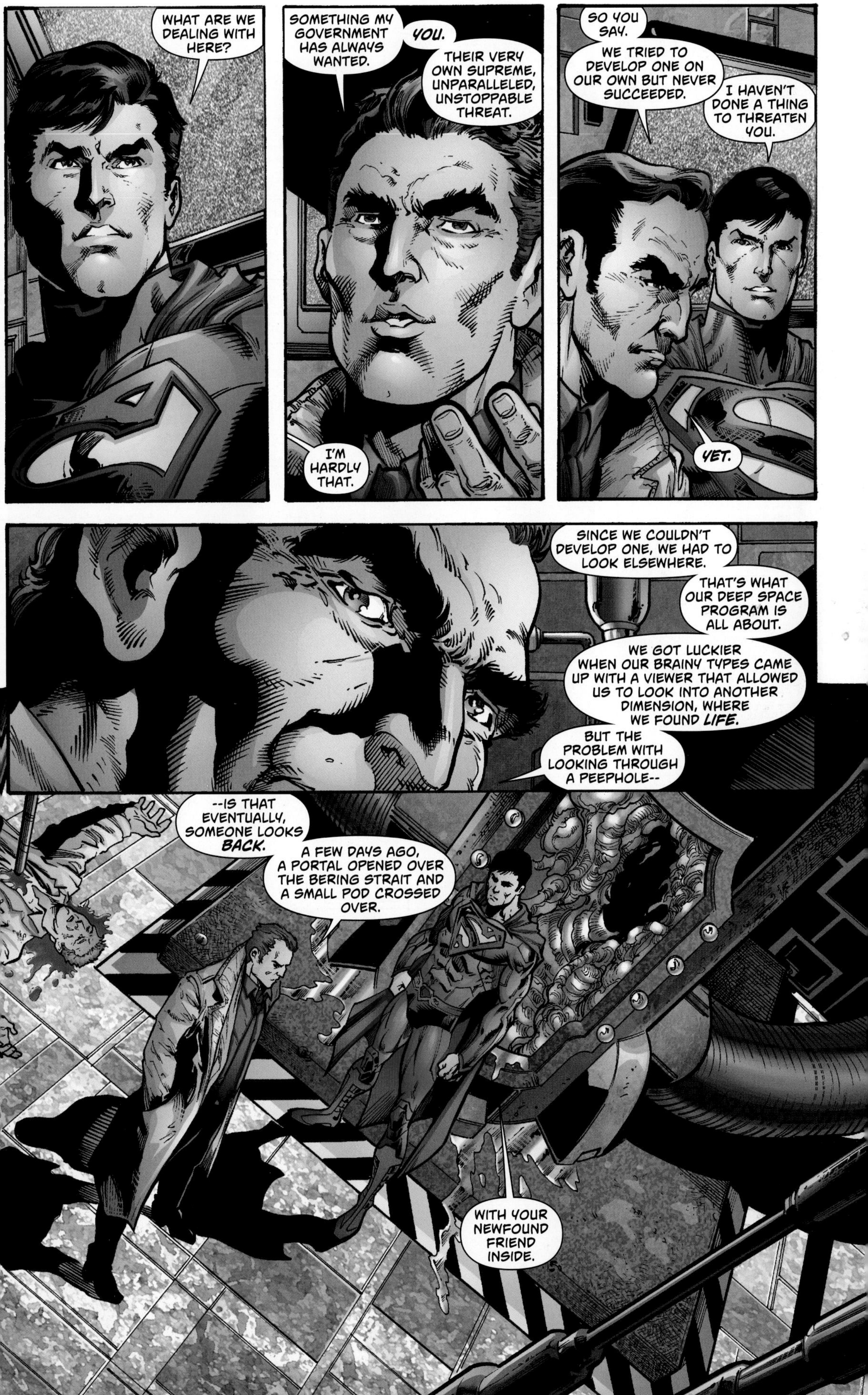
WHAT ARE WE DEALING WITH HERE?
SOMETHING MY GOVERNMENT HAS ALWAYS WANTED.
YOU.
THEIR VERY OWN SUPREME, UNPARALLELED, UNSTOPPABLE THREAT.
I'M HARDLY THAT.
SO YOU SAY.
WE TRIED TO DEVELOP ONE ON OUR OWN BUT NEVER SUCCEEDED.
I HAVEN'T DONE A THING TO THREATEN YOU.
YET.
SINCE WE COULDN'T DEVELOP ONE, WE HAD TO LOOK ELSEWHERE.
THAT'S WHAT OUR DEEP SPACE PROGRAM IS ALL ABOUT.
WE GOT LUCKIER WHEN OUR BRAINY TYPES CAME UP WITH A VIEWER THAT ALLOWED US TO LOOK INTO ANOTHER DIMENSION, WHERE WE FOUND LIFE.
BUT THE PROBLEM WITH LOOKING THROUGH A PEEPHOLE--
--IS THAT EVENTUALLY, SOMEONE LOOKS BACK.
A FEW DAYS AGO, A PORTAL OPENED OVER THE BERING STRAIT AND A SMALL POD CROSSED OVER.
WITH YOUR NEWFOUND FRIEND INSIDE.

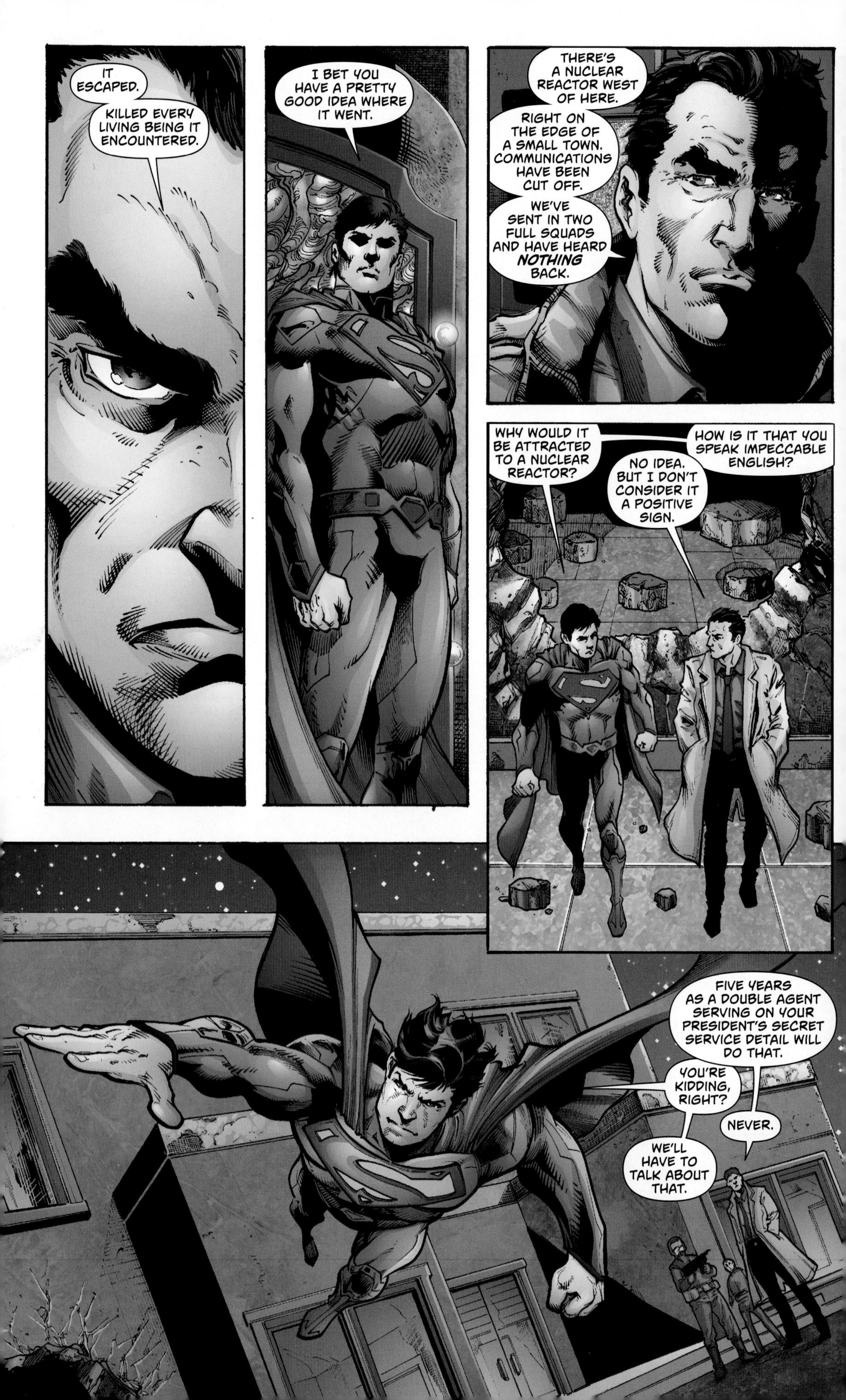
IT ESCAPED.
KILLED EVERY LIVING BEING IT ENCOUNTERED.
I BET YOU HAVE A PRETTY GOOD IDEA WHERE IT WENT.
THERE'S A NUCLEAR REACTOR WEST OF HERE.
RIGHT ON THE EDGE OF A SMALL TOWN. COMMUNICATIONS HAVE BEEN CUT OFF.
WE'VE SENT IN TWO FULL SQUADS AND HAVE HEARD NOTHING BACK.
WHY WOULD IT BE ATTRACTED TO A NUCLEAR REACTOR?
NO IDEA. BUT I DON'T CONSIDER IT A POSITIVE SIGN.
HOW IS IT THAT YOU SPEAK IMPECCABLE ENGLISH?
FIVE YEARS AS A DOUBLE AGENT SERVING ON YOUR PRESIDENT'S SECRET SERVICE DETAIL WILL DO THAT.
YOU'RE KIDDING, RIGHT?
NEVER.
WE'LL HAVE TO TALK ABOUT THAT.

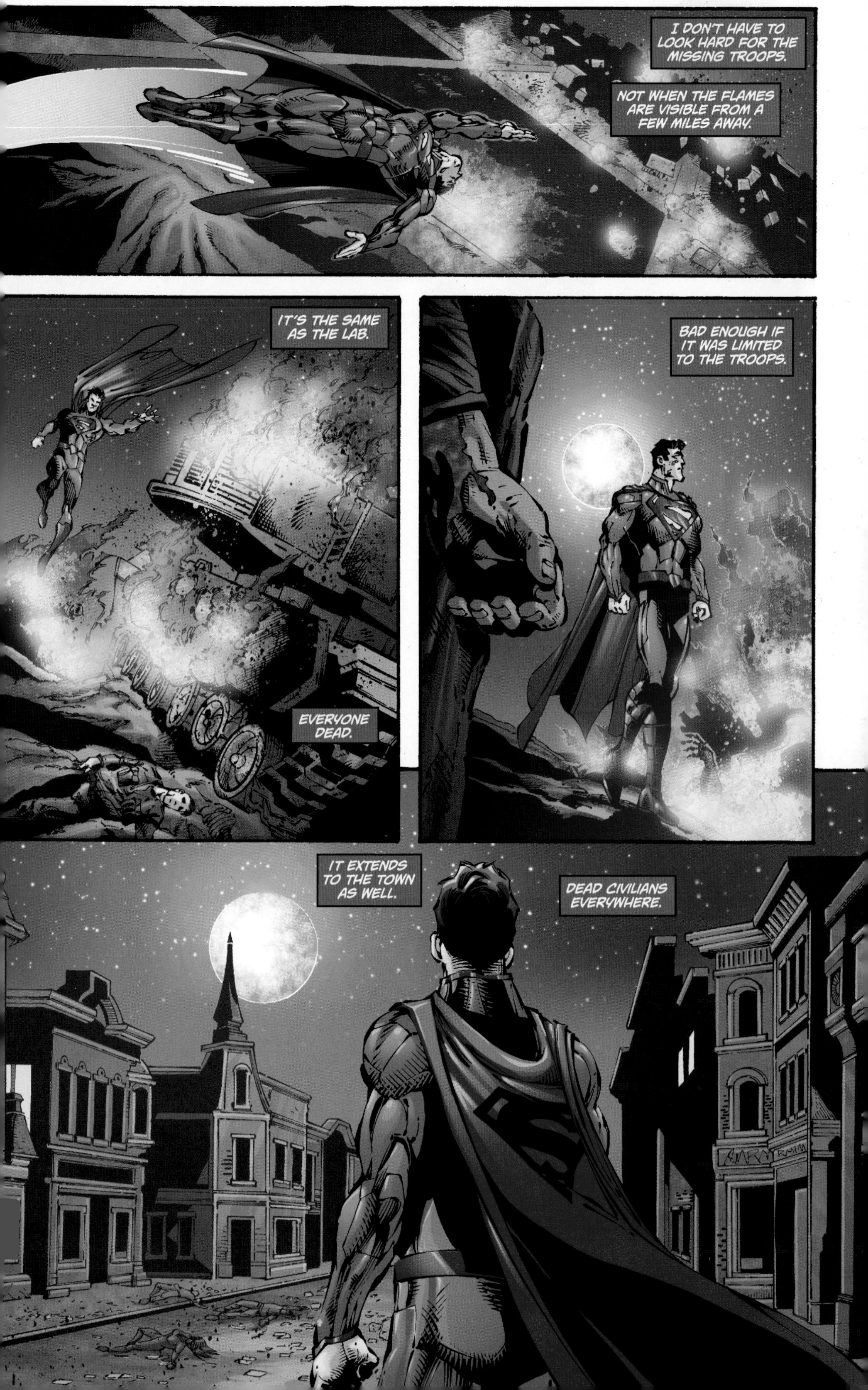
I DON'T HAVE TO LOOK HARD FOR THE MISSING TROOPS.
NOT WHEN THE FLAMES ARE VISIBLE FROM A FEW MILES AWAY.
IT'S THE SAME AS THE LAB.
EVERYONE DEAD.
BAD ENOUGH IF IT WAS LIMITED TO THE TROOPS.
IT EXTENDS TO THE TOWN AS WELL.
DEAD CIVILIANS EVERYWHERE.

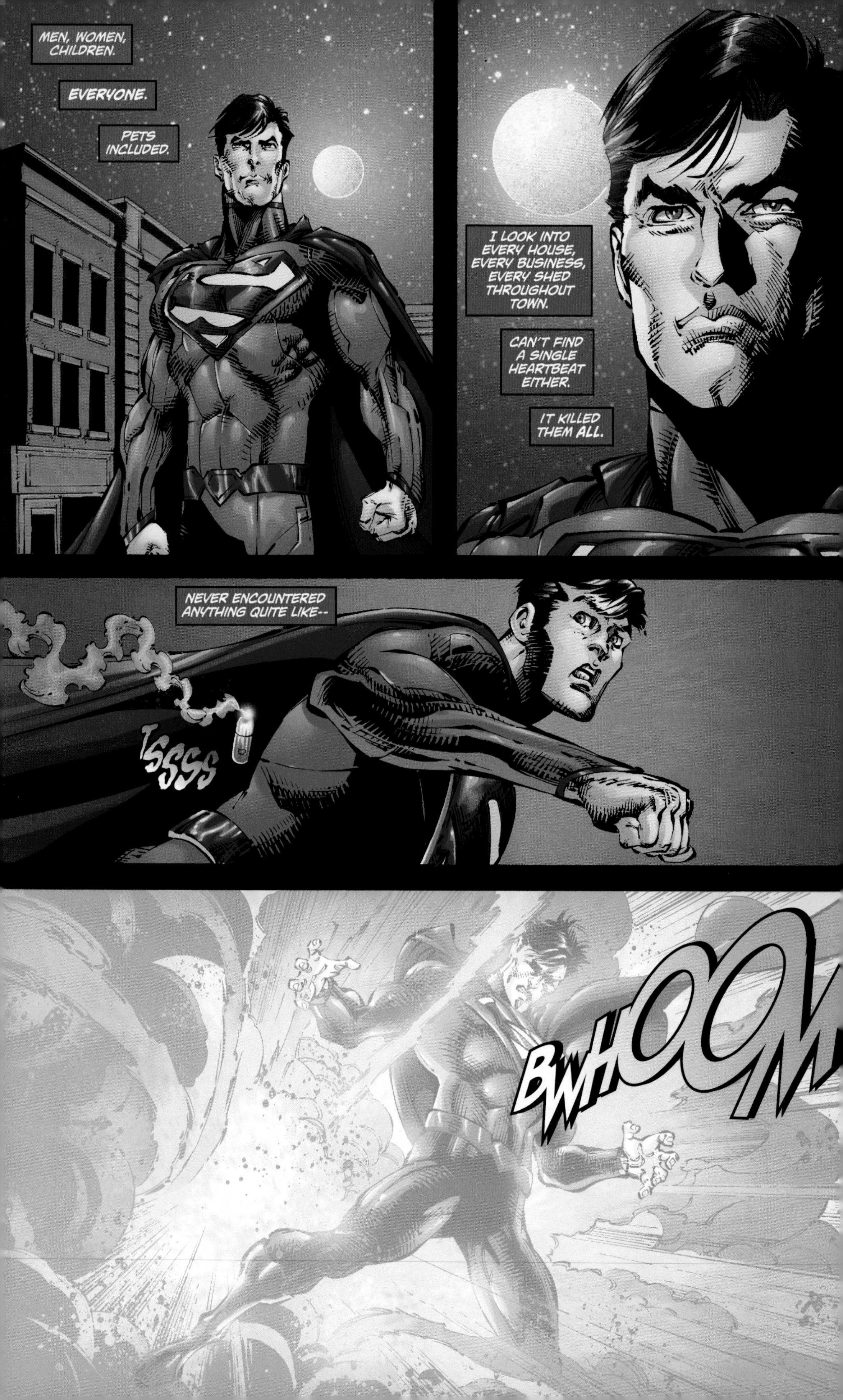
MEN, WOMEN, CHILDREN.
EVERYONE.
PETS INCLUDED.
I LOOK INTO EVERY HOUSE, EVERY BUSINESS, EVERY SHED THROUGHOUT TOWN.
CAN'T FIND A SINGLE HEARTBEAT EITHER.
IT KILLED THEM ALL.
NEVER ENCOUNTERED ANYTHING QUITE LIKE--
TSSSS
BWHOOM

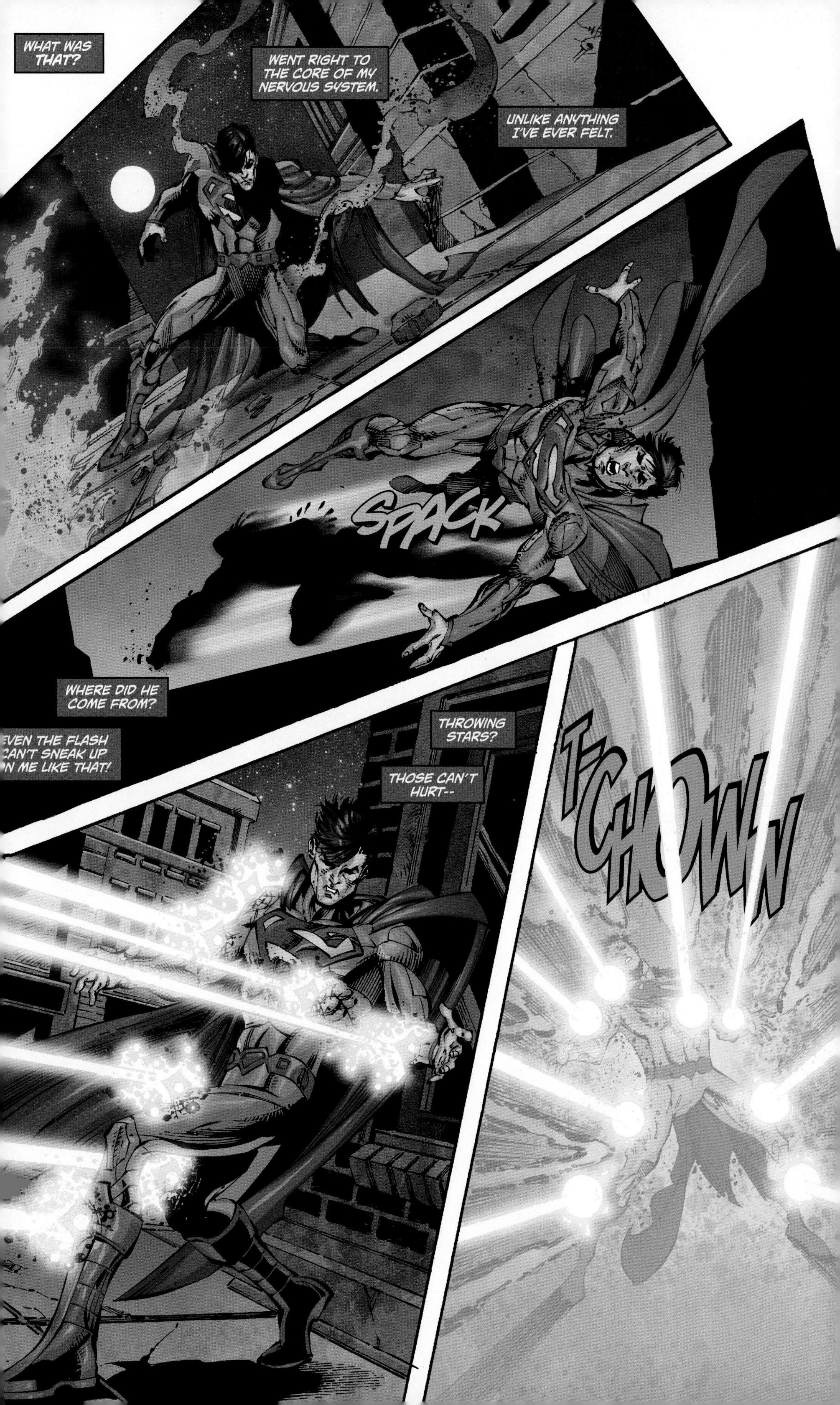
WHAT WAS THAT?
WENT RIGHT TO THE CORE OF MY NERVOUS SYSTEM.
UNLIKE ANYTHING I'VE EVER FELT.
SPACK
WHERE DID HE COME FROM?
EVEN THE FLASH CAN'T SNEAK UP ON ME LIKE THAT!
THROWING STARS?
THOSE CAN'T HURT--
T-CHOWWN

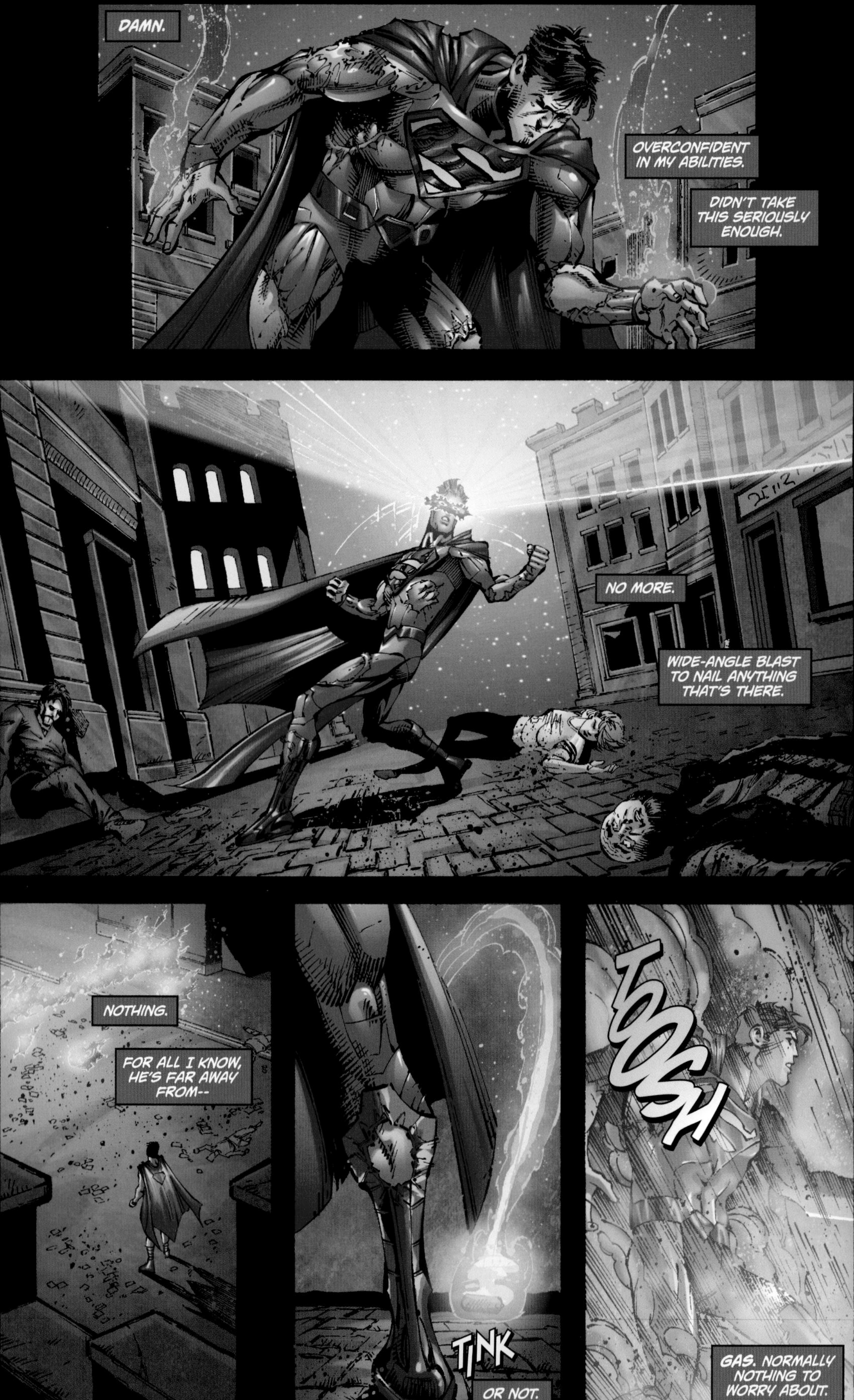
DAMN.
OVERCONFIDENT IN MY ABILITIES.
DIDN'T TAKE THIS SERIOUSLY ENOUGH.
NO MORE.
WIDE-ANGLE BLAST TO NAIL ANYTHING THAT'S THERE.
NOTHING.
FOR ALL I KNOW, HE'S FAR AWAY FROM--
TINK
OR NOT.
FOOOSH
GAS. NORMALLY NOTHING TO WORRY ABOUT.

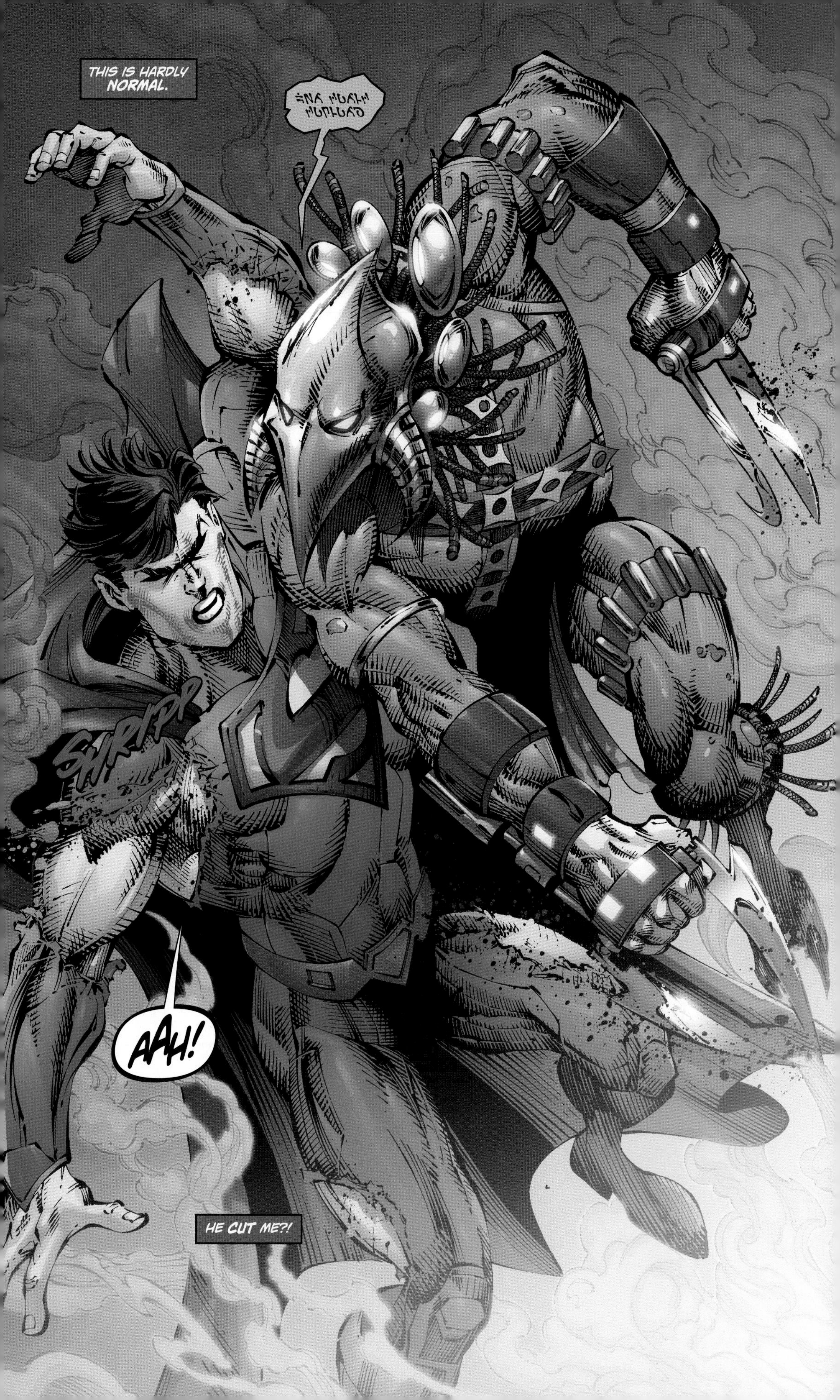
THIS IS HARDLY NORMAL.
SHRIPP
AAH!
HE CUT ME?!

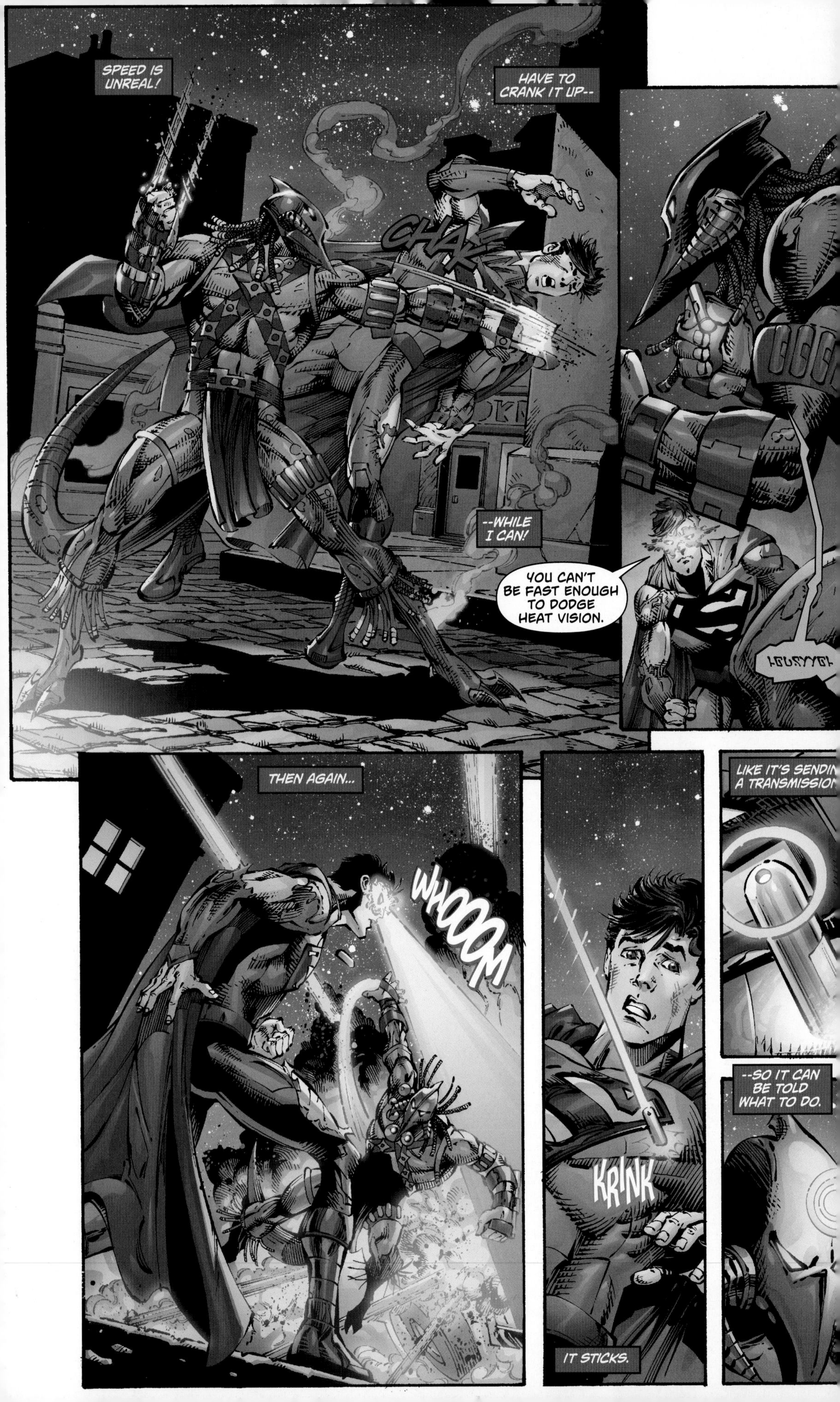

SPEED IS UNREAL!
CHAK
HAVE TO CRANK IT UP--
--WHILE I CAN!
YOU CAN'T BE FAST ENOUGH TO DODGE HEAT VISION.
THEN AGAIN...
WHOOOM
KRINK
IT STICKS.
LIKE IT'S SENDIN
A TRANSMISSIO
--SO IT CAN BE TOLD WHAT TO DO.

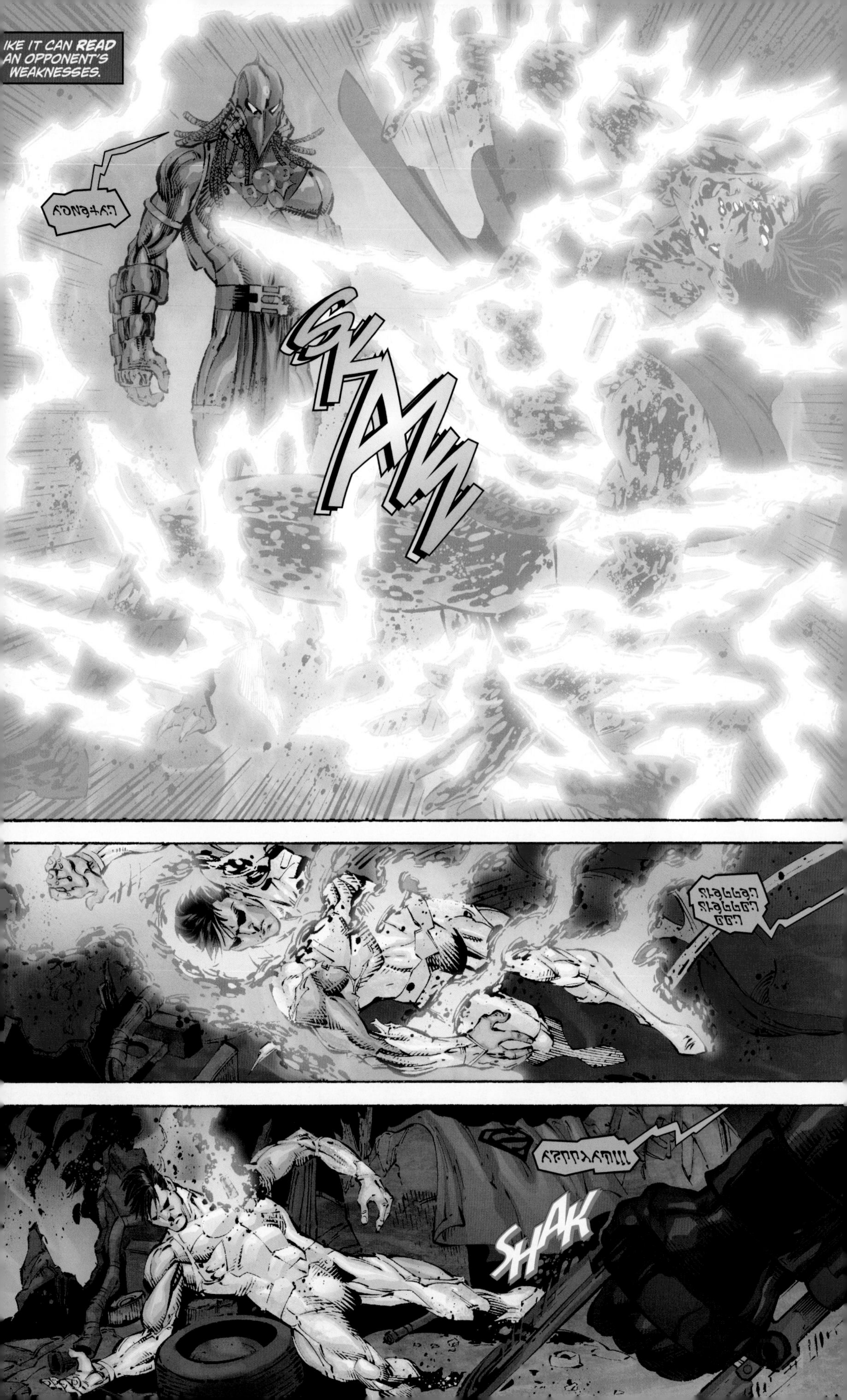
IKE IT CAN READ AN OPPONENT'S WEAKNESSES.
SHAK

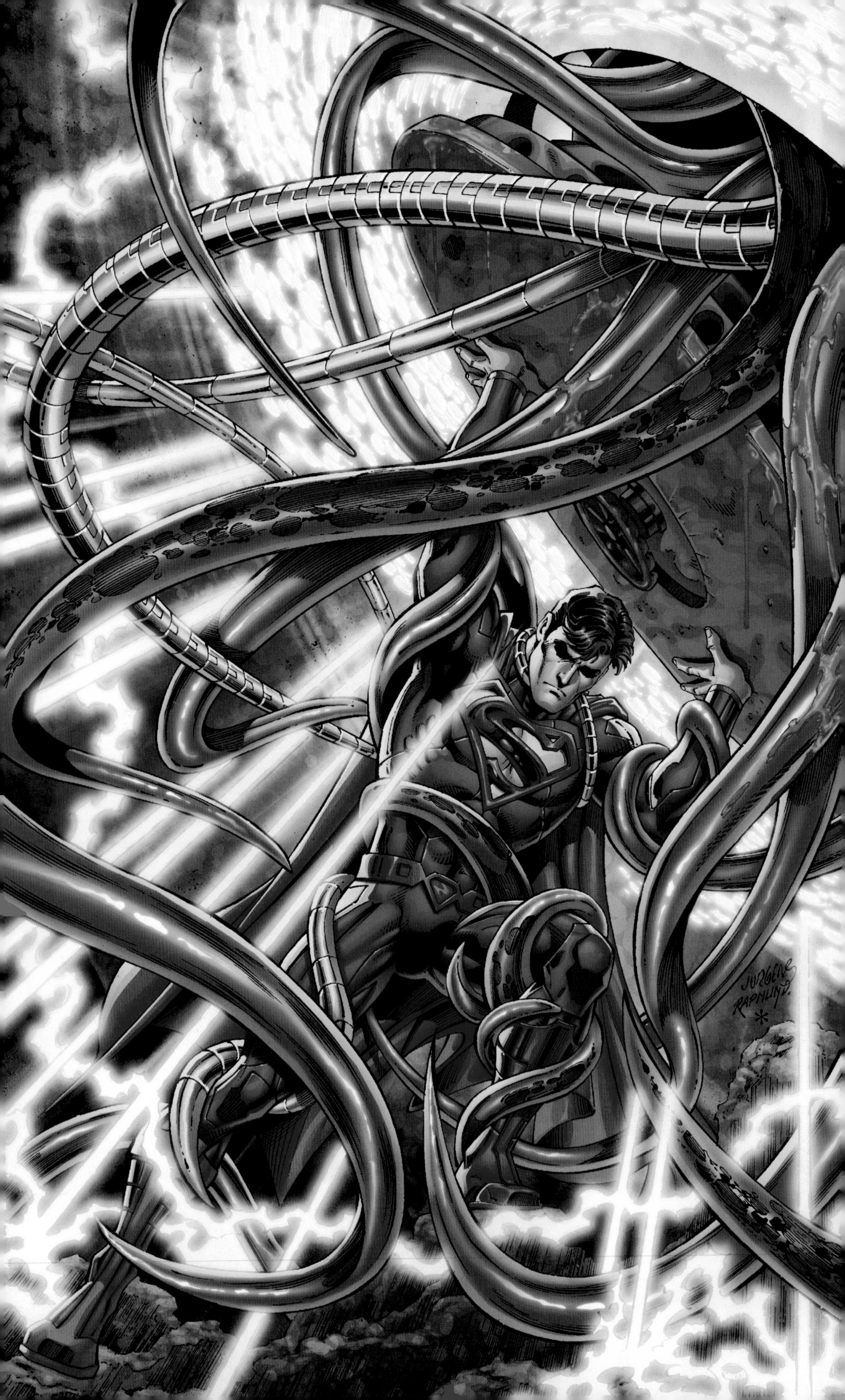
JURGENS
RAPMUND

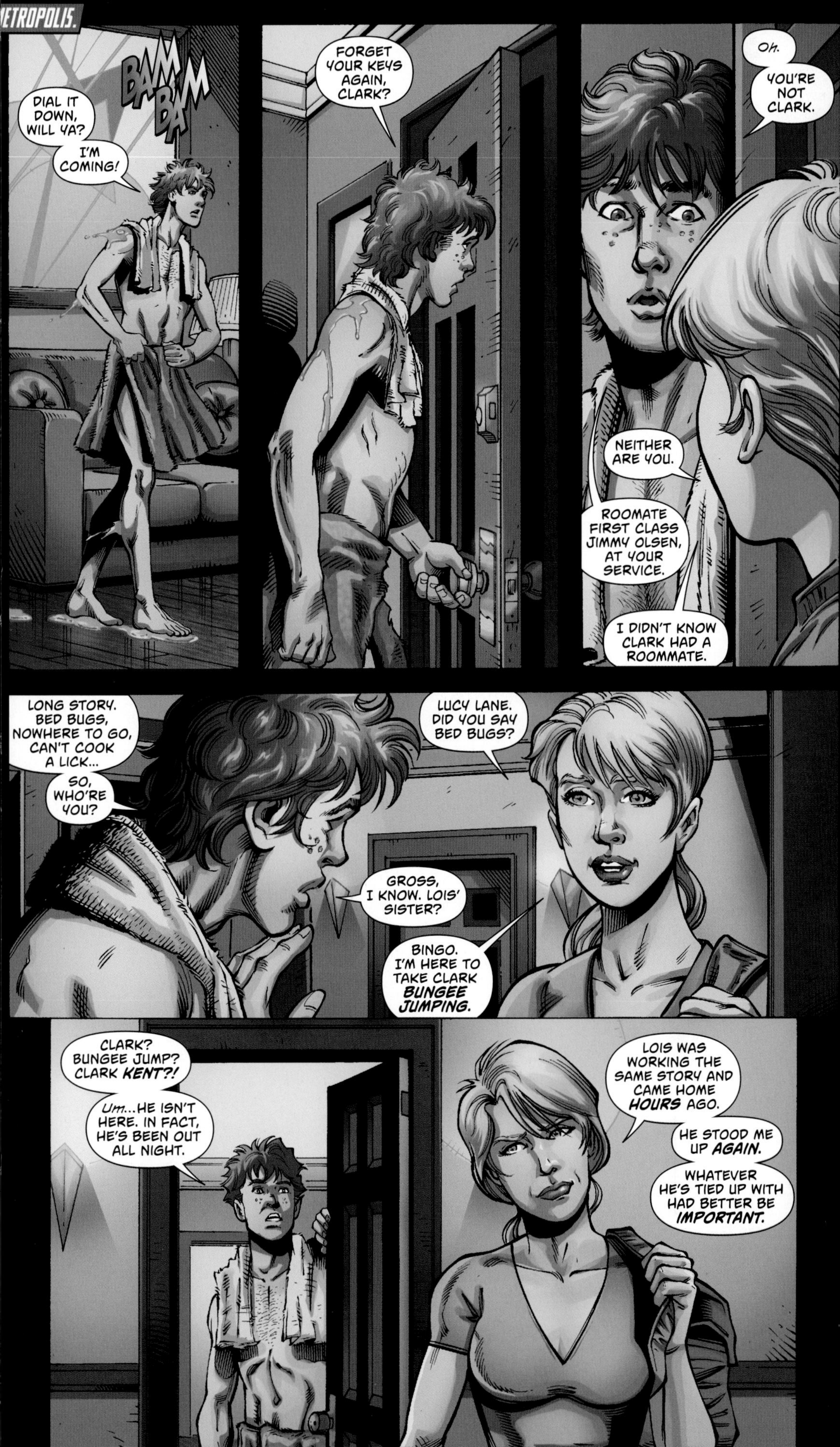
METROPOLIS.
BAM BAM BAM
DIAL IT DOWN, WILL YA?
I'M COMING!
FORGET YOUR KEYS AGAIN, CLARK?
Oh.
YOU'RE NOT CLARK.
NEITHER ARE YOU.
ROOMATE FIRST CLASS JIMMY OLSEN, AT YOUR SERVICE.
I DIDN'T KNOW CLARK HAD A ROOMMATE.
LONG STORY. BED BUGS, NOWHERE TO GO, CAN'T COOK A LICK...
SO, WHO'RE YOU?
LUCY LANE. DID YOU SAY BED BUGS?
GROSS, I KNOW. LOIS' SISTER?
BINGO. I'M HERE TO TAKE CLARK BUNGEE JUMPING.
CLARK? BUNGEE JUMP? CLARK KENT?!
Um...HE ISN'T HERE. IN FACT, HE'S BEEN OUT ALL NIGHT.
LOIS WAS WORKING THE SAME STORY AND CAME HOME HOURS AGO.
HE STOOD ME UP AGAIN.
WHATEVER HE'S TIED UP WITH HAD BETTER BE IMPORTANT.

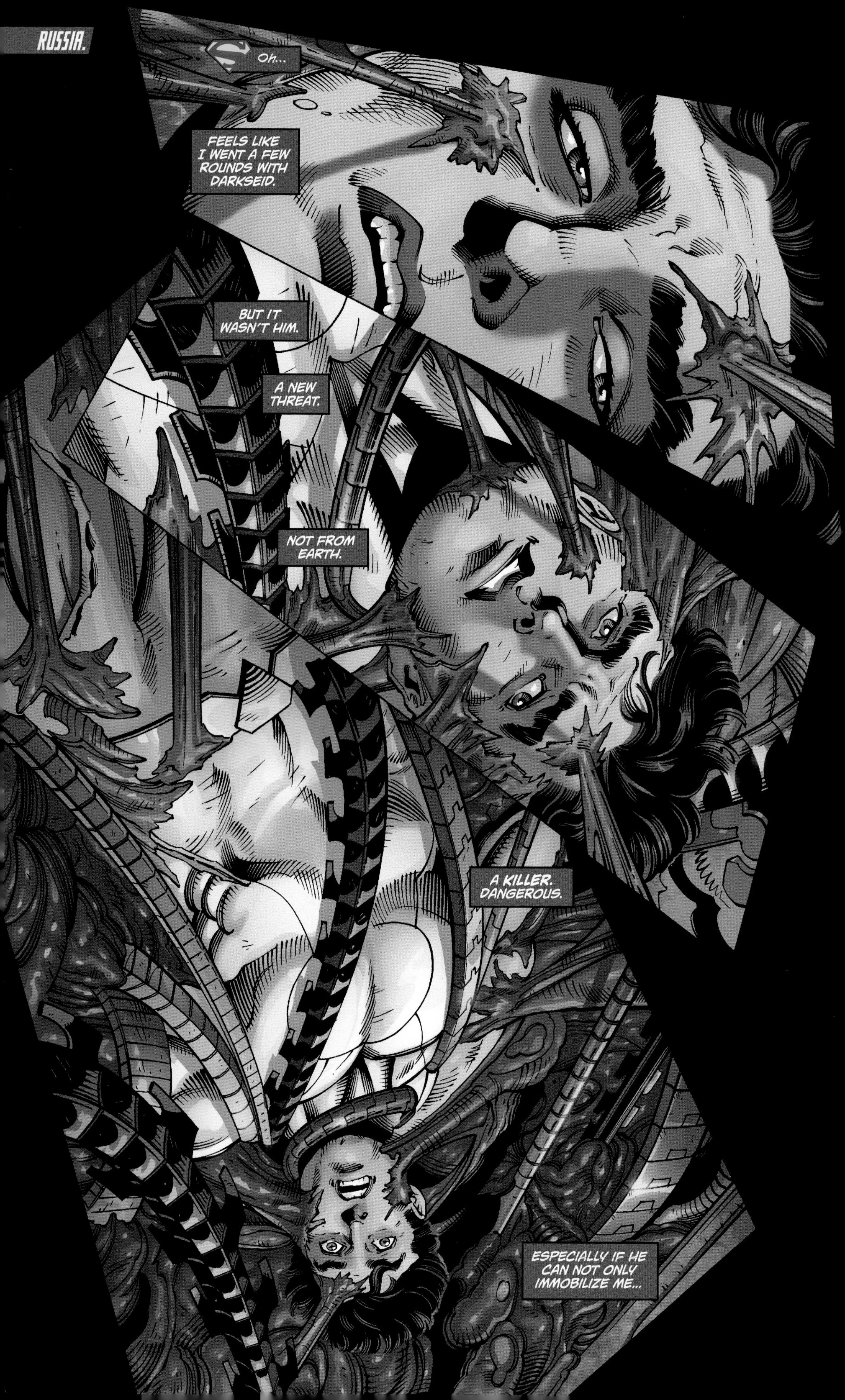
RUSSIA.
Oh...
FEELS LIKE I WENT A FEW ROUNDS WITH DARKSEID.
BUT IT WASN'T HIM.
A NEW THREAT.
NOT FROM EARTH.
A KILLER. DANGEROUS.
ESPECIALLY IF HE CAN NOT ONLY IMMOBILIZE ME...

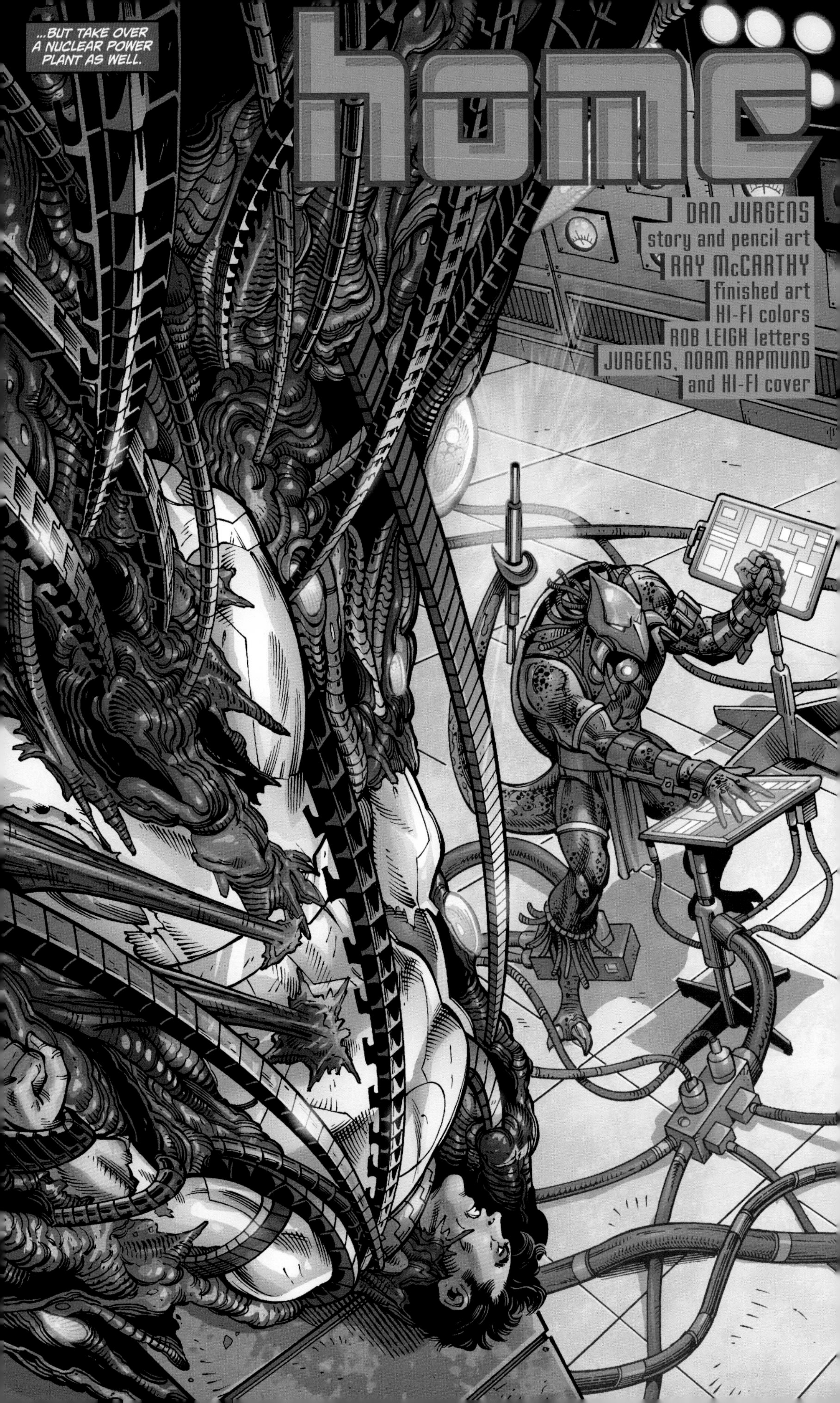
...BUT TAKE OVER A NUCLEAR POWER PLANT AS WELL.
HOME
DAN JURGENS story and pencil art
RAY McCARTHY finished art
HI-FI colors
ROB LEIGH letters
JURGENS, NORM RAPMUND and HI-FI cover

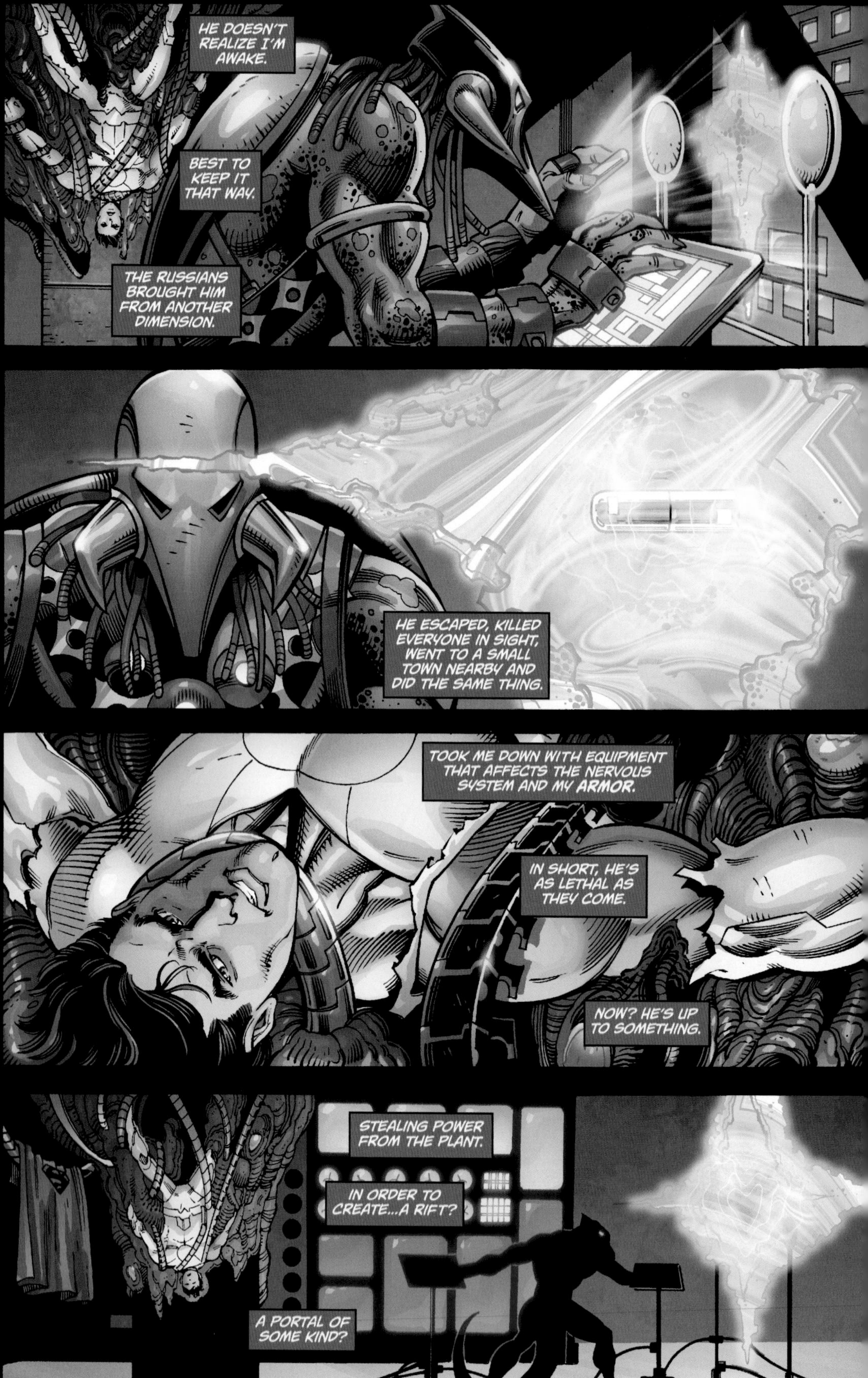
HE DOESN'T REALIZE I'M AWAKE.
BEST TO KEEP IT THAT WAY.
THE RUSSIANS BROUGHT HIM FROM ANOTHER DIMENSION.
HE ESCAPED, KILLED EVERYONE IN SIGHT, WENT TO A SMALL TOWN NEARBY AND DID THE SAME THING.
TOOK ME DOWN WITH EQUIPMENT THAT AFFECTS THE NERVOUS SYSTEM AND MY ARMOR.
IN SHORT, HE'S AS LETHAL AS THEY COME.
NOW? HE'S UP TO SOMETHING.
STEALING POWER FROM THE PLANT.
IN ORDER TO CREATE...A RIFT?
A PORTAL OF SOME KIND?

GATEWAY.

FOR OTHERS OF HIS KIND.

TO BRING THEM HERE.

AN ARMY OF CREATURES, WILLING TO WIPE OUT HUMAN LIFE.

HAVE TO CHANGE THE EQUATION.

NO MORE WATCHING.

TIME TO ACT.

TOOSH

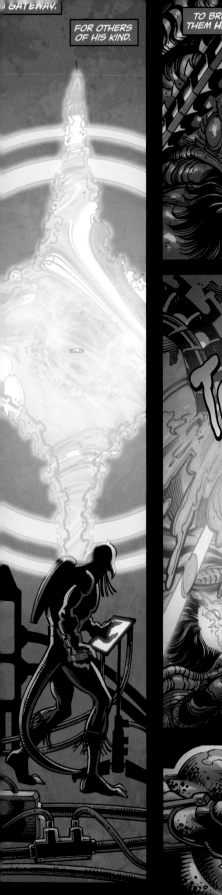

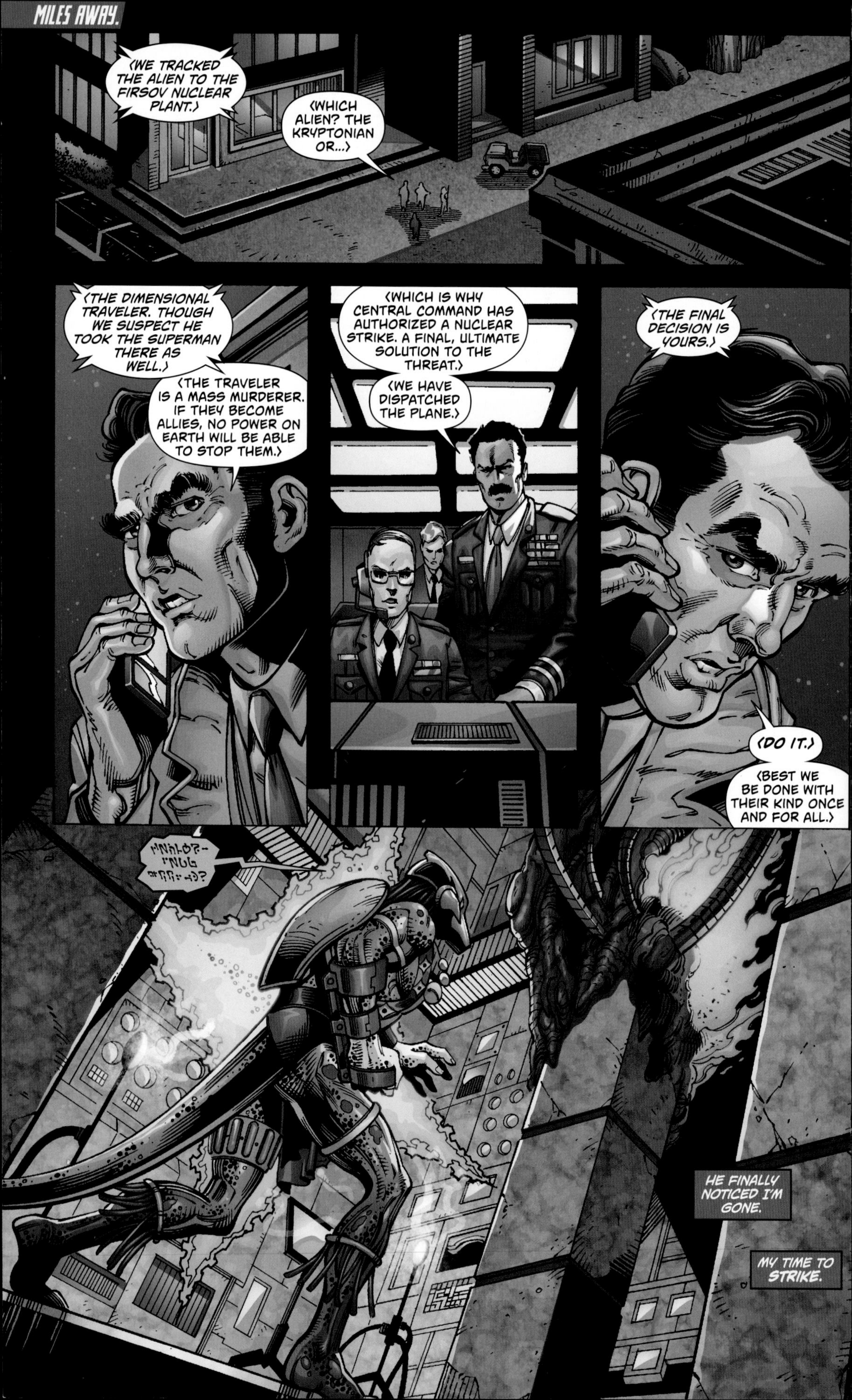
MILES AWAY.
⟨WE TRACKED THE ALIEN TO THE FIRSOV NUCLEAR PLANT.⟩
⟨WHICH ALIEN? THE KRYPTONIAN OR...⟩
⟨THE DIMENSIONAL TRAVELER. THOUGH WE SUSPECT HE TOOK THE SUPERMAN THERE AS WELL.⟩
⟨THE TRAVELER IS A MASS MURDERER. IF THEY BECOME ALLIES, NO POWER ON EARTH WILL BE ABLE TO STOP THEM.⟩
⟨WHICH IS WHY CENTRAL COMMAND HAS AUTHORIZED A NUCLEAR STRIKE. A FINAL, ULTIMATE SOLUTION TO THE THREAT.⟩
⟨WE HAVE DISPATCHED THE PLANE.⟩
⟨THE FINAL DECISION IS YOURS.⟩
⟨DO IT.⟩
⟨BEST WE BE DONE WITH THEIR KIND ONCE AND FOR ALL.⟩
HE FINALLY NOTICED I'M GONE.
MY TIME TO STRIKE.

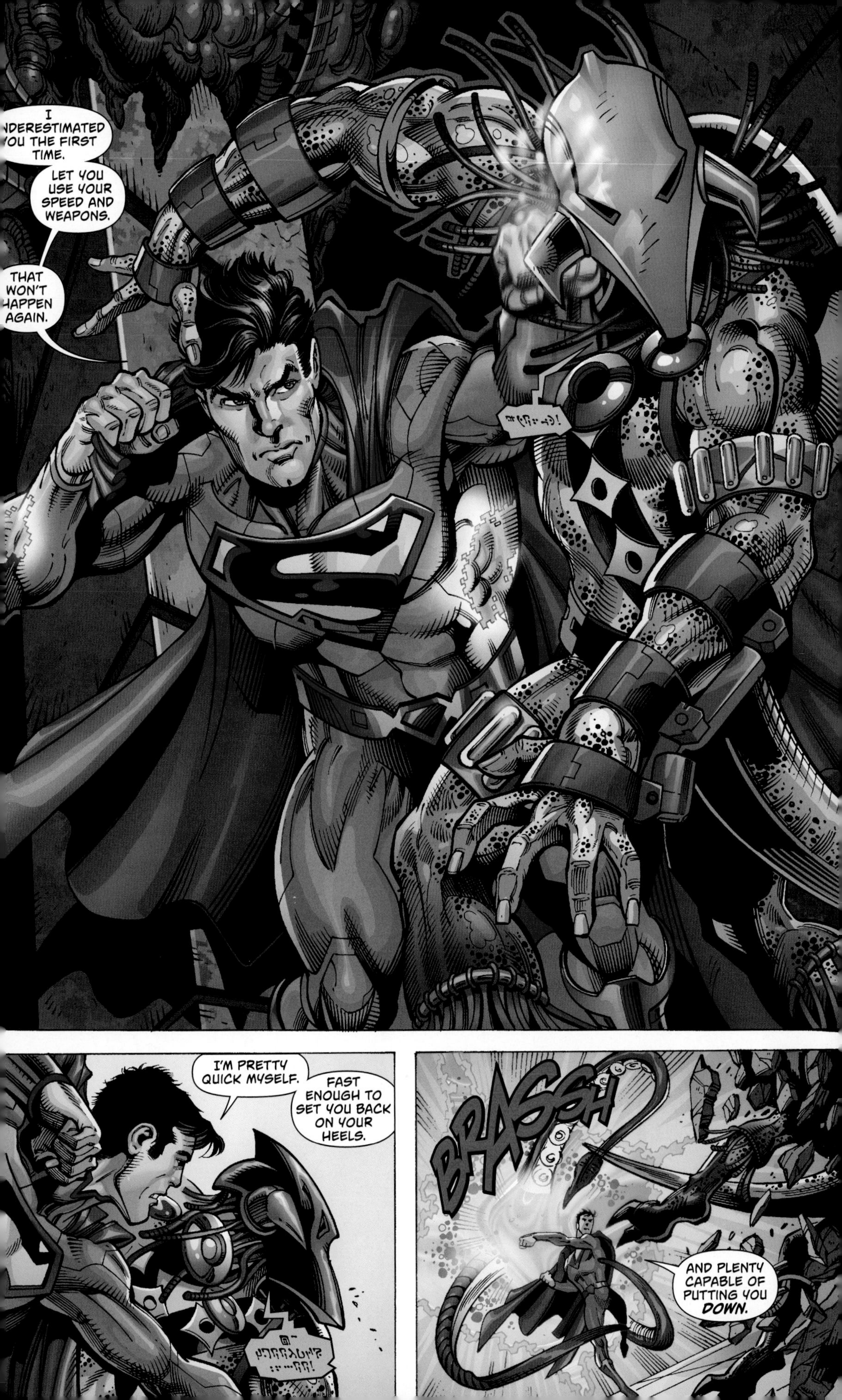

I NDERESTIMATED OU THE FIRST TIME.
LET YOU USE YOUR SPEED AND WEAPONS.
THAT WON'T HAPPEN AGAIN.
I'M PRETTY QUICK MYSELF.
FAST ENOUGH TO SET YOU BACK ON YOUR HEELS.
BRASSH
AND PLENTY CAPABLE OF PUTTING YOU *DOWN.*

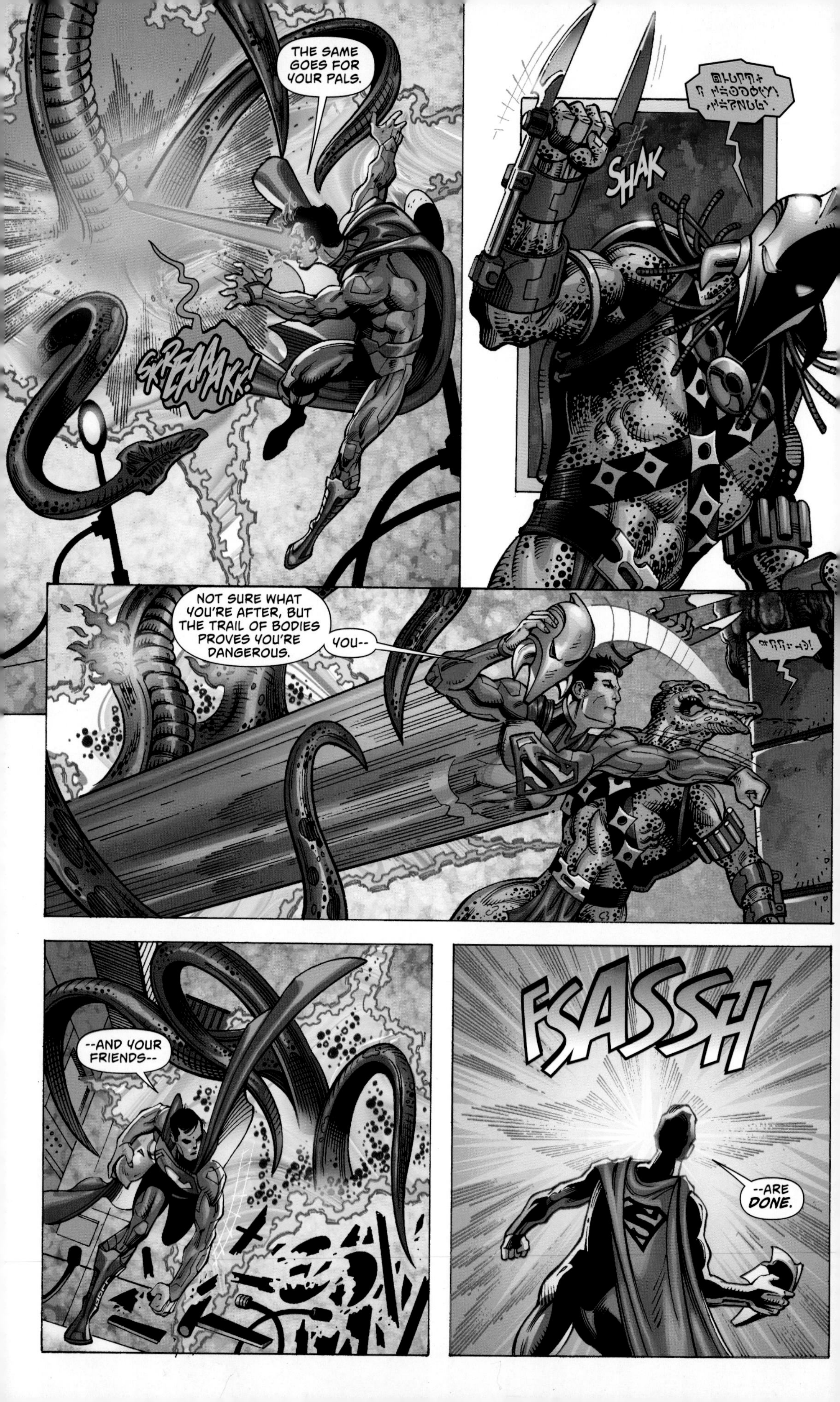

THE SAME GOES FOR YOUR PALS.
SKREAAAKK!
SHAK
NOT SURE WHAT YOU'RE AFTER, BUT THE TRAIL OF BODIES PROVES YOU'RE DANGEROUS.
YOU--
--AND YOUR FRIENDS--
FSASSH
--ARE DONE.

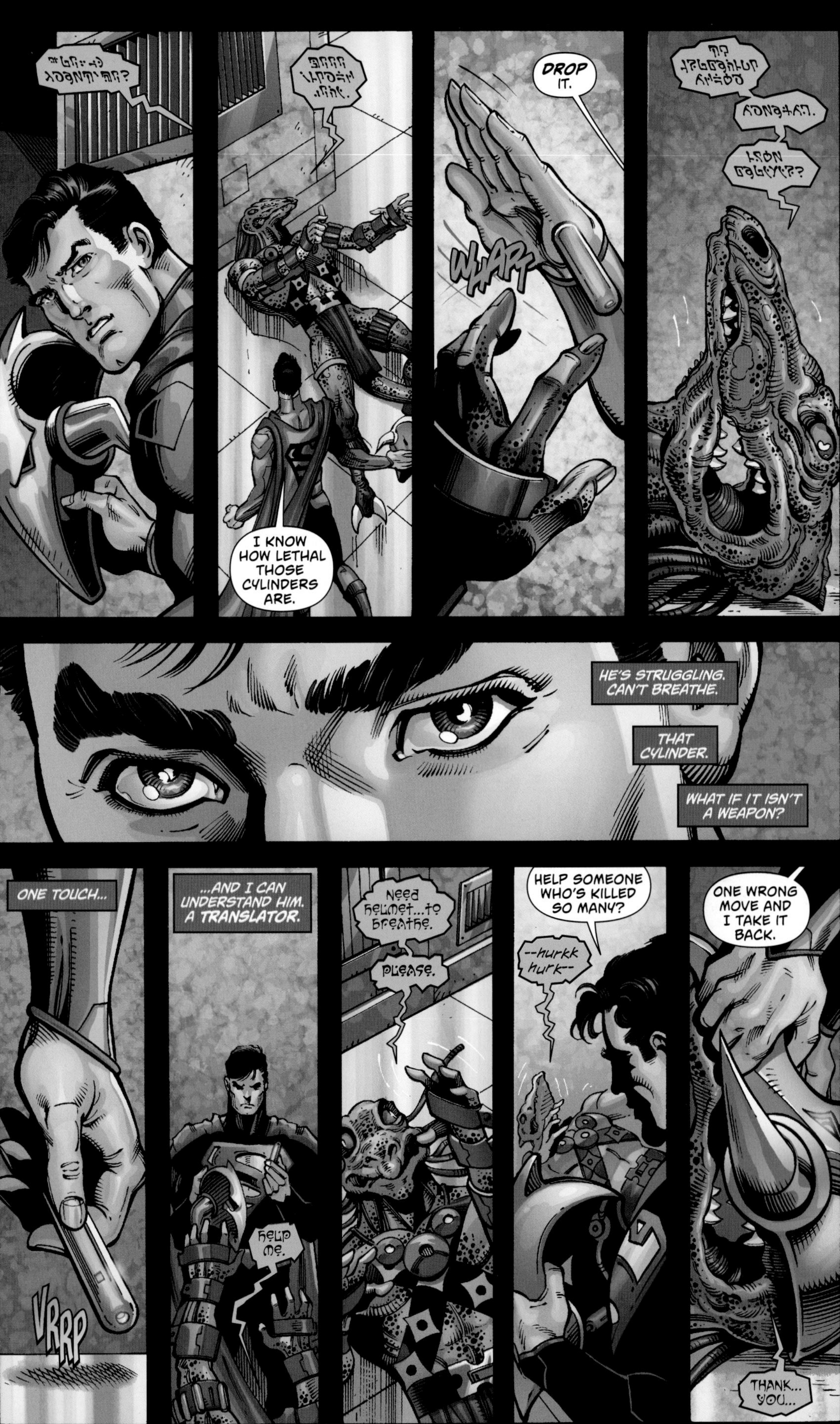
DROP IT.
WHAP
I KNOW HOW LETHAL THOSE CYLINDERS ARE.
HE'S STRUGGLING. CAN'T BREATHE.
THAT CYLINDER.
WHAT IF IT ISN'T A WEAPON?
ONE TOUCH...
VRRP
...AND I CAN UNDERSTAND HIM. A TRANSLATOR.
HELP ME.
NEED HELMET...TO BREATHE.
PLEASE.
HELP SOMEONE WHO'S KILLED SO MANY?
--HURKK HURK--
ONE WRONG MOVE AND I TAKE IT BACK.
THANK... YOU...

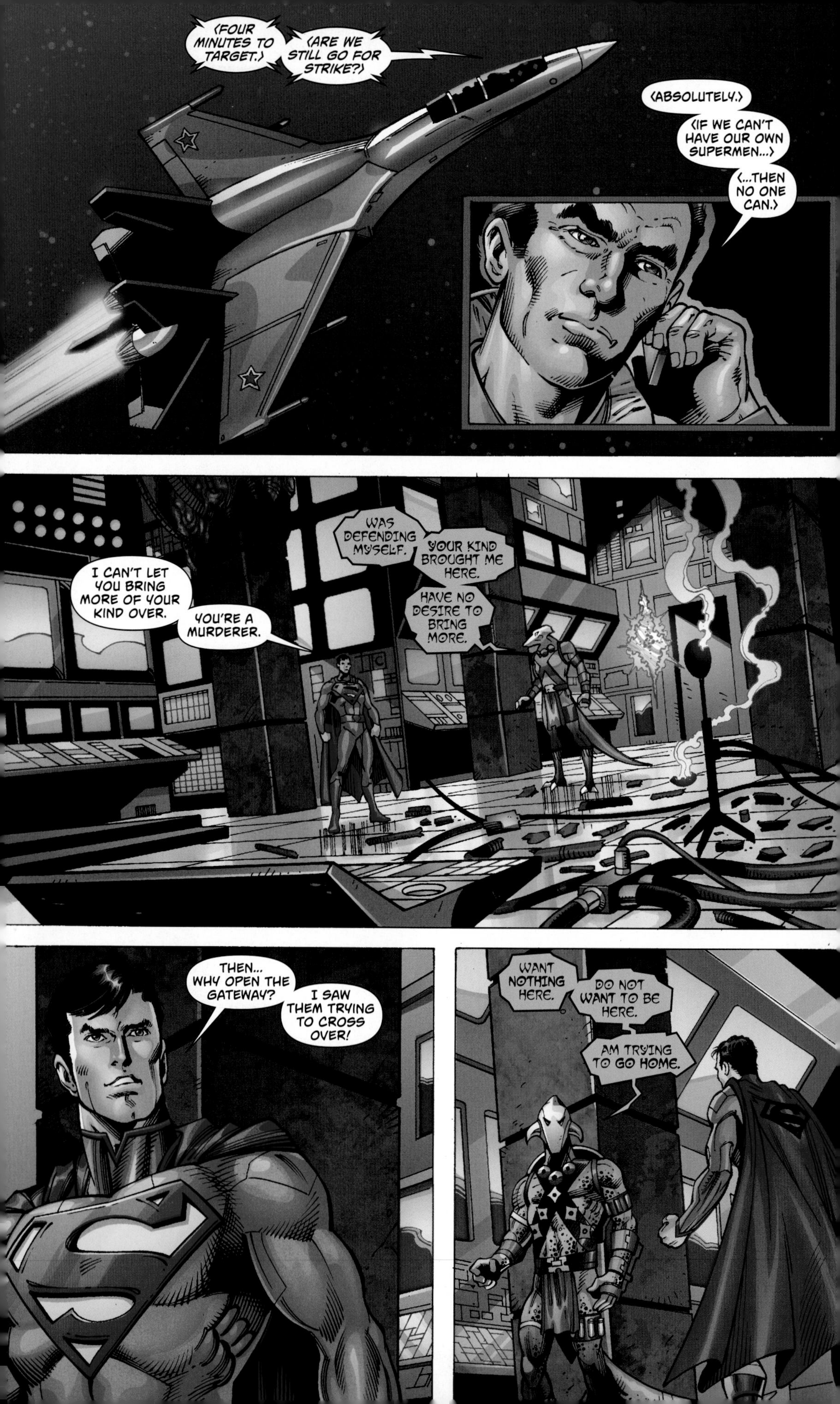
‹FOUR MINUTES TO TARGET.›
‹ARE WE STILL GO FOR STRIKE?›
‹ABSOLUTELY.›
‹IF WE CAN'T HAVE OUR OWN SUPERMEN...›
‹...THEN NO ONE CAN.›
I CAN'T LET YOU BRING MORE OF YOUR KIND OVER.
YOU'RE A MURDERER.
WAS DEFENDING MYSELF.
YOUR KIND BROUGHT ME HERE.
HAVE NO DESIRE TO BRING MORE.
THEN... WHY OPEN THE GATEWAY?
I SAW THEM TRYING TO CROSS OVER!
WANT NOTHING HERE.
DO NOT WANT TO BE HERE.
AM TRYING TO GO HOME.

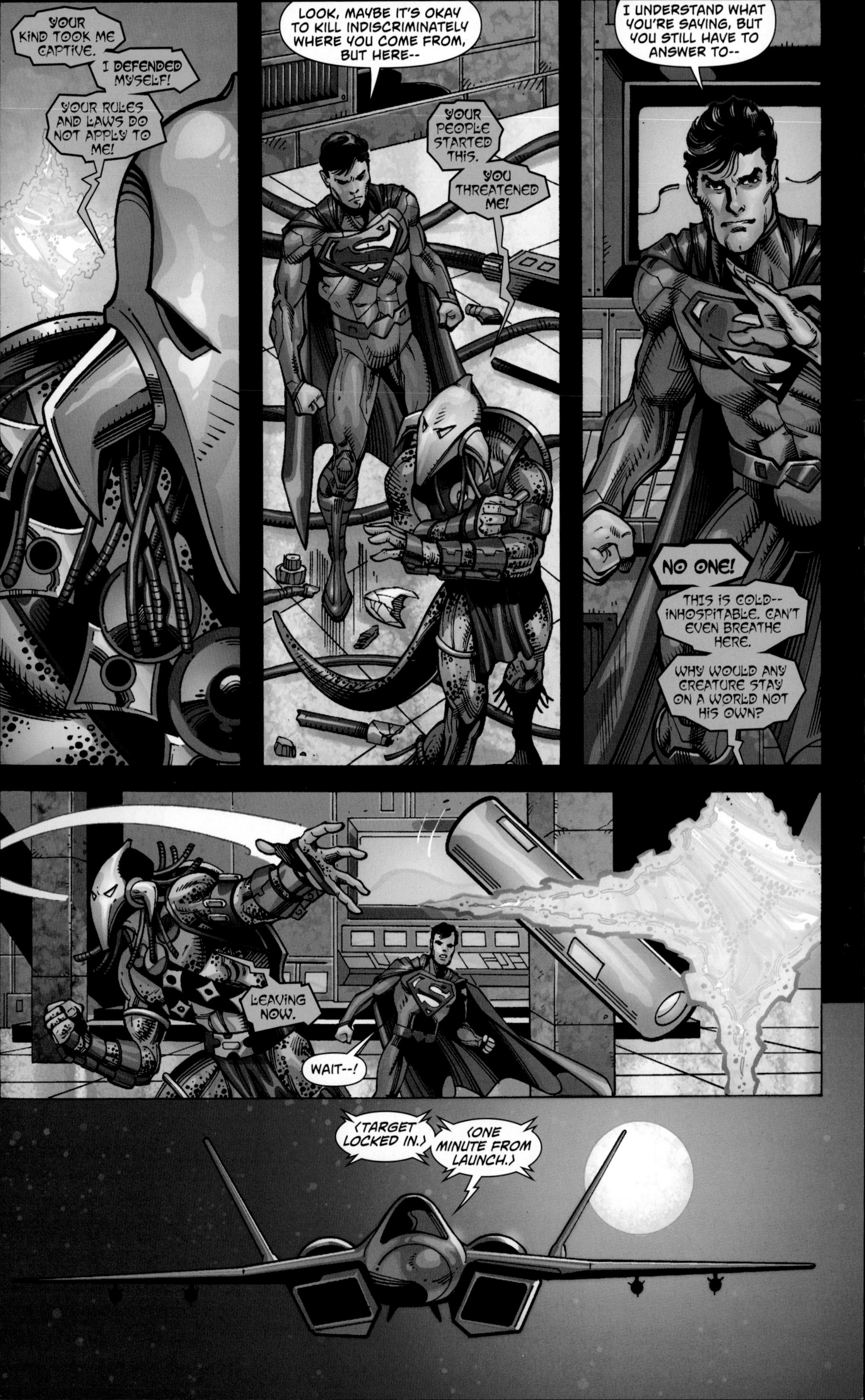
YOUR KIND TOOK ME CAPTIVE.
I DEFENDED MYSELF!
YOUR RULES AND LAWS DO NOT APPLY TO ME!
LOOK, MAYBE IT'S OKAY TO KILL INDISCRIMINATELY WHERE YOU COME FROM, BUT HERE--
YOUR PEOPLE STARTED THIS.
YOU THREATENED ME!
I UNDERSTAND WHAT YOU'RE SAYING, BUT YOU STILL HAVE TO ANSWER TO--
NO ONE!
THIS IS COLD-- INHOSPITABLE. CAN'T EVEN BREATHE HERE.
WHY WOULD ANY CREATURE STAY ON A WORLD NOT HIS OWN?
LEAVING NOW.
WAIT--!
‹TARGET LOCKED IN.›
‹ONE MINUTE FROM LAUNCH.›

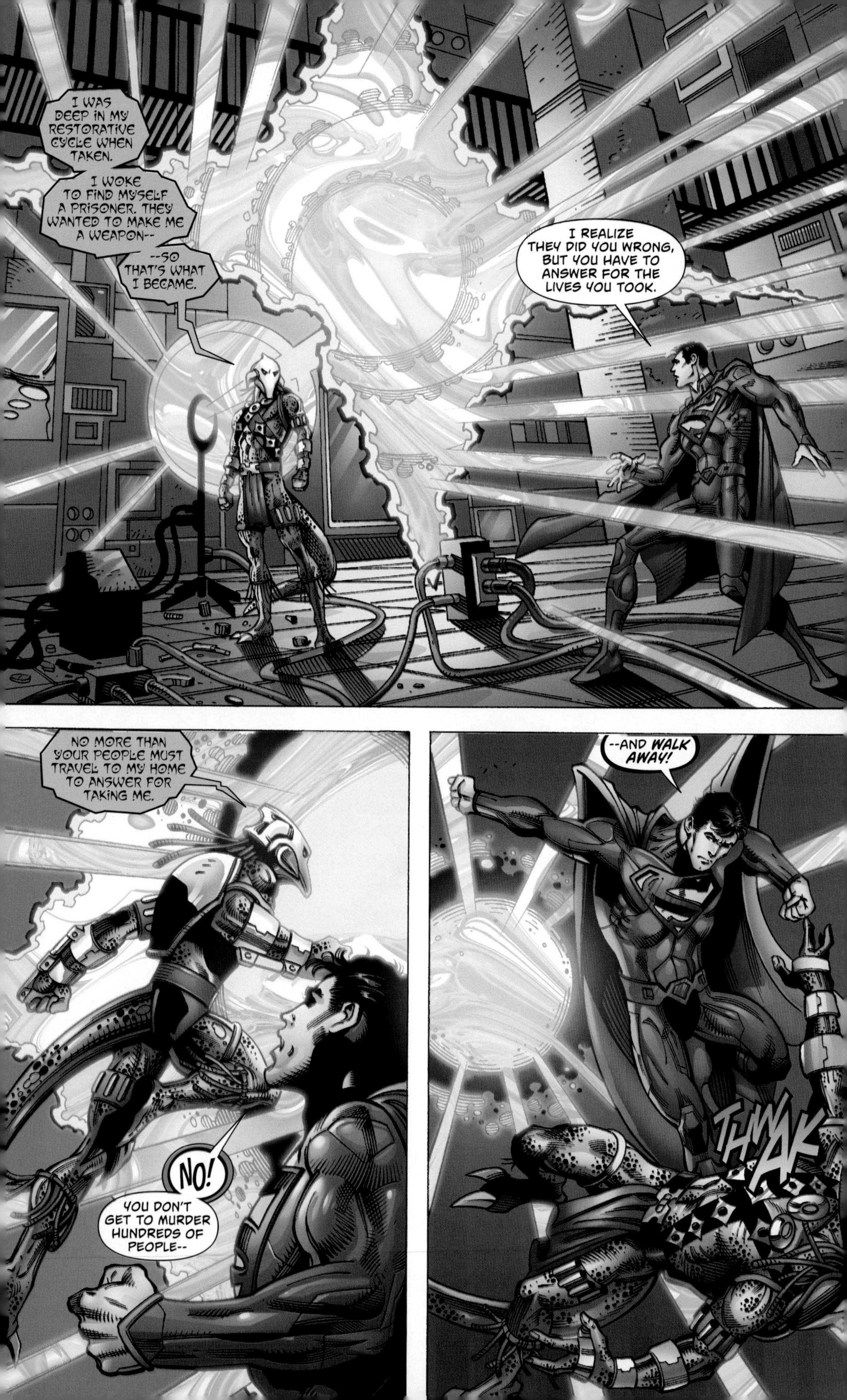
I WAS DEEP IN MY RESTORATIVE CYCLE WHEN TAKEN.
I WOKE TO FIND MYSELF A PRISONER. THEY WANTED TO MAKE ME A WEAPON--
--SO THAT'S WHAT I BECAME.
I REALIZE THEY DID YOU WRONG, BUT YOU HAVE TO ANSWER FOR THE LIVES YOU TOOK.
NO MORE THAN YOUR PEOPLE MUST TRAVEL TO MY HOME TO ANSWER FOR TAKING ME.
NO!
YOU DON'T GET TO MURDER HUNDREDS OF PEOPLE--
--AND WALK AWAY!
THWAK

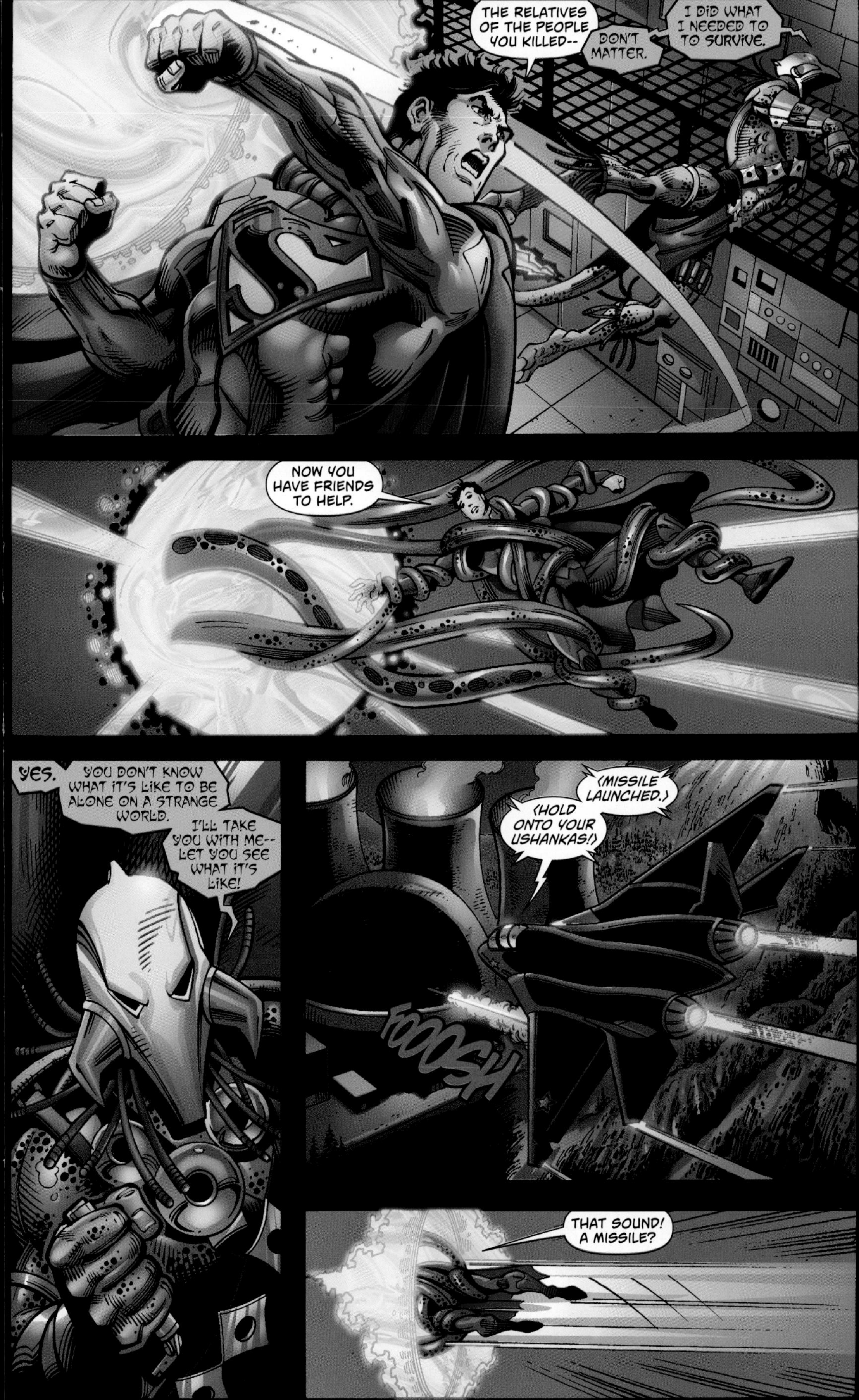
THE RELATIVES OF THE PEOPLE YOU KILLED--
DON'T MATTER.
I DID WHAT I NEEDED TO TO SURVIVE.
NOW YOU HAVE FRIENDS TO HELP.
YES.
YOU DON'T KNOW WHAT IT'S LIKE TO BE ALONE ON A STRANGE WORLD.
I'LL TAKE YOU WITH ME-- LET YOU SEE WHAT IT'S LIKE!
(MISSILE LAUNCHED.)
(HOLD ONTO YOUR USHANKAS!)
FOOOSH
THAT SOUND! A MISSILE?

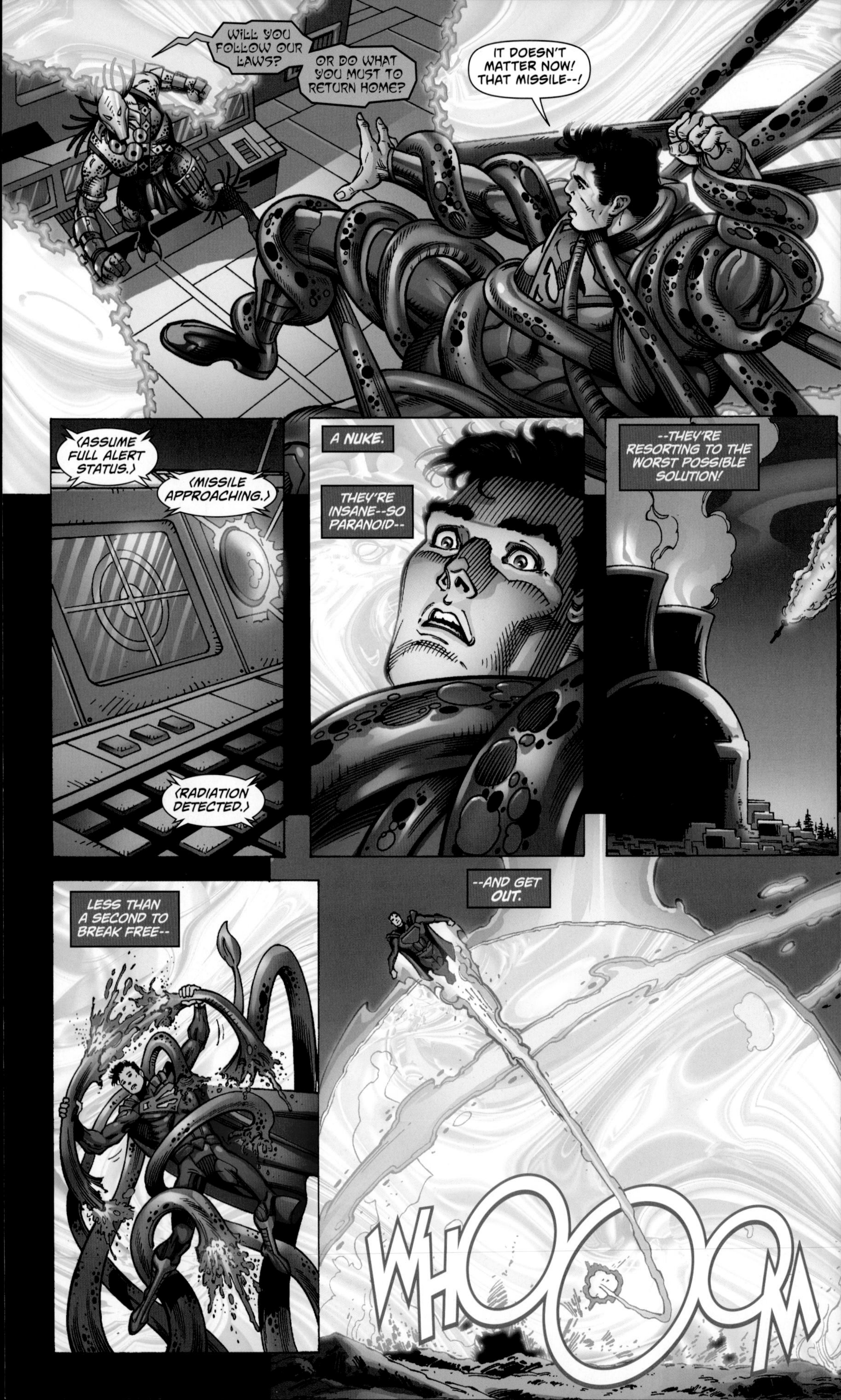
WILL YOU FOLLOW OUR LAWS?
OR DO WHAT YOU MUST TO RETURN HOME?
IT DOESN'T MATTER NOW! THAT MISSILE--!
(ASSUME FULL ALERT STATUS.)
(MISSILE APPROACHING.)
(RADIATION DETECTED.)
A NUKE.
THEY'RE INSANE--SO PARANOID--
--THEY'RE RESORTING TO THE WORST POSSIBLE SOLUTION!
LESS THAN A SECOND TO BREAK FREE--
--AND GET OUT.
WHOOOOM

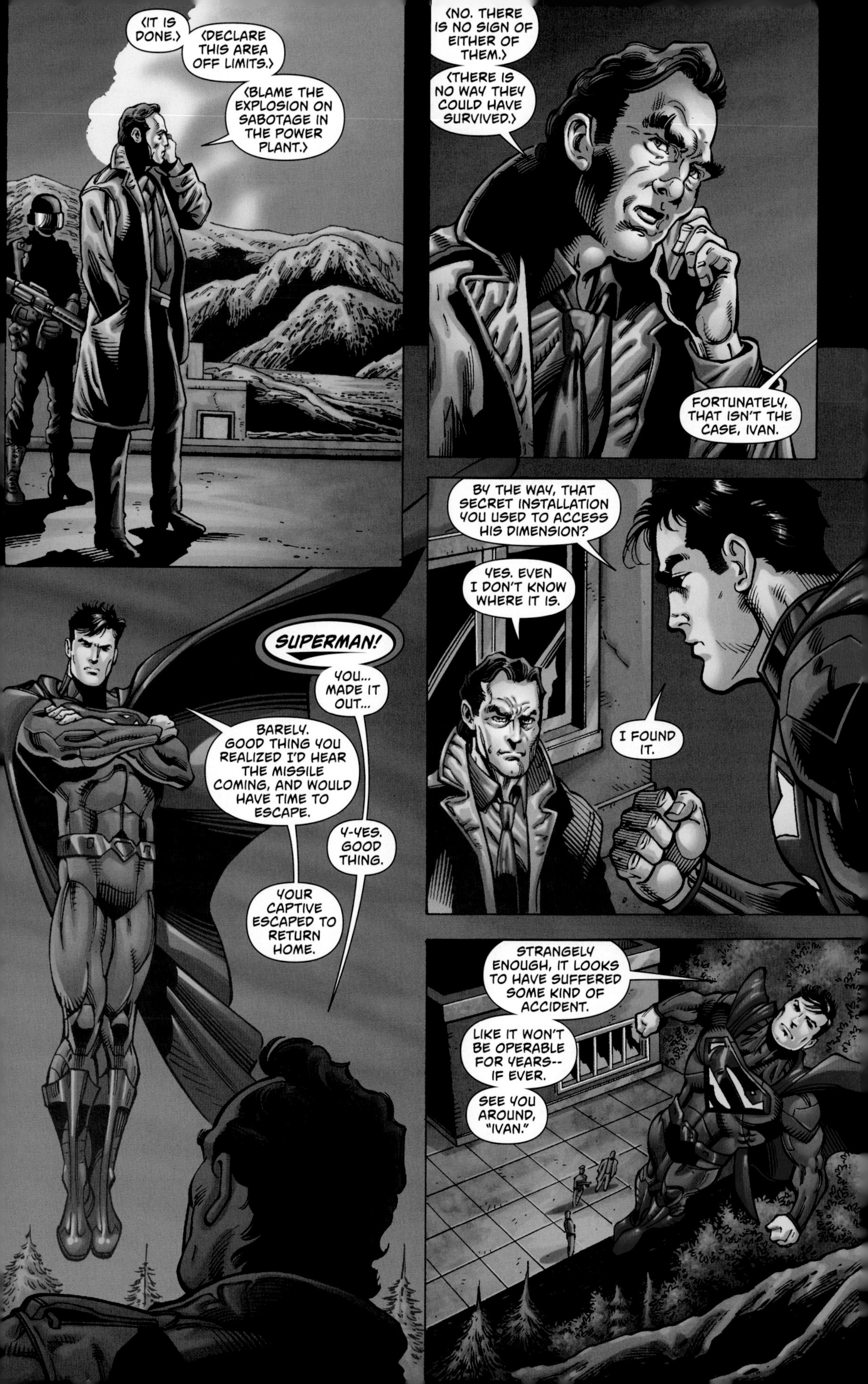
‹IT IS DONE.›
‹DECLARE THIS AREA OFF LIMITS.›
‹BLAME THE EXPLOSION ON SABOTAGE IN THE POWER PLANT.›
‹NO. THERE IS NO SIGN OF EITHER OF THEM.›
‹THERE IS NO WAY THEY COULD HAVE SURVIVED.›
FORTUNATELY, THAT ISN'T THE CASE, IVAN.
SUPERMAN!
YOU... MADE IT OUT...
BARELY. GOOD THING YOU REALIZED I'D HEAR THE MISSILE COMING, AND WOULD HAVE TIME TO ESCAPE.
Y-YES. GOOD THING.
YOUR CAPTIVE ESCAPED TO RETURN HOME.
BY THE WAY, THAT SECRET INSTALLATION YOU USED TO ACCESS HIS DIMENSION?
YES. EVEN I DON'T KNOW WHERE IT IS.
I FOUND IT.
STRANGELY ENOUGH, IT LOOKS TO HAVE SUFFERED SOME KIND OF ACCIDENT.
LIKE IT WON'T BE OPERABLE FOR YEARS-- IF EVER.
SEE YOU AROUND, "IVAN."

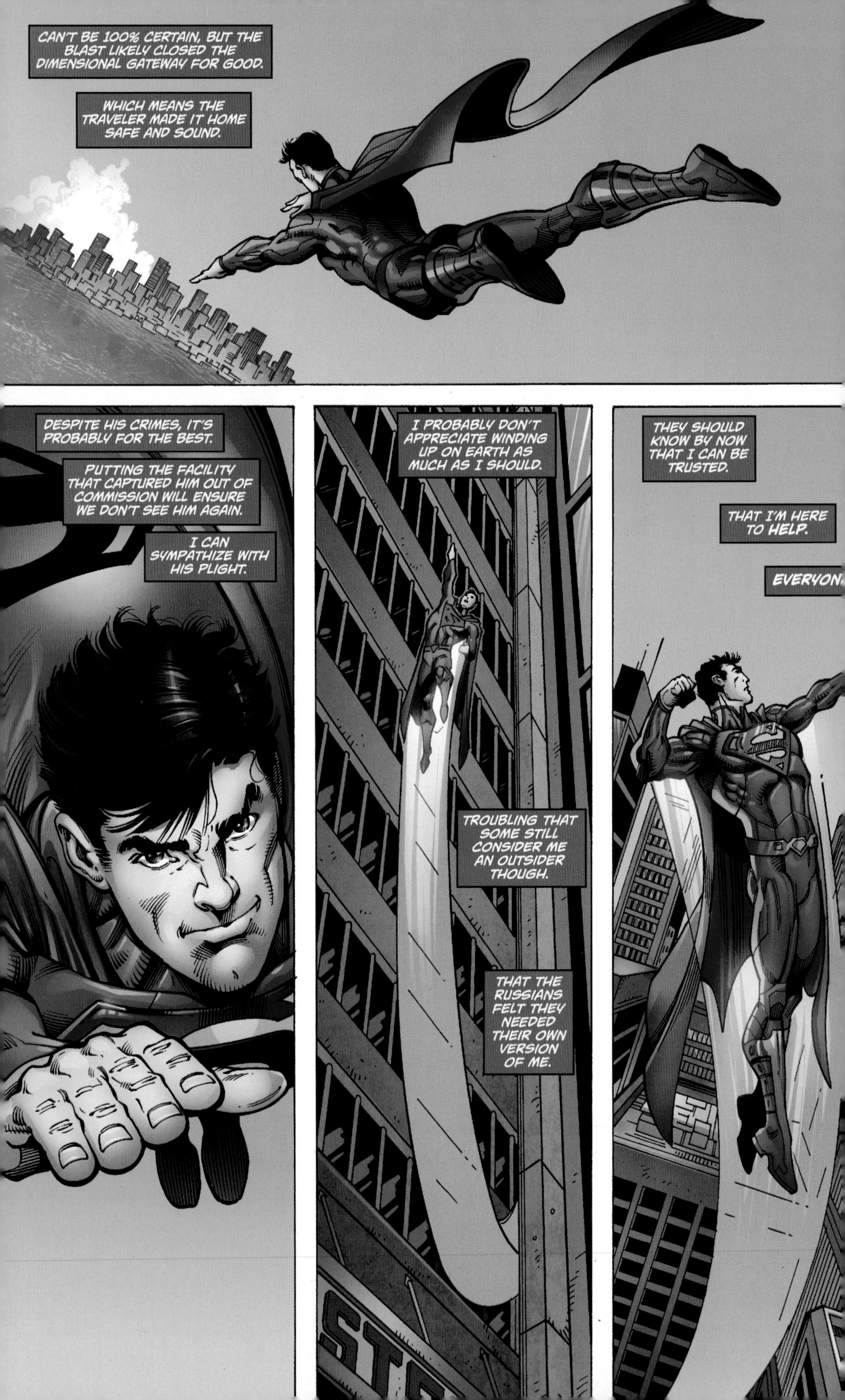
CAN'T BE 100% CERTAIN, BUT THE BLAST LIKELY CLOSED THE DIMENSIONAL GATEWAY FOR GOOD.
WHICH MEANS THE TRAVELER MADE IT HOME SAFE AND SOUND.
DESPITE HIS CRIMES, IT'S PROBABLY FOR THE BEST.
PUTTING THE FACILITY THAT CAPTURED HIM OUT OF COMMISSION WILL ENSURE WE DON'T SEE HIM AGAIN.
I CAN SYMPATHIZE WITH HIS PLIGHT.
I PROBABLY DON'T APPRECIATE WINDING UP ON EARTH AS MUCH AS I SHOULD.
TROUBLING THAT SOME STILL CONSIDER ME AN OUTSIDER THOUGH.
THAT THE RUSSIANS FELT THEY NEEDED THEIR OWN VERSION OF ME.
THEY SHOULD KNOW BY NOW THAT I CAN BE TRUSTED.
THAT I'M HERE TO HELP.
EVERYON

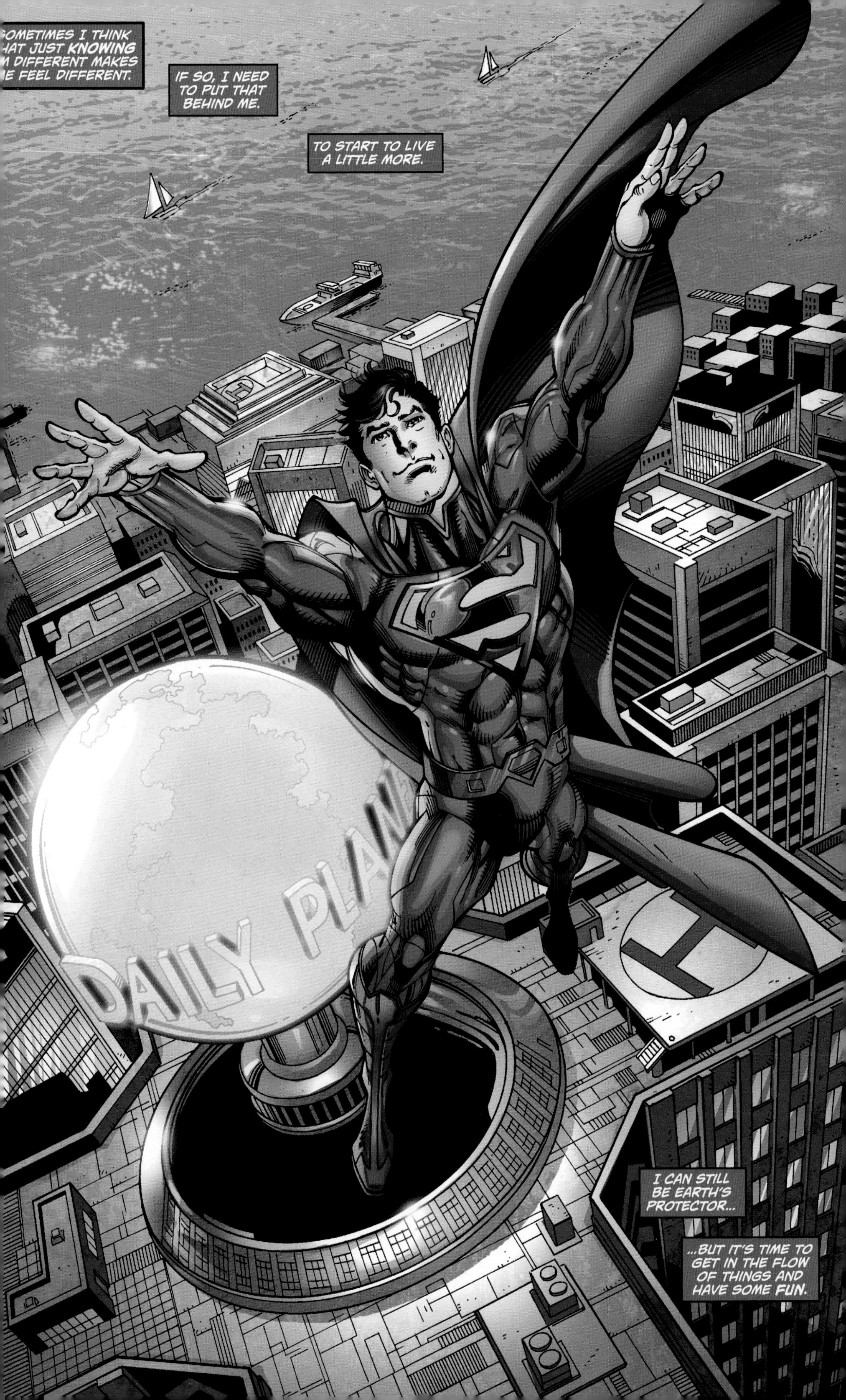
SOMETIMES I THINK THAT JUST KNOWING I'M DIFFERENT MAKES ME FEEL DIFFERENT.
IF SO, I NEED TO PUT THAT BEHIND ME.
TO START TO LIVE A LITTLE MORE.
DAILY PLAN
I CAN STILL BE EARTH'S PROTECTOR...
...BUT IT'S TIME TO GET IN THE FLOW OF THINGS AND HAVE SOME FUN.

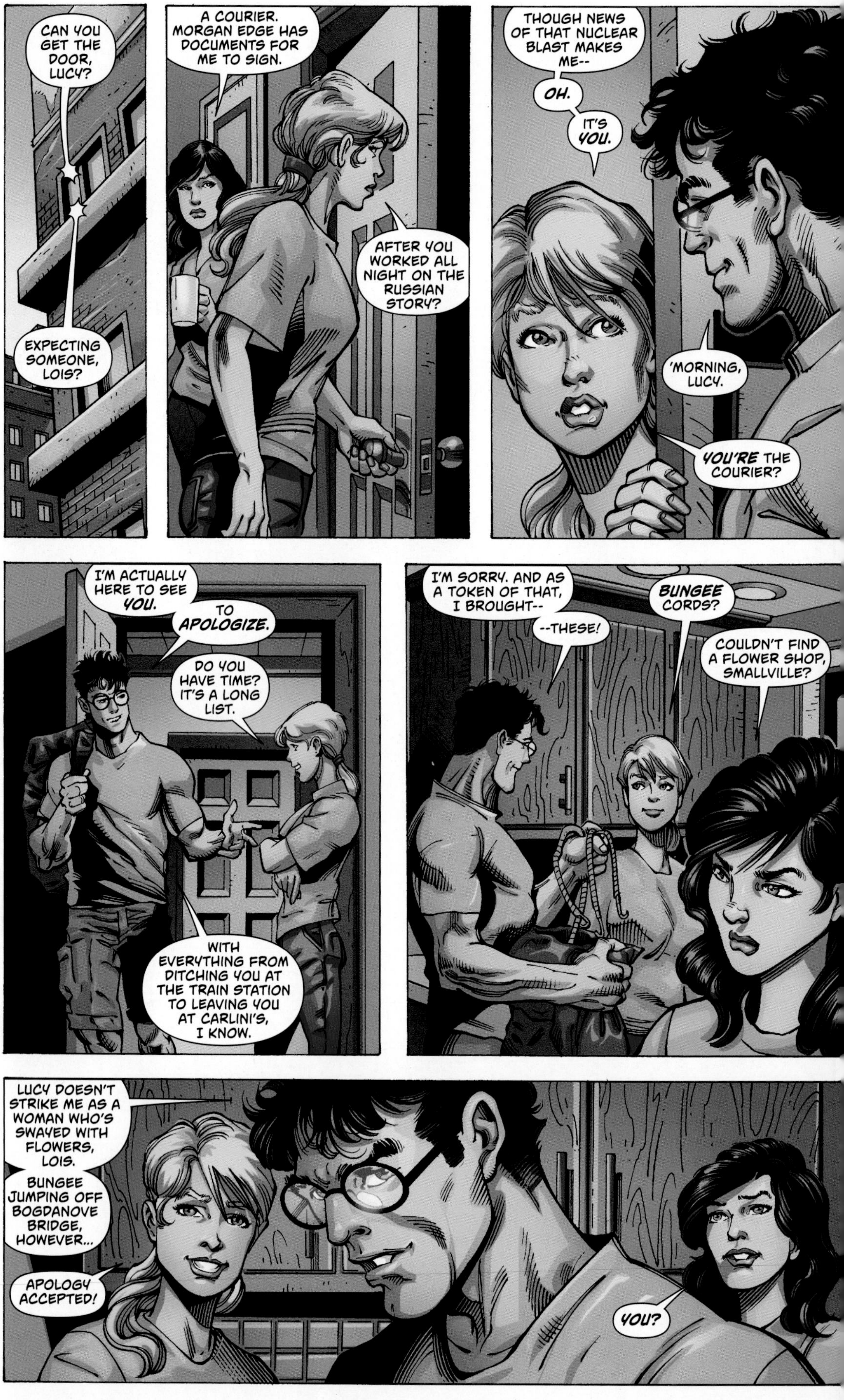
CAN YOU GET THE DOOR, LUCY?
EXPECTING SOMEONE, LOIS?
A COURIER. MORGAN EDGE HAS DOCUMENTS FOR ME TO SIGN.
AFTER YOU WORKED ALL NIGHT ON THE RUSSIAN STORY?
THOUGH NEWS OF THAT NUCLEAR BLAST MAKES ME--
OH.
IT'S YOU.
'MORNING, LUCY.
YOU'RE THE COURIER?
I'M ACTUALLY HERE TO SEE YOU.
TO APOLOGIZE.
DO YOU HAVE TIME? IT'S A LONG LIST.
WITH EVERYTHING FROM DITCHING YOU AT THE TRAIN STATION TO LEAVING YOU AT CARLINI'S, I KNOW.
I'M SORRY. AND AS A TOKEN OF THAT, I BROUGHT--
--THESE!
BUNGEE CORDS?
COULDN'T FIND A FLOWER SHOP, SMALLVILLE?
LUCY DOESN'T STRIKE ME AS A WOMAN WHO'S SWAYED WITH FLOWERS, LOIS.
BUNGEE JUMPING OFF BOGDANOVE BRIDGE, HOWEVER...
APOLOGY ACCEPTED!
YOU?

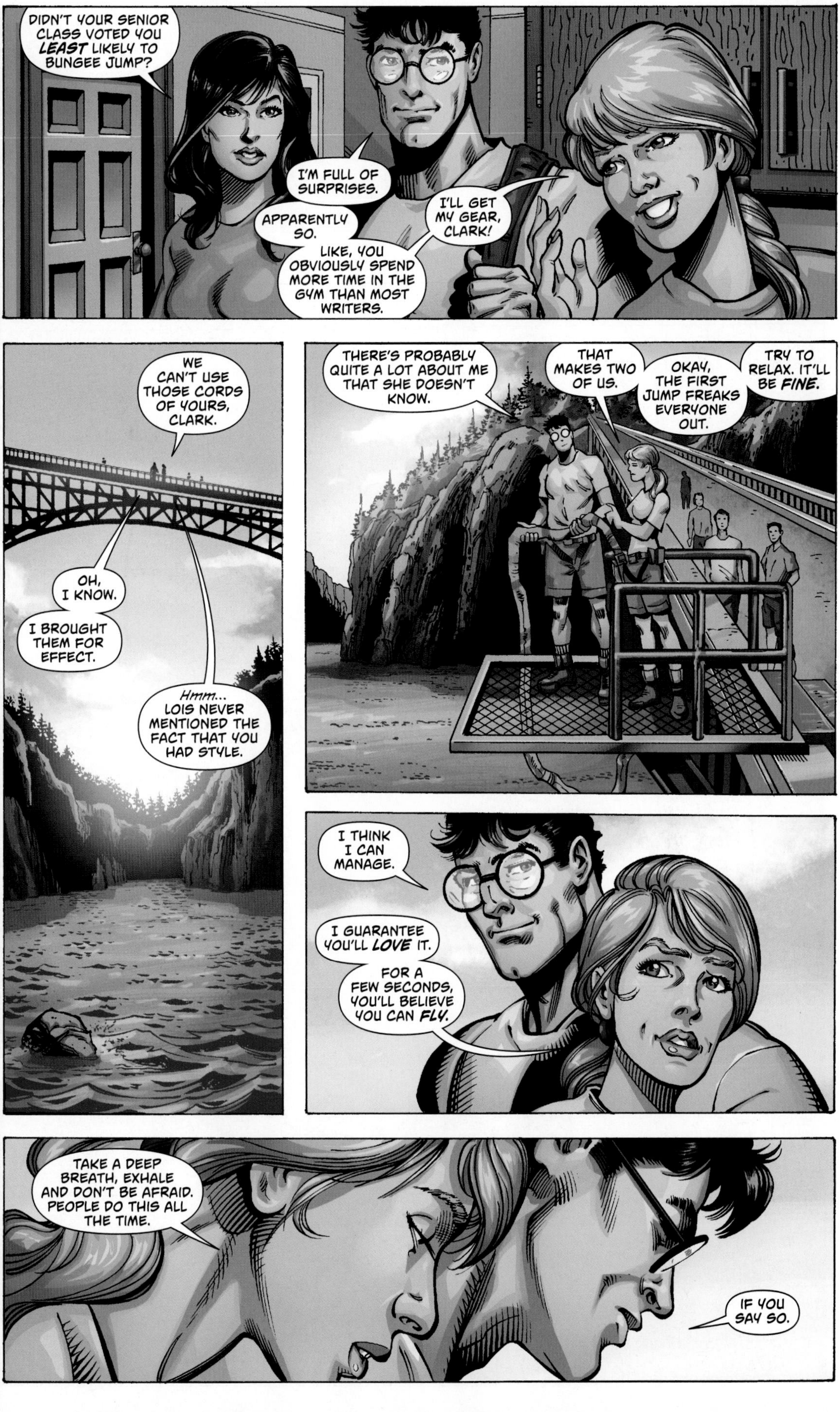
DIDN'T YOUR SENIOR CLASS VOTED YOU LEAST LIKELY TO BUNGEE JUMP?
I'M FULL OF SURPRISES.
APPARENTLY SO.
LIKE, YOU OBVIOUSLY SPEND MORE TIME IN THE GYM THAN MOST WRITERS.
I'LL GET MY GEAR, CLARK!
WE CAN'T USE THOSE CORDS OF YOURS, CLARK.
OH, I KNOW.
I BROUGHT THEM FOR EFFECT.
Hmm... LOIS NEVER MENTIONED THE FACT THAT YOU HAD STYLE.
THERE'S PROBABLY QUITE A LOT ABOUT ME THAT SHE DOESN'T KNOW.
THAT MAKES TWO OF US.
OKAY, THE FIRST JUMP FREAKS EVERYONE OUT.
TRY TO RELAX. IT'LL BE FINE.
I THINK I CAN MANAGE.
I GUARANTEE YOU'LL LOVE IT.
FOR A FEW SECONDS, YOU'LL BELIEVE YOU CAN FLY.
TAKE A DEEP BREATH, EXHALE AND DON'T BE AFRAID. PEOPLE DO THIS ALL THE TIME.
IF YOU SAY SO.

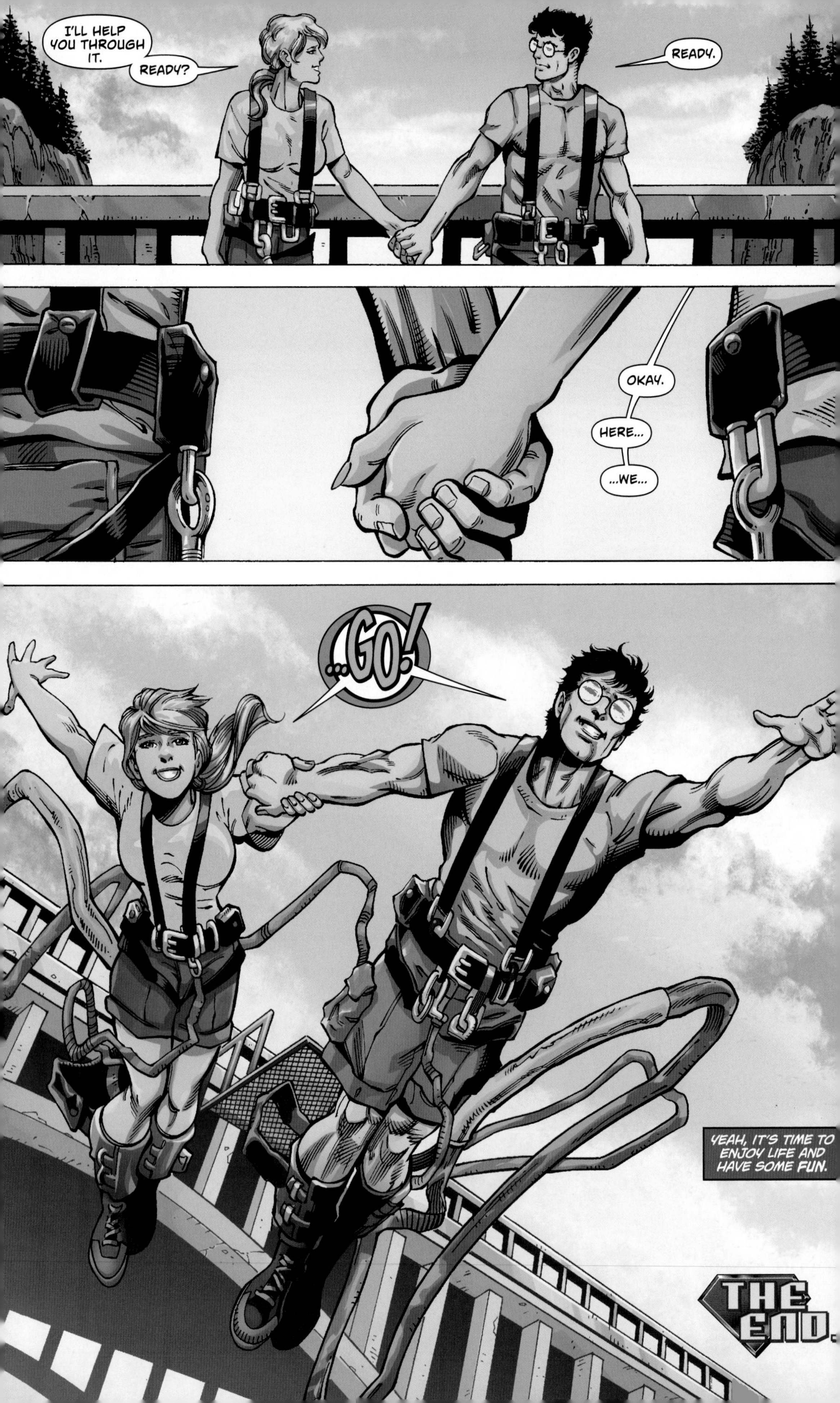
I'LL HELP YOU THROUGH IT.
READY?
READY.
OKAY.
HERE...
...WE...
...GO!
YEAH, IT'S TIME TO ENJOY LIFE AND HAVE SOME FUN.
THE END.

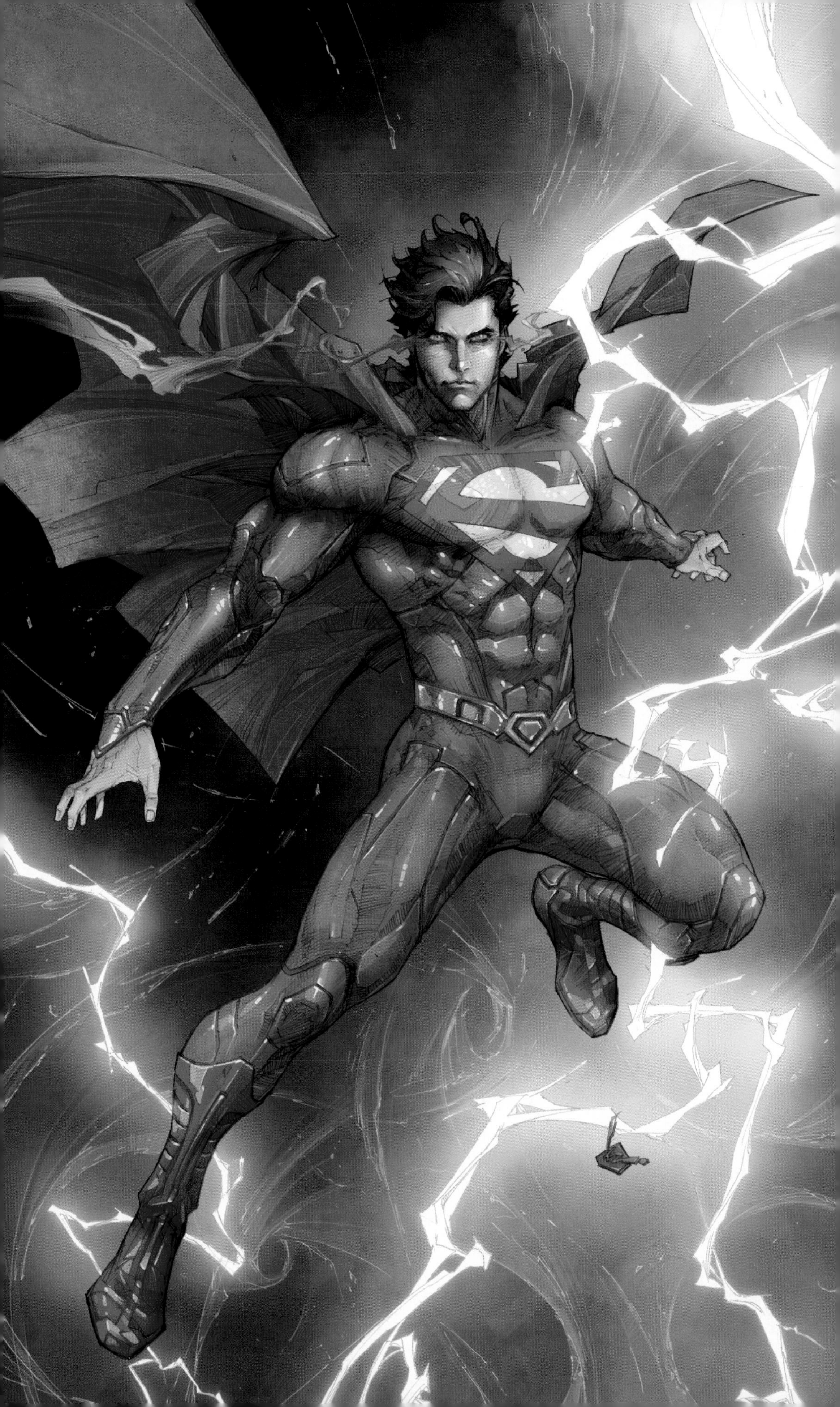

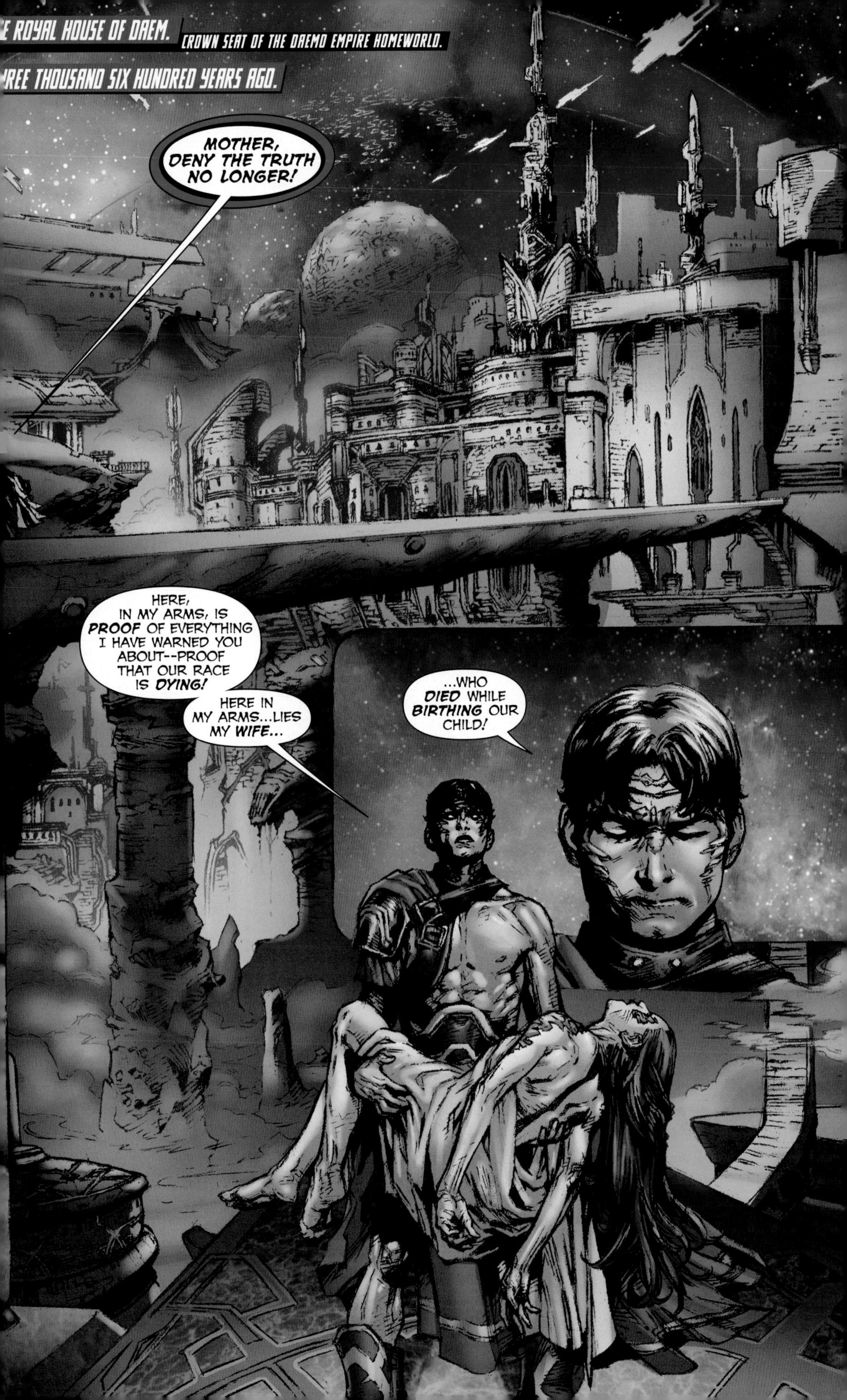

E ROYAL HOUSE OF DAEM.
CROWN SEAT OF THE DAEMO EMPIRE HOMEWORLD.
REE THOUSAND SIX HUNDRED YEARS AGO.
MOTHER, DENY THE TRUTH NO LONGER!
HERE, IN MY ARMS, IS PROOF OF EVERYTHING I HAVE WARNED YOU ABOUT--PROOF THAT OUR RACE IS DYING!
HERE IN MY ARMS...LIES MY WIFE...
...WHO DIED WHILE BIRTHING OUR CHILD!

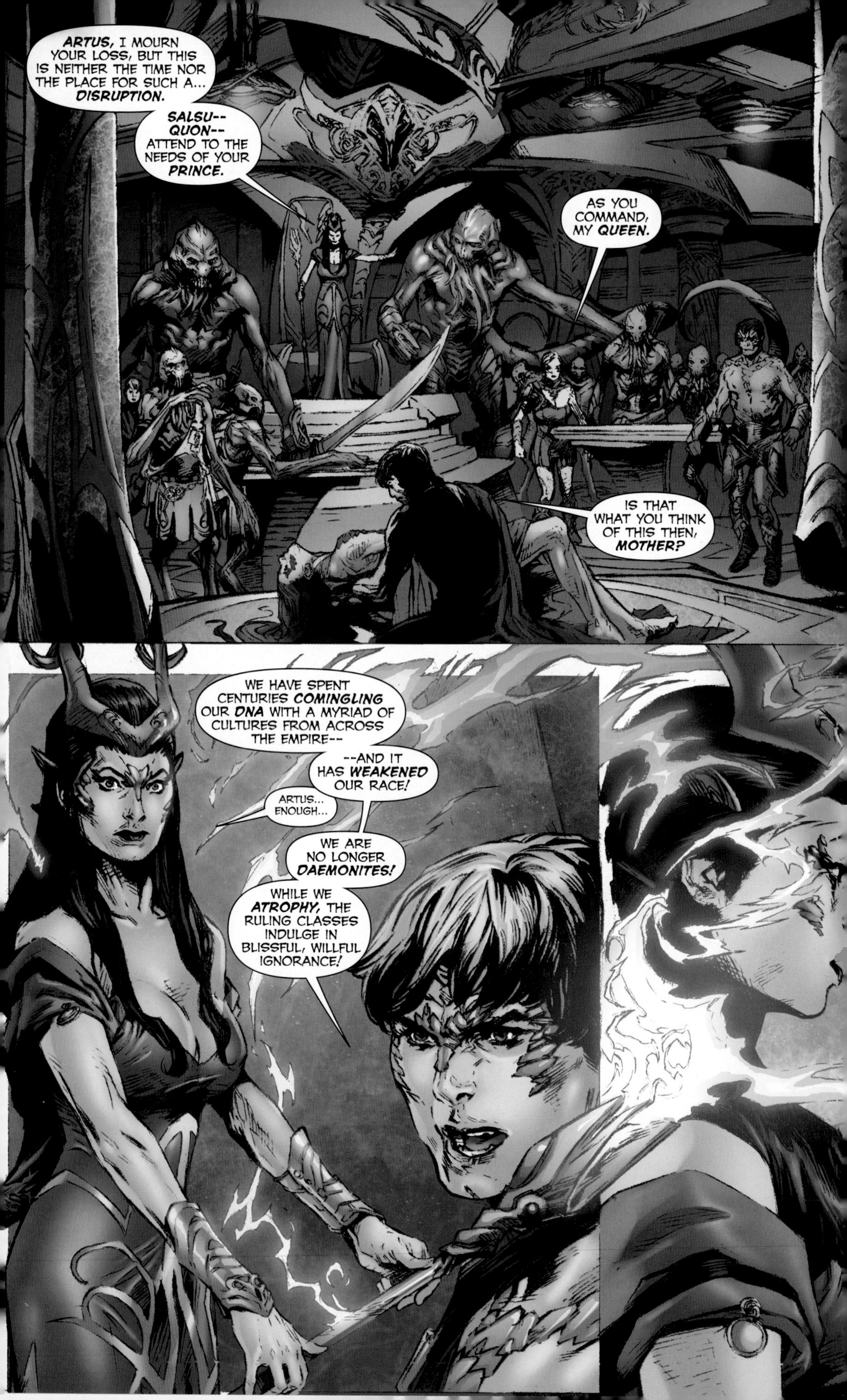
ARTUS, I MOURN YOUR LOSS, BUT THIS IS NEITHER THE TIME NOR THE PLACE FOR SUCH A... DISRUPTION.
SALSU-- QUON-- ATTEND TO THE NEEDS OF YOUR PRINCE.
AS YOU COMMAND, MY QUEEN.
IS THAT WHAT YOU THINK OF THIS THEN, MOTHER?
WE HAVE SPENT CENTURIES COMINGLING OUR DNA WITH A MYRIAD OF CULTURES FROM ACROSS THE EMPIRE--
--AND IT HAS WEAKENED OUR RACE!
ARTUS... ENOUGH...
WE ARE NO LONGER DAEMONITES!
WHILE WE ATROPHY, THE RULING CLASSES INDULGE IN BLISSFUL, WILLFUL IGNORANCE!

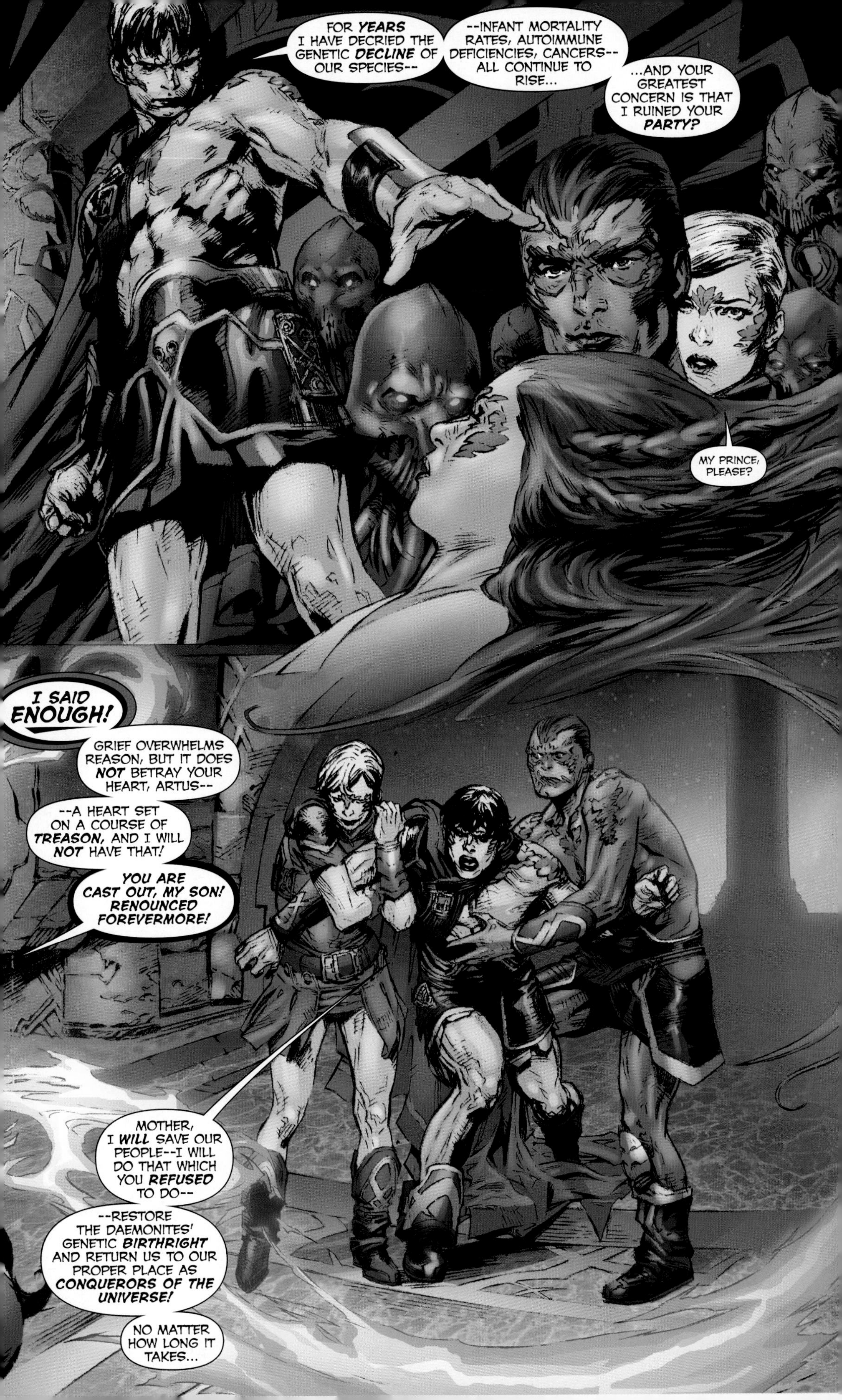

FOR YEARS I HAVE DECRIED THE GENETIC DECLINE OF OUR SPECIES--
--INFANT MORTALITY RATES, AUTOIMMUNE DEFICIENCIES, CANCERS-- ALL CONTINUE TO RISE...
...AND YOUR GREATEST CONCERN IS THAT I RUINED YOUR PARTY?
MY PRINCE, PLEASE?
I SAID ENOUGH!
GRIEF OVERWHELMS REASON, BUT IT DOES NOT BETRAY YOUR HEART, ARTUS--
--A HEART SET ON A COURSE OF TREASON, AND I WILL NOT HAVE THAT!
YOU ARE CAST OUT, MY SON! RENOUNCED FOREVERMORE!
MOTHER, I WILL SAVE OUR PEOPLE--I WILL DO THAT WHICH YOU REFUSED TO DO--
--RESTORE THE DAEMONITES' GENETIC BIRTHRIGHT AND RETURN US TO OUR PROPER PLACE AS CONQUERORS OF THE UNIVERSE!
NO MATTER HOW LONG IT TAKES...

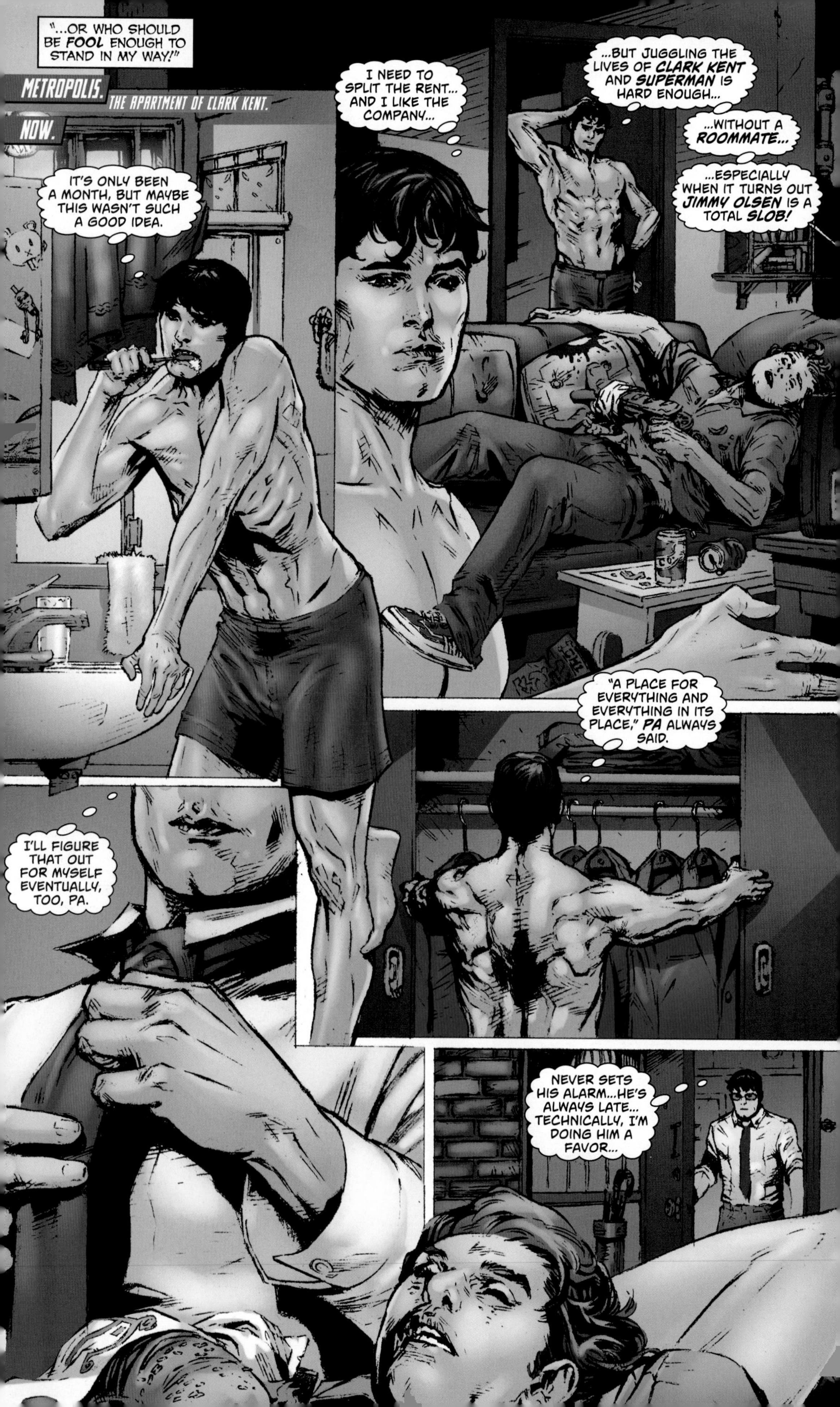

"...OR WHO SHOULD BE FOOL ENOUGH TO STAND IN MY WAY!"
METROPOLIS.
THE APARTMENT OF CLARK KENT.
NOW.
IT'S ONLY BEEN A MONTH, BUT MAYBE THIS WASN'T SUCH A GOOD IDEA.
I NEED TO SPLIT THE RENT... AND I LIKE THE COMPANY...
...BUT JUGGLING THE LIVES OF CLARK KENT AND SUPERMAN IS HARD ENOUGH...
...WITHOUT A ROOMMATE...
...ESPECIALLY WHEN IT TURNS OUT JIMMY OLSEN IS A TOTAL SLOB!
"A PLACE FOR EVERYTHING AND EVERYTHING IN ITS PLACE," PA ALWAYS SAID.
I'LL FIGURE THAT OUT FOR MYSELF EVENTUALLY, TOO, PA.
NEVER SETS HIS ALARM...HE'S ALWAYS LATE... TECHNICALLY, I'M DOING HIM A FAVOR...

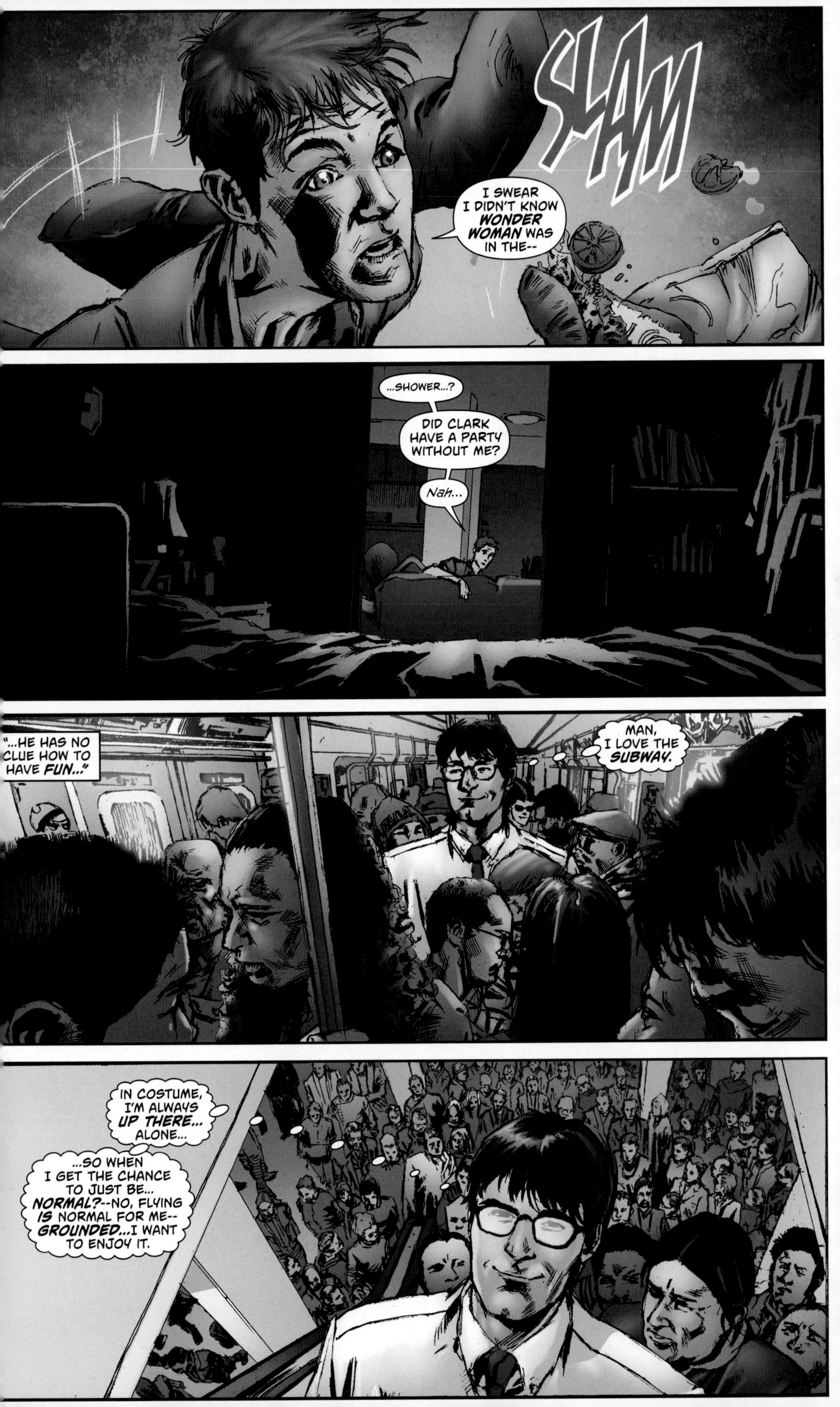
SLAM
I SWEAR I DIDN'T KNOW WONDER WOMAN WAS IN THE--
...SHOWER...?
DID CLARK HAVE A PARTY WITHOUT ME?
Nah...
"...HE HAS NO CLUE HOW TO HAVE FUN..."
MAN, I LOVE THE SUBWAY.
IN COSTUME, I'M ALWAYS UP THERE... ALONE...
...SO WHEN I GET THE CHANCE TO JUST BE... NORMAL?--NO, FLYING IS NORMAL FOR ME-- GROUNDED...I WANT TO ENJOY IT.

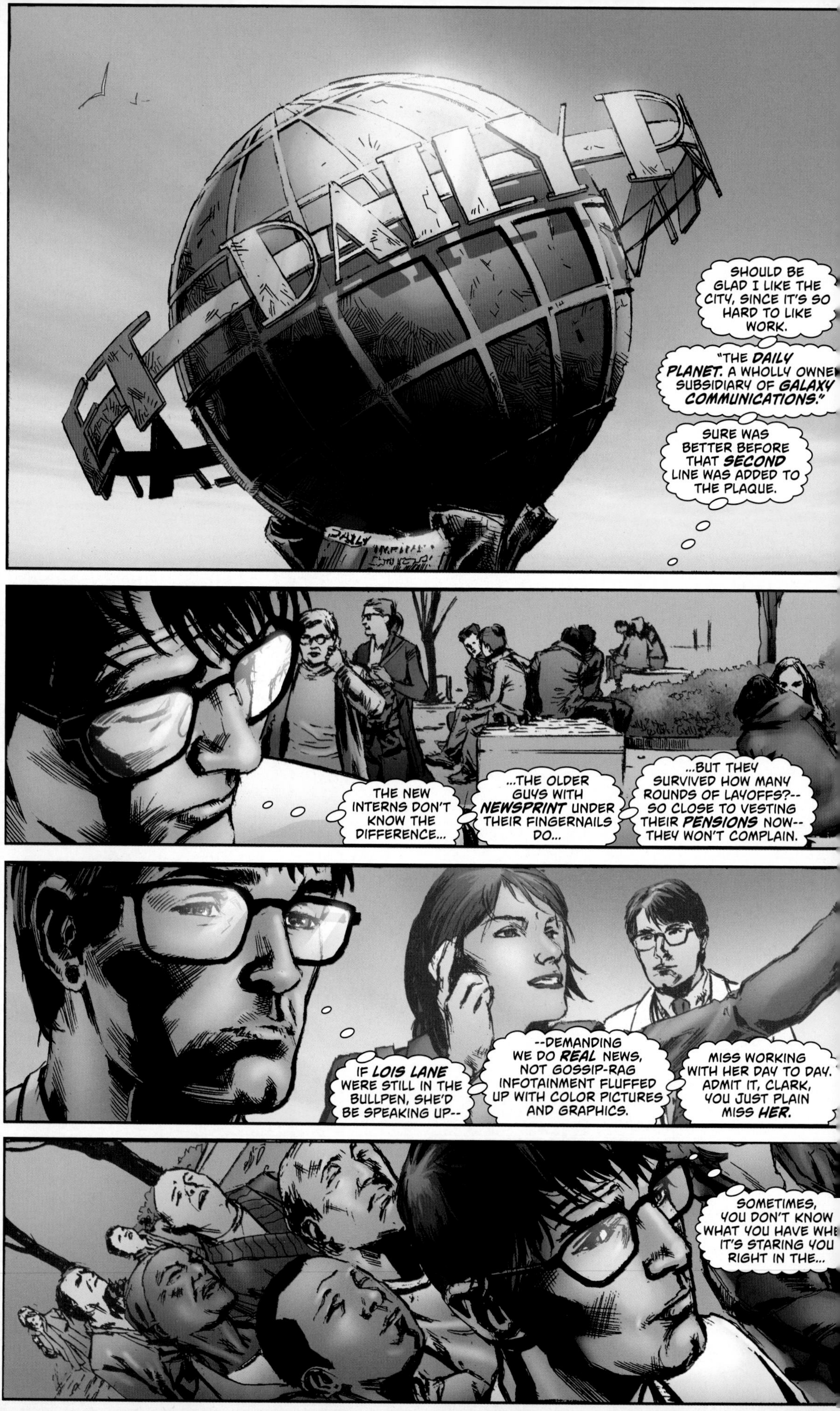

SHOULD BE GLAD I LIKE THE CITY, SINCE IT'S SO HARD TO LIKE WORK.
"THE DAILY PLANET. A WHOLLY OWNE SUBSIDIARY OF GALAXY COMMUNICATIONS."
SURE WAS BETTER BEFORE THAT SECOND LINE WAS ADDED TO THE PLAQUE.
THE NEW INTERNS DON'T KNOW THE DIFFERENCE...
...THE OLDER GUYS WITH NEWSPRINT UNDER THEIR FINGERNAILS DO...
...BUT THEY SURVIVED HOW MANY ROUNDS OF LAYOFFS?--SO CLOSE TO VESTING THEIR PENSIONS NOW--THEY WON'T COMPLAIN.
IF LOIS LANE WERE STILL IN THE BULLPEN, SHE'D BE SPEAKING UP--
--DEMANDING WE DO REAL NEWS, NOT GOSSIP-RAG INFOTAINMENT FLUFFED UP WITH COLOR PICTURES AND GRAPHICS.
MISS WORKING WITH HER DAY TO DAY. ADMIT IT, CLARK, YOU JUST PLAIN MISS HER.
SOMETIMES, YOU DON'T KNOW WHAT YOU HAVE WHE IT'S STARING YOU RIGHT IN THE...

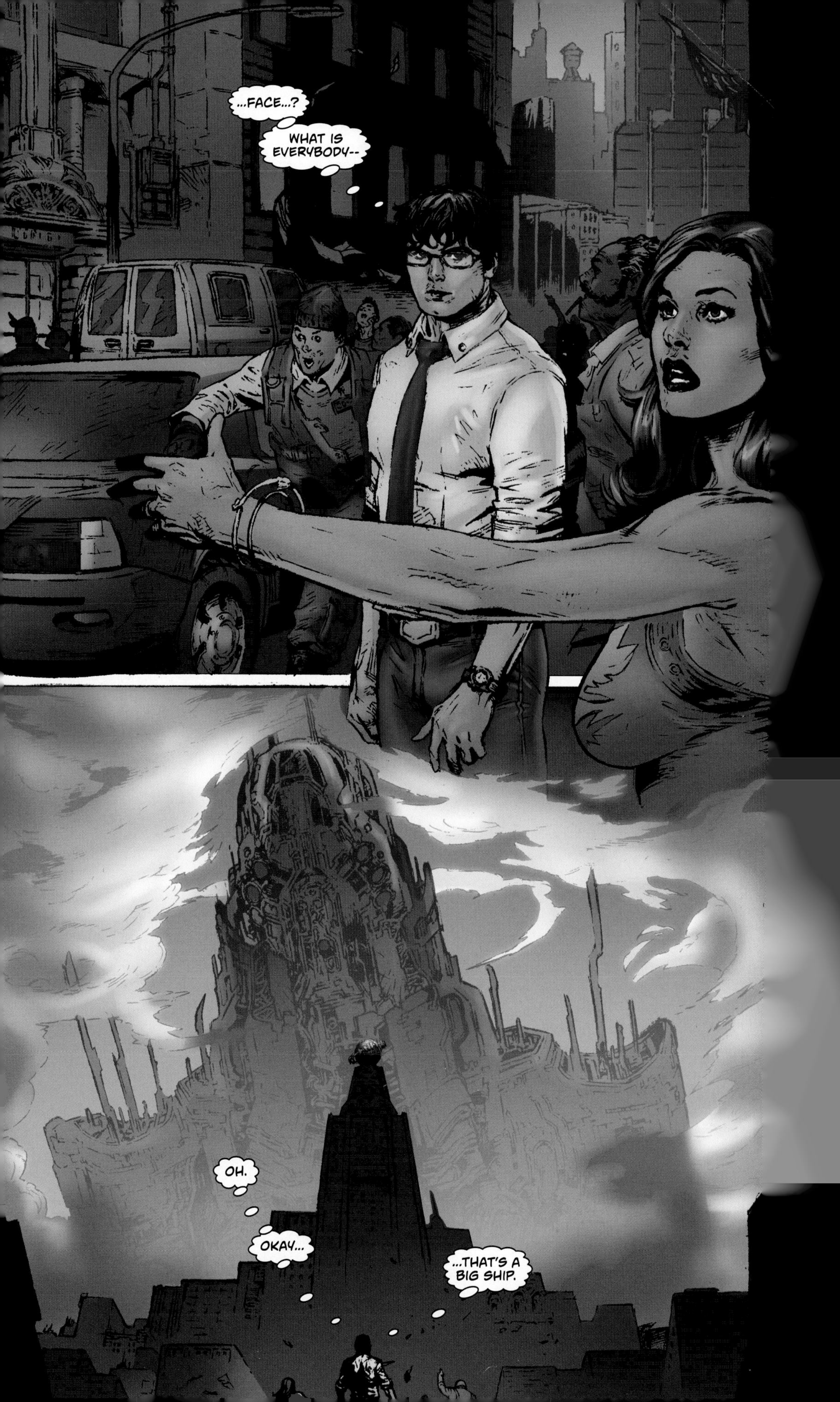
...FACE...?
WHAT IS EVERYBODY--
OH.
OKAY...
...THAT'S A BIG SHIP.

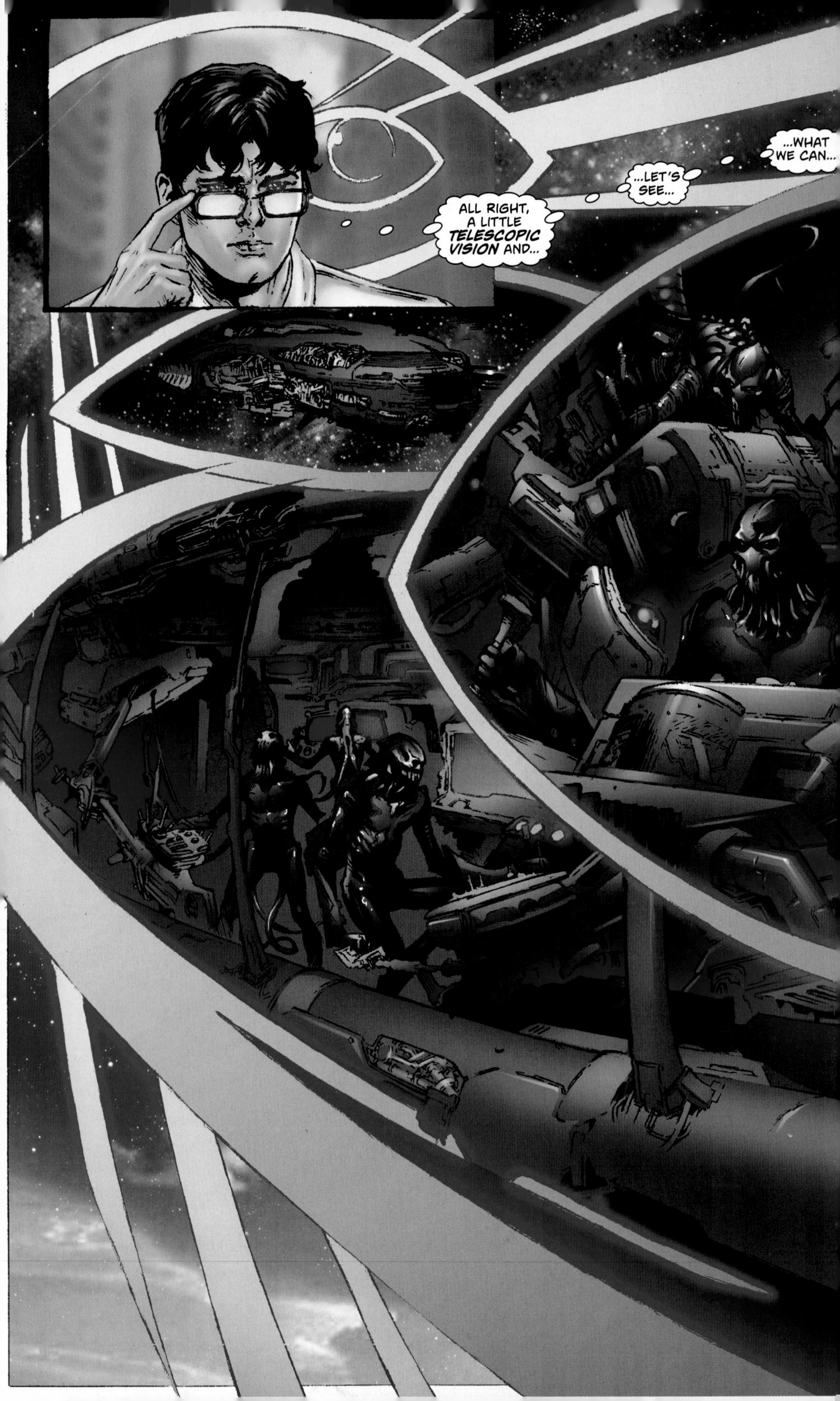

ALL RIGHT, A LITTLE TELESCOPIC VISION AND...
...LET'S SEE...
...WHAT WE CAN...

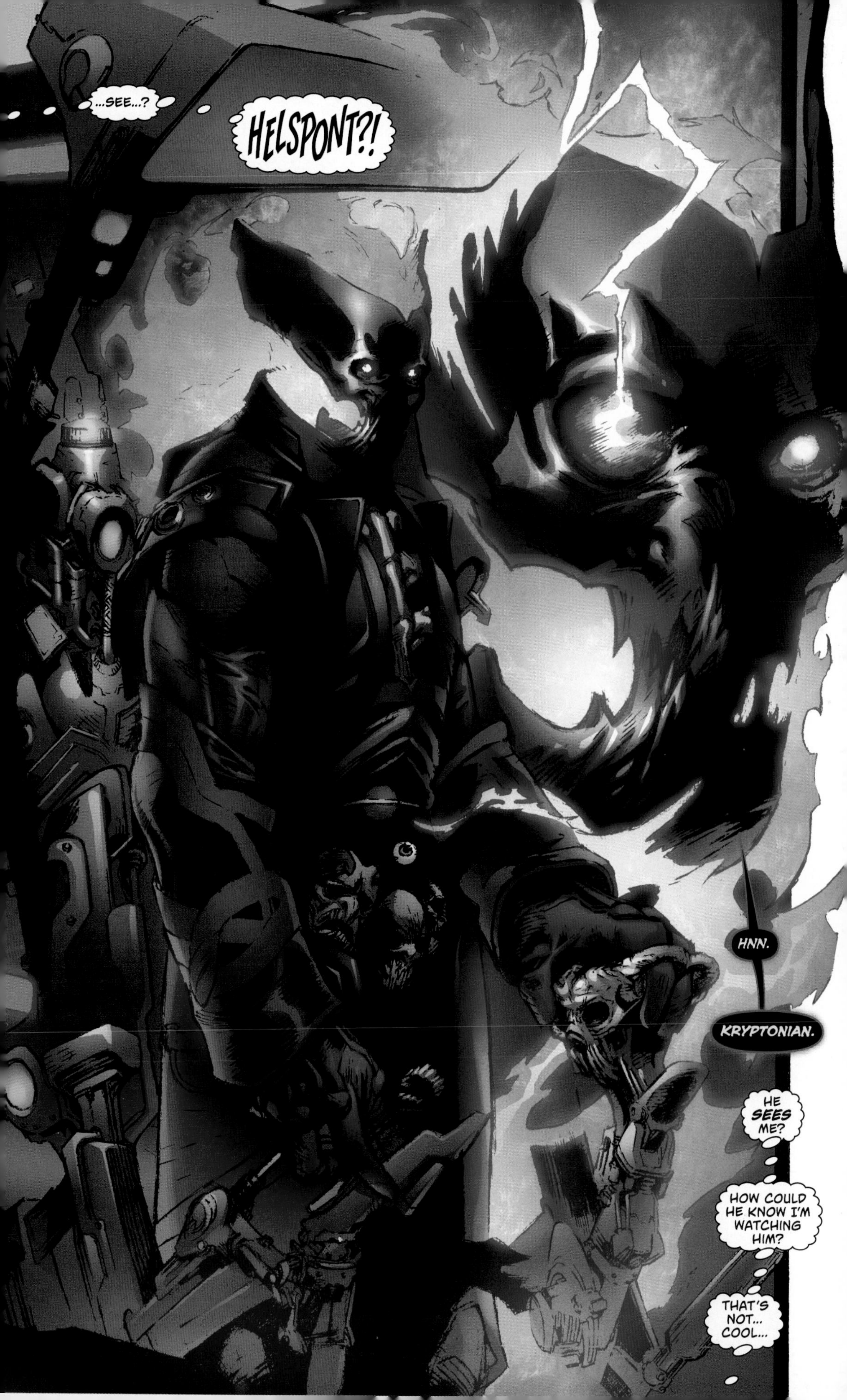
...SEE...?
HELSPONT?!
HNN.
KRYPTONIAN.
HE SEES ME?
HOW COULD HE KNOW I'M WATCHING HIM?
THAT'S NOT... COOL...

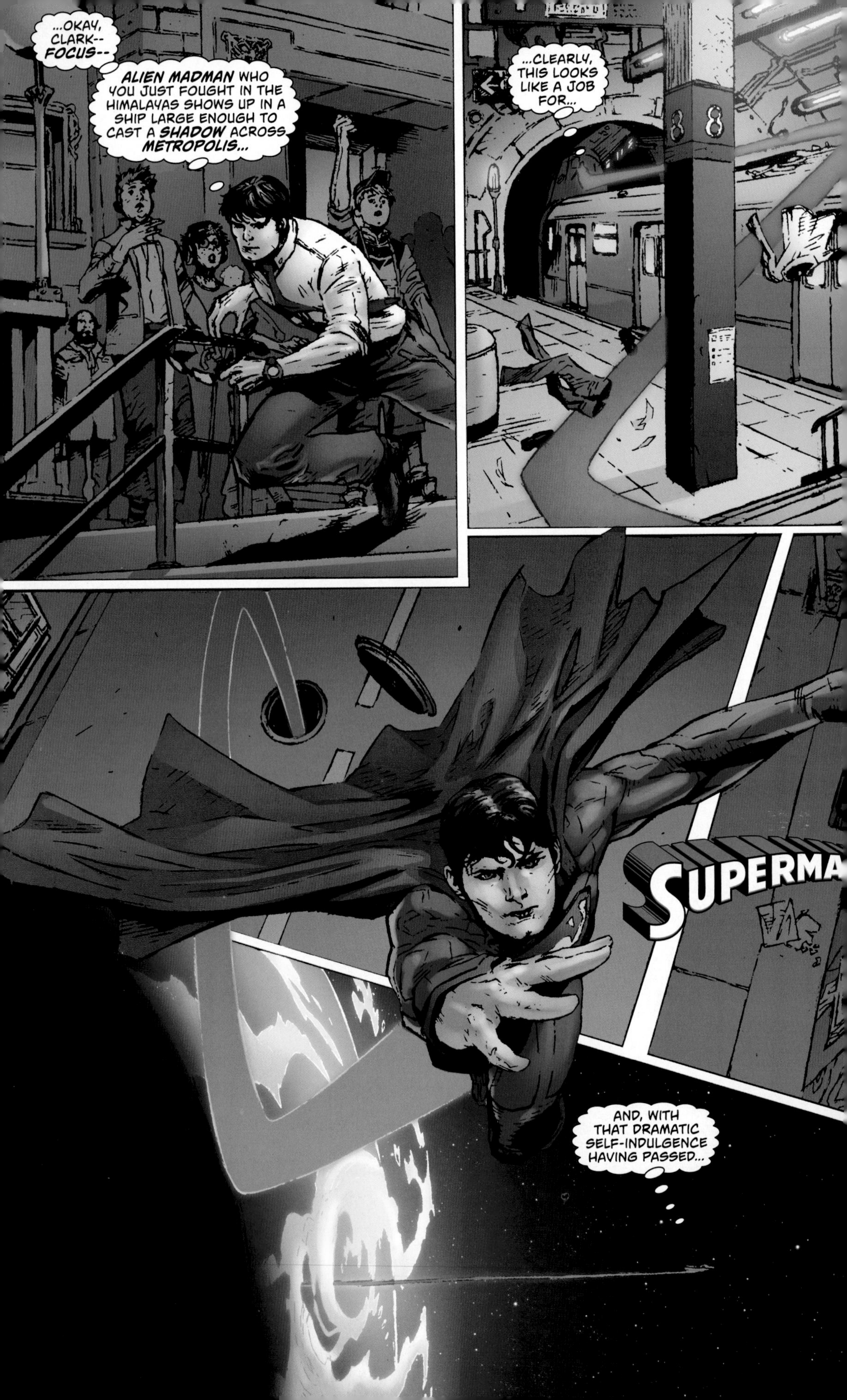
...OKAY, CLARK-- FOCUS--
ALIEN MADMAN WHO YOU JUST FOUGHT IN THE HIMALAYAS SHOWS UP IN A SHIP LARGE ENOUGH TO CAST A SHADOW ACROSS METROPOLIS...
...CLEARLY, THIS LOOKS LIKE A JOB FOR...
SUPERMA
AND, WITH THAT DRAMATIC SELF-INDULGENCE HAVING PASSED...

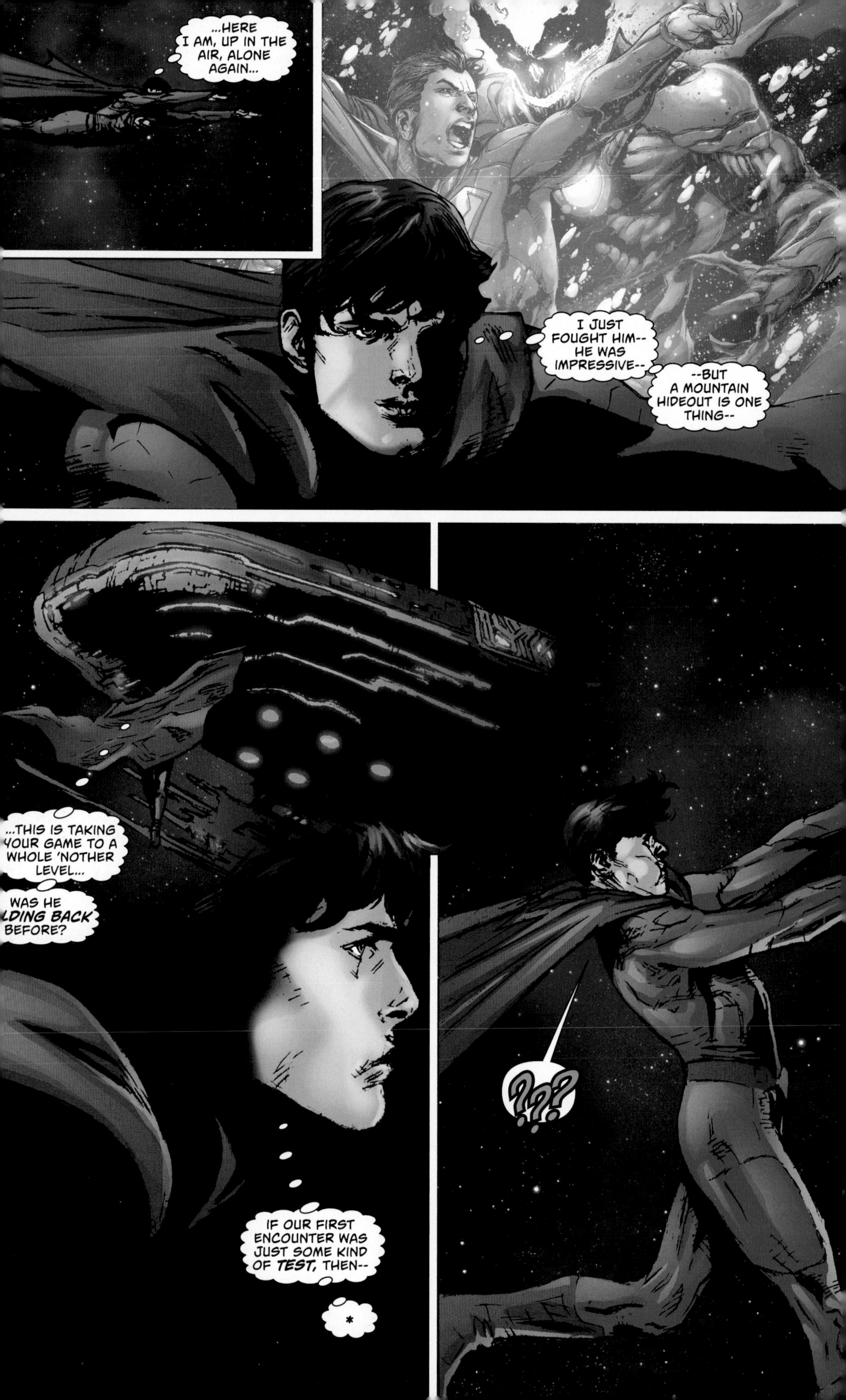
...HERE I AM, UP IN THE AIR, ALONE AGAIN...
I JUST FOUGHT HIM-- HE WAS IMPRESSIVE--
--BUT A MOUNTAIN HIDEOUT IS ONE THING--
...THIS IS TAKING YOUR GAME TO A WHOLE 'NOTHER LEVEL...
WAS HE LDING BACK BEFORE?
IF OUR FIRST ENCOUNTER WAS JUST SOME KIND OF TEST, THEN--
*
???

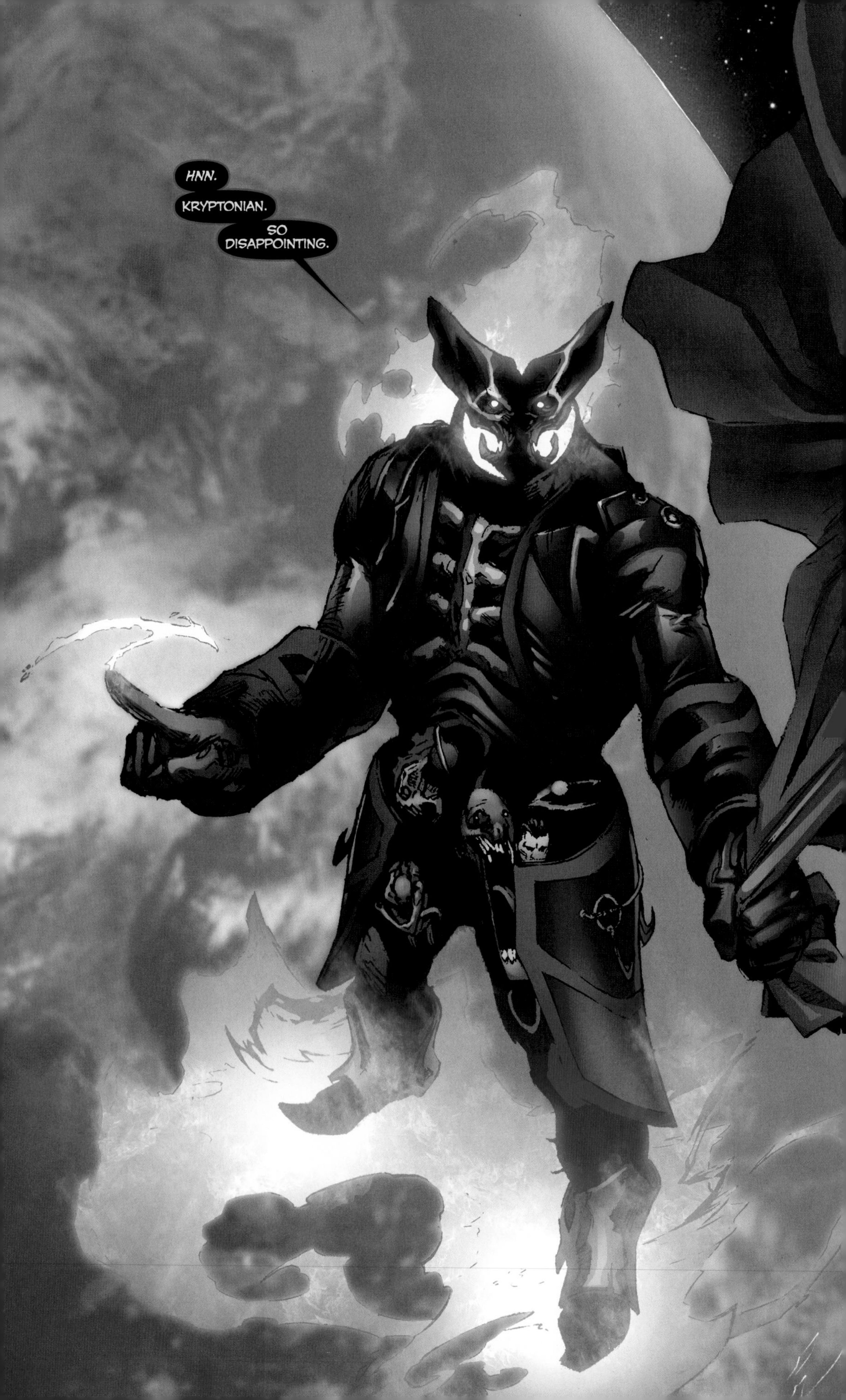
HNN.
KRYPTONIAN.
SO DISAPPOINTING.

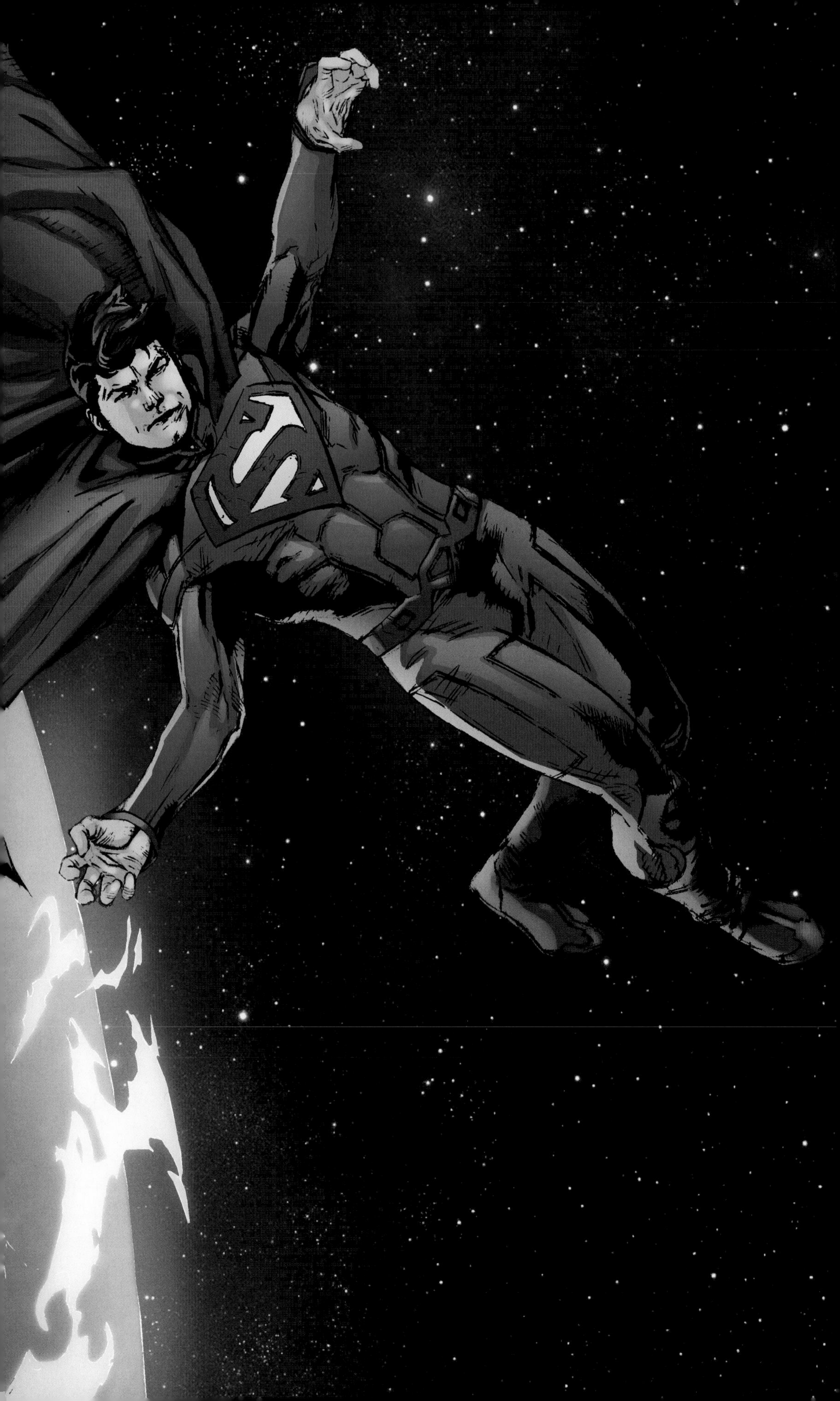

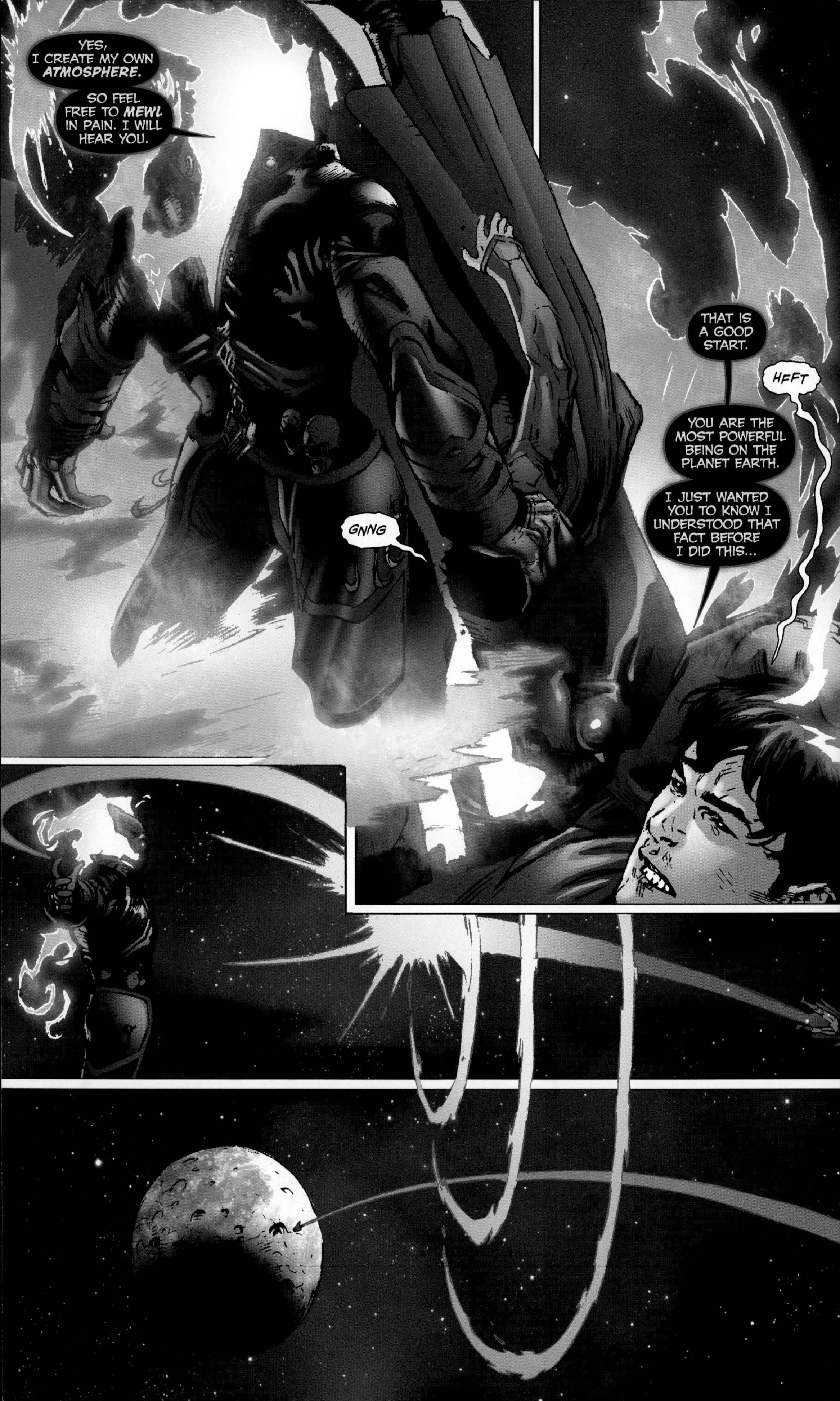
YES, I CREATE MY OWN ATMOSPHERE.
SO FEEL FREE TO MEWL IN PAIN. I WILL HEAR YOU.
GNNG
THAT IS A GOOD START.
HFFT
YOU ARE THE MOST POWERFUL BEING ON THE PLANET EARTH.
I JUST WANTED YOU TO KNOW I UNDERSTOOD THAT FACT BEFORE I DID THIS...

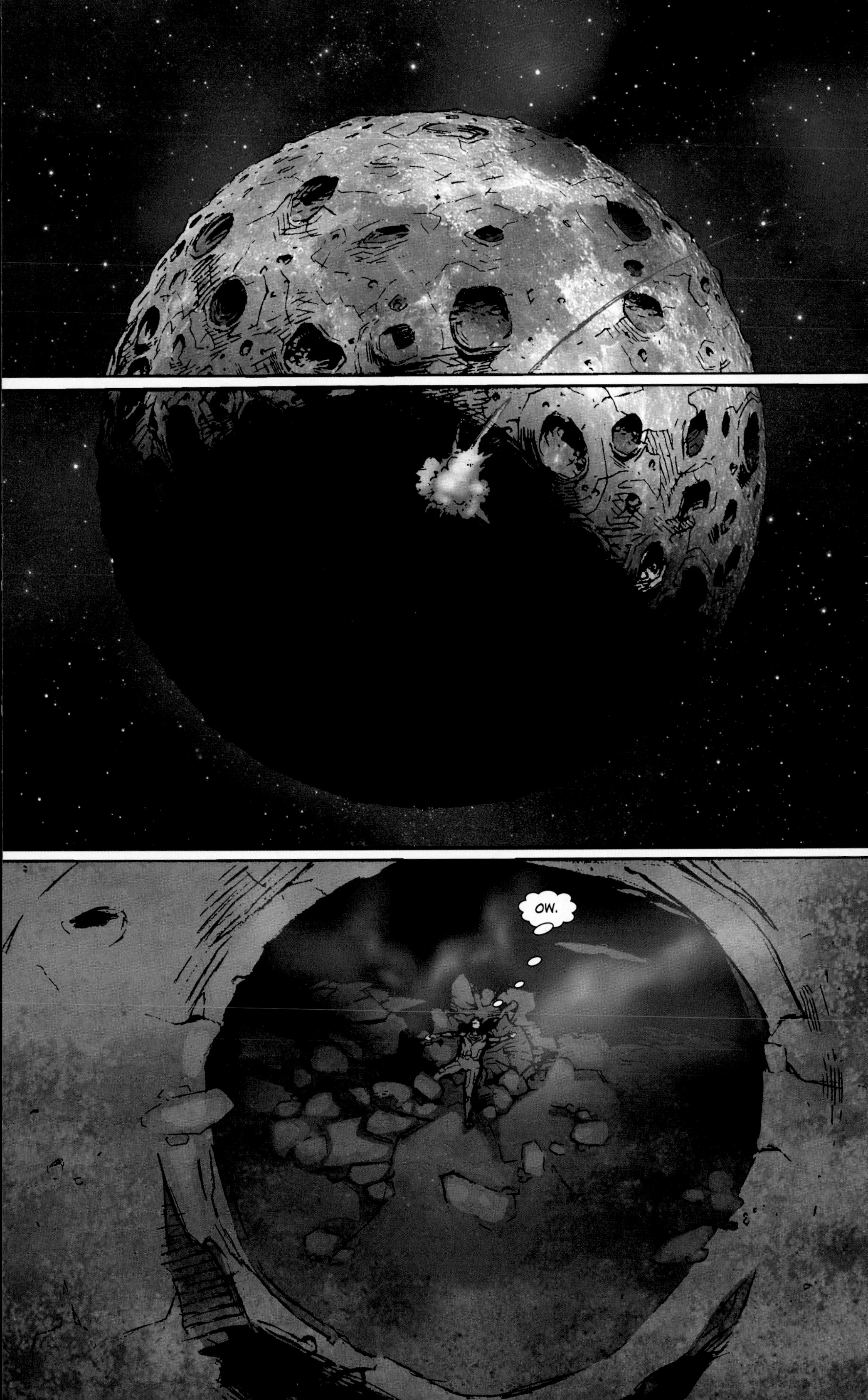
OW.

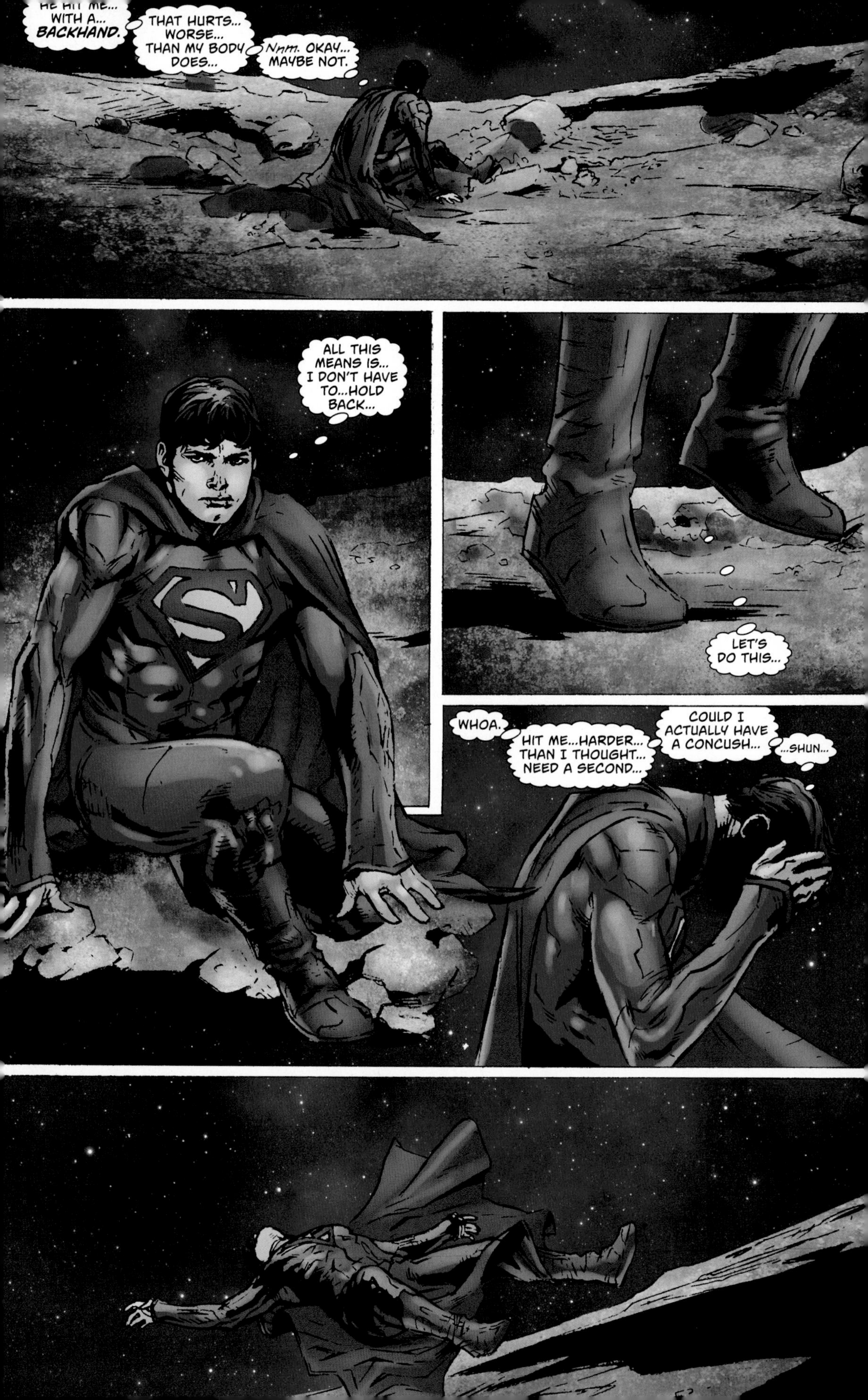
HE HIT ME... WITH A... BACKHAND.
THAT HURTS... WORSE... THAN MY BODY DOES...
Nnm. OKAY... MAYBE NOT.
ALL THIS MEANS IS... I DON'T HAVE TO...HOLD BACK...
LET'S DO THIS...
WHOA.
HIT ME...HARDER... THAN I THOUGHT... NEED A SECOND...
COULD I ACTUALLY HAVE A CONCUSH...
...SHUN...

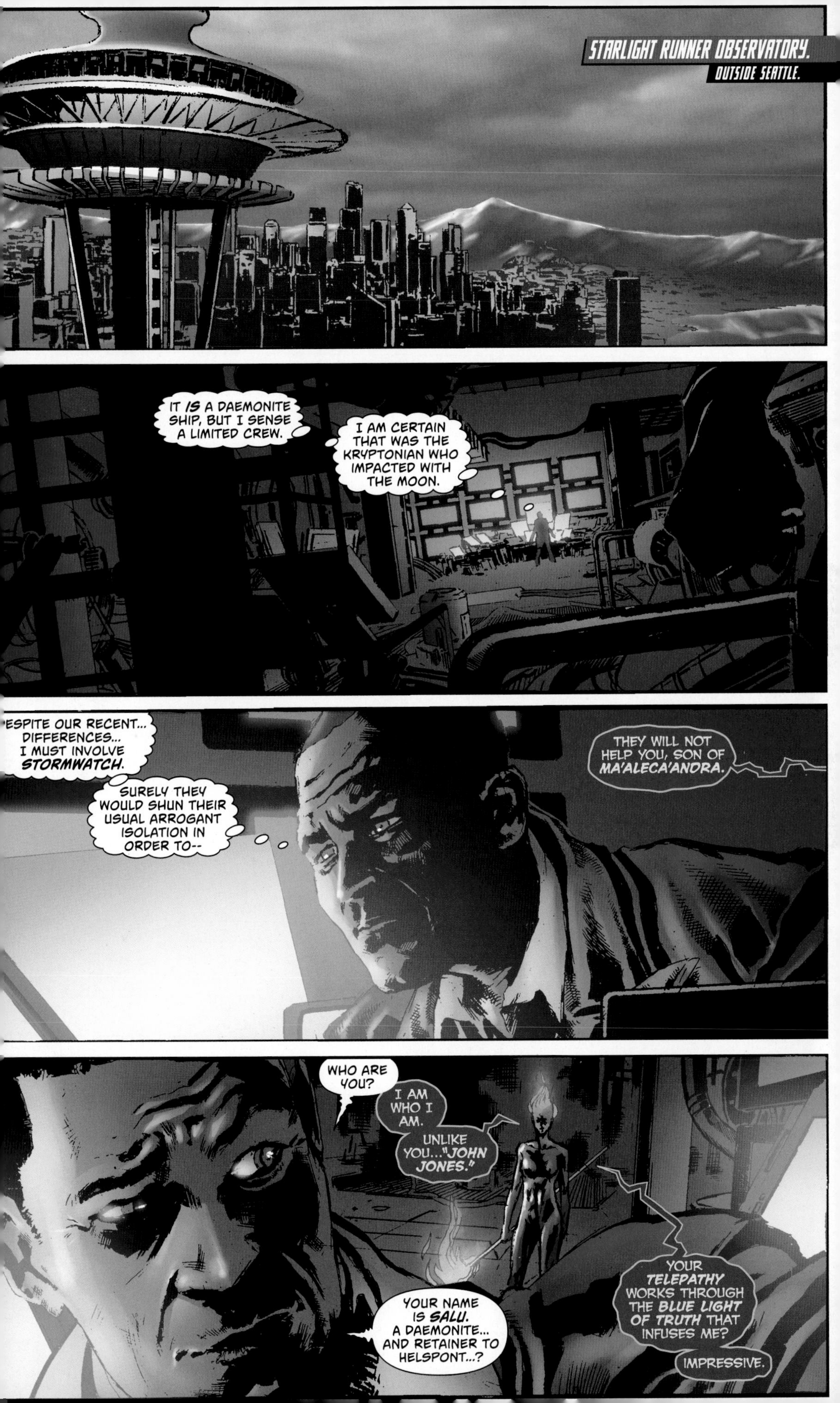
STARLIGHT RUNNER OBSERVATORY.
OUTSIDE SEATTLE.
IT IS A DAEMONITE SHIP, BUT I SENSE A LIMITED CREW.
I AM CERTAIN THAT WAS THE KRYPTONIAN WHO IMPACTED WITH THE MOON.
ESPITE OUR RECENT... DIFFERENCES... I MUST INVOLVE STORMWATCH.
SURELY THEY WOULD SHUN THEIR USUAL ARROGANT ISOLATION IN ORDER TO--
THEY WILL NOT HELP YOU, SON OF MA'ALECA'ANDRA.
WHO ARE YOU?
I AM WHO I AM.
UNLIKE YOU..."JOHN JONES."
YOUR NAME IS SALU. A DAEMONITE... AND RETAINER TO HELSPONT...?
YOUR TELEPATHY WORKS THROUGH THE BLUE LIGHT OF TRUTH THAT INFUSES ME?
IMPRESSIVE.

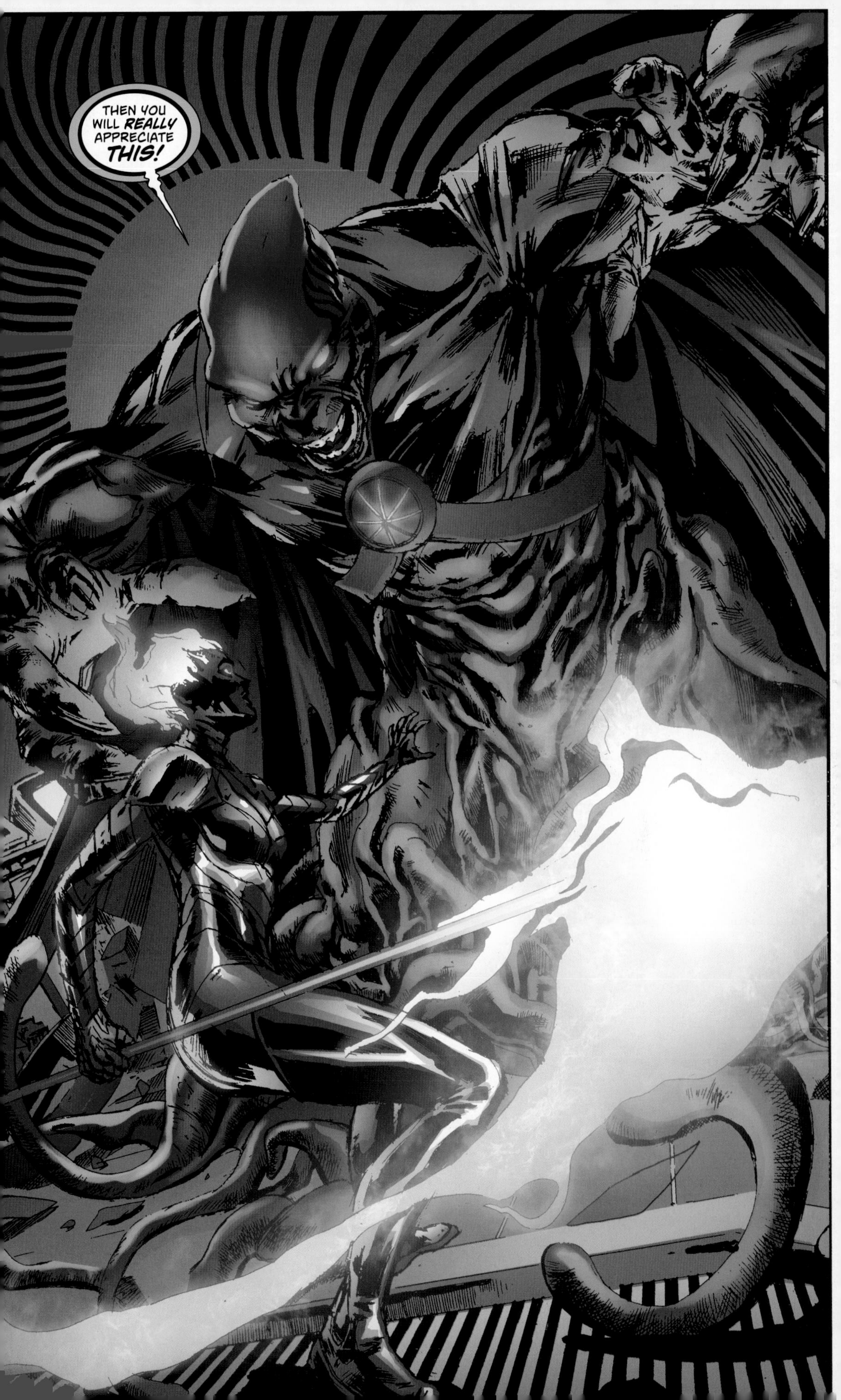
THEN YOU WILL REALLY APPRECIATE THIS!

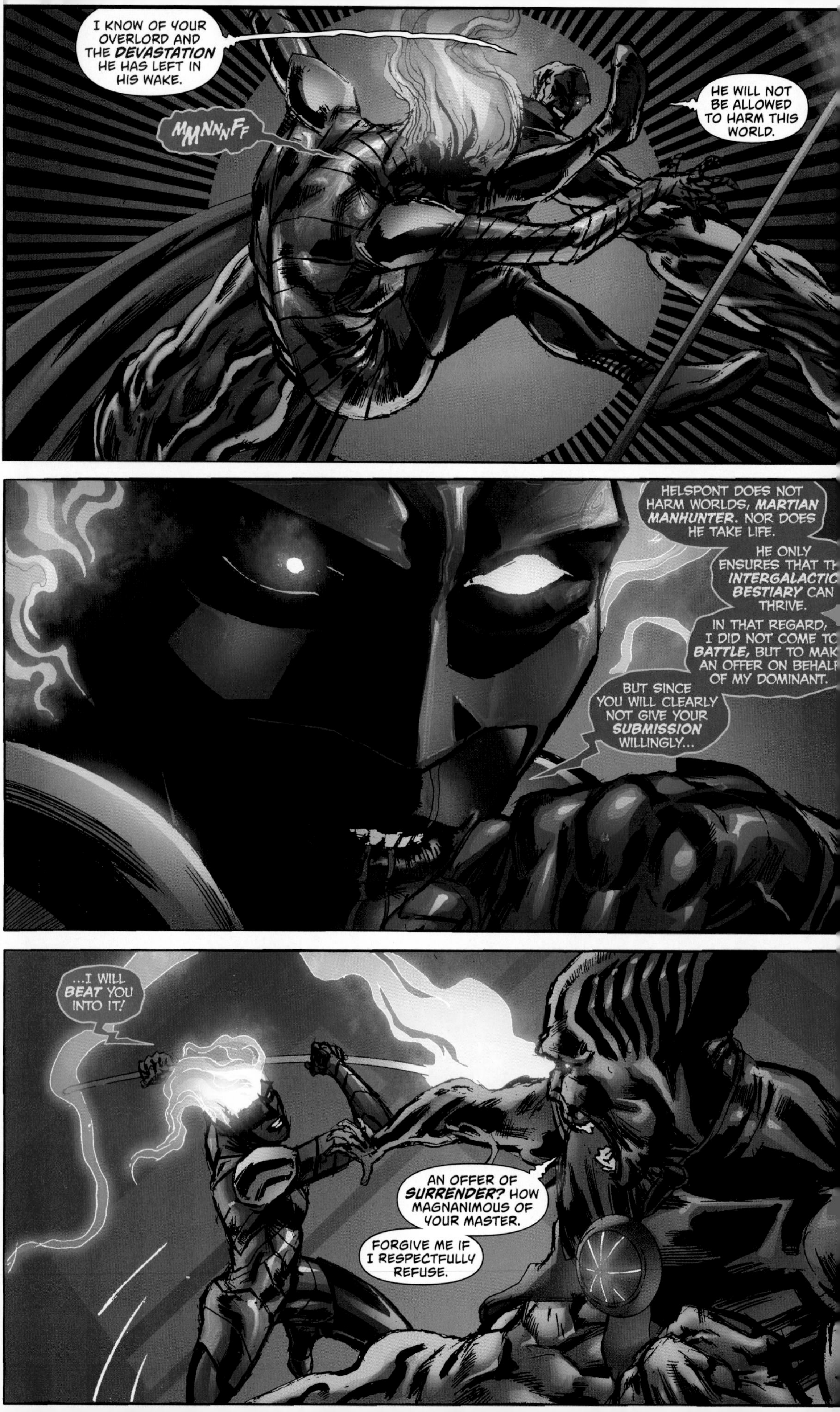

I KNOW OF YOUR OVERLORD AND THE DEVASTATION HE HAS LEFT IN HIS WAKE.
MMNNNFF
HE WILL NOT BE ALLOWED TO HARM THIS WORLD.
HELSPONT DOES NOT HARM WORLDS, MARTIAN MANHUNTER. NOR DOES HE TAKE LIFE.
HE ONLY ENSURES THAT TH INTERGALACTIC BESTIARY CAN THRIVE.
IN THAT REGARD, I DID NOT COME TO BATTLE, BUT TO MAK AN OFFER ON BEHALF OF MY DOMINANT.
BUT SINCE YOU WILL CLEARLY NOT GIVE YOUR SUBMISSION WILLINGLY...
...I WILL BEAT YOU INTO IT!
AN OFFER OF SURRENDER? HOW MAGNANIMOUS OF YOUR MASTER.
FORGIVE ME IF I RESPECTFULLY REFUSE.

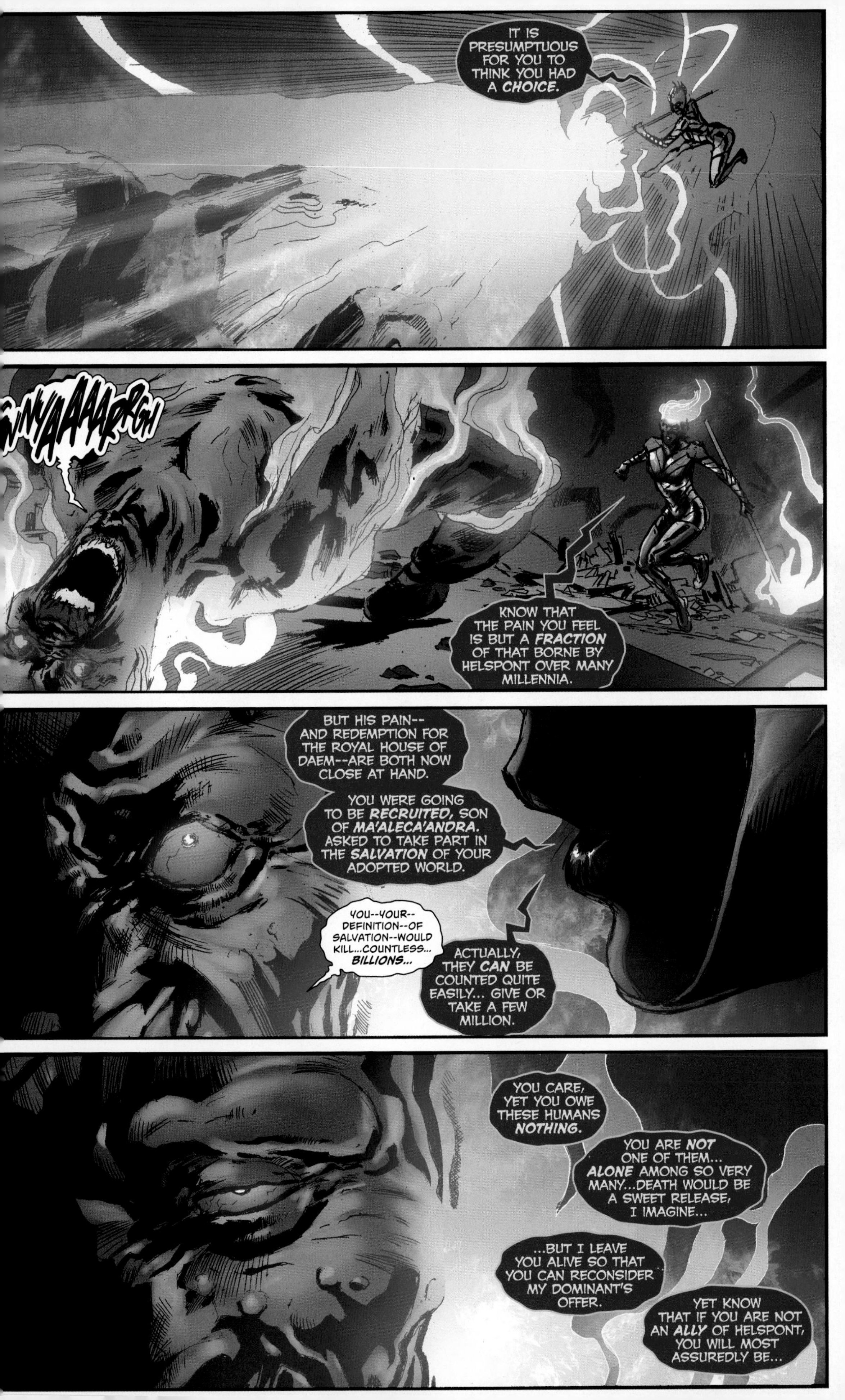

IT IS PRESUMPTUOUS FOR YOU TO THINK YOU HAD A CHOICE.
NNYAAAARRGH
KNOW THAT THE PAIN YOU FEEL IS BUT A FRACTION OF THAT BORNE BY HELSPONT OVER MANY MILLENNIA.
BUT HIS PAIN-- AND REDEMPTION FOR THE ROYAL HOUSE OF DAEM--ARE BOTH NOW CLOSE AT HAND.
YOU WERE GOING TO BE RECRUITED, SON OF MA'ALECA'ANDRA. ASKED TO TAKE PART IN THE SALVATION OF YOUR ADOPTED WORLD.
YOU--YOUR-- DEFINITION--OF SALVATION--WOULD KILL...COUNTLESS... BILLIONS...
ACTUALLY, THEY CAN BE COUNTED QUITE EASILY... GIVE OR TAKE A FEW MILLION.
YOU CARE, YET YOU OWE THESE HUMANS NOTHING.
YOU ARE NOT ONE OF THEM... ALONE AMONG SO VERY MANY...DEATH WOULD BE A SWEET RELEASE, I IMAGINE...
...BUT I LEAVE YOU ALIVE SO THAT YOU CAN RECONSIDER MY DOMINANT'S OFFER.
YET KNOW THAT IF YOU ARE NOT AN ALLY OF HELSPONT, YOU WILL MOST ASSUREDLY BE...

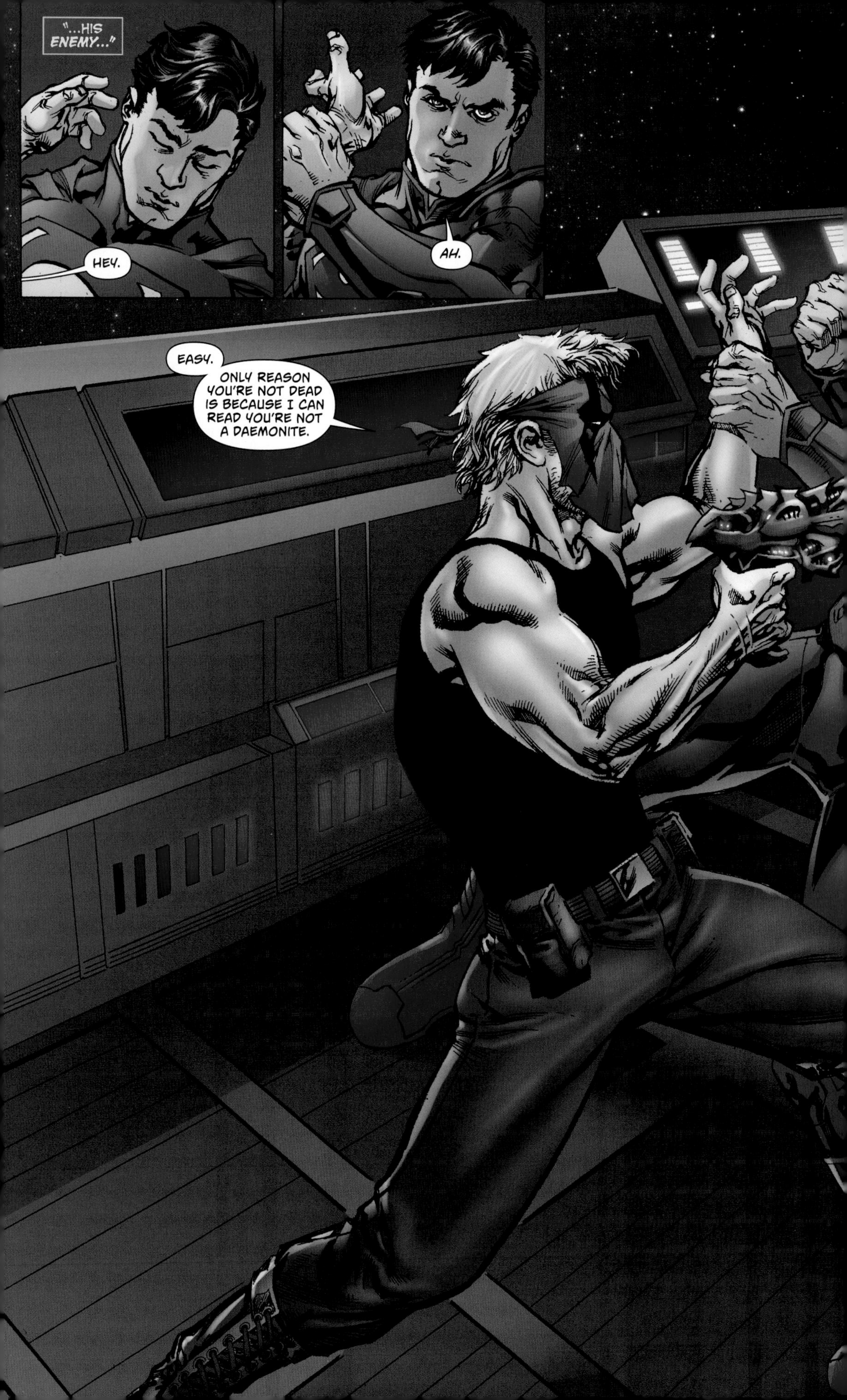

"...HIS ENEMY..."
HEY.
AH.
EASY.
ONLY REASON YOU'RE NOT DEAD IS BECAUSE I CAN READ YOU'RE NOT A DAEMONITE.

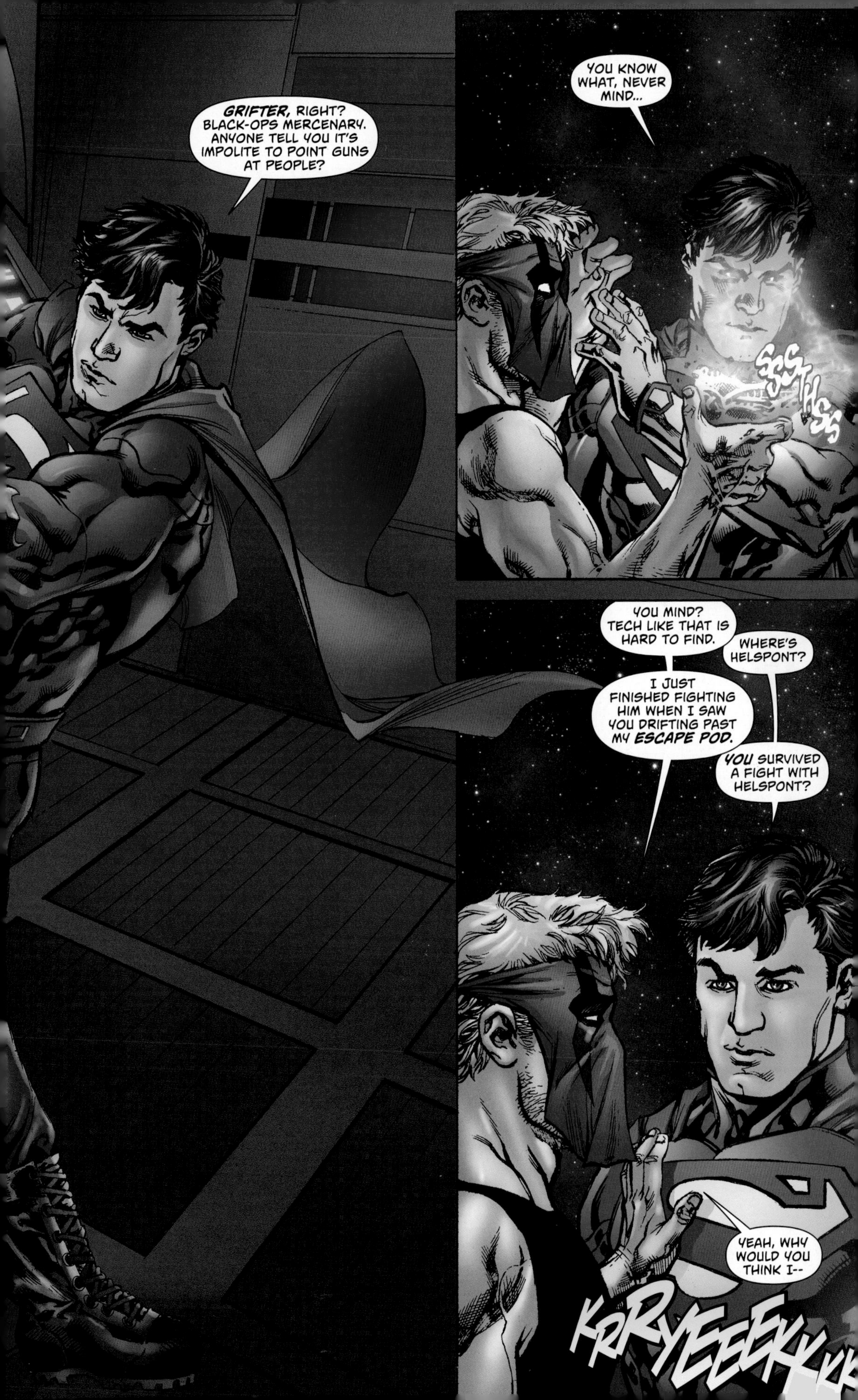
GRIFTER, RIGHT? BLACK-OPS MERCENARY. ANYONE TELL YOU IT'S IMPOLITE TO POINT GUNS AT PEOPLE?
YOU KNOW WHAT, NEVER MIND...
SSSTHSSS
YOU MIND? TECH LIKE THAT IS HARD TO FIND.
WHERE'S HELSPONT?
I JUST FINISHED FIGHTING HIM WHEN I SAW YOU DRIFTING PAST MY ESCAPE POD.
YOU SURVIVED A FIGHT WITH HELSPONT?
YEAH, WHY WOULD YOU THINK I--
KRRYEEEKKKK

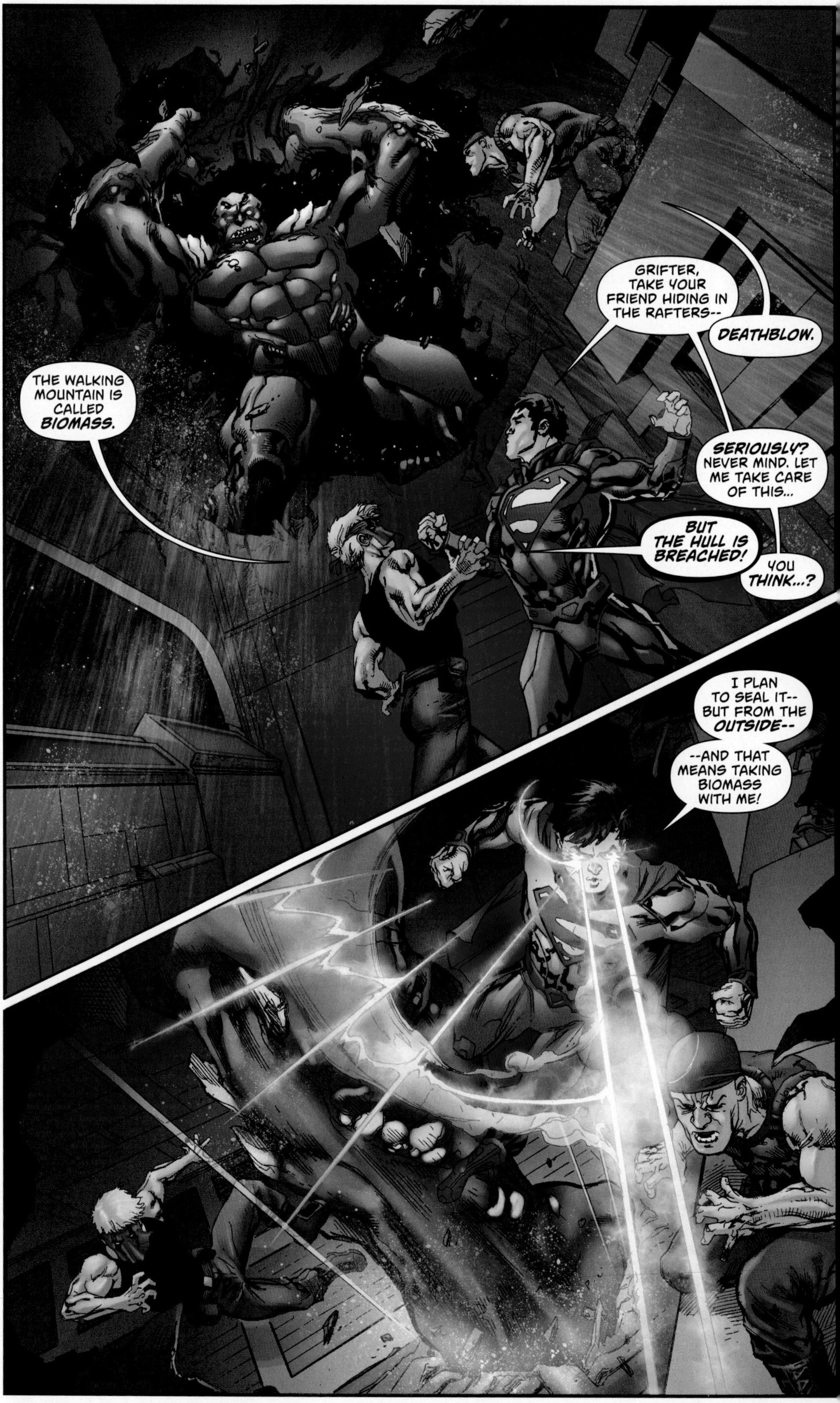
GRIFTER, TAKE YOUR FRIEND HIDING IN THE RAFTERS--
DEATHBLOW.
THE WALKING MOUNTAIN IS CALLED BIOMASS.
SERIOUSLY? NEVER MIND. LET ME TAKE CARE OF THIS...
BUT THE HULL IS BREACHED!
YOU THINK...?
I PLAN TO SEAL IT-- BUT FROM THE OUTSIDE--
--AND THAT MEANS TAKING BIOMASS WITH ME!

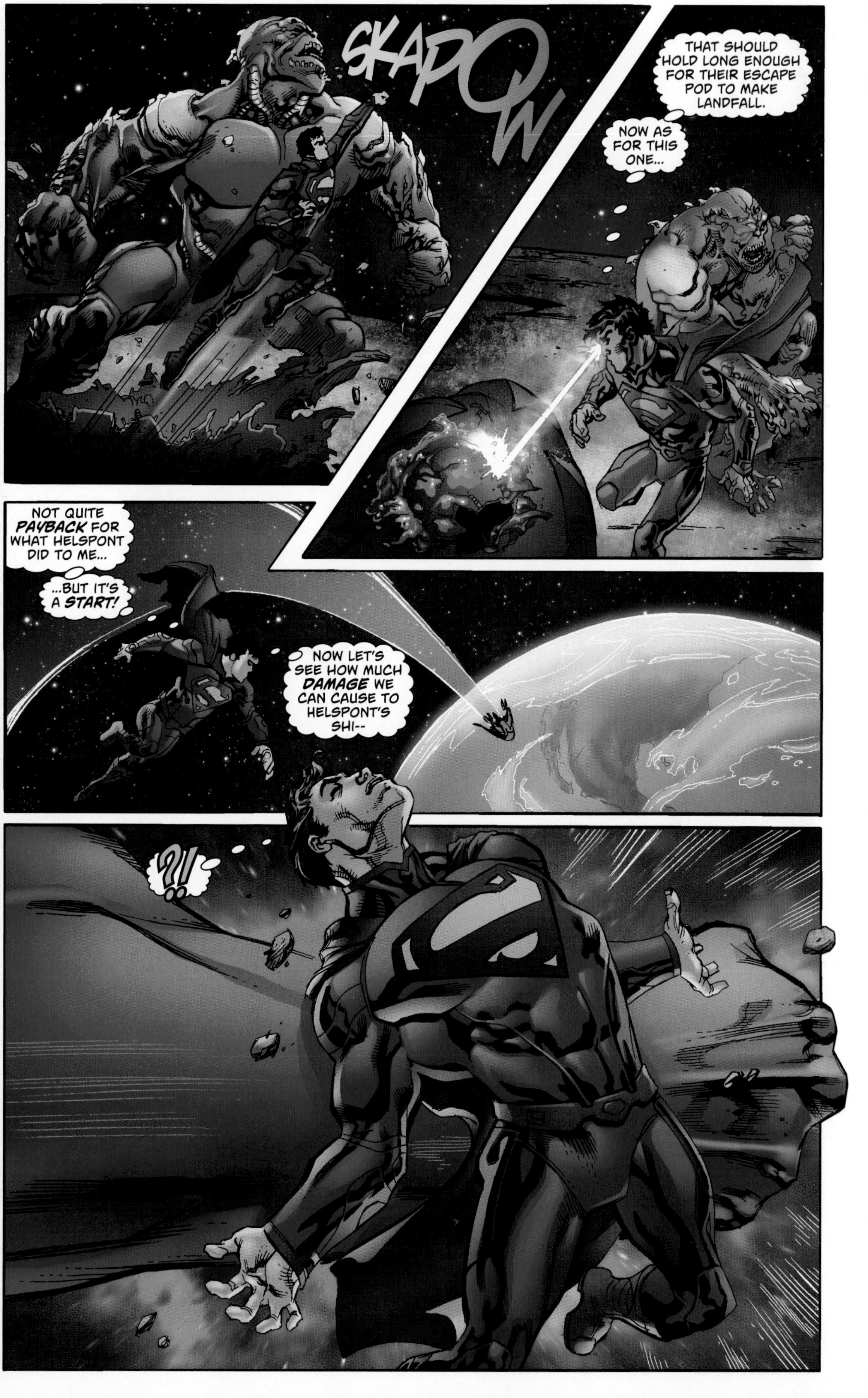
SKAPOW
THAT SHOULD HOLD LONG ENOUGH FOR THEIR ESCAPE POD TO MAKE LANDFALL.
NOW AS FOR THIS ONE...
NOT QUITE PAYBACK FOR WHAT HELSPONT DID TO ME...
...BUT IT'S A START!
NOW LET'S SEE HOW MUCH DAMAGE WE CAN CAUSE TO HELSPONT'S SHI--
?!

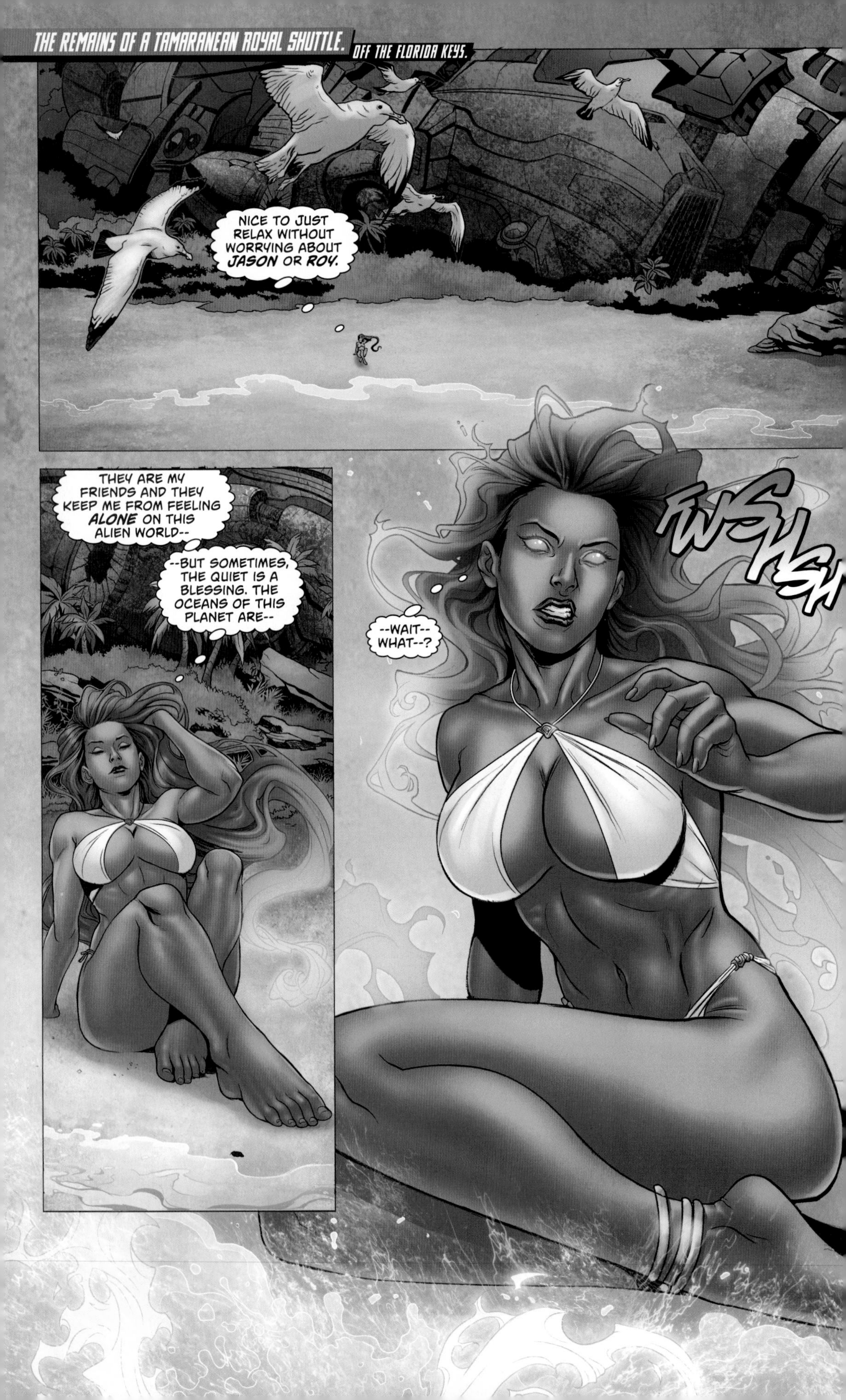
THE REMAINS OF A TAMARANEAN ROYAL SHUTTLE.
OFF THE FLORIDA KEYS.
NICE TO JUST RELAX WITHOUT WORRYING ABOUT JASON OR ROY.
THEY ARE MY FRIENDS AND THEY KEEP ME FROM FEELING ALONE ON THIS ALIEN WORLD--
--BUT SOMETIMES, THE QUIET IS A BLESSING. THE OCEANS OF THIS PLANET ARE--
--WAIT-- WHAT--?
FWSHSH

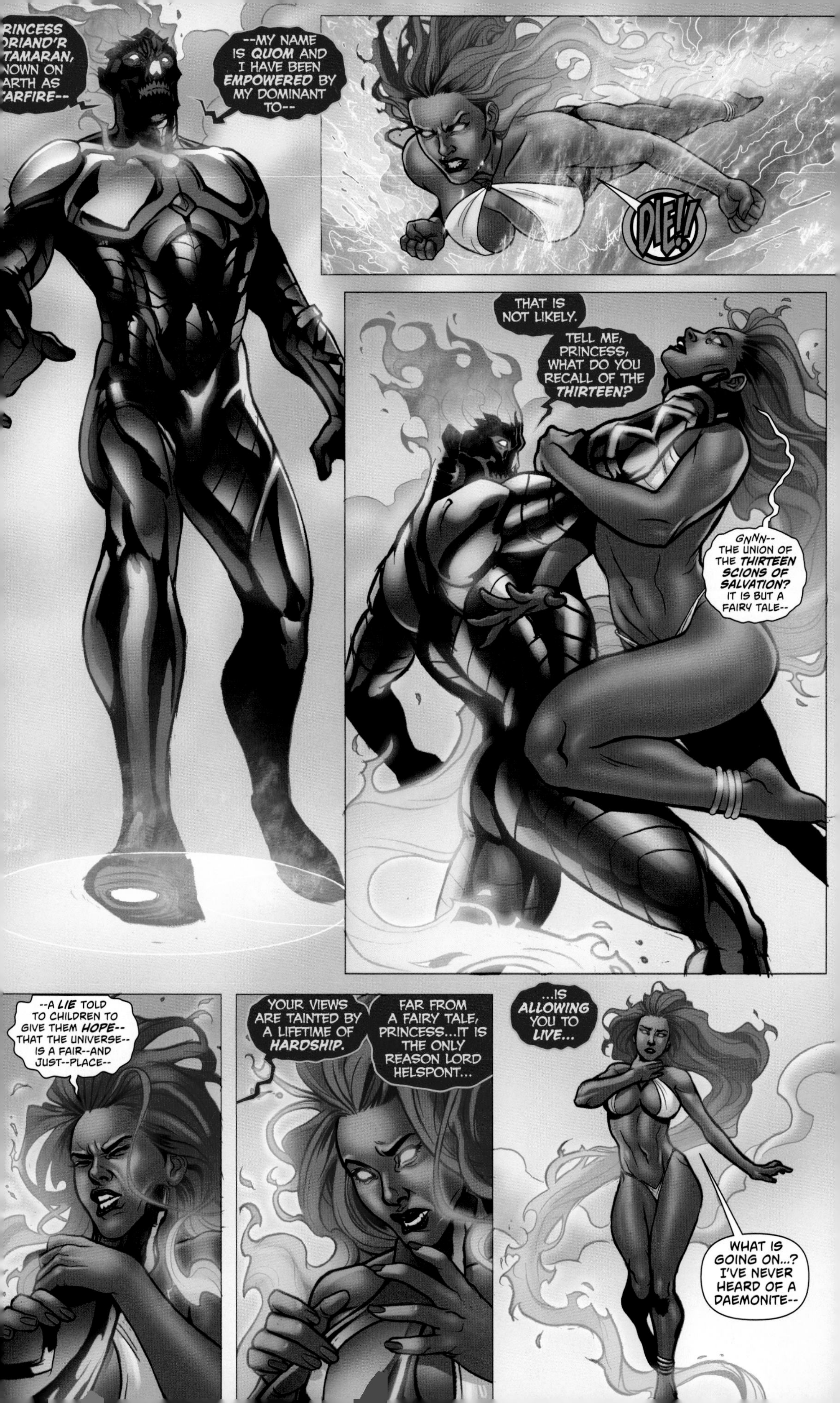
PRINCESS
ORIAND'R
TAMARAN,
NOWN ON
ARTH AS
TARFIRE--
--MY NAME
IS QUOM AND
I HAVE BEEN
EMPOWERED BY
MY DOMINANT
TO--
DIE!!
THAT IS
NOT LIKELY.
TELL ME,
PRINCESS,
WHAT DO YOU
RECALL OF THE
THIRTEEN?
GNNN--
THE UNION OF
THE THIRTEEN
SCIONS OF
SALVATION?
IT IS BUT A
FAIRY TALE--
--A LIE TOLD
TO CHILDREN TO
GIVE THEM HOPE--
THAT THE UNIVERSE--
IS A FAIR--AND
JUST--PLACE--
YOUR VIEWS
ARE TAINTED BY
A LIFETIME OF
HARDSHIP.
FAR FROM
A FAIRY TALE,
PRINCESS...IT IS
THE ONLY
REASON LORD
HELSPONT...
...IS
ALLOWING
YOU TO
LIVE...
WHAT IS
GOING ON...?
I'VE NEVER
HEARD OF A
DAEMONITE--

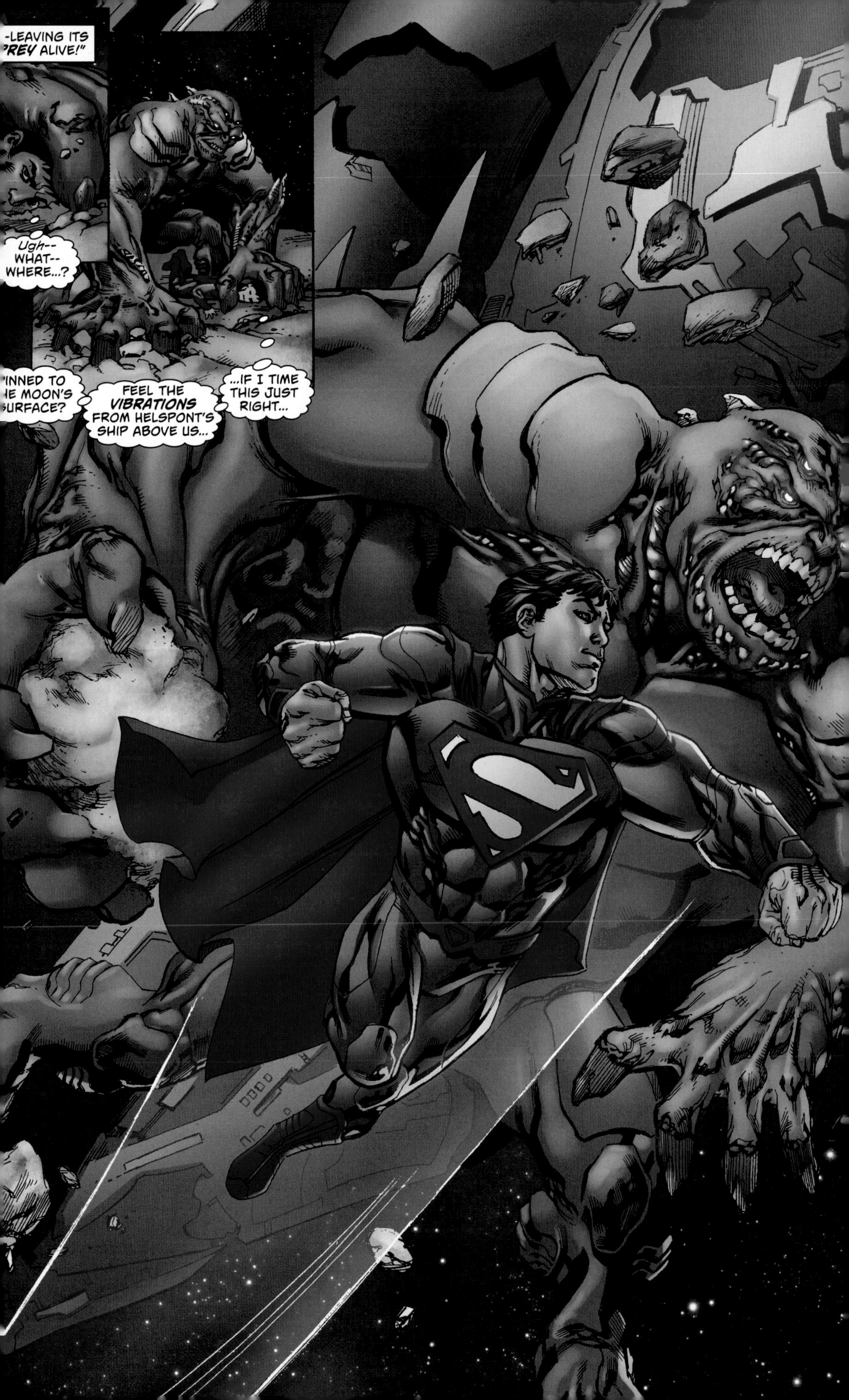
-LEAVING ITS
PREY ALIVE!"
Ugh-- WHAT-- WHERE...?
PINNED TO
HE MOON'S
SURFACE?
FEEL THE VIBRATIONS FROM HELSPONT'S SHIP ABOVE US...
...IF I TIME THIS JUST RIGHT...

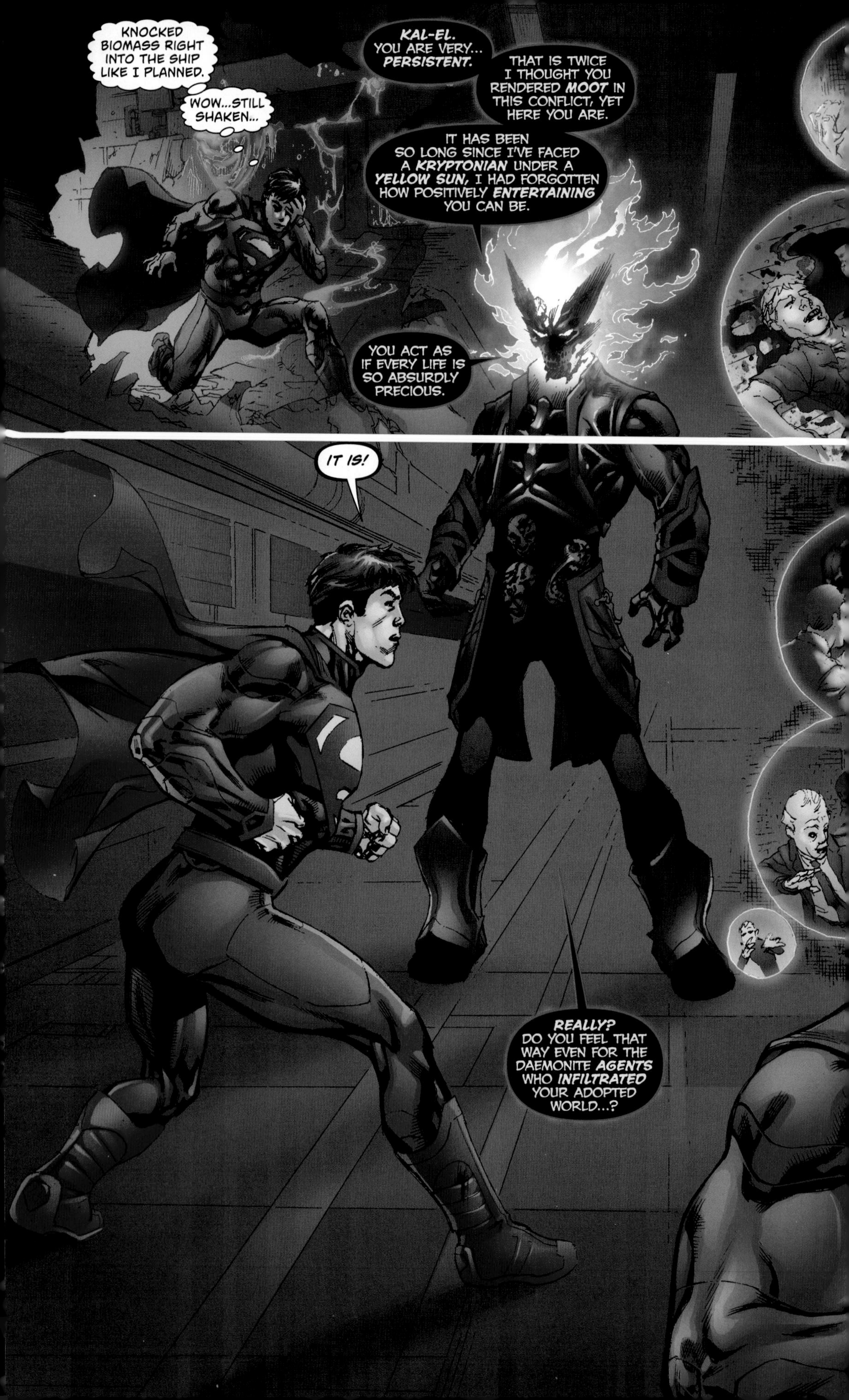
KNOCKED BIOMASS RIGHT INTO THE SHIP LIKE I PLANNED.
WOW...STILL SHAKEN...
KAL-EL. YOU ARE VERY... PERSISTENT.
THAT IS TWICE I THOUGHT YOU RENDERED MOOT IN THIS CONFLICT, YET HERE YOU ARE.
IT HAS BEEN SO LONG SINCE I'VE FACED A KRYPTONIAN UNDER A YELLOW SUN, I HAD FORGOTTEN HOW POSITIVELY ENTERTAINING YOU CAN BE.
YOU ACT AS IF EVERY LIFE IS SO ABSURDLY PRECIOUS.
IT IS!
REALLY? DO YOU FEEL THAT WAY EVEN FOR THE DAEMONITE AGENTS WHO INFILTRATED YOUR ADOPTED WORLD...?

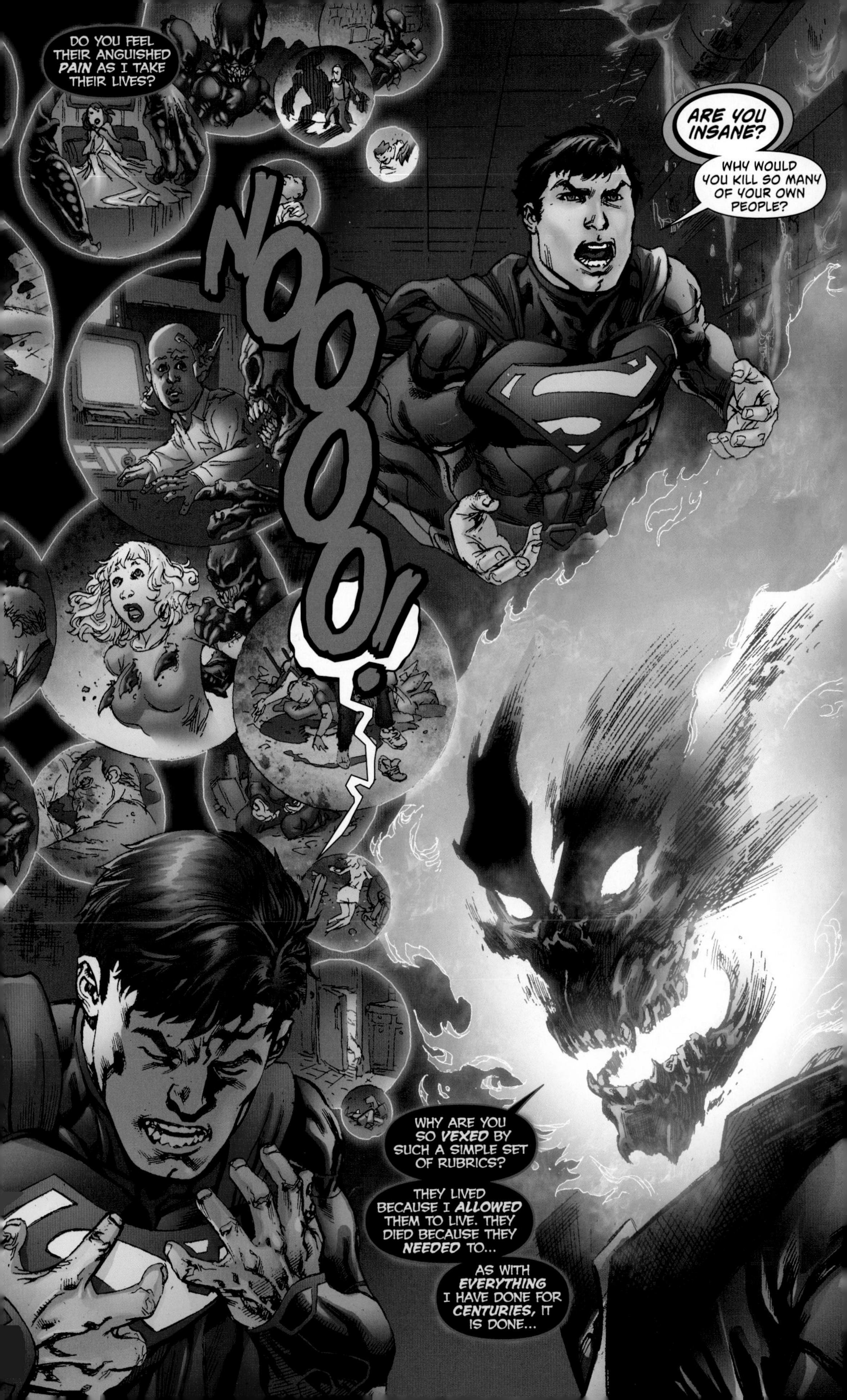

DO YOU FEEL THEIR ANGUISHED PAIN AS I TAKE THEIR LIVES?
ARE YOU INSANE?
WHY WOULD YOU KILL SO MANY OF YOUR OWN PEOPLE?
NOOOOO!
WHY ARE YOU SO VEXED BY SUCH A SIMPLE SET OF RUBRICS?
THEY LIVED BECAUSE I ALLOWED THEM TO LIVE. THEY DIED BECAUSE THEY NEEDED TO...
AS WITH EVERYTHING I HAVE DONE FOR CENTURIES, IT IS DONE...

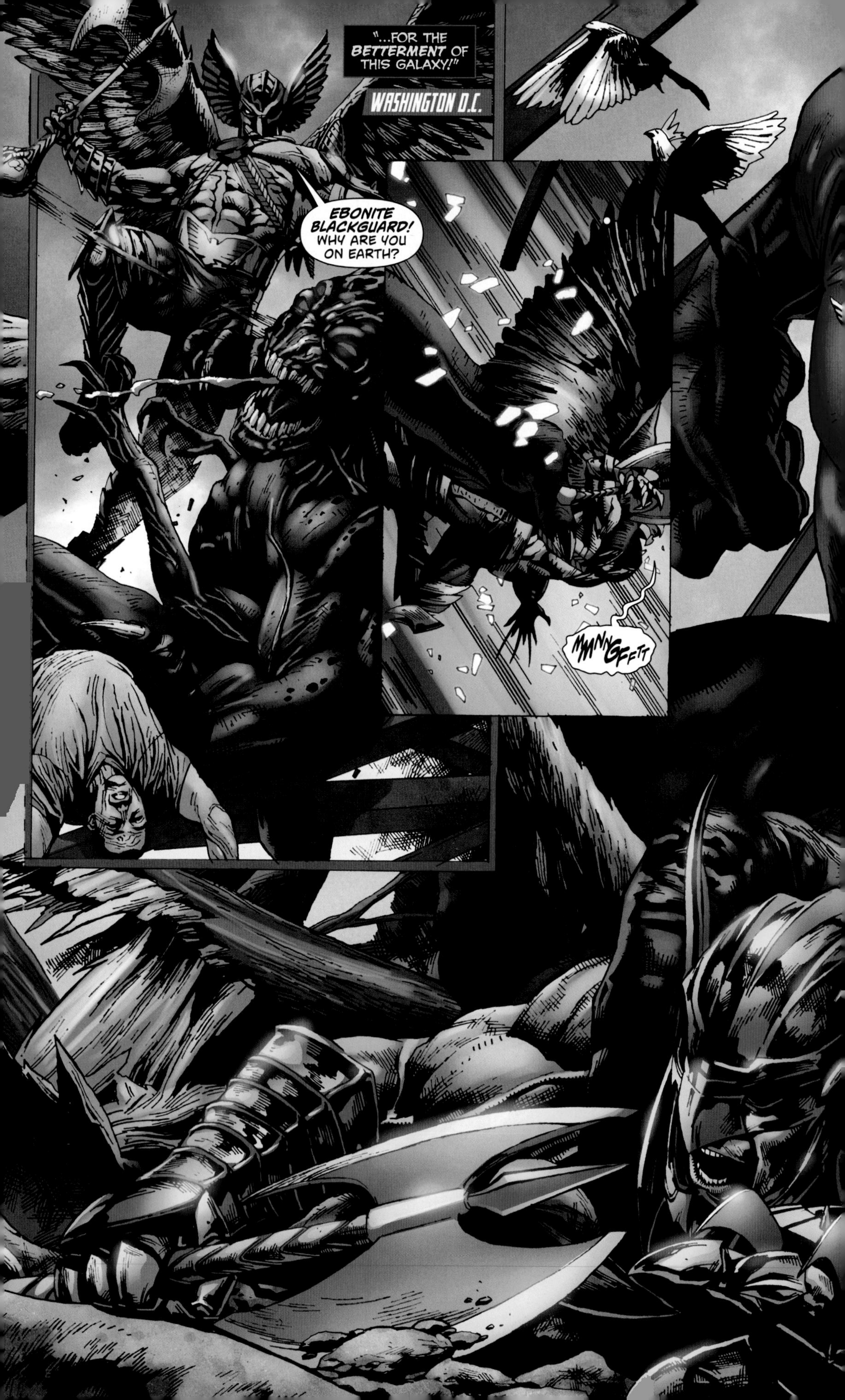
"...FOR THE *BETTERMENT* OF THIS GALAXY!"
WASHINGTON D.C.
EBONITE BLACKGUARD! WHY ARE YOU ON EARTH?
MMNNGFFTT

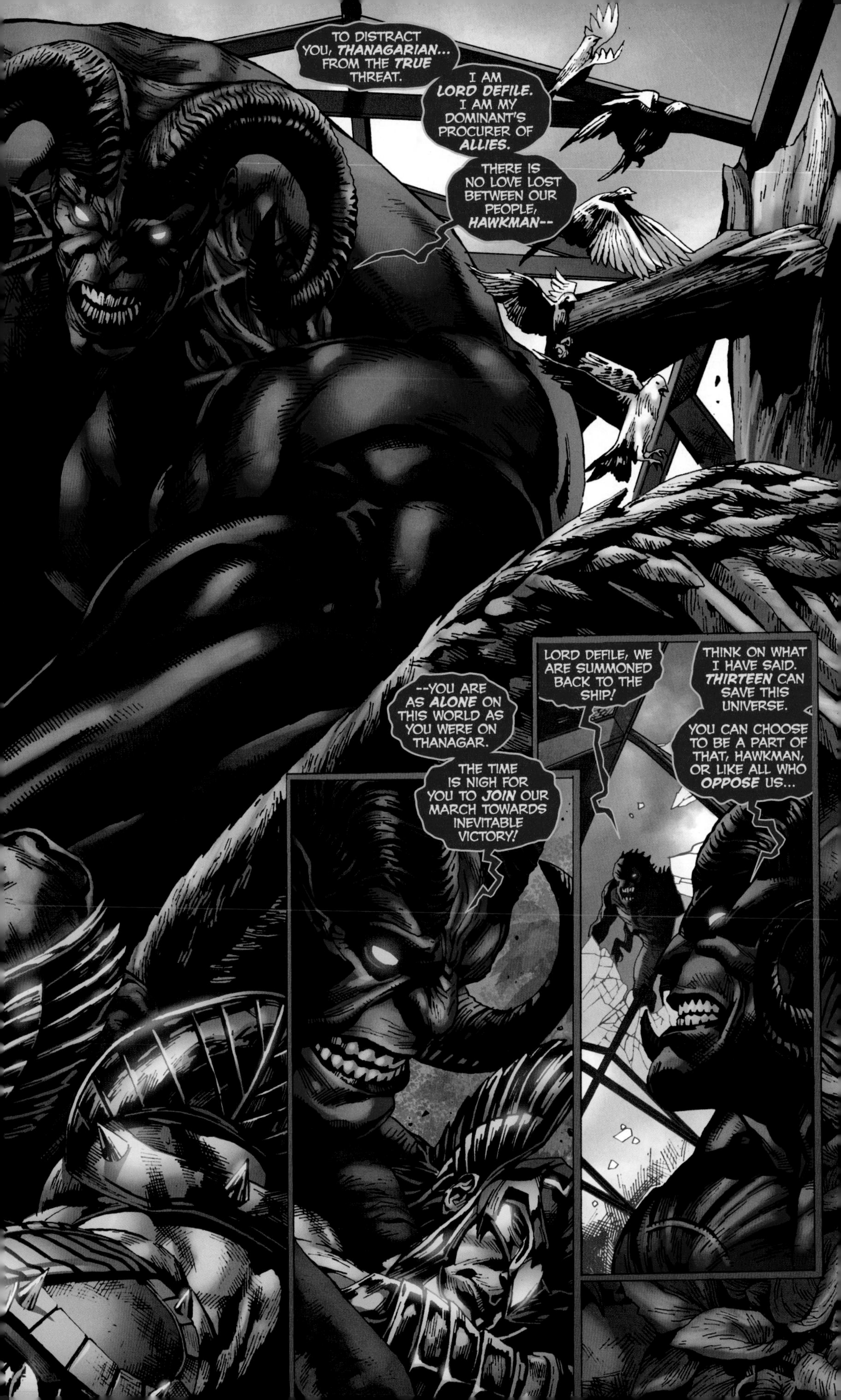
TO DISTRACT YOU, THANAGARIAN... FROM THE TRUE THREAT.
I AM LORD DEFILE. I AM MY DOMINANT'S PROCURER OF ALLIES.
THERE IS NO LOVE LOST BETWEEN OUR PEOPLE, HAWKMAN--
--YOU ARE AS ALONE ON THIS WORLD AS YOU WERE ON THANAGAR.
THE TIME IS NIGH FOR YOU TO JOIN OUR MARCH TOWARDS INEVITABLE VICTORY!
LORD DEFILE, WE ARE SUMMONED BACK TO THE SHIP!
THINK ON WHAT I HAVE SAID. THIRTEEN CAN SAVE THIS UNIVERSE.
YOU CAN CHOOSE TO BE A PART OF THAT, HAWKMAN, OR LIKE ALL WHO OPPOSE US...

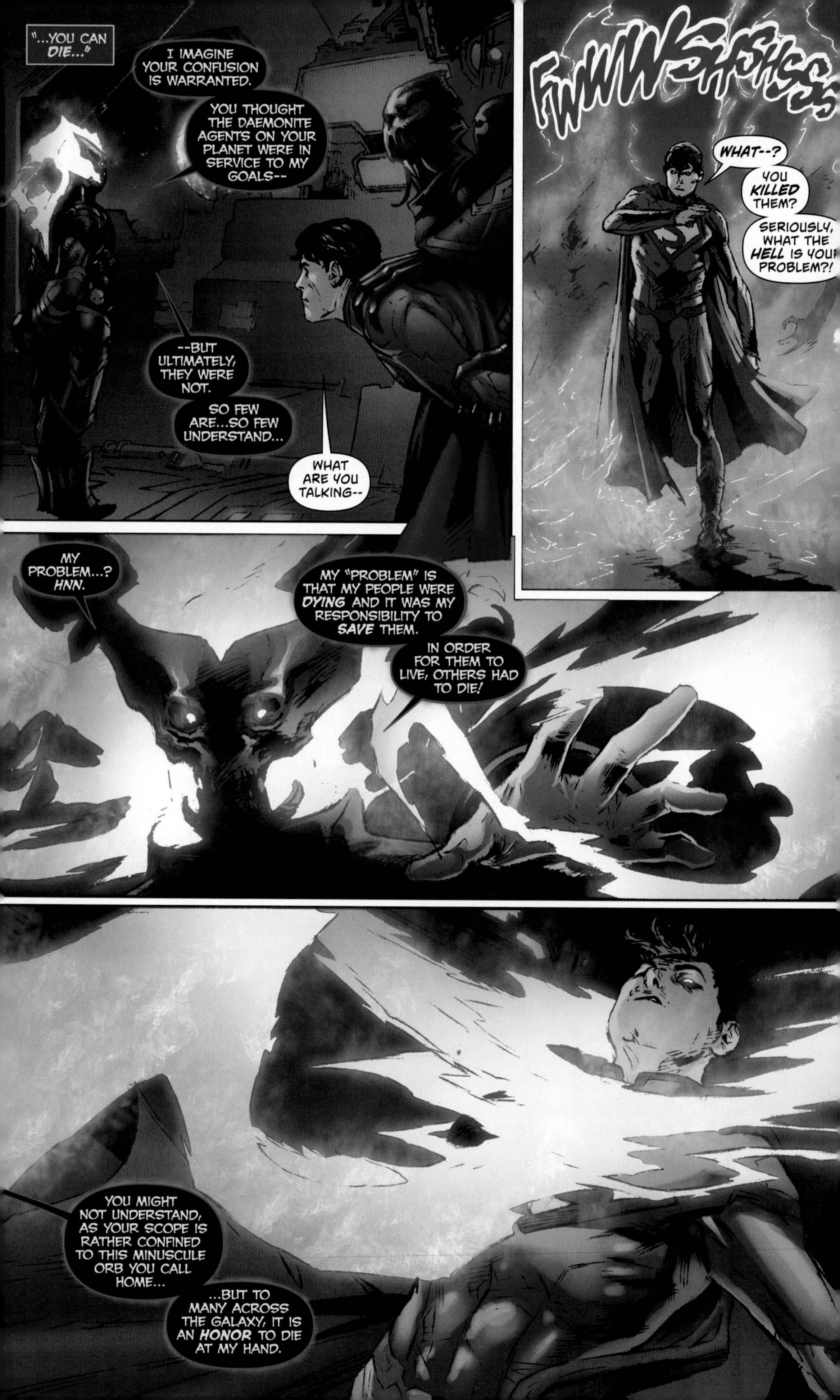
"...YOU CAN DIE..."
I IMAGINE YOUR CONFUSION IS WARRANTED.
YOU THOUGHT THE DAEMONITE AGENTS ON YOUR PLANET WERE IN SERVICE TO MY GOALS--
--BUT ULTIMATELY, THEY WERE NOT.
SO FEW ARE...SO FEW UNDERSTAND...
WHAT ARE YOU TALKING--
FWWWSHSHSSS
WHAT--?
YOU KILLED THEM?
SERIOUSLY, WHAT THE HELL IS YOUR PROBLEM?!
MY PROBLEM...? HNN.
MY "PROBLEM" IS THAT MY PEOPLE WERE DYING AND IT WAS MY RESPONSIBILITY TO SAVE THEM.
IN ORDER FOR THEM TO LIVE, OTHERS HAD TO DIE!
YOU MIGHT NOT UNDERSTAND, AS YOUR SCOPE IS RATHER CONFINED TO THIS MINUSCULE ORB YOU CALL HOME...
...BUT TO MANY ACROSS THE GALAXY, IT IS AN HONOR TO DIE AT MY HAND.

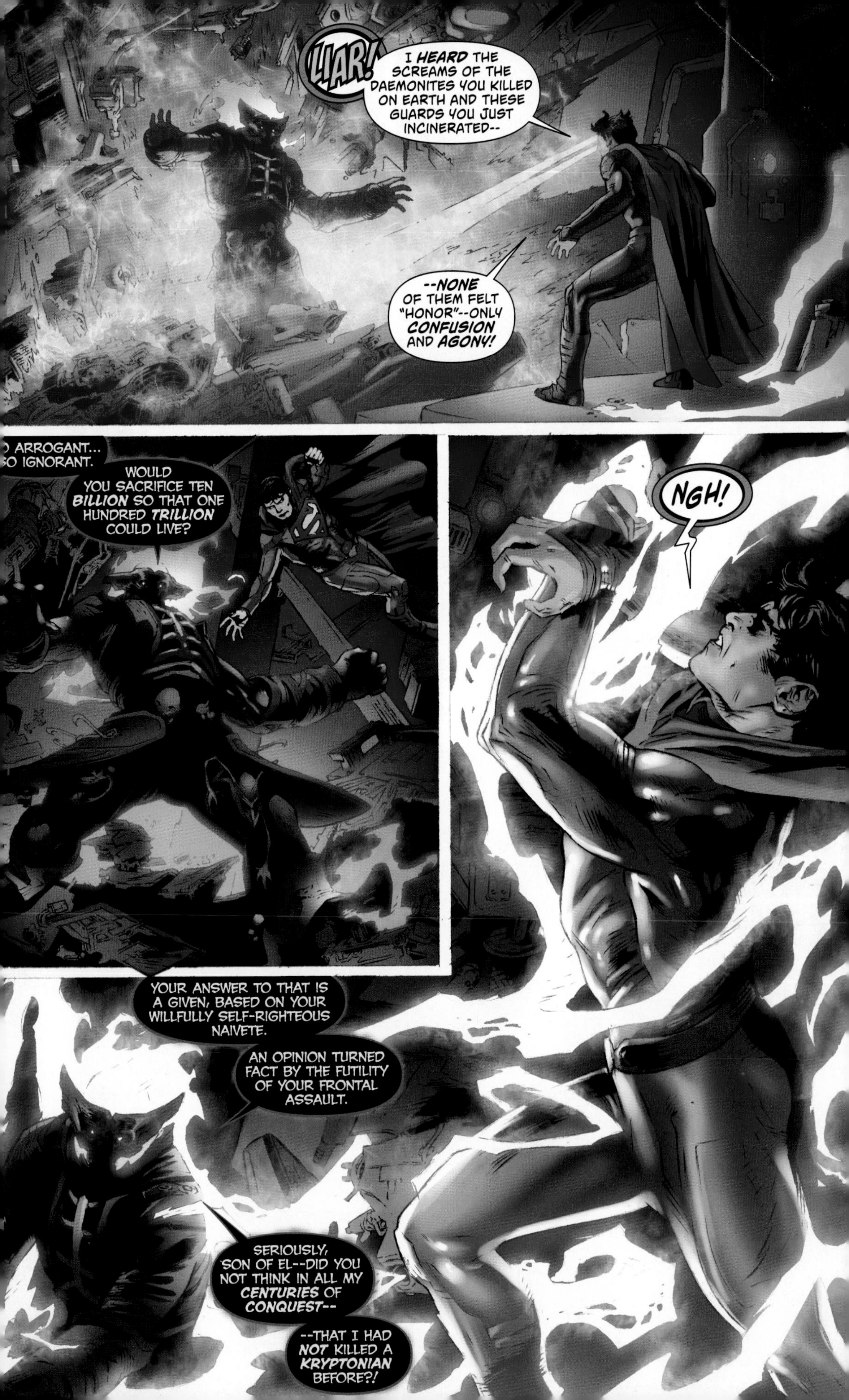
LIAR!
I HEARD THE SCREAMS OF THE DAEMONITES YOU KILLED ON EARTH AND THESE GUARDS YOU JUST INCINERATED--
--NONE OF THEM FELT "HONOR"--ONLY CONFUSION AND AGONY!
O ARROGANT... SO IGNORANT.
WOULD YOU SACRIFICE TEN BILLION SO THAT ONE HUNDRED TRILLION COULD LIVE?
NGH!
YOUR ANSWER TO THAT IS A GIVEN, BASED ON YOUR WILLFULLY SELF-RIGHTEOUS NAIVETE.
AN OPINION TURNED FACT BY THE FUTILITY OF YOUR FRONTAL ASSAULT.
SERIOUSLY, SON OF EL--DID YOU NOT THINK IN ALL MY CENTURIES OF CONQUEST--
--THAT I HAD NOT KILLED A KRYPTONIAN BEFORE?!

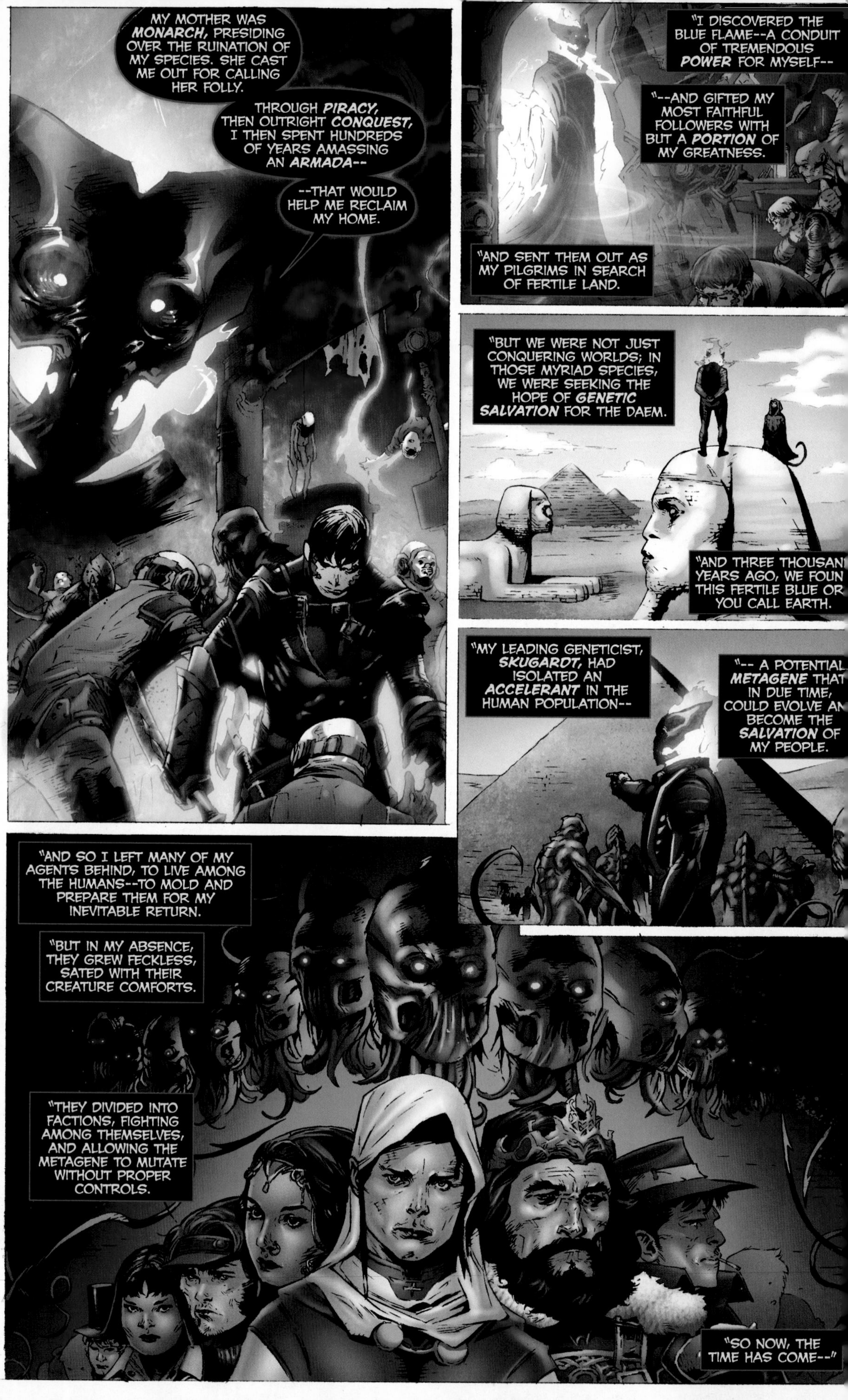
MY MOTHER WAS MONARCH, PRESIDING OVER THE RUINATION OF MY SPECIES. SHE CAST ME OUT FOR CALLING HER FOLLY.
THROUGH PIRACY, THEN OUTRIGHT CONQUEST, I THEN SPENT HUNDREDS OF YEARS AMASSING AN ARMADA--
--THAT WOULD HELP ME RECLAIM MY HOME.
"I DISCOVERED THE BLUE FLAME--A CONDUIT OF TREMENDOUS POWER FOR MYSELF--
"--AND GIFTED MY MOST FAITHFUL FOLLOWERS WITH BUT A PORTION OF MY GREATNESS.
"AND SENT THEM OUT AS MY PILGRIMS IN SEARCH OF FERTILE LAND.
"BUT WE WERE NOT JUST CONQUERING WORLDS; IN THOSE MYRIAD SPECIES, WE WERE SEEKING THE HOPE OF GENETIC SALVATION FOR THE DAEM.
"AND THREE THOUSAN YEARS AGO, WE FOUN THIS FERTILE BLUE OR YOU CALL EARTH.
"MY LEADING GENETICIST, SKUGARDT, HAD ISOLATED AN ACCELERANT IN THE HUMAN POPULATION--
"-- A POTENTIAL METAGENE THAT IN DUE TIME, COULD EVOLVE AN BECOME THE SALVATION OF MY PEOPLE.
"AND SO I LEFT MANY OF MY AGENTS BEHIND, TO LIVE AMONG THE HUMANS--TO MOLD AND PREPARE THEM FOR MY INEVITABLE RETURN.
"BUT IN MY ABSENCE, THEY GREW FECKLESS, SATED WITH THEIR CREATURE COMFORTS.
"THEY DIVIDED INTO FACTIONS, FIGHTING AMONG THEMSELVES, AND ALLOWING THE METAGENE TO MUTATE WITHOUT PROPER CONTROLS.
"SO NOW, THE TIME HAS COME--"

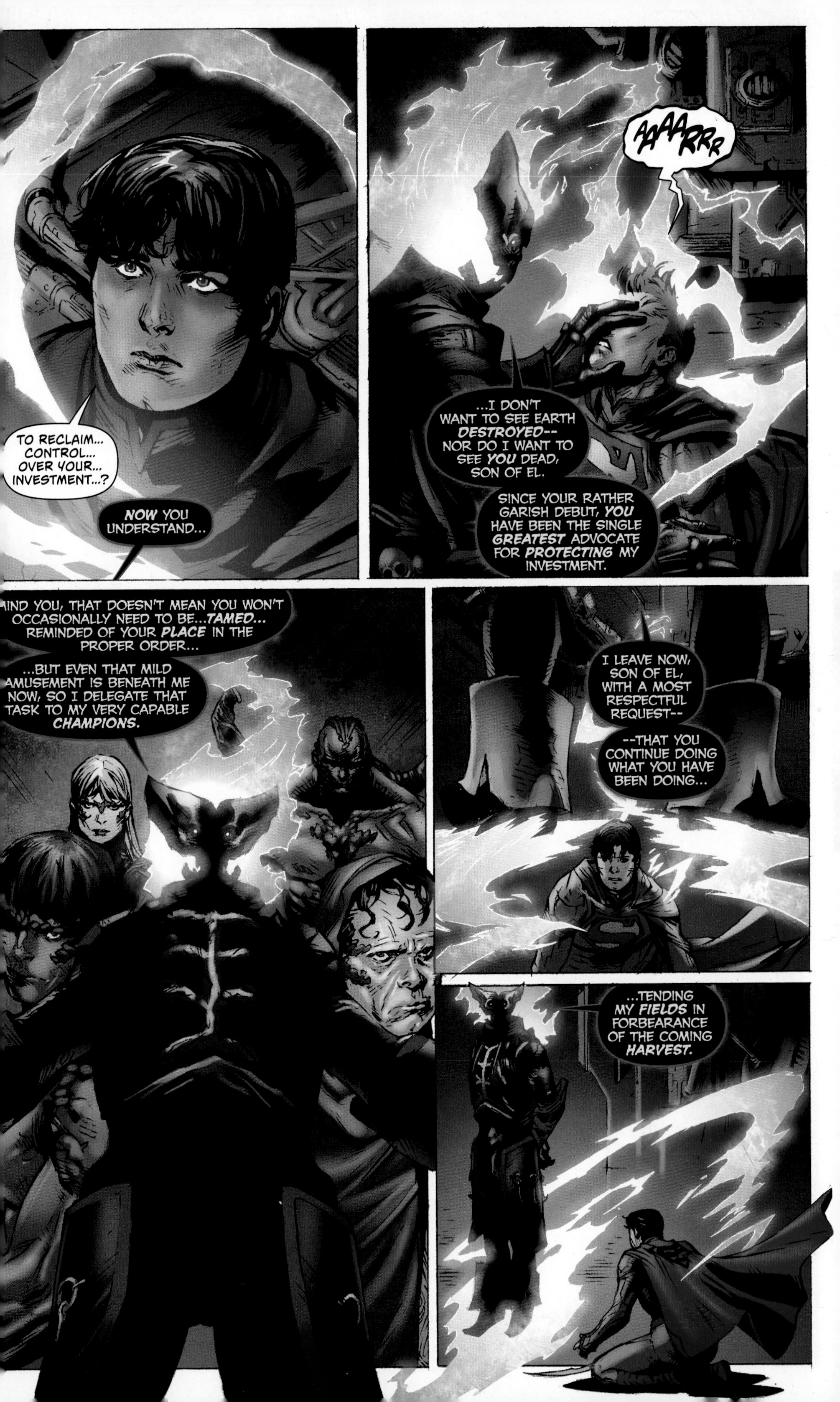
TO RECLAIM... CONTROL... OVER YOUR... INVESTMENT...?
NOW YOU UNDERSTAND...
AAAARRR
...I DON'T WANT TO SEE EARTH DESTROYED-- NOR DO I WANT TO SEE YOU DEAD, SON OF EL.
SINCE YOUR RATHER GARISH DEBUT, YOU HAVE BEEN THE SINGLE GREATEST ADVOCATE FOR PROTECTING MY INVESTMENT.
MIND YOU, THAT DOESN'T MEAN YOU WON'T OCCASIONALLY NEED TO BE...TAMED... REMINDED OF YOUR PLACE IN THE PROPER ORDER...
...BUT EVEN THAT MILD AMUSEMENT IS BENEATH ME NOW, SO I DELEGATE THAT TASK TO MY VERY CAPABLE CHAMPIONS.
I LEAVE NOW, SON OF EL, WITH A MOST RESPECTFUL REQUEST--
--THAT YOU CONTINUE DOING WHAT YOU HAVE BEEN DOING...
...TENDING MY FIELDS IN FORBEARANCE OF THE COMING HARVEST.

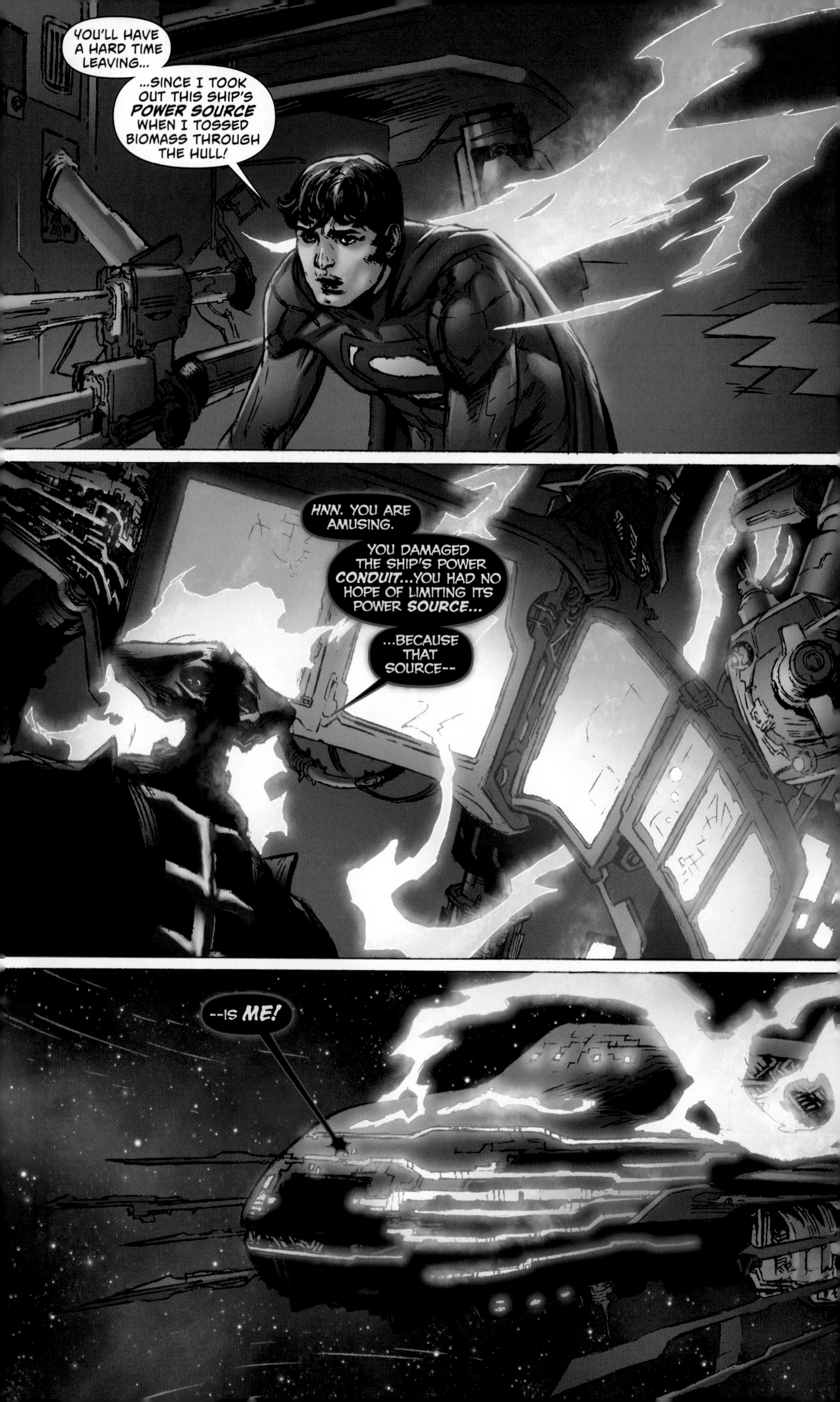
YOU'LL HAVE A HARD TIME LEAVING...
...SINCE I TOOK OUT THIS SHIP'S **POWER SOURCE** WHEN I TOSSED BIOMASS THROUGH THE HULL!
HNN. YOU ARE AMUSING.
YOU DAMAGED THE SHIP'S POWER **CONDUIT...**YOU HAD NO HOPE OF LIMITING ITS POWER **SOURCE...**
...BECAUSE THAT SOURCE--
--IS **ME!**

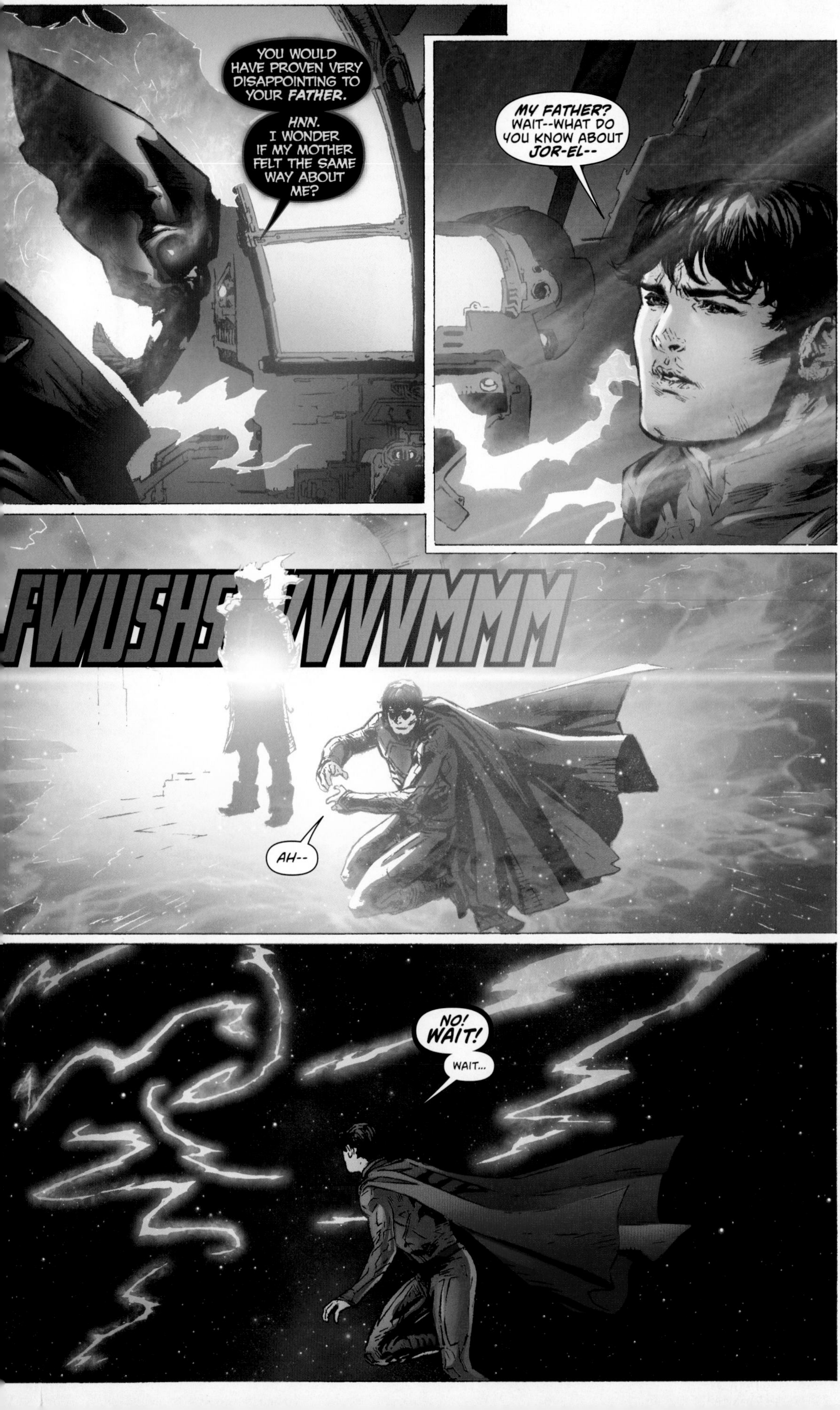
YOU WOULD HAVE PROVEN VERY DISAPPOINTING TO YOUR FATHER.
HNN. I WONDER IF MY MOTHER FELT THE SAME WAY ABOUT ME?
MY FATHER? WAIT--WHAT DO YOU KNOW ABOUT JOR-EL--
FWUSHSVVVVMMM
AH--
NO! WAIT!
WAIT...

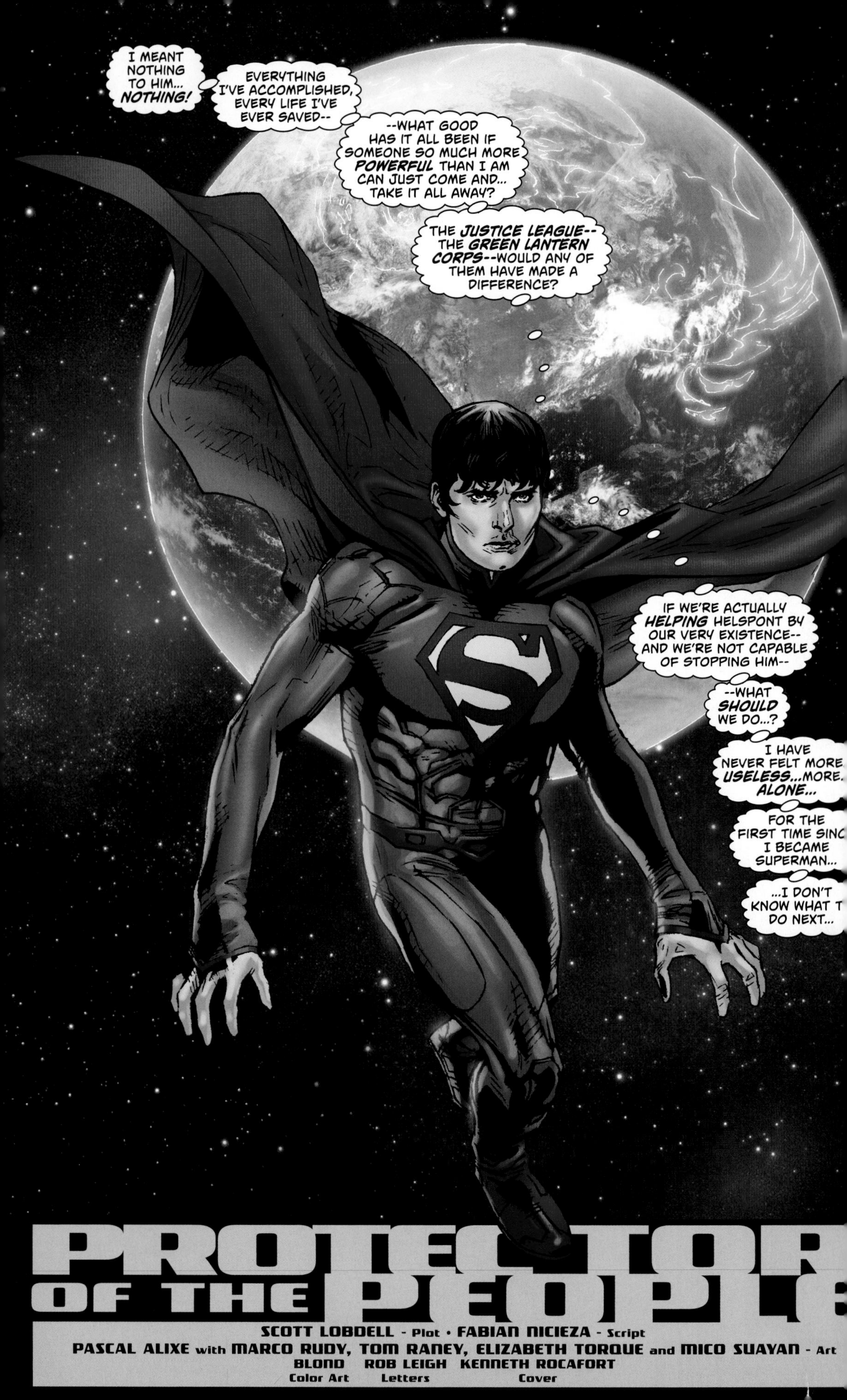
I MEANT NOTHING TO HIM... NOTHING!
EVERYTHING I'VE ACCOMPLISHED, EVERY LIFE I'VE EVER SAVED--
--WHAT GOOD HAS IT ALL BEEN IF SOMEONE SO MUCH MORE POWERFUL THAN I AM CAN JUST COME AND... TAKE IT ALL AWAY?
THE JUSTICE LEAGUE-- THE GREEN LANTERN CORPS--WOULD ANY OF THEM HAVE MADE A DIFFERENCE?
IF WE'RE ACTUALLY HELPING HELSPONT BY OUR VERY EXISTENCE-- AND WE'RE NOT CAPABLE OF STOPPING HIM--
--WHAT SHOULD WE DO...?
I HAVE NEVER FELT MORE USELESS...MORE. ALONE...
FOR THE FIRST TIME SINC I BECAME SUPERMAN...
...I DON'T KNOW WHAT T DO NEXT...
PROTECTOR OF THE PEOPLE
SCOTT LOBDELL - Plot • FABIAN NICIEZA - Script
PASCAL ALIXE with MARCO RUDY, TOM RANEY, ELIZABETH TORQUE and MICO SUAYAN - Art
BLOND Color Art ROB LEIGH Letters KENNETH ROCAFORT Cover

"It's fresh air. I like this all-too-human Superman, and I think a lot of you will, too."
—SCRIPPS HOWARD NEWS SERVICE

START AT THE BEGINNING!

SUPERMAN: ACTION COMICS VOLUME 1: SUPERMAN AND THE MEN OF STEEL

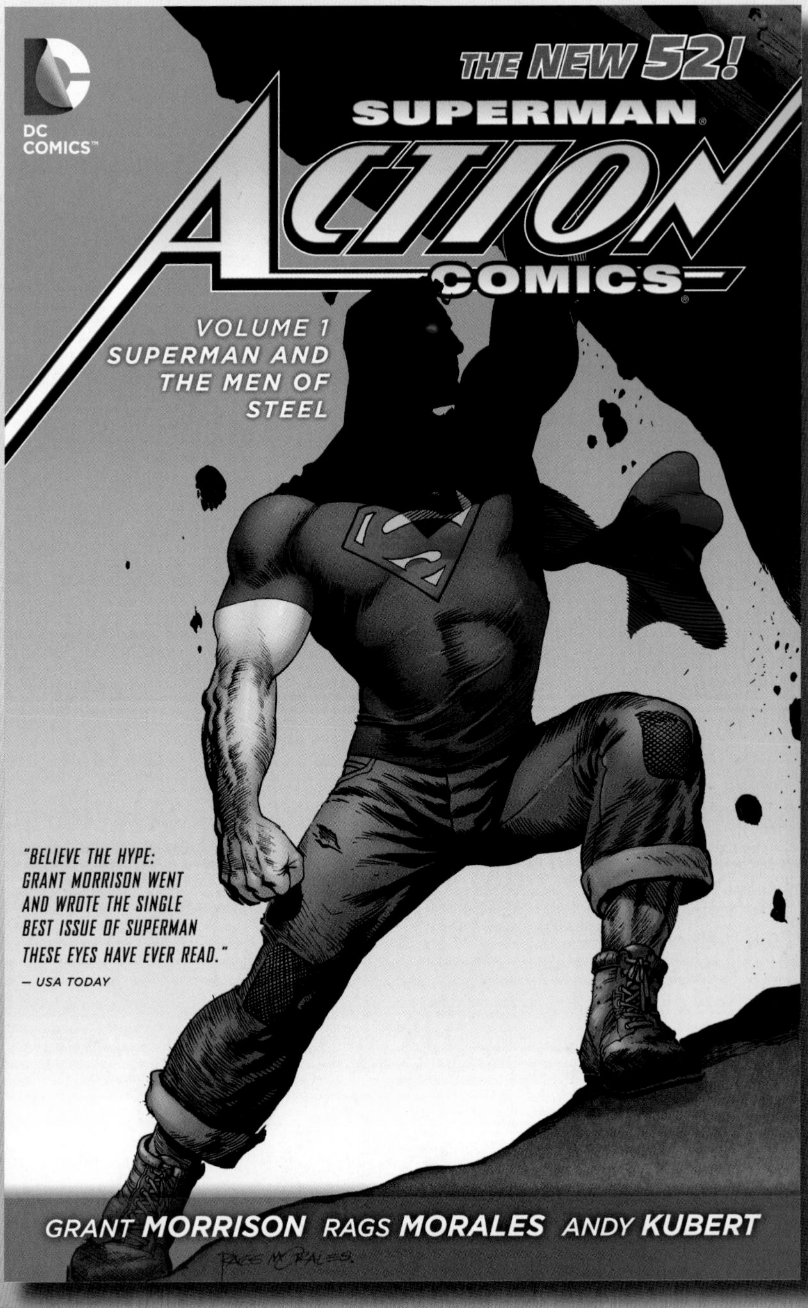

SUPERMAN VOLUME 1: WHAT PRICE TOMORROW?

GEORGE PEREZ JESUS MERINO NICOLA SCOTT

SUPERGIRL VOLUME 1: THE LAST DAUGHTER OF KRYPTON

MICHAEL GREEN MIKE JOHNSON MAHMUD ASRAR

SUPERBOY VOLUME 1: INCUBATION

SCOTT LOBDELL R.B. SILVA ROB LEAN

DC COMICS™

THE NEW 52!

SUPERMAN®

ACTION COMICS™

VOLUME 1
SUPERMAN AND THE MEN OF STEEL

"BELIEVE THE HYPE: GRANT MORRISON WENT AND WROTE THE SINGLE BEST ISSUE OF SUPERMAN THESE EYES HAVE EVER READ."
— USA TODAY

GRANT **MORRISON** RAGS **MORALES** ANDY **KUBERT**